Introduction to Container Ship Operations and Onboard Safety

Alexander Arnfinn Olsen

LONDON AND NEW YORK

Cover image: by author

First published 2022
by Routledge
2 Park Square, Milton Park, Abingdon, Oxon OX14 4RN

and by Routledge
605 Third Avenue, New York, NY 10158
Routledge is an imprint of the Taylor & Francis Group, an informa business

© 2022 Alexander Arnfinn Olsen

The right of Alexander Arnfinn Olsen to be identified as author of this work has been asserted in accordance with sections 77 and 78 of the Copyright, Designs and Patents Act 1988.

All rights reserved. No part of this book may be reprinted or reproduced or utilised in any form or by any electronic, mechanical, or other means, now known or hereafter invented, including photocopying and recording, or in any information storage or retrieval system, without permission in writing from the publishers.

Trademark notice: Product or corporate names may be trademarks or registered trademarks, and are used only for identification and explanation without intent to infringe.

British Library Cataloguing-in-Publication Data
A catalogue record for this book is available from the British Library

Library of Congress Cataloging-in-Publication Data
Names: Olsen, Alexander Arnfinn, author.
Title: Introduction to container ship operations and onboard safety/ Alexander Arnfinn Olsen.
Description: Abingdon, Oxon; New York, NY: Routledge, [2022] | Includes index.
Identifiers: LCCN 2021044019 (print) | LCCN 2021044020 (ebook) | ISBN 9781032155432 (hardback) | ISBN 9781032155425 (paperback) | ISBN 9781003244615 (ebook)
Subjects: LCSH: Merchant marine—Handbooks, manuals, etc. | Merchant marine—Great Britain. | Seamanship—Handbooks, manuals, etc.
Classification: LCC VK155 .O47 2022 (print) | LCC VK155 (ebook) | DDC 387.5—dc23
LC record available at https://lccn.loc.gov/2021044019
LC ebook record available at https://lccn.loc.gov/2021044020

ISBN: 978-1-032-15543-2 (hbk)
ISBN: 978-1-032-15542-5 (pbk)
ISBN: 978-1-003-24461-5 (ebk)

DOI: 10.1201/9781003244615

Typeset in Sabon
by Deanta Global Publishing Services, Chennai, India

Contents

List of tables	vii
Preface	viii
Acknowledgements	ix
Author's note	x
Abbreviations	xi

PART I
The merchant mercantile 1

1	The merchant mercantile	3
2	Officer training and professional development	10
3	Ranks, roles, and responsibilities	18
4	Health and safety	26
5	Container and RORO ships	49
6	Maritime regulatory framework	61

PART II
Principles of ship architecture and engineering 77

7	Basic container ship architecture	79
8	Primary ship engineering systems	101
9	Auxiliary ship engineering systems	119
10	Principles of ship stability	134

vi Contents

PART III
Ship operations 153

11 Deck operations 155

12 Engine room operations 163

13 Bridge operations 187

14 Passage planning and navigation 202

15 Stowaways, piracy, and drug trafficking 209

PART IV
Cargo operations 217

16 Hague–Visby Rules and bills of lading 219

17 Dangerous cargoes 227

18 Container specifications 235

19 Container planning, handling, stowing, and lashing 247

PART V
Maritime emergencies 263

20 Maritime incidents and emergencies 265

21 Ship fires, firefighting systems, and firefighter equipment 273

22 Emergency distress equipment and signals 291

23 Lifesaving appliances 299

24 Abandoning ship 304

Index 311

Tables

1.1	Comparison of dry cargo ship sizes	6
1.2	Comparison of wet cargo ship sizes	6
2.1	Ancillary and safety course certification	13
2.2	Deck merchant navy Certificate of Competency structure	16
2.3	Certificate of Competency endorsements	16
4.1	Types of PPE	30
5.1	Generations of container ship design and development	52
5.2	Largest container ships by class and TEU capacity (2021)	57
5.3	Six largest ship registries by number of ships registered (2021)	58
5.4	Average container freight market rates (2009–2014)	59
5.5	Container industry alliances (2021)	60
6.1	Summary of the shipping industry regulatory framework	62
13.1	Beaufort Wind Scale	192
17.1	Classification of dangerous goods	230
18.1	20 ft ISO container dimensions	236
18.2	40 ft ISO container dimensions	237
18.3	45 ft ISO container dimensions	237
21.1	Classes of fires, fuel, and extinguishing media	286
21.2	Approximate air consumption limits for SCBA	289
22.1	GMDSS areas, ranges, and bands	292
22.2	GMDSS frequencies	292

Preface

Approximately 71% of the Earth's surface is covered by water; of that, 96.5% forms the world's oceans. It is not surprising therefore that maritime transport forms the backbone of the global economy. Roughly 80% of global trade by volume and over 70% of global trade by value is carried by sea and handled by ports worldwide. To put that into perspective, in 2016 alone the international liner industry shipped in the region of 130 million containers with an estimated value in excess of US $4 trillion. As of July 2021, there were over 88,000 ships in the global merchant fleet and 1,647,500 seafarers. The life and work of a seafarer are complex and challenging. There are many aspects to being a seafarer. The purpose of this book is to introduce the reader to the fundamental aspects of container ship operations. This book covers many of the basics including ship architecture and engineering, stability, navigation, crew management, health, and safety, and responding to emergencies. The chapters have been written in such a way as to be accessible for the casual reader, the student, and the maritime professional. A blend of theory and practical steps provides the reader with an overview of living and working onboard container ships.

Alexander Arnfinn Olsen

Acknowledgements

I would like to personally thank everyone involved in putting together this book, with particular thanks going to Fidaa Karkori, Pamela Rossi Ciampolini, Richard Rossi Ciampolini, Ari Matthew Olsen, and the team at Routledge et al. without whose assistance and support this book would not have been possible.

Author's note

I would like to draw the reader's attention, if I may, to the use of terminology throughout this book. As with most professions, seafaring uses specific terms and words, many of which are interchangeable. 'Ship' and 'vessel' are two examples of terms which mean the same thing and can be used interchangeably. Other examples include 'officer' and 'mate'; 'seafarer' and 'mariner', and many more besides. I have chosen to use certain terms in place of others; please be assured the reason for doing so is purely personal preference, and no inference should be taken unless otherwise stated.

Abbreviations

1O	First Officer
2E	Second Engineer
2O	Second Officer
3E	Third Engineer
3O	Third Officer
4E	Fourth Engineer
5E	Fifth Engineer
AB	Able Seaman
ACGIH	American Conference of Governmental Industrial Hygienists
AED	Automatic External Defibrillator
AFRA	Average Freight Rate Assessment
AHT	Anchor Handling Tug
AIS	Automatic Identification System (SART)
ALARP	As Low As Reasonably Possible
AW	Anchor Winch
B	Bosun
BAECO	Breathing Apparatus Entry Control Officer
BC	Bulk Cargo
BIBO	Bulk In, Bags Out
BSc	Bachelor of Science (degree)
BT	Bow Thruster
CABA	Compressed Air Breathing Apparatus
CC	Chief Cook
CDC	Centers for Disease Control (US)
CDC	Continuous Discharge Certificate
CE	Chief Engineer
CM	Centimetre
CO	Chief Officer
CoC	Certificate of Competency
CONRO	Container Roll On / Roll Off
C-OSV	Code of Safe Practices for Offshore Supply Vessels
COSWP	Code of Safe Working Practices
CS	Cable Ship
CSO	Company Security Officer
CSS	Code of Safe Practice for Cargo Stowage and Securing
CTC	Carbon Tetrachloride
CVD	Cardiovascular Disease

DCP	Dry Chemical Powder
DOC	Document of Compliance
DP	Designated Person
DSC	Digital Selective Calling
DSV	Diving Support Vessel
DWT	Deadweight Tonnage
ECR	Engine Control Room
EEBD	Emergency Escape Breathing Device
EMCIP	European Marine Casualty Information Platform
EMSA	European Maritime Safety Agency
ENG1	Medical Certificate
EOW	Engineer Officer of the Watch
EPIRB	Emergency Personal Indicating Locator Beacon
ERT	Engine Response Team
ETO	Electrical Techno Officer
F	Fitter
FFA	Firefighting Appliances
FPSO	Floating Production, Storage and Offloading Unit
FRV	Fisheries Research Vessel
FSA	Formal Safety Assessment
FV	Fishing Vessel
GCSE	General Certificate of Secondary Education (UK)
GENRO	General Roll On/Roll Off
GMDSS	Global Maritime Distress Signal System
GP	General Purpose (Rating)
GPS	Global Positioning Satellite/System
GTS	Gas Turbine Ship
HAVS	Hand Arm Vibration Syndrome
HAZMAT	Hazardous Material
HFL	Higher Flammable Limit
HIV/AIDS	Human Immunodeficiency Virus/Acquired Immune Deficiency Syndrome
HMCG	Her Majesty's Coastguard (UK)
HMS	Her Majesty's Ship (UK)
HOD	Head of Department
HRU	Hydrostatic Release Unit
HSC	High Speed Code
HSE	Health, Safety and Environment
IACS	International Association of Classification Societies
IAEA	International Atomic Energy Agency
IG	Inert Gas
IGC	International Code of the Construction and Equipment of Ships Carrying Liquefied Gases in Bulk
ILO	International Labour Organisation
IMCSTDG	International Maritime Code for the Storage and Transportation of Dangerous Goods
IMDG	International Maritime Dangerous Goods
IMO	International Maritime Organisation
IMSBC	International Maritime Solid Bulk Cargoes Code
INF	Code for the Safe Carriage of Irradiated Nuclear Fuel, Plutonium and High-Level Radioactive Wastes On Board Ships

INMARSAT	International Maritime Satellite System
IOPP	International Oil Pollution Prevention Certificate
ISM	International Safety Manual
ISPS	International Ship and Port Security Code
LB	Lifeboat
LFL	Lower Flammable Limit
LNG	Liquefied Natural Gas
LNG/C	Liquefied Natural Gas Carrier
LPG	Liquefied Petroleum Gas
LPG/C	Liquefied Petroleum Gas Carrier
LSA	Lifesaving Appliances
LUT	Local User Terminal
M	Motorman
MAIB	Maritime Accident Investigation Branch (UK)
MARPOL	Regulation for the Prevention of Pollution by Oil
MARSEC	Maritime Security
MAS	Maritime Assistance Service
MCA	Maritime and Coastguard Agency (UK)
MEL	Maximum Exposure Limit
MES	Maritime Evacuation System
MF	Medium Frequency
MFA	Medical First Aid
MM	Master Mariner
MOB	Man-Overboard
MODU	Mobile Offshore Drilling Unit
MRCC	Maritime Rescue Coordination Centre
MS	Motor Ship
MSC	Marine Stewardship Council
MSD	Musculoskeletal Disorder
MSDS	Material Safety Data Sheet
MSI	Maritime Safety Information
MT	Motor Tanker
MV	Motor Vessel
MW	Mooring Winch
MY	Motor Yacht
NS	Nuclear Ship
OEM	Original Equipment Manufacturer
OES	Occupational Exposure Standard
OOW	Officer of the Watch
OS	Ordinary Seaman
OWS	Oily Water Separator
PAS	Public Address System
PCC	Pure Car Carrier
PCM	Physical Science, Chemistry and Mathematics
PCTC	Pure Car and Truck Carrier
PFSO	Port Facility Security Officer
PFSP	Port Facility Security Plan
PLB	Personal Locating Beacon
PMR	Portable Marine Radio
PPE	Personal Protective Equipment

PS	Portside
PSC	Port State Control
PSSR	Personal Safety and Social Responsibilities Certificate
PSV	Platform Support Vessel
PTSD	Posttraumatic Stress Disorder
PTW	Permit to Work
RB	Rescue Boat
RC	Rescue Craft
RFA	Royal Fleet Auxiliary
RMS	Royal Mail Ship
RORO	Roll On/Roll Off
RPE	Respiratory Protective Equipment
RV	Research Vessel
S	Steward
SAR	Search and Rescue
SART	Search and Rescue Transponder
SCBA	Self-Contained Breathing Apparatus
SDID	Sodium Dichloroisocyanurate Dihydrate
SLW	Safe Lifting Weight
SSM	Ship Safety Manual
SMS	Safety Management System
SOLAS	Safety of Life at Sea
SOPEP	Shipboard Oil Pollution Emergency Plan
SPS	Special Purpose Ships Code
SS	Steamship
SSAS	Ship Security Alert System
SSO	Ship Safety Officer
SSP	Ship Security Plan
STBD	Starboard
STCW	Standards of Training, Certification, and Watchkeeping
SV	Sailing Vessel
SWATH	Small Water Airplane Twin Hull
T/F	Trainee Fitter
T/M	Trainee Motorman
T/OS	Trainee Ordinary Seaman
T/W	Trainee Wiper
TB	Tuberculosis
TDC	Timber Deck Cargo
TLV	Threshold Limit Value
TLV-C	Threshold Limit Value – Ceiling Limit
TLV-STEL	Threshold Limit Value – Short Term Exposure Limit
TLV-TWA	Threshold Limit Value – Time Weighted Average
TME	Trainee Marine Engineer
TPA	Thermal Protective Aids
TS	Training Ship
UHF	Ultrahigh Frequency
UIN	Unique Identifier Number
ULCC	Ultra Large Crude Carrier
UMS	Unmanned Machinery Space
UN	United Nations

UNCLOS	United Nations Convention on the Law of the Sea
UNCTAD	United Nations Conference on Trade and Development
USCG	United States Coastguard
USS	United States Ship
VDR	Voyage Data Recorder
VHF	Very High Frequency
VLCC	Very Large Crude Carrier
W	Wiper
WHO	World Health Organisation
WIG	Wing in Ground Aircraft

Part I

The merchant mercantile

Chapter 1

The merchant mercantile

In the United Kingdom, there are three pillars to Britain's seagoing presence. The first is what is technically called the *merchant mercantile*. The merchant mercantile is the official maritime register of the UK and comprises all UK commercial registered ships and their crews. Many people refer to this as *the merchant navy* though in fact no such organisation exists. This misunderstanding often arises from confusion with the second pillar, the *Royal Navy*, which is Britain's Senior Service and naval defence force. Unlike ships of the *Royal Navy*, which are military in purpose and whose officers and ratings are bound by the *Articles of War*,[1] merchant ships are used for peaceful commercial shipping.[2] That said, merchant ships may – and have been – 'pressed into service' by the British Government during times of national emergency. The last time this happened was in 1982 when Britain went to war with Argentina over the Falkland Islands.[3] The third pillar is an odd combination of the two. The *Royal Fleet Auxiliary* (RFA) consists of ships under the control of the *Royal Navy* but which are manned by civilian crews. Though civilians, RFA officers and ratings are subject to the same regulations as their Naval counterparts.

BRITAIN AS A SEAFARING NATION

Britain has a long and illustrious seafaring history. This is largely down to her position of isolation, an island situated off the northern coasts of the European mainland. Sea trade has forever been a necessity as well as a way of life. In terms of the modern merchant mercantile, its origins can be traced as far back as the 17th century. An attempt was made by the Admiralty to impress all civilian seafarers as a potential pool of labour for the navy. That attempt met stiff opposition, and it was not until 1835 that a civilian register of seafarers was drawn up by the Board of Trade in London. This was to become the founding stone of Britain's modern merchant mercantile. Throughout the 18th and 19th centuries, Britain's merchant fleet expanded relentlessly, benefitting considerably from her trade with the British colonial possessions in the Caribbean, India, and across Africa and the Far East. By 1913 the merchant mercantile was the largest in the world. World War One (WWI) (1914–1918) however was to cost the merchant mercantile dearly with some 5,000 ships or 7,759,090 tonnes sunk, and 14,661 lives lost, mostly to the unrestricted warfare waged by German U-boats. In 1919, as recognition of the sacrifices made by Britain's merchant seafarers during the war, King George V (1910–1936) bestowed the moniker 'the Merchant Navy' on the service though it would be another ten years before the merchant mercantile would become formally known as the *Merchant Navy*. On 14 February 1928 King George V conferred on Edward, Prince of Wales, the title of *Master of the Merchant Navy and Fishing Fleets*, a position he held after his coronation in January 1936 until his abdication in December 1936.

DOI: 10.1201/9781003244615-2

4 The merchant mercantile

Following King Edward VIII's abdication, the royal patronage passed to King George VI (1936–1952) and is currently held by Queen Elizabeth II (1952–present).

During World War Two (WWII) (1939–1945) the merchant mercantile would again sustain heavy losses with the sinking of 14.7 million tonnes of shipping (approximately 54% of Britain's total pre-war tonnage) and the loss of over 32,000 men. Despite best efforts to maintain a position of dominance after the end of WWII, from the mid-1950s to the 1980s the merchant mercantile underwent a process of gradual decline. This was caused in part by the break-up of the British Empire, which at its zenith controlled over one-quarter of the world's landmass and by the rise of the flag of convenience. By way of comparison, in 1939 the merchant mercantile controlled over 33% of all global tonnage. By 2012 this number had fallen to 1,504 ships. By 2021, only 1,304 ships were flying the *Red Ensign*[4] out of a global fleet of 98,140 ships.[5] Whereas once the merchant mercantile was number one, by 2021 its position had fallen to 24th place. Although Britain is credited with establishing the world's first civilian merchant fleet, other countries were quick to follow suit, many of which have adopted the title and customs of the British merchant mercantile including its rank structure, uniform, and terminology. One such country is Greece, which like Britain, is a maritime nation by tradition. Shipping has been a mainstay of Greek economic activity since ancient times. The modern Greek maritime fleet consists of merchant vessels owned and operated by Greek companies and ships sailing under the Hellenic flag of convenience. According to Lloyds of London, in 2015 the Greek Merchant Marine controlled the world's largest merchant fleet in terms of tonnage with a total DWT of 334,649,089 tonnes and a fleet of 5,226 Greek owned vessels, with the majority being bulk carriers and oil tankers. Many other countries have their own merchant fleets, with ships sailing under their own flag or under flags of convenience. Denmark is a world leader in container shipping. Japan and Norway have long dominated the car carrier industry. Oddly enough, even landlocked Switzerland has a fleet of 28 ships.[6]

CONTAINER SHIPS

As we may have noticed, there are many different types of ships that form the merchant mercantile. We have mentioned some of them already though the list really is endless. The United Nations Conference on Trade and Development (UNCTAD) categorises merchant ships into six different categories: container ships, oil tankers, bulk (and combination) carriers, general cargo ships, and 'other ships' which include liquefied petroleum gas carriers, liquefied natural gas carriers, parcel (chemical) tankers, specialised tankers, reefers, offshore supply, tugs, dredgers, cruise ships, ferries, and other non-cargo vessels. The one we are interested in here is the *container ship*. Thousands of container ships sail the world's seas and oceans each year, handling the bulk of international trade.

The modern ocean shipping industry is separated into two main sectors:

1. The *liner sector*, which typically – but not always – involves container ships that carry 'general cargo' and operate as 'common carriers' calling at scheduled ports of call
2. The *tramp sector*, where ships go from port to port picking up cargo and discharging it wherever the customer demands

Today, container ships are almost always built from welded steel and, with some exceptions, have a lifecycle of between 25 to 30 years before they are scrapped. Container ships, like all ships, come in many different sizes though the shape is almost always universal. We will discuss the shape of container ships later in this book, but suffice it to say that container ships are specially designed to do two main things: (a) carry as much cargo as safely as possible; and (b) get from one port to another as quickly as possible. There are three main types of container ships. The first is the type most people are familiar with: vast floating behemoths that transport tens of thousands of cargoes in big metal boxes called *containers*. The containers are manufactured from corrugated steel and come in a variety of sizes though the two most common are the 40-foot equivalent unit (FEU) and the less common 20-foot equivalent unit (TEU). These containers are also called ISO containers as their shape and dimensions comply with the standards set by the *International Standardisation Organisation* (ISO). These ships are called *box ships* because they only carry containers. In some limited circumstances, they may carry gauge (oversized) cargoes such as yachts and heavy machinery though this is very rare. The majority of box ships are owned by shipping lines and follow regular set routes.

The second type of container ship is also a box ship but is much smaller than the container liners. These ships may either work as tramps, flitting from one port to another, or as feeders, going from one port to another port on a regular service. Feeders tend to operate in shallower waters and between ports that can handle larger container ships and ports that cannot. The third type of container ship is the *Roll-On Roll-Off* (RORO) ship. These are unique in the sense that they can carry both rolling cargo and containerised cargo. Rolling cargo is categorised as cargo which can be moved on wheels. This may be under its own power (for example, combine harvesters, mining rigs, and trucks) or by being pulled on a trailer by a separate power unit (for example, static heavy machinery). With the latter, the cargo is loaded onto a flatbed trailer and pulled on board. As well as carrying rolling cargo, ROROs can load containers onto their main deck (more about that later). The rolling cargo is brought on board via a stern ramp, and containers are loaded on deck by shore gantry cranes.

In addition to their type, container ships are categorised according to their size. This typically means the ship's length overall (LOA), width (beam), the amount of hull submerged in water when the ship is empty or laden (draught), and the ship's height above water level. These are important considerations for the ship's officers. In theory, from a safety perspective, a ship can be any size so long as it is well balanced and maintains an even keel in all situations. From a commercial perspective, it makes sense for ships to be big. Bigger ships mean more cargo. Practically, however, ships are limited to the areas they are intended to serve. Oil tankers, for example, are gigantic because they are long, wide, and have a relatively high draught. This means they are perfect for shipping oil from the Middle East to Europe or Asia. There are no major obstacles in the way of oil tanker design once the ship is safe, navigable, and sufficiently economical to operate. Container ships are a completely different affair. Unlike oil tankers, which are slow and lumbering, container ships must be swift and manoeuvrable. For this reason, container ships are considered 'fast ships' in the sense that they move at speed (on average between eight and twelve knots[7]) and spend very little time in each port. Compare this to oil tankers (which typically make way at six knots) and the difference is quite clear. In addition to their speed, container ship designs are very different to other types of ships in that they necessarily have deeper draughts and higher sideboards. This places a limit on how far container ships can grow and still remain competitive.

If you recall from earlier, we mentioned there are two types of container ships – liners and freighters. We know that freighters tend to be smaller and more agile. This means they can go from one port to another quite easily without the fear of exceeding any depths or physical obstructions. Liner ships tend to be much longer, heavier, and higher. Though they can carry more cargo, which means they generate more profit per cargo tonne carried, they are restricted in where they can go. The largest liner ships can visit a very select few ports.

6 The merchant mercantile

The majority though are limited by two geographical locations: the Panama Canal, Panama and the Suez Canal, Egypt. The largest ships capable of navigating the Panama Canal are called *Panamax Ships*, a portmanteau of *Panama* and *maximum*. This means the vessel's beam and draught[8] are the maximum that is permitted to enter the canal. The largest ships that can enter the Suez Canal are called *Suezmax*. Ships that are too wide or have a draught too deep to enter either canal are called 'post-'; so, a ship that is too wide or has a draught that is too deep for the Panama Canal is called a *Post Panamax* ship. Ship categorisation is quite a complex task as there are many different factors that must be considered, but for the sake of brevity, container ships (i.e., dry cargo ships) can be categorised as seen in Table 1.1.

The categories in Table 1.1 do not just apply to container ships; they apply to all types of dry cargo vessels including cruise ships, bulk carriers, ferries, and any other type of vessel which does not transport liquid cargoes. This is because a separate but similar system exists for wet cargo ships such as oil and product tankers and gas carriers.

Table 1.1 Comparison of dry cargo ship sizes

Small Handy Size	20,000 to 28,000 gross tonnes (GT) deadweight (DWT)
Seaway Max	28,000 DWT. These are the largest sized ships that can enter and navigate the St Lawrence Seaway[a] and have maximum dimensions of length overall (LOA) 225.6m (740ft); beam (width) 23.8m (106ft); draught of 8.08m (26.51ft); and a height above the waterline not exceeding 35.5m (116ft)
Handy Size	28,000 to 40,000 DWT
Handymax	40,000 to 50,000 DWT
Panamax	52,000 DWT loaded or 80,000 DWT empty. These were the largest sized ships capable of navigating the Panama Canal prior to the widening works completed in 2015. Panamax ships have maximum dimensions of LOA 294.13m (965ft); beam 32.2m (106ft); draught 12.04m (39.5ft); and a maximum height above the waterline not exceeding 57.91m (190ft)
Neo Panamax	120,000 DWT. These ships are the successor to the Panamax and have LOA 366m (1,201ft); beam 55m (180ft); draught 18m (59ft)
Capesize	On average up to 156,000 DWT, though some ore bulk carriers may be as large as 400,000 DWT. These ships are larger than Neo Panamax and Suezmax and are not permitted to enter the Panama or Suez Canals. This means to travel between oceans, Capesize ships must traverse the Cape of Good Hope (South Africa) or Cape Horn (Chile)
Chinamax	380,000 to 400,000 DWT. Maximum LOA 360m (1,180ft); beam 65m (213ft); draught 24m (79ft). These dimensions are limited by port infrastructure in China

[a] Canal and Lock System allowing navigation from the Atlantic Ocean to the Great Lakes of the US and Canada.

Table 1.2 Comparison of wet cargo ship sizes

Aframax	Oil tankers between 75,000 and 115,000 DWT. This is the largest size defined by the average freight rate assessment (AFRA) scheme
Q-Max	Liquified natural gas carriers for Qatar exports. LOA 345m (1,132ft); beam 53.8m (177ft); draught 12m (39ft)
Suezmax	160,000 DWT. Beam 77.5m (254ft); draught 20.1m (66ft); and maximum height above the waterline not exceeding 68m (223ft)
Very Large Crude Carrier (VLCC)	150,000 to 320,000 DWT
Malaccamax	Ships with a maximum draught of 20.5m (67.3ft) and typically 300,000 DWT capable of traversing the Malacca Strait (Malaysia-Indonesia)
Ultra Large Crude Carrier (ULCC)	320,000 to 550,000 DWT

Regardless of their type or size, all ships are given a name by their owner. This name helps to differentiate one vessel from another. Naming conventions differ from one shipowner to another, though some established companies have longstanding traditions over the names they assign to their vessels. A common practice is for shipowners to combine existing or new builds into *classes*. This means ships that share common characteristics such as size and carrying capacity all form part of the same class. One example is the *Hamburg Express Class* operated by the German company, *Hapag-Lloyd*. There are ten sister ships in the *Hamburg Express Class*, with the class leader being the *Hamburg Express* herself. In addition to their name, ships are assigned a prefix. The prefix consists of two or more letters and goes before the ship's name. The prefix indicates what type of vessel the ship is. For example, the prefix 'SS' indicates the vessel is propelled by steam and is therefore a 'steamship'. Some common forms of prefix include MV which is an abbreviation for 'motor vessel', RV which denotes the ship is a research vessel, and MT which denotes the ship is a motor tanker. Whilst this might not seem immediately relevant, it is an important factor to consider when the ship is caught in an emergency. Most people are probably more familiar with the prefixes used by naval vessels. In the UK for example, all Royal Navy ship names are prefixed with HMS, which is the abbreviated form of 'His/Her Majesty's Ship'. In the US, a similar system exists where military vessels are assigned the prefix USS or 'United States Ship'. It is quite common for other non-military government vessels to also use prefixes assigned to their names, such as HMC (His/Her Majesty's Cutter) or UKBA (UK Border Agency).

CREW STRUCTURE AND HIERARCHY

Seafaring is a tradition that encompasses a variety of professions and ranks. Each of these roles carries unique responsibilities that are integral to the efficient operation of the ship. As such, the UK is a founding signatory to the *International Convention on Standards of Training, Certification and Watchkeeping for Seafarers, 1978*, more commonly known as the STCW Convention. Under the convention, all merchant ships must have a minimum of two departments: the deck department, responsible for navigation and cargo management; and an engineering department, responsible for overseeing and operating the ship's machinery and propulsion systems. Ships with complex electronics and communications systems may have a separate electro-technical department. Cruise ships and large passenger ferries typically have a hospitality or steward's department on board and specialist ships often have a medical department depending on their size and type of work. The ship is commanded by a licenced master (captain) who is the most senior person on board and has ultimate authority and responsibility for the ship, her cargo, and her crew. The master is nominally a member of the deck department, though unlike the other deck officers the master is not responsible for standing watch. Bridge watchkeeping and navigational duties are performed by licenced deck officers; this means safely sailing the ship from one port to another on time and without causing damage to the ship or her cargo. The maintenance and operation of machinery and systems is overseen by licenced engineering officers. Supporting the officers are unlicenced deck ratings.

The officer in charge of the deck department is the chief officer or chief mate (CO). Immediately below the chief officer is the first officer (1O), followed by the second officer (2O), and then the third officer (3O). Some companies employ a fourth officer though this is increasingly rare. We will not go into too much detail about their roles and responsibilities here as this is covered later. On the engineering side, the chief engineer (ChEng or CE) is in command of the engine room. Immediately below the chief engineer is the second engineer (2E) or the chief engineer's deputy. Below the 2E is the third engineer (3E), followed by the

8 The merchant mercantile

fourth engineer (4E). Some ships may employ a fifth engineer (5E) who is licenced but has yet to acquire the seagoing experience to be promoted to 4E. In years gone by it was quite common for ships to sail with a radio officer (sparky) on board. This role is now obsolete as deck officers must be trained and proficient in the use of emergency distress radio tele-communications equipment (GMDSS). That said, ships with complex telecommunications and electrical or electronic systems may employ an Electro-Technical Officer (ETO). The ETO is separate to both the deck and engineering departments and answers directly to the chief officer. Furthermore, reefer ships may also carry refrigeration technicians and officers whose responsibility it is to maintain the onboard refrigeration systems.

Ratings are unlicenced members of the ship's crew and carry out the day-to-day tasks involved in maintaining the seaworthiness of the ship. For deck ratings, this typically involves quite menial jobs such as chipping and painting, scrubbing the deck plates, polishing, wash-ing down the bridge windows, and generally keeping the ship in a clean and tidy condition. Deck ratings also support the deck officers when the ship is coming into port and pulling alongside. This involves handling the ropes and wires and operating deck machinery. When cargo is loaded, it is the deck ratings that assist the shore stevedores to lash the containers in place. This is physically demanding work and is often quite dangerous. Engineering ratings support the engineering officers in maintaining the systems on board. This means keeping the engine room machinery well lubricated, fixing minor mechanical problems, carrying out repairs, and performing regular preventative maintenance.

Separate to both the deck and engineering departments is the steward's department. This is often the smallest department on board with only two members, both of whom are rat-ings. The department head is the chief cook, whose responsibilities include drawing up the menus, preparing and cooking three square meals each day, and managing the ship's sup-plies and perishables. Subordinate to the chief cook is the steward, whose job it is to clean and maintain the common areas[9] of the accommodation and clean the officers' cabins and day offices. For a small remuneration, the steward may even launder the officers' clothes and bedding. Ratings are generally responsible for their own upkeep and for cleaning their personal quarters.

Officer cadets (OC) are nominally above the most senior rating (the Bosun), though in a practical sense any officer cadet is well advised to remember they are the least experienced member of the ship's crew and should act accordingly. Officer cadets are student officers who are training to become either a deck (navigation) officer or an engineering officer. Depending on their chosen career path, officer cadets spend their seagoing time shadowing the officers in their department and working on deck/in the engine room with the ratings to gain invaluable insight and seamanship skills.

In this chapter, we have covered the basics of what the merchant mercantile is and how it was established. We have discussed the various types of container ships and what differenti-ates one from another. We have also briefly looked at the crew structure and the hierarchy on board. In the next chapter, we will explore how to become an officer of the merchant mercantile, what career streams are available, and what training and professional develop-ment is needed.

NOTES

1. Armed Forces Act 2006 (as amended).
2. Code of Conduct for the Merchant Navy, August 2013.
3. 2 April 1982–14 June 1982.

The merchant mercantile 9

4. Consisting of 147 bulk carriers: 59 container ships: 116 general cargo ships; 99 oil tankers; and 883 others including cruise ships, ferries, and support vessels.
5. Consisting of 11,965 bulk carriers; 5,371 container ships; 19,116 general cargoes; 11,201 oil tankers; and 50,487 others including cruise ships, ferries, and support vessels.
6. Consisting of 21 bulk carriers, three general cargo ships, one oil tanker, and three non-classified vessels.
7. 1 knot equals 1.15 mph or 1.8 kmph; therefore, a ship making way at 12 knots is effectively travelling at 13.8 mph (22.2 kmph).
8. Beam is the width of the ship from one side to the other. Draught is the height of the submerged portion of the vessel from the waterline to the keel.
9. This may include passageways and hallways, meeting rooms, pilot's cabins, the bridge, mess and galley, gym, and any other common areas.

Chapter 2

Officer training and professional development

In the previous chapter, we began by exploring the merchant mercantile and what it is and what it does. We also briefly looked at the rank structure and what everyone who lives and works on board merchant ships does. In this chapter, we will explore how to become a qualified and licenced officer of the merchant mercantile. Although all officers must be trained to the universal standard set out in the STCW Convention, the quality of training and qualified officer proficiency differs greatly. For that reason, this chapter will focus specifically on UK officer training and professional development.

OFFICER TRAINING AND PROFESSIONAL DEVELOPMENT

In the UK there are two academic routes into the maritime profession. Irrespective of which route is taken, the starting point is to apply for a cadetship. A cadetship is a sponsored placement on a recognised course of study that is paid for by a shipping company. The aspiring officer may either apply directly to a sponsoring company or through a sponsorship agency. Once the aspiring officer has secured sponsorship, they are ready to apply to any of the world-leading, UK-based maritime training colleges. If accepted, the sponsoring company pays for the cadet's course fees and the mandatory STCW training modules. As part of the officer training, the company also provides the mandatory seagoing experience on board their ships. This seagoing experience is needed to apply for a *Certificate of Competency* (CoC).

Students starting out at the beginning of their careers will study towards a qualification that enables them to apply for a Certificate of Competency. This is the licence which entitles the holder to seek employment on board a merchant ship. Certificates of Competency come in different levels, with each level either applying restrictions on what type and tonnage of vessel the holder can work on and at what rank. We will discuss Certificates of Competency in greater detail later in this chapter, but it is perhaps useful to explain the main differences in brief now. Certificates of Competency are issued in accordance with the provisions of the STCW Convention. There are two main levels: limited and unlimited. A limited certificate restricts the holder to certain types and tonnages of ships and navigational areas (ocean or coastal) that they can operate in. By contrast, an unlimited certificate entitles the holder to work on any type and any tonnage of ship, anywhere in the world, provided the holder also has the mandatory STCW certificates relevant to the vessel. The requirements for working on a container ship operating in the Indian Ocean, for example, is very different to the requirements needed to work on an oil tanker in the North Sea. As stated above, we need not concern ourselves with this too much now as we will cover it in greater depth later. As stated above, there are two academic routes to becoming an officer. The first is the degree route and the second is the Higher National Diploma (HND) route. Both routes ultimately lead to the same outcome – a recognised qualification with which the officer cadet can apply

10   DOI: 10.1201/9781003244615-3

for their Certificate of Competency. Remember – it is the Certificate of Competency as well as the other mandatory training that permit the officer cadet to seek employment as a licenced officer and not the academic certificate itself.

The officer cadet training syllabus is developed under the auspices of the Merchant Navy Training Board (MNTB), with approval given by the Maritime and Coastguard Agency (MCA). All training delivery must conform to the provisions set out in the STCW Convention and, in so doing, prepares the student to take the final oral examination that leads to the Certificate of Competency. The officer training syllabus encompasses a wide range of subject areas including traditional maritime competencies such as celestial navigation, ship stability, general cargo management, and seamanship, as well as modern disciplines including business management, maritime law, and information technology (for deck officers), and marine engineering principles, workshop technology, steam propulsion, motor (diesel) propulsion, auxiliaries, mechanics, thermodynamics, engineering drawing, ship construction, and marine electrics as well as practical workshop training (for engineering officers).

Depending on the pathway, training to become a deck or engineering officer usually takes between three to four years to complete. This period is called the cadetship. The training programme is divided into two main components: instructor-led classroom studies and seagoing service. Some of the leading providers of officer training in the UK include Warsash Maritime Academy (Southampton), South Tyneside College (Newcastle), Fleetwood Maritime Academy (Lancashire), Plymouth University, and City of Glasgow College. A small number of universities also provide maritime courses that can lead to STCW certifications including Solent University (Southampton) and John Moore University (Liverpool), though these courses tend to prepare the student for work within the wider maritime industry rather than specifically as deck or engineering officers.

The degree route

As mentioned above, the first route to becoming an officer is to study towards a MNTB accredited degree programme approved by the MCA. This pathway is called the *MNTB Deck Officer Cadet Training Programme (Degree Route)* and leads to the award of either an honours degree (HD), a foundation degree (FD) or – in Scotland – the Scottish Professional Diploma (SPD). In addition, provided the required certificates are obtained, on graduation the student can apply for their Unlimited II/1 licence, which is the minimum required to become an Officer of the Watch (OOW) on any sized vessel. After graduating, it is common for the newly qualified officer to start as a third officer, after which they can begin to make their way up the ranks up to and including chief officer. Obtaining the chief officer's Certificate of Competency (Unlimited II/2) requires extensive seagoing experience and onshore training. It also means qualifying for the master's Certificate of Competency (Unlimited II/3) in the event the chief officer must stand in for the master. Though each rank in the hierarchy requires additional training, the initial qualification remains extant. The HD/FD/SPD programme consists of alternating periods of classroom-based learning and seagoing service. To successfully complete the programme, the student must achieve an overall examination pass average of 50% or higher. This requires a minimum pass average of 65% in *Navigation* and 60% in *Stability and Operations*.[1] On successful completion of the programme of study, the officer has seven years to acquire their Chief Officer Unlimited II/2 Certificate of Competency.

HND route

The Higher National Diploma (HND) route offers an alternative pathway into the maritime profession leading to the award of a HND or Higher National Certificate (HNC). On completion of the HND, the student is entitled to apply for an Unlimited II/1 Certificate of Competency, which is the minimum required to become an OOW notwithstanding any restrictions endorsed on the licence. The HNC does not qualify the student for a Certificate of Competency. Where the student completes a HNC, they have seven years to fulfil the requirements needed to apply for an OOW II/1 Certificate of Competency. If the student does not obtain their Certificate of Competency within the seven-year period, and later wishes to, they must complete the applicable study programme again. For each officer rank below chief officer, that means resitting their HNC course. For chief officer rank, that means reattending the full HND.

Other routes

The *Experienced Seafarer Pathway* is a route open to all ratings currently employed on board UK-registered vessels who wish to advance to officer level by obtaining the required qualifications leading to a Certificate of Competency. This route entails completing several modules from the HND/HNC course and sitting the required examinations. The rating must also provide evidence of not less than 36 months' seagoing service and meet all STCW requirements. On successful completion, the rating may apply for their Certificate of Competency and thereafter seek employment as an officer. For non-UK residents, it is possible to undertake a HND/HNC course of study that leads to the award of a Certificate of Competency. This is done via the MCA-approved overseas 'one plus one' route and forms part of the *MCA-approved Overseas Collaborative Programme* (OCP). The programme is overseen by the MCA and is offered by participating UK nautical colleges. Seagoing service requirements may differ from those for UK students; therefore, it is strongly advisable for anyone looking to apply to the OCP to seek advice before applying to the scheme. There is a separate entry route for serving and ex-Royal Navy personnel who wish to transfer into the merchant service. Warfare officers, who are also the ship's navigating officer, must apply to the MCA for a *Certificate of Equivalent Competency* (CEC). They must also hold a *Royal Navy Navigational Watch Keeping Officers Course* (NWKC) certificate. For Senior Rates (i.e., petty officer and above) they must hold a *First Line Management 'Leadership and Management'* (L&M) certificate, which is akin to the *Human Element and Leadership and Management* (HELM) certificate issued to civilian officers; and for Junior Rates at Able Seaman level, they must hold the *Royal Navy Senior Ratings' Command Course* certificate. Whilst having any one of these certificates may ease the transition from military to merchant service, they are not in themselves an exemption from the STCW prerequisites. This inevitably means additional training will be required to reconcile any discrepancies between military and civilian training. It is worth noting that a similar relationship exists between civilian seafarers wishing to join the Naval Service as a Naval Reservist.[2,3]

Ancillary technical training and safety course certification

All entry routes require the officer cadet to successfully undertake ancillary technical training and safety course certification in accordance with the provisions set out in the STCW Convention. On successful completion of each course the officer cadet is issued with a STCW approved certificate of proficiency. The ancillary technical courses form part of the education and training requirement as specified in sections A-II/1, A-II/2, and A-II/3 of the STCW Convention. The safety courses form part of the mandatory training requirement for emergency response, occupational safety, ship security, medical care, and sea survival

Officer training, professional development 13

Table 2.1 Ancillary and safety course certification

Ancillary and safety course certification	II/1[a]	II/2[b]	II/3[c]	STCW code reference
Personal Survival Techniques	✓	✓	✓	A-VI/1-1
Fire Prevention and Firefighting	✓	✓	✓	A/VI/1-2
Elementary First Aid	✓	✓	✓	A-VI/1-3
Personal Safety and Social Responsibility	✓	✓	✓	A-VI/1-4
Proficiency in Security Awareness	✓	✓	✓	A-VI/6-1
Proficiency in Survival Craft and Rescue Boats	✓	✓	✓	A-VI/2
Advanced Firefighting	✓	✓	✓	A-VI/3
Medical First Aid	✓	✓	✓	A-VI/4-1
Medical Care		✓		A-VI/4-2
NAEST[d] (Operational)	✓	✓	✓	A-II/1
NAEST (Management)		✓		A-II/2
Efficient Deck Hand (EDH)	✓	✓	✓	N/A
HELM[e] (Operational)	✓		✓	N/A
HELM (Management)		✓		N/A
GMDSS[f] (GOC)	✓	✓		A-IV/2
GMDSS (ROC)			✓	A-IV/2

[a] OOW
[b] Chief officer
[c] Master
[d] Human Element and Leadership and Management (HELM)
[e] Navigation Aids and Equipment Simulator Training (NAEST)
[f] Global Maritime Distress and Safety System (GMDSS)

as specified in chapter A-VI of the STCW Convention. A summary of the ancillary technical training and safety course requirement per each type of Certificate of Competency is provided below:

Personal Survival Techniques (PST)

PST is a STCW basic training module which provides essential knowledge of survival at sea. It includes both theoretical and practical training which investigate the causes of distress, knowledge and use of emergency equipment, the launch and recovery of life rafts, preparation for survival, personal survival skills, and the role of Search and Rescue (SAR) organisations. PST training must be retaken every five years to maintain currency.

STCW Maritime Fire Prevention and Firefighting

The Maritime Firefighter course forms part of the mandatory basic safety training that all seafarers must complete. It deals with the precautions needed to minimise the risk of fires, how fires are caused, and how to extinguish them safely. The aim of the course is to provide seafarers with the essential knowledge and training in firefighting and fire prevention, with a particular focus on understanding the risk of fire on board and how to minimise those risks; learning how to fight and extinguish fires as well as search for and recover casualties from smoke-enveloped compartments; and covers how to wear firefighting equipment including personal breathing apparatus and the safe use of fire extinguishers.

Elementary First Aid

This progressive first aid course (A-VI/4-1) is designed to provide seafarers the skills and essential knowledge to take action when encountering medical emergencies at sea.

Medical Care[4]

The *Proficiency for Persons in Charge of Medical Care on Board Ship* is a component module for MCA OOW certification. It offers a natural progression from the MCA Proficiency in Medical First Aid course and is designed for officers with responsibility for medical care on board. The course provides knowledge of medical care at sea and aims to develop the confidence to respond safely to any medical situation.

Proficiency in Survival Craft and Rescue Boats

This ancillary course is part of the training required to obtain an OOW Certificate of Competency. The course provides the knowledge and practical training for officers whose duties include commanding survival craft in emergency situations. The course is intended only for personnel serving on vessels not equipped with davit launched lifeboats and is intended as a direct replacement for the existing *Advanced Sea Survival* certificate. It should be noted this certificate does not qualify the holder to operate fast rescue boats, which requires separate training and assessment.

Human Element and Leadership and Management (HELM)

HELM forms part of the education and training requirements necessary to obtain a UK-endorsed Certificate of Competency. It is aimed at providing the leadership and managerial skills required of officers as mandated by the STCW Convention. There are two levels to HELM: Operational (O) and Management (M). Most MNTB officer training courses include O level HELM in their syllabus. The Management level of HELM is a standalone course and must be completed before an II/2 Certificate of Competency may be awarded.

Navigation Aids and Equipment Simulator Training (NAEST)

NAEST forms part of the education and training required to obtain a Certificate of Competency. It provides the fundamental knowledge and skills required to maintain a safe navigational watch, to use electronic navigational aids to determine vessel positioning, and to use the equipment for safety of navigation in anti-collision modes. There are two levels to NAEST: Operational (O) and Management (M). OCs who have completed the NAEST (O) course (formally NARAS) after 1 July 2005 will have covered the use of Electronic Chart Display Information Systems (ECDIS) as required by the STCW Code. If ECDIS training has not been completed, this will need to be done before undertaking the NAEST (M) course.

Efficient Deck Hand (EDH)

EDH forms part of the education and training required to obtain a UK Certificate of Competency. The EDH course provides an understanding of safe working practices with regards to seamanship, cargo handling, anchor procedures, pilot ladders, and means of access, shipboard organisation, and associated topics.[5]

Global Maritime Distress and Safety System (GMDSS)

Any member of the ship's crew whose duties involve operating radio equipment must be appropriately qualified. The GMDSS course forms part of the education and training required to obtain a UK Certificate of Competency. To obtain a Certificate of Competency, the officer cadet must hold a valid GMDSS certificate issued by the UK, or an administration recognised by the MCA. The certificate must have a STCW endorsement.[6]

Each of these certificates (unless otherwise stated) is valid for a period of five years. Upon expiration, each certificate must be renewed by undertaking the appropriate training. Further information regarding Personal Survival Techniques (PST), Fire Prevention and Fire Fighting, Elementary First Aid, Personal Safety and Social Responsibility (PSSR), Proficiency in Survival Craft and Rescue Boats, Advanced Fire Fighting, Medical First Aid, Medical Care, and other required shipboard courses can be found in MSN 1865. As mentioned above, during the three to four years of training to become an officer, the officer cadet must spend a minimum period of 12 months on seagoing service. During this time on board, the officer cadet compiles a portfolio of their onboard experience. The seagoing service is spread across the entire cadetship usually in three-month blocks. At the end of the cadetship, which includes the academic, ancillary technical and safety course training, the officer cadet is required to sit an oral examination invigilated by an MCA appointed master mariner. Upon passing the oral examination, the officer cadet is entitled to apply for their Certificate of Competency. To do this, the officer cadet submits their academic certificate, seagoing service portfolio, and training certificates for appraisal by the MCA. Provided the officer cadet meets the requirements set by the MCA and everything is in order, the Certificate of Competency is issued usually within 12 weeks of the application being received.

CERTIFICATE OF COMPETENCY

As per the provisions of the *Merchant Shipping (Standards of Training, Certification and Watchkeeping) Regulations 2015*, which implemented the requirements of STCW 1978 into English law, as amended including the provisions prescribing the mandatory minimum requirements for the certification of OOW, the officer is now considered competent to undertake watchkeeping duties as a licenced OOW. The Certificate of Competency is an official document issued by the MCA to all deck and engineering officers and is internationally recognised as per STCW 2010, section A-II/1 – chapter II (Resolution 2). The Certificate of Competency will clearly state what, if any, restrictions are placed on the officer. There are two limitations – tonnage and operational area. An unlimited endorsement means the officer can perform watchkeeping duties on any vessel over 500 gross tonnes anywhere in the world. A limited endorsement limits the holder to vessels between 500 gross tonnes and 200 gross tonnes, and the vessel must remain within near coastal limits.[7] Where such limitations apply, the officer is issued with an II/3 endorsement. Officers without limitation may work on any vessel of any tonnage provided they hold an II/1 endorsement. When an officer successfully obtains their *chief's ticket*, i.e., a chief officer's endorsement, they must exchange their current Certificate of Competency for an II/2 endorsement. This permits the officer to assume the duties of a chief officer. This is important as the chief officer is the master's deputy, and as such, is expected to stand in during the master's absence. Interestingly, the STCW Convention makes no provision for vessels which operate on inland waterways, nor for vessels with a gross tonnage of less than 200 gross tonnes and uninspected vessels.[8] Separate Certificates of Competency are issued for deck and engineering officers serving on fishing vessels, and for engineering officers on yachts.

16 The merchant mercantile

Table 2.1 summarises each type of Certificate of Competency and the corresponding limitations that apply.

In addition to the endorsements discussed above, the Certificate of Competency will also contain annotations relating to specific STCW functions. These include navigation (function 1), cargo handling and stowage (function 2), controlling the operation of the ship (function 3), and radiocommunications (function 7). The endorsement is matched with a STCW capacity level, which is either Operational, identified with an 'O'; or Management, identified with an 'M' on the Certificate of Competency. The required functions and capability for each Certificate of Competency are provided in Table 2.2.

As a final thought on Certificates of Competency, the UK offers no restrictions to foreign nationals who wish to serve on UK-registered ships. The only exception is the master of strategic vessels and RFA ships. Non-UK qualified officers wanting to work on UK-registered commercial vessels can apply to the MCA for a *Certificate of Equivalent Competency* (CEC) provided the applicant holds a recognised STCW approved Certificate of Competency from a country whose standards of training are considered equal to those of the UK. The applicant must also prove sufficient proficiency of the English language and demonstrate an understanding of the laws relating to the management of UK-registered ships.[9] It should be noted that some countries do apply restrictions on crew nationalities. For instance, in accordance with section 27 of the *Merchant Marine Act of 1920* (the Jones Act) only US citizens may serve on US-registered vessels engaged in cabotage.[10]

In this chapter we have covered the training pipeline for merchant mercantile officers.

We have focused on officer training, as there is no formal training requirement for ratings other than the STCW mandated safety training that applies to all seafarers. In the next chapter, *Ranks and Responsibilities*, we will begin to examine the onboard hierarchy in much finer detail. We will also examine the role of each member of the crew, their general duties, and their responsibilities.

Table 2.2 Deck merchant navy Certificate of Competency structure

CoC	Area limitation	Tonnage limitation	STCW convention regulation
Officer of the Watch (OOW)	Near Coastal	Less than 500GT	II/3
	Unlimited	Unlimited	II/1
Chief officer	Near Coastal	Unlimited	II/2
	Near Coastal	Less than 3,000GT	II/2
	Unlimited	Less than 3,000GT	II/2
	Unlimited	Unlimited	II/2
Master	Near Coastal	Less than 500GT	II/3
	Specified Area	Less than 3,000GT domestic vessels	II/3
	Near Coastal	Unlimited	II/2
	Unlimited	Less than 3,000GT	II/2
	Unlimited	Unlimited	II/2

Table 2.3 Certificate of Competency endorsements

Function	OOW	Chief officer/master
1	O	M
2	O	M
3	O	M
7	O	O

NOTES

1. Where the student fails to achieve the required pass mark, they may be able to resit the examination for the failed module. Provided the pass mark is achieved the second time round, , the student will be awarded the appropriate qualification.
2. JSP 532 Reservists and Civilian Employment (Part 2: Guidance).
3. JSP 545 Tri-Service Regulations for Recruitment (Part 2: Guidance).
4. When serving on a European Union (EU)-registered vessel as a master or person otherwise responsible for providing medical care on a vessel operating in an unlimited area, it is mandatory under Article 4(1)(b) of Directive 92/29 EEC to undertake an approved Medical Care training course. It should be noted on 1 January 2021 the UK officially left the EU. This means the EU regulations previously applicable to UK seafarers may no longer apply in their present form. Though the Medical Care requirement will remain for British seafarers working on EU-registered vessels, the requirement may change for UK seafarers working on UK-registered vessels.
5. Further information about the EDH course requirements can be found in MSN 1862.
6. For further information about the GMDSS including recognised administrations, refer to MSN 1864.
7. The *Merchant Shipping (Training and Certification) Regulations 1997* define 'near-coastal voyage' as 'a voyage during which the vessel is never more than 150 nautical miles from a safe haven in the United Kingdom, or never more than 30 nautical miles from a safe haven in the Republic of Ireland'. The area within these limits is sometimes referred to as the 'UK near-coastal area'.
8. For instance, private pleasure craft and yachts under 200GT.
9. For example, the Provision and Use of Work Equipment Regulations (PUWER) (1998), Working at Height Regulations (DROPS) (2005), and the Code of Safe Working Practices for Merchant Seafarers (2015, incorporating amendment 1, October 2016).
10. Cabotage is the transport of goods and/or passengers between two ports in the same country by a ship registered in another country. Originally, the term applied only to sea trade but now applies to aviation, railways, and road transport.

Chapter 3

Ranks, roles, and responsibilities

In the previous chapter, we briefly touched on the rank structure within the merchant mercantile, and the roles and responsibilities of the deck and engineering departments. Over the next few pages, we will examine this structure more closely as well as explore in greater detail the responsibilities and day-to-day duties of the officers and ratings who work on board container ships. We know there are two core departments: the deck and engineering department, and that each department has its officer cadre and ratings. Sitting at the top of the hierarchy is the master, who is nominally a member of the deck department. To start with, we will begin by examining the roles and responsibilities of the deck department, followed by the engineering department.

THE DECK DEPARTMENT

Within the deck department, most container ships have between three and four officers. Though each officer has specific duties assigned to their rank, which we will discuss shortly, there are common duties that all deck officers perform with the notable exception of the ship's master. The term *master* descends from the Latin *magister navis*, which was used extensively throughout the Roman Empire to indicate the patrician (nobleman) who was in command of a vessel. The *magister navis* had the right to wear the *laurus*[1] or *corona laurèa* and the *corona navalis*.[2] Today, this tradition has continued as ship's masters signify their rank by wearing cap visors adorned with stitched gold laurel or oak leaves. The master is the most senior licensed mariner on board and holds ultimate command and responsibility for the ship, her cargo, and her crew. Although specific duties and responsibilities may be delegated to subordinate officers, the master remains personally responsible for the ship and for the actions of the officers on board. It is the duty of the master to ensure that the ship complies with all local and international laws and adheres to company policies and Flag State regulations. This includes, but is not necessarily limited to, all aspects of operation such as the safe navigation of the ship, its cleanliness and seaworthiness, safe handling of all cargo, management of all personnel, inventory of the ship's cash and stores, and maintaining the ship's certificates and documentation.

One of the most important duties the master has is ensuring the vessel's compliance with the ship security plan. This is a mandatory requirement under the *International Ship and Port Facility Security Code, 2004* (ISPS Code). The ISPS Code is an amendment to the SOLAS Convention (1974/1988) and provides for maritime security including the minimum-security arrangements for ships, port facilities, and government agencies. The ship security plan must be customised to meet the needs of each individual ship and sets out the relevant duties for the ship's officers and crew such as conducting searches and inspections, securing restricted spaces, and responding to threats from terrorists, hijackers, pirates,

DOI: 10.1201/9781003244615-4

and stowaways. The ship security plan also provides provision for responding to refugees and asylum seekers, smugglers, and saboteurs. On international voyages, the master is responsible for satisfying the requirements of local immigration and customs regulations. Immigration issues may include oncoming and off-going crew members, handling crew members who are caught attempting to desert the ship, and managing accommodation for foreign national crew members (such as visas and letters of passage). Customs and excise officials may require the master to provide a cargo declaration, a ship's stores declaration, a declaration of crew members' personal effects, crewing lists, and – if relevant – passenger lists. Although these documents are usually drawn up by subordinate officers, the master's signature certifies the authenticity of the document, thereby making the master responsible for the document's accuracy.

The master has special responsibilities when the ship or its cargo are damaged or when the ship causes damage to other vessels or facilities. In these situations, the master acts as the point of contact for local investigators and is responsible for providing complete and accurate logbooks, reports, witness statements, and evidence. Examples of common incidents include external damage caused by collisions with other ships or with fixed infrastructure such as buoys and quaysides, running aground, and dragging anchor. Common causes of cargo damage include heavy weather, water damage, pilferage, and damage caused during loading and unloading. The latter may be caused by poor lashing by the crew or rough handling by shoreside stevedores. All persons present on board the ship – including public authorities, the crew, and any passengers – fall under the master's authority and are the master's responsibility. In the event of injury, the master must provide any medical treatment that is available and appropriate. If the injury is so severe that it requires expert medical attention, the master must take appropriate steps to deliver the casualty to an onshore medical facility. If a death occurs on board, the master must investigate the likely cause of death and make provision for returning the body to the deceased's family. Finally, there is a common misconception that masters can perform marriages at sea. Whilst this is entirely dependent on the laws of each Flag State, most maritime authorities do not recognise and bestow this power. That said, since 1854, any marriages presided over on UK-registered ships must be recorded in the official ship's log.

The chief officer or chief mate, also synonymous with the first officer or first mate, is the highest-ranking officer in the deck department. Oddly, despite the chief officer in effect being the master's deputy, the chief engineer holds the same rank as the master, effectively making the chief engineer second in seniority. The title varies according to the ship's employment, type, nationality, and trade: for instance, the title of chief mate is not normally used on board British and Commonwealth ships, though it is commonly used on US and Norwegian ships. In addition to watchkeeping, the chief officer holds a wide variety of responsibilities including overseeing crew welfare and managing training in areas such as safety, firefighting, and man overboard (MOB) recovery. The chief officer also holds various appointments such as the *Head of the Deck Department*, *Head of Cargo/Stowage Operations*, *Head of Safety/Fire Fighting*, *Head of Onboard Security* (akin to the Ship Security Officer (SSO)), *Head of Environment and Quality*, and so on. As the senior officer in charge of cargo operations, the chief officer oversees cargo loading, stowage, securing, and discharging. Moreover, the chief officer is accountable for the care of the cargo from the time the cargo is brought on board the ship to the time it is offloaded.[3] Managing cargo correctly is a very complex process that requires experience and powerful computer aided technology to ensure maximum capacity is achieved and the ship remains safe and stable. Even under the best sea conditions, a ship is precariously balanced in the water and is subject to numerous competing forces which act on the ship's hull. The chief officer is the most senior watchkeeper. At sea, the chief officer keeps the 4–8 (0400 to 0800hrs and 1600 to 2000hrs)

20 The merchant mercantile

watch. When in port, the chief officer focuses on their other duties such as overseeing cargo operations, maintaining fire and security watches, monitoring communications, and managing the anchor or mooring lines.

Subordinate to the chief officer is the second officer, who is also a licensed member of the deck department. The second officer is third in command after the master and the chief officer. The second officer is customarily the ship's navigator. This means the second officer prepares and drafts the passage plan. The passage plan is the route that the ship will take from one port to the next and must account for the ship's draught and beam, cargoes carried, weather conditions, and any other factors that could adversely impact on the ship's schedule.[4] As well as being the ship's navigator, the second officer is also a watchkeeper. On most ships, this means standing the 12–4 (0000 to 0400hrs and 1200 to 1600hrs) watch. Other duties vary from ship to ship, but the second officer is often the ship's medical officer and may have responsibility delegated to them for maintaining the ship's distress equipment. When responsible for maintaining distress equipment, the second officer may assume the GMDSS officer role, a task involving the testing, maintenance, and proper log keeping of the ship's GMDSS equipment. This includes the Emergency Position-Indicating Radio Beacon (EPIRB), Navigational Telex (NAVTEX) unit, Inmarsat consoles, various radios, the Search and Rescue Transponder (SART), and Digital Selective Calling (DSC) systems. Below the second officer is the third officer, who is also the most junior licensed officer in the deck department. Like the chief and second officers, the third officer is a watchkeeper and stands the 8–12 (0800 to 1200hrs and 2000 to 0000hrs) watch. In addition to their watchkeeping duties, the third officer is usually tasked with overseeing the management and maintenance of the ship's lifesaving equipment and appliances (LSA). This typically includes all firefighting systems, the lifeboats and life rafts, the rescue boat (if relevant), and any other emergency equipment.

Watchkeeping is the primary occupation of the deck officer when the ship is underway. When an officer is standing watch, they are referred to as the Officer of the Watch (OOW). We have already come across this term in a previous chapter when we covered Certificates of Competency, but to remind ourselves, the Certificate of Competency is evidence that the officer is trained and competent to stand watch. The OOW has three fundamental duties: to navigate the ship, to safely avoid marine traffic, and to respond to emergencies. The OOW generally stands watch on the bridge with an able seaman who acts as the helmsman. Some ships may post an additional lookout. The helmsman executes turns according to the passage plan and the lookout reports dangers such as approaching ships. The ability to handle the ship is key to safe watchkeeping. In much the same way as a car turns and stops, the ship's draught, trim, speed, and under-keel clearance all affect its turning radius and stopping distance. Other factors include the effects of wind and current, squat, shallow water, and other similar effects. Despite the development of modern telecommunications systems, the OOW must also be able to transmit and interpret Morse Code signals and correctly use and interpret flag signals in accordance with the *International Code of Signals* (ICS).

Managing communications between ships and coastal stations is one of the key responsibilities of the OOW. Subsequently, all officers are required to be fluent in both spoken and written English. By having a common language it is easier to produce and use nautical charts and publications, to understand weather and safety broadcasts, to understand and respond to distress signals, and to communicate with other ships and coastal stations. It also enables multinational and multilingual crews to work together. On par with managing the ships communications is the navigation of the ship itself. Celestial, terrestrial, electronic, and coastal navigation techniques[5] are used to fix the ship's position on a navigational chart. A position is the exact location of the ship at any given time in reference to its latitude and longitude. To get from one port to another, the ship follows a predetermined route or 'track'.

To ensure the ship is 'on track', the OOW must constantly determine the ship's position. The OOW does this by taking *fixes* every so often. Out at sea, this may be once every hour; in congested and coastal areas, a fix may be required every few minutes. The fix is then annotated on the ship's chart. When calculating progress underway, the OOW has to take into consideration various factors that impede on the ship. These include the effects of wind, tides, currents, weight, and speed. To ensure accuracy insofar as is possible, the OOW uses supplemental information from nautical publications such as Sailing Directions, tide tables, Notices to Mariners, and radio broadcasts. With all things being equal, the passage should be smooth and relatively eventless. In the event the vessel should suffer a navigation-related calamity, the OOW must react quickly and appropriately.

A considerable amount of the OOW's time is spent avoiding other vessels, floating jetsam, and static infrastructure. The *International Regulations for Preventing Collisions at Sea* or the COLREGs are the cornerstone of safe watchkeeping. To assist the OOW, modern ships are fitted with radar and Automatic Radar Plotting Aids (ARPA). These systems are located on the bridge and help the ship to pass safely between other vessels and marine obstacles. They do this by feeding critical information to the OOW including the range, bearing, course, and speed of any approaching objects, the time and distance of closest point of approach, and any changes to course and speed. This information can then be used by the OOW to apply COLREG principles to safely manoeuvre the vessel out of harm's way. Whilst radar and ARPA are excellent tools to be used by the OOW, they are systems and not a substitute for good watchkeeping and seamanship. Radar has various limitations, and ARPA inherits those limitations and adds several of its own. Factors such as rain, turbulent seas, and dense cloud cover can prevent the radar from detecting other vessels. Furthermore, dense traffic and constant course or speed changes can confuse ARPA. Finally, human errors such as inaccurate speed inputs and confusion between true and relative vectors also limit the accuracy of radar and ARPA equipment. Subsequently, under the best sea conditions, radar and ARPA should be used to confirm mechanical observations. In poor and adverse sea conditions, radar and ARPA may be used as a guide, but the OOW should refrain from substituting their own professional judgement and reckoning by relying solely on the radar and ARPA.

It is an unfortunate fact that emergencies can, and do, happen at any time. Deck and engineering officers are trained and equipped to respond to the vast array of incidents and emergencies that could happen on board their ship. Although most incidents can be broadly categorised – such as fire or flooding – the complex design and nature of container ships means that no two incidents are the same. This is simply because there are far too many variables. A galley fire might seem at face value innocuous but if left unattended the consequences can be dire. Likewise, light smouldering in a container bay may not warrant immediate attention if the ship is entering into a precautionary zone, but again, left unattended, smouldering can quite easily escalate into a full-blown hold fire. Fires are by far the most dangerous threat to any ship. They can start small and undetected and within a few minutes engulf an entire section of the ship. Add into the mix vast quantities of heavy fuel oil, lubricating oil, compressed gases, flammable cargoes, and dangerous goods, and the risk to human life and the marine environment becomes immediately obvious. This is why fire prevention and firefighting are so heavily ingrained both in initial officer cadet training and through continuous professional development (CPD). Should a fire break out on board, it is the chief officer who assumes command of the situation as the *Incident Leader*, assigning each crew member to an *Emergency Response Team* (ERT). Under the authority of the chief officer, each ERT is assigned specific duties such as firefighting, casualty evacuation, or first aid response. Knowing how to respond to an incident on board is only part of the role of being an officer. Officers must also understand how to communicate distress using any of the prescribed methods, which we will cover in greater detail later.

Finally, although it is the chief officer who is operationally in charge of cargo operations, all deck officers must be able to oversee the loading, stowage, lashing, and unloading of containers. This requires an understanding of the hazards associated with heavy lift loads, cargo stowage, care of cargo, intact and damaged ship stability – both in and out of port – buoyancy, and managing dangerous goods.

Unlicensed seafarers without a Certificate of Competency are called ratings. Like officers, ratings can belong to either the deck or the engineering department. Deck ratings carry out the day-to-day business of running the ship. At sea, this involves chipping and painting, checking the lashings on containers, securing the ship for rough weather, welding loose fittings and fixtures, swabbing the decks, and generally keeping the vessel in a clean and seaworthy condition. When coming alongside and in port, ratings assist the deck officers in handling the painter ropes and mooring lines, bringing the ship safely alongside, and assisting the stevedores to load and unload efficiently. The job of a rating is a physically demanding one, which involves being outside in all weathers, sea states, and climatic conditions. Engine ratings support the engineers in keeping the power and propulsion systems, the steering gear, and all ancillary systems and machinery in good working order.

The most senior rating on board is the *bosun*. The bosun belongs to the deck department and, although subordinate to all officers, typically reports directly to the chief officer. The role of the bosun is to plan the day's work, assign tasks to the deck crew, and ensure all preventative and corrective maintenance is carried out. The bosun must be skilled in all matters relating to marlinespike seamanship.[6] Outside their supervisory role, the bosun regularly inspects the vessel and performs a variety of routine, skilled, and semi-skilled duties to maintain all areas of the ship not maintained by the engine department. These duties may include cleaning, painting, and maintaining the vessel's hull, superstructure, and deck equipment as well as executing preventative maintenance. An experienced bosun will be an expert in cargo rigging, winch operations, deck maintenance, working aloft, and a variety of other deck-related duties. During anchoring operations, the bosun usually operates the ship's windlasses when letting go and heaving up the anchors. Finally, the bosun also acts as the rating's foreman, bringing any issues or problems to the attention of the senior officers. Unless the ship has an especially small crew, the bosun rarely stands watch.

Second to the bosun in the deck department are the Able Seamen (Deck) or (AB(D)). AB(D)s are ratings with at least two years' seagoing experience and who are proven to be well acquainted with their duties. Unlike the bosun, the AB(D) may be required to work as a 'watch-stander' (as opposed to a watchkeeper), a dayworker, or both. Once the AB(D) has gained sufficient seagoing experience, they may seek advancement to officer level through the *Experienced Seafarer Route* (see Chapter 2). As a watch-stander at sea, the AB(D)s duties include assisting the OOW as the helmsman, lookout, or both. The helmsman is required to maintain a steady course, to properly execute all rudder orders, and to liaise with the OOW using the correct navigational terms relating to heading and steering. Alternatively, when the ship is in port, the watch-standing AB(D) is usually tasked with security watches over the gangway or anchors. An AB(D) who is employed as a day worker performs general maintenance, repair, sanitation, and upkeep of material, equipment, and areas managed by the deck department. This includes maintenance of the ship's metal structures such as chipping, scraping, cleaning, priming, and painting. Areas frequently in need of such maintenance include the hull, decks, superstructure, cargo gear, and smokestack. Dayworkers also frequently perform maintenance on the lifeboats, rescue boats, and life rafts, and emergency and damage control equipment. On many vessels, being a dayworker is a position granted to senior ABs, as it generally allows more time for rest and relaxation. In emergencies, AB(D)s are usually called upon to carry out damage control, operate firefighting equipment and, in the worst situations, launch the lifeboats.

Sitting below the AB(D) is the Ordinary Seaman (Deck) or (OS(D)). The OS(D) is the most junior rating in the deck department having less than two years' seagoing experience. On most ships, the OS(D) is an apprentice working towards gaining sufficient experience to become an AB(D). OS(D) are not required to keep watch but must pass examinations relating to watchkeeping skills such as performing helmsman and lookout duties. This requires much practical experience and so it is quite common to find the OS(D) on the bridge after working hours. During the apprenticeship, the OS(D) performs a variety of duties related to the operation and upkeep of deck department areas and equipment. These duties vary from ship to ship, the type of voyage, the number of crewmembers on board, prevailing weather and climatic conditions, the bosun, and any number of other variables. In any case, the OS(D) can certainly look forward to spending days on end attending to descaling, buffing, and painting the decks and superstructure; sweeping and swabbing the deck; splicing wires and ropes; breaking out, rigging, overhauling, and stowing cargo-handling gear, stationary rigging, and running gears; securing cargo; and launching and recovering the rescue boats.

THE ENGINEERING DEPARTMENT

The chief engineer, commonly referred to as the 'ChEng' or 'Chief', is the most senior engineering officer on board with responsibility for overseeing the maintenance and operation of the ships mechanical, electrical, and electronic systems. To become a chief engineer, a marine engineer must acquire the appropriate chief engineer Certificate of Competency or *ticket* appropriate to the tonnage, power rating, and type of ship that the engineer is employed on. As mentioned previously, the chief engineer holds the same rank as the master but is operationally subordinate to the master in all matters outside the confines of the engine room. Although the master has the authority to command the chief engineer to carry out an action, it would be a very foolhardy master indeed that overrides the professional judgement of the most senior engineer on board. The chief engineer is not an engine watchkeeping officer. Subordinate to the chief engineer is the second engineer (2E). The second engineer deputises for the chief engineer when off duty and assigns the daily workload to the third, fourth, and fifth engineers and the engine ratings. As the chief engineer may not be able to attend the engine room every day due to their ever increasing administrative duties, it is the second engineer's responsibility to oversee and report on the plant conditions and needs. This means the second engineer must be familiar with the ship's systems, repair schedules, and test results as obtained from regular oil soundings and water samples. Daily tasks are generally given in order of seniority or necessity, with officers receiving the most important jobs and ratings being given the more laborious duties. Like the chief officer, the second engineer stands the 4–8 (0400 to 0800hrs and 1600 to 2000hrs) engine room watch.

The third engineer is subordinate to the second engineer and senior to the fourth engineer. The third engineer's duties usually involve managing the auxiliary boilers, auxiliary engines, incinerators, air compressors, fuel systems, fuel oil purifiers, and the condensate and feed systems. Depending on the ship, the third engineer may be given charge of bunkering operations (taking on fuel) provided they hold a *Fuel Transfer Operation Person in Charge* (PIC) endorsement. The third engineer is a watchkeeping rank and stands the 12–4 (0000 to 0400hrs and 1200 to 1600hrs) watch. The fourth engineer is the most junior officer of the engineering department and is often tasked with carrying out general duties. Depending on the ship, the fourth engineer may assist the third officer in maintaining the condition of the lifeboats. On a day-to-day basis, the fourth engineer is often assigned duties such as keeping the main plant operating, overseeing the propulsion, sewage processing, and treatment systems, maintaining the electrical systems, and general preventative maintenance. As part of their CPD, fourth engineers are trained in HVAC, electronics, and emergency first aid with an emphasis on different burns. The fourth engineer is also a watchkeeping rank and stands the 8–12 (0800 to 1200hrs and 2000 to 0000hrs) watch.

Like the deck department, engineering ratings also have a hierarchical structure. Unlike the deck department, engine ratings have specific job roles as well as ranks. The most senior rating is the Able Seafarer (Engine) or AB(E) who may be assigned duties commensurate with the role of the former *motorman* or *oiler*. This new rank structure was implemented as per the amendments to the STCW Convention, which sought to equalise the rank structure between the deck and engineering rates. The motorman performs a variety of tasks connected to the maintenance and repair of engine room, fireroom, machine shop, ice-machine room, and steering room equipment. The motorman's duties include inspecting equipment such as pumps, turbines, distilling plants, and condensers, and preparing records of condition. The motorman is also responsible for lubricating and maintaining critical machinery and plant such as generators, steering systems, the lifeboat winches, and grey, brown, and black water disposal systems.[7] Although motorman certification differs from country to country, there is some universality through international conventions. This means that even though individual maritime administrations can set their own benchmarks, they must subscribe to a minimum level of competency that meets suitably qualified and experienced person (SQEP) criteria in the UK or qualified member of the engine department (QMED) in the US. Second to the motorman is the oiler or greaser. Their main duty is to lubricate the engine room machinery and plant and maintain the 'hotel' facilities on board including the sewage, lighting, air conditioning, and water systems. In years gone by oilers were employed across a variety of industries from steel milling to mining. Today, oilers are almost exclusively employed on board ships. The oiler is the second junior rate and sits directly above the wiper. With sufficient seagoing experience, the oiler can seek advancement and become a licensed marine engineer.

Subordinate to the AB(E) is the Ordinary Seaman (Engine) (OS(E)). The OS(E) typically performs the duties previously assigned to the wiper. The job of the OS(E) is to clean the engine spaces and machinery, and assist the marine engineers as directed. Similar to the OS(D), the position is an apprenticeship to becoming an AB(E).

Separate and distinct from both the deck and engineering departments, though nominally under the authority of the chief engineer, is the Electro-Technical Officer or ETO. It is very rare for container ships to carry ETOs on board as there is generally very little demand for their expertise. That said, interestingly, as ships have become increasingly dependent on electronic systems, shipping companies and ship operators are slowly recognising the benefits of having electronic expertise on board. This is especially true on diesel electric ships and vessels equipped with specialised systems such as dynamic positioning (DP). Unlike the marine engineers, the ETO does not stand an engine room watch. Instead, they are on call 24 hours a day. On larger vessels such as cruise ships, ETOs often have their own department and rank structure.[8] The final department found on all container ships is the galley department. On most ships, this is simply a chief cook and assistant cook, who also carries out general housekeeping duties. Large passenger vessels such as cruise ships and ferries often have a dedicated stewards department, led by a chief steward and or chief purser, and assisted by hospitality staff. Container ships are almost exclusively devoid of such comforts.

In this chapter we have covered the rank structure on board container vessels relating to the officers and ratings of the deck and engineering departments, as well as the roles, responsibilities, and functions of each member of the ship's crew. In the next chapter we will begin to explore the conditions on board container ships such as working and rest times, the onboarding procedure, working in foul weather, heavy seas, and extreme heat. We will also begin to look at some of the health and safety considerations associated with working on board container ships.

NOTES

1. The Laurus was a crown made from Laurus leaves.
2. The *corona navalis* or naval crown was a sign of authority worn by the commander of Roman vessels. Senior naval officers at commander rank and above and senior personnel of the civilian emergency services (police, fire, and ambulance) also have depictions of gold or silver Laurus leaves on their cap visors as an indication of their rank.
3. This is a simplification as each cargo is loaded according to a contract, or *bill of lading*. The bill of lading will state whether the shipper is only responsible for the cargo during transit, or whether the shipper is responsible for the delivery of the cargo to the end customer.
4. This may include international and civil war coastal zones, sea areas subject to terrorist attack and piracy, trade embargoes, and any specific navigational challenges such as the Panama and Suez Canals.
5. Celestial navigation refers to the use of stars and planetary references; terrestrial navigation comprises dead reckoning, visual navigation, and some other generic position fixing techniques. Dead reckoning means relative positioning with respect to previous positions. Electronic navigation involves the use of radar and electronic charts (ECDIS); coastal navigation involves relative positioning with respect to coastal marks such buoys, church steeples, lighthouses, and any other visual mark.
6. Marlinespike is the art of seamanship and includes the tying of various types of knots, splicing, and working with cable or wire rope.
7. Grey water is wastewater from sinks and showers; deck wash; and any other source of wastewater that is not categorised as brown or black water. Brown water is sewage waste (i.e., toilet waste). Black water is oily water from the bilges, fuel tanks, and ballast tanks.
8. For example, Lead ETO, First Electrician, Chief Electrical Officer, or Chief Electrical Engineer.

Chapter 4

Health and safety

Joining a ship for the first time can often be an exciting yet daunting experience. To ease the transition, all crew members must participate in some form of familiarisation training. This usually takes place before joining the vessel, where specific equipment is used on board, and always after joining the vessel. Onboard familiarisation is overseen by the master but delegated to an appropriate officer. It is important that familiarisation is provided as soon as possible but certainly within 14 days of joining the ship. As a minimum, familiarisation training should provide the crew member with a brief of their duties and responsibilities, the location of their cabin or quarters, rest and work areas, positions of emergency equipment and lifesaving appliances, emergency response procedures and emergency evacuation routes, the onboard firefighting procedures, an outline of the ship's alarms, and ship abandonment protocols. It is best practice for new crew members to join the vessel before the outgoing crew member departs the vessel, with at least one to two days overlap. This ensures there is sufficient time for the crew members to acquaint themselves with their new surroundings and duties. It also allows a short period where the incoming crew member can shadow their opposite number. The crew member familiarisation process is a formal process and is delivered best when planned well in advance. In the run up to shore leave, it is very easy to forget important points that need to be shared, especially as the crew member must carry out their own duties as well as preparing for the handover. Writing out a summary sheet with bullet points is an effective way of ensuring critical information is passed on including the location and operation of job specific equipment, the ship's watchkeeping roster and handover procedures, and indeed any other information specific to the vessel. If the replacement crew member is an officer of the deck department, they will need to be familiarised with the navigation systems, the location of charts and publications on the bridge, the GMDSS equipment, the steering system, mooring equipment, cargo handling procedures and equipment, and so forth. Engineering personnel will need to be familiarised with their assigned machinery, maintenance procedures, engine control room (ECR) watchkeeping procedures, and emergency response and firefighting procedures. In addition to their duties, oncoming crew members should also be briefed on the master's or chief engineer's standing, day and night orders, the Garbage Management Plan (GMP) and how rubbish/garbage is handled on board, the Oil Pollution Prevention Plan (OPPP), the Ship Security Plan (SSP), the lifeboat release procedure, life raft release procedure, and the procedures for the authorised use of maritime distress signals and flares. All these procedures are contained in the ship's formal Safety Management System (SMS), which we now examine in greater detail.

SAFETY MANAGEMENT SYSTEM

All ships must have a Safety Management System (SMS) which is a formal procedure that ensures the safe management and operation of the ship, with an additional onus on

26   DOI: 10.1201/9781003244615-5

protecting the marine environment. The SMS is a key requirement of the *International Safety Management* (ISM) *Code*. Every SMS must satisfy the functional requirements set out in the ISM, which includes procedures and guidelines for responding to emergency situations; a safety and environmental protection policy; procedures and guidelines for reporting accidents or any other form of non-compliance; clear and concise information relating to the various levels of authority and attendant lines of communication; procedures and guidelines for complying with international and Flag State regulations; procedures for conducting internal audits and management reviews; and general and specific vessel details. The key outcome of the SMS is the ship's Safety Management Plan (SMP) which is typically drafted by the shipowner/onshore designated person with input from the master and any other relevant stakeholders. The SMS is usually provided to the ship as an abridged document consisting of various sections. These include a general summary of the SMS and SMP; a Safety and Environmental Policy; details of the onshore designated person or vessel manager; details pertaining to the ship's personnel and onboard resources and training; a detailed summary of the master's responsibilities and authority; a detailed summary of the company's responsibilities and authority; key operational procedures; emergency response procedures; accident and emergency reporting procedures; a detailed summary of ship maintenance requirements and record keeping; a list of all statutory and regulatory documents to be maintained on board; and a detailed summary of the review and future evaluation process.

Although working at sea is by definition a hazardous occupation, various measures can be taken by seafarers to reduce the risks they face. One such measure is the *Formal Safety Assessment* (FSA). Formal Safety Assessment is a supplementary system that supports the SMS and is described by the IMO as a 'rational and systematic process for assessing the risks associated with shipping activity and for evaluating the costs and benefits of reducing those risks'. In effect, Formal Safety Assessment is a five-step process that covers critical aspects of safety analysis and proposes recommendations for implementing suitable safeguards against areas of concern. The concept of Formal Safety Assessment was first proposed in 1988 in response to the *Pipa Alpha* incident.[1] *Pipa Alpha* was an offshore oil platform located 120 miles north-east of Aberdeen, Scotland, and was owned and operated by *Occidental Petroleum Limited*. On 6 July 1988 an explosion occurred, killing 167 men including two crewmen of an offshore rescue vessel. Sixty-one workers survived and 30 bodies were never recovered. The total insured loss resulting from the incident was about £1.7 billion making it one of the costliest manmade incidents of all time. The severity of the *Pipa Alpha* incident was sufficiently grave for maritime authorities to recognise the need for a formal methodology to analyse maritime-related safety risks. According to the IMO, the benefits of Formal Safety Assessment are transparent decision-making; decision-making based on the thorough understanding of risk and evaluation of alternative options; and justification for measures based on methodological analysis and evaluation. Carrying out a Formal Safety Assessment involves following a five-step process: (1) identify risk or hazards; (2) carry out a detailed risk analysis; (3) carry out risk control options analysis; (4) carry out cost benefit assessment; and (5) present recommendations. Once the Formal Safety Assessment has been completed, and the options evaluated against their costs and benefits, the outcome is then incorporated into the SMS.

Once the SMS is in place, implementing the recommendations of the Formal Safety Assessment, the next step is to communicate these recommendations to the onboard safety committee, which sits under the chairmanship of the master. The safety committee comprises the Ship's Safety Officer, a safety representative from the deck and engineering rating departments, and any other relevant stakeholders. Additional crew members may be invited to attend safety committee meetings as and when the need arises. The purpose of the safety committee is to implement the SMS and to enhance the standard of safety on

28 The merchant mercantile

board. It does this by monitoring safety procedures and practices. The safety committee is an important agency and has the same powers as safety representatives onshore. The main tasks of the safety committee include – but are not limited to – fostering and improving safe working attitudes and practices. The safety committee also functions as the crew's forum for addressing safety concerns. As the onboard safety representatives, the safety committee is empowered to propose recommendations for the enhancement of occupational health and safety measures and has the authority to inspect the Safety Officer's records. Where the safety committee identifies deficiencies in the systems and practices on board, the committee is further empowered to implement actions designed to improve the state of onboard occupational health as well as recommend amendments to safety policies and procedures. In addition to their core duties, the safety committee also has ancillary responsibilities such as maintaining official minutes of safety meetings and recording suggestions, progress, and any actions agreed; ensuring safety tools and personal protective equipment is available to crew members; ensuring the availability of safety-related publications; ensuring the accuracy of accident reports; and holding safety meetings at least every four to six weeks.

Although the matter of health and safety ultimately lies with the master, the ISM Code (which came into force under the premise of SOLAS to meet the requirements of the *Merchant Shipping and Fishing Ships (Health and Safety at Work) Regulations 1997 (SI 1997 No. 2962) (the Regulations)* and the *Code of Safe Working Practice for Merchant Mariners* (COSWP), ships are legally required to appoint a designated person (DP). The designated person is a two-person role. The first is the shore-based vessel manager and the second is any member of the ships' senior management team[2] appointed to the role of Ship's Safety Officer (SSO). The SSO role involves overseeing the safety of the crew and promoting an effective safety culture by engendering safe working practices. The SSO is a critical role especially during Port State Authority audits, as ship safety is almost universally the first aspect of the ship's operational regime to be inspected. As might be expected, detailed guidance on the qualifications and training for SSOs is provided in the STCW Convention, at table A-II/2 and A-III/2 and in *IMO Model Course 3.11 (Marine Accident and Incident Investigation)*. Accordingly, the ISM Code states the SSO must have a minimum of two years consecutive seagoing service.[3] The SSO role is usually held by one of the ship's senior officers. The appointment is contingent on the appointee having the relevant seagoing experience **and** completing the Ship Safety Officer Course. Though not expressly prohibited in the regulations, it is accepted practice for the master not to appoint themselves as the SSO, the reason being the master is generally considered overwhelmed by their normal duties without adding yet another layer of responsibility. Although the position of SSO is a static appointment, it is customary to delegate the responsibility of SSO to the OOW. This ensures the responsibilities contingent with the role are rotated accordingly.

The appointment of a SSO requires various personal qualities that enable the appointee to enforce the responsibilities imposed under the relevant ISM provisions. The main duties incumbent on the SSO are surveying the ship for potential hazards which may directly affect the health and safety of the crew. It also involves overseeing compliance with the SMS; coordinating safety measures with port representatives; identifying deficiencies in existing safety and security plans; and bringing said deficiencies to the attention of the master; carrying out safety inspections of the entire ship at least once every three months; promoting and enhancing crew safety awareness; carrying out continuous crew safety training; ensuring work practices are compliant with safety regulations; investigating crew complaints relating to health and safety issues; investigating onboard accidents and drafting the accident investigation report; maintaining accurate records involving near misses; ensuring all equipment mandated under the ISM Code and SMS is present, maintained, tested, and calibrated; and if necessary stopping operations should they pose a threat to the safety of the ship or her crew. As we can see, the SSO role is quite an involved responsibility which is why it requires specific training and personal qualities. It should be noted however that the SSO is **not** required to perform any of the above duties during emergencies nor are they responsible for the provision of medical treatment or emergency first aid.

As mentioned above, the SSO is responsible for carrying out whole-of-vessel safety checks. These must be performed at least once every three months. The SSO safety check involves testing the various machineries, alarms, and safety equipment on board, the aim being to confirm they are in working condition. In addition to the SSO safety check, periodic safety checks also need to be carried out on specific systems and equipment in accordance with the ship's SMS. Some periodic safety checks must be performed weekly whilst others are carried out monthly. Periodic safety checks are an integral part of the ship's preventative maintenance schedule (PMS). Weekly checks include the emergency generator, fuel oil levels, lube oil levels, and radiator water levels. It also includes starting the emergency fire pump which should be left to run for a reasonable time which allows the pressure to be recorded. Machinery space dampers must be inspected and greased weekly, and the watertight bulkheads operated on location and remotely from the bridge. Monthly checks include visually inspecting the carbon dioxide storage room. This involves releasing the box door to test the alarm. By doing so, the engine room ventilation fans should trip. Fire detection equipment such as individual smoke detector circuits should be checked by spraying an aerosol directly beneath the sensor and observing the fire alarm panel. Fire extinguishers and hoses should be inspected visually. The emergency batteries should be checked for specific gravity and 'topped up' if required. Emergency lighting should be inspected and replaced if found defective. Remote operated valves should be checked monthly. Bilge alarms should be checked on location and remotely. Finally, the engines should be run for a reasonable time at least once a month, together with manipulation of the rudder, to check the lube oil levels, fuel oil levels, and battery charge. The outcome and results of each of these tests and checks must be formally recorded and retained on the bridge/in the engine control room as appropriate for future inspection.

PERSONAL PROTECTIVE EQUIPMENT

Ships are by nature extremely hazardous places to live and work. In such environments, the provision and use of personal protective equipment (PPE) is critical. PPE is designed to provide the wearer with a last line of defence against injury. It is not designed to be, nor should it be seen as, an alternative or replacement for safe working practices. Under SOLAS, the IMS Code, and UK law, all employers are required to provide their employees with PPE that is appropriate for the work that is performed. In most cases, this means providing as a minimum overalls, boots, gloves, hardhats, and goggles. It is also enforced under MLC regulation 4.3 – Health and Safety Protection and Accident Prevention. The regulation states that 'each [Flag State] Member shall ensure that mariners on ships that fly its flag are provided with occupational health protection and live, work and train on board ship in a safe and hygienic environment'. Chapter 8 of the *Code of Safe Working Practices for Seamen* (COSWP) provides comprehensive advice on the different types of PPE and their use. All UK registered vessels must carry – by law – a copy of COSWP on board. Indeed, COSWP is so highly regarded it has become the maritime industry's standard in terms of seafarer occupational health and safety. COSWP outlines the various types of PPE required to be carried on board, which is summarised in Table 4.1.

The law of each Flag State dictates the precise requirements regarding the provision and use of PPE on board ships, though as mentioned above all companies are required to adhere to the regulations set out by the MLC in regulation 4.3. For British seafarers, a helpful explanation

30 The merchant mercantile

Table 4.1 Types of PPE

Type of PPE	Examples
Head protection	Safety helmet, bump caps, hair net
Hearing protection	Earmuffs, ear plugs
Face and eye protection	Goggles, face shield
Respiratory protection	Dust mask, respirator, breathing apparatus
Body protection	High visibility boiler suit, safety belt, harnesses, aprons
Hand and foot protection	Gloves, safety boots, shoes
Protection against drowning	Lifejackets, life vests, buoyancy aids, lifebuoys
Protection against hypothermia	Immersion suit, anti-exposure suit

of the mariner occupational health regulations enforceable on UK flagged ships is provided in MSN 1870 (M+F). Although this applies specifically to UK flagged ships, it should be considered a useful guideline for all ships sailing under any flag. UK law states that shipowners must provide their employees with PPE at no cost to the individual. Many other Flag States have adopted a similar requirement. This obligation is also usually supported by the seafarer's contract of employment. This is particularly important for seafarers engaged under agency contracts. Other significant shipowner obligations under MSN 1870 (M+F) include regulation 8(4), which states 'a competent person should inspect each item of protective equipment at regular intervals and in all cases before and after use. All inspections should be recorded. Equipment should always be properly stowed in a safe place after use'. Furthermore, regulation 9 states 'defective or ineffective protective equipment provides no defence. It is therefore essential that the correct items of equipment are selected and that they are properly maintained'. To ensure maximum effectiveness, the manufacturer's instructions should be kept with the relevant equipment and, if necessary, referred to before use and during inspections. Though there are obligations on employers regarding the provision of PPE, there are also obligations on employees on wearing PPE. There is very little point in shipowners going to the expense of providing their crews with expensive personal equipment if seafarers do not use them. This is a considerable source of concern for the maritime industry. Lax supervision and management from senior officers and the complacent attitude of crew members have been linked to a number of entirely avoidable injuries occurring on board ships. Subsequently, ships require assertive leadership by example combined with continuous training. Wearing PPE should not become a burdensome exercise, but rather, should be seen as part of a positive top-down safety culture. Crew members who fail to 'suit up' or do not use the PPE provided should be reminded of their legal obligations and that they are not only putting themselves at risk but their fellow crew members as well. Continued misuse of PPE should and can amount to gross negligence and be grounds for dismissal. Where injuries have been sustained, and the investigation shows that PPE was neither used nor worn properly, this can negate any entitlement to compensation. It is important for crew members to recognise that protective equipment is a vital component of their working lives and can often be the difference between walking away from an incident intact and being permanent injured and maimed. It should also be reinforced that personal equipment is really the last defence against injury and should never be seen or used as a replacement for safe systems of work.

WORKING TIME AND REST

Almost all ships operate on a continuous 24 hour, seven days a week schedule, and container ships are no exception. This often places extreme pressure on the officers and crew.

To equalise the work/rest balance for seafarers, the IMO implemented the *Maritime Labour Convention* (MLC) in 2006, which came into force on 20 August 2013. Pursuant to title 2 of the MLC, crew members must not exceed a working time of 14 hours in any 24-hour period. Furthermore, the MLC states that seafarers are not permitted to exceed a total working time of 72 hours in any 168-hour period.[4] Rest periods must not be less than ten hours in any 24-hour period and 77 hours in any 168-hour period. That said, the MLC does provide some very specific exemptions to the work/rest regulation. Where these exemptions are applied, it is on the proviso that there is no discernible impact on crew safety, which must always be the overriding priority. To ensure seafarers maintain a healthy work/rest balance, seafarers cannot be requested, formally or otherwise, to exceed their workhours past the maximum allowed. It is also illegal to entice crew members to exceed their workhours through financial inducement. Although the standards set by the MLC are similar to the 2010 Manila amendments to the STCW Convention, both texts stop short of actually defining what a 'rest' period is. This is important as official health and welfare guidelines recommend a minimum eight hours' uninterrupted sleep in any 24-hour period. Such is the work regime on container ships that it is not uncommon for crew members to snatch rest as and when they can. As neither the MLC or STCW stipulate that the eight hours rest period must be consecutive, it is entirely legal for crew members to rest for two hours, work for six hours, rest for two hours, and so on. Obviously, this type of work regimen is far from ideal and would lead to severe fatigue and health complications. Even so, it is inadvisable but not illegal.

Short-sea conditions tend to be worse than on ocean-going ships. The reason is that passages are shorter, there is a higher density of local traffic, and hazards tend to be more numerous. It is not uncommon, especially on offshore support vessels to the oil and gas industry, for officers to work a 12 hours on, 12 hours off watch pattern, often for days and weeks at a time. On top of their watch duties, the officers also have their other duties to attend to when not on watch. This can make the working day extremely long and arduous, especially in heavy seas. Furthermore, with respect to the regulations, this watch pattern leaves very little margin for error, with industry research showing that seafarers who follow this routine are most likely to breach the regulations than those who follow the standard four on, eight off.[5] Seafarers who are fortunate enough to serve on vessels following the standard watch pattern should aim to achieve as much sleep as possible during one rest period, rather than splitting their sleep between the two rest periods. Unfortunately, that is often easier said than done, as the practical reality on board the ship often determines when crew members can get the rest they need. During sea passages this is not often a problem, but when approaching port, during anchorage, or navigating busy sea lanes, it is often necessary to have all 'hands on deck' – and often so for extended periods of time. Whilst this clearly contravenes the letter of the regulations, the safety of the ship is the greater priority, therefore crew members may be exempted from the work/rest restrictions. This requires careful monitoring and management not just by the onboard crew but also by the onshore vessel manager. As a case in point, a study of deck officers employed on English Channel ferries found that 41% of respondents who remained compliant with the regulations over a 28-day period also reported experiencing elevated levels of tiredness and fatigue.

Fatigue is by far one the worst and yet also one of the most common conditions to afflict seafarers. Without sufficient undisturbed sleep, the body begins to slow down and lose control of vital functions. The brain becomes groggy and easily confused. Metabolism slows resulting in loss of appetite, lower energy, apathy, and depression. If left unattended, the brain may eventually shut down completely causing the seafarer to unintentionally fall asleep. Sleeping on duty is inexcusable, but sleeping on watch puts the seafarer, their colleagues, and the ship in immediate danger. Furthermore, long term sleep deprivation

32 The merchant mercantile

– of which fatigue is a symptom – can lead to psychological issues later in life including dementia and Alzheimer's. With proper planning and monitoring, seafarers should be able to manage their work/rest balance without causing undue harm to themselves or endangering the vessel.

Work and rest time violations

Legally speaking, every individual on board is responsible for their own health and safety, which includes ensuring sufficient rest and sleep. Unfortunately, the fast paced nature of working and living on board container ships means achieving a work/life balance is difficult. Container ships, unlike other types of merchant vessels, often run to extremely tight schedules. Frequent port calls and little time spent in port can often mean crew members exceed their work/rest times through no fault of their own. This is an issue that affects many sectors and industries, but the maritime industry is perhaps one of the worst offenders. Add to that foul weather and heavy seas, and it is understandable why many seafarers begin to exhibit signs of fatigue. To combat this, the master has a responsibility to ensure their vessel is operated in a safe manner. This means managing the officers and ratings in such a way that if the work/rest limit is violated, sufficient rest time is allocated as soon as practicably possible. In any case, work/rest time violations should never become a frequent occurrence, as working time records are often the first documents to be inspected following an accident or incident. Any indication that the crew have frequently exceeded their work/rest times, and any evidence that suggests master knowingly permitted it, is a serious offence and the consequences can be severe.

WORKING IN EXTREME CONDITIONS

Foul weather and heavy seas

A fair wind and calm seas. This is what every seafarer wishes for each time they set sail. Foul weather makes navigation difficult and heavy seas are just nasty. Even seasoned seafarers suffer from seasickness! Unfortunately, nature often feels the need to conspire against sailors and rarely is a passage completely uneventful. Despite ships having the benefit of advanced technology, such as meteorological sensors and regular weather updates, it is common for squalls to develop without a moment's notice. This can make for very unpleasant conditions on board. Whenever advance warning is given that sea conditions are going to deteriorate, it is vital that the officers and crew take every possible precaution. This means checking and tightening the container lashings and rolling stock tensioners, securing loose tools and equipment, stowing personal items in cabins and offices, and securing the galley and mess. When sea conditions are especially rough, it is normal practice to man the bridge with the full complement of deck officers including the master, and to post additional lookouts.

Further to securing the deck and accommodation areas, it is equally important for the engine room personnel to prepare the machinery and plant for adverse sea conditions. In open waters the ship is ordinarily set to autopilot. At the onset of rough weather, it is strongly advised to revert to manual steering. This helps to prevent excessive hunting on the rudder. The engineers should also check and monitor the lube oil levels, linkages, and other critical parameters of the steering gear. Where the ship has more than one motor, and only one motor is running, it is good practice to switch on the second motor and operate both together. This provides maximum torque for turning the rudder. It is becoming increasingly popular for ships to have an unmanned machinery space (UMS). On traditional ships, there is always an engineer on watch (EOW). With UMS engine rooms, normal engine operating parameters are set by the engineers, which means the engine control room can be left unattended. When the ship encounters rough weather, it is imperative that the UMS function is disabled and the engine control room is fully manned. This is important as in heavy seas, it is highly likely the propeller(s) will rise out of and fall back into the water. When the propeller(s) rise and fall this causes fluctuations on the engine load, which in turn can damage the engines. To prevent this from happening, the engines should either be put on foul weather mode (where installed) or the rpm should be reduced accordingly. Furthermore, the engineers must maintain a regular check on the oil sump levels and tank levels. Failure to do so can set off false alarms, which may trip the engine causing internal damage. If the tank levels are not monitored, the flow level may fall below the pump inlets causing the engines to lose suction. To prevent power outages or blackouts, it is important for the standby generator to be kept onload.

Water ingress is more likely during heavy seas when waves can wash over the main decks. It is therefore imperative that all cargo holds, watertight bulkheads, watertight doors, and portals are closed and locked. Water ingress to the cargo holds can cause the ship to lose stability. As the volume of water increases, it can cause the ship to roll. As the ship tries to correct itself by righting to the opposite side, the effect is magnified by the added weight of the free-flowing water causing the ship to capsize. This is referred to as *free surface effect*. Admittedly, free surface effect is less likely to occur on box ships, as the container holds are subdivided. This restricts the free movement of water inside the hull. RORO ships, by virtue of having open internal decks, are more at risk of free surface effect, as are passenger ferries. Ships designed to carry liquids, such as oil tankers, have specially designed holds which are subdivided into smaller tanks. This prevents the fluids from building sufficient momentum to capsize the vessel. The types of ship most likely to suffer from free surface effect are bulk carriers. This is because they tend to have large open holds and carry vast quantities of free-flowing cargoes such as coal and grain. In the wrong conditions, free-flowing solid cargoes can behave in much the same way as fluids. Given bulk carriers lack the same degree of compartmentalisation found on oil tankers, it is easy to understand why free-surface effect is more of a concern than with most other types of vessels.

When the ship is about to encounter inclement conditions, it is strongly advisable for the crew to put in place other restrictions and precautions. Accessing the main and open decks during heavy seas should be avoided wherever possible. This reduces the potential for man-overboard incidents. All loose deck items such as mooring ropes, lashing equipment, and drums should be securely stowed and lashed to prevent them from breaking loose. As mentioned above, all openings in the deck for cargo and other spaces should be closed and locked, including non-essential vents. Wherever possible, internal access spaces and passageways should be used with extra care taken on stairs. It is always good practice to maintain three points of contact when going up or down stairways. This can be two feet and one hand or two hands and one foot. Under no circumstances should mechanical lifts be operated during rough weather. These should be isolated and closed off. Depending on the severity of the conditions, the OOW may make an announcement on the public address system advising crew members to take up positions as per the Muster List. This usually means posting extra lookouts either side of the bridge, at specific vantage points about the vessel, and in the engine room. It is likely the galley will go into restricted service with cold meals served instead of the usual selection of hot and cold meals.

Extreme heat and extreme cold

Depending on where and when the ship is operating, the crew may find themselves working in intolerable conditions. Ships operating around the equator, the Middle East, and in

Asia often encounter extreme heat and humidity. At the opposite end, ships operating in the polar regions, northern Europe, and the southern tip of South America experience extreme cold. Both conditions are problematic for the ship and her crew, and it is important that the correct precautions are taken. There are two potential effects which can cause the crew to lose effectiveness. The first is related to heat sickness caused by working in hot and humid conditions. Importantly, these need not necessarily be related to the ambient climate, as the engine room and cargo holds can often be of themselves quite inhospitable. *Heat exhaustion* is the first serious consequence of working in a hot environment. Heat exhaustion develops gradually and is caused by the loss of salt and water from the body through excessive perspiration (sweating). Perspiration is the body's natural heat control mechanism. As heat radiates out through the skin, vital fluids and salts are lost. These must be replaced. Salt is best ingested with food and supplemented by salt-containing fluids. When working in moderate heat (between 25°C and 32°C) at least four litres (seven pints) of fluids should be consumed daily; in hotter temperatures (between 32°C (90°F) and 40°C (105°F)) this should be increased to six litres (ten pints) daily. Fluid intake should be spaced out equally throughout the day and not consumed in one go. Doing so can cause other health effects which are best avoided. Although the body is good at regulating its internal temperature, it is not always able to accurately determine the ambient temperature. In other words, the brain can be fooled into thinking the temperature outside the body is cooler or warmer than it actually is. For example, if the air temperature reads 29°C (85°F) but there is zero humidity, the temperature will actually feel like it is closer to 26°C (78°F). Alternatively, if the air temperature reads 29°C (85°F) and there is 80% humidity, it will actually feel more like 36°C (97°F). Heat exhaustion is most likely to occur in high environmental temperatures within the range of 32°C and 40°C (90°F and 105°F). Temperatures above 54°C (130°F) can lead to heatstroke.[6]

Heat stroke is the most serious consequence from being in hot ambient temperatures. In simple terms, heat stroke is caused by the thermostat in the brain failing. In this situation the body cannot regulate its temperature and becomes dangerously overheated. It is quite common for heat stroke to follow heat exhaustion, as natural perspiration can no longer cool the body. Heat stroke can occur suddenly causing unconsciousness within minutes. If left untreated, it can be lethal. Symptoms of heat stroke include headache, dizziness, and discomfort; restlessness and confusion; hot, flushed, and dry skin; a rapid deterioration in motor and verbal response; full, pounding pulse; and a body temperature above 40°C (70°F). Anyone exhibiting symptoms of heat stroke should be wrapped in a cold, wet sheet until the body temperature has fallen to below 38°C (68°F). Once the casualty's temperature has cooled sufficiently, replace the wet sheet with a dry sheet. The dry sheet helps to prevent the body temperature from falling too much. It is important to monitor the casualty for at least a couple of hours in case their condition deteriorates or they fall unconscious. If the casualty's condition does deteriorate and shows no signs of improvement, seek immediate onshore medical assistance.

When working in cold weather regions it is just as important to take appropriate steps towards personal health and safety as it is in warmer tropical climates. The risks of being exposed to the extreme cold when out on deck or on the bridge wings are numerous and dangerous. To avoid hypothermia, always wear appropriate clothing. It is advisable to don several layers of clothing rather one or two thick layers. Each layer should fit loosely, as tight clothing restricts blood circulation. It is critical for warm blood to reach the vital organs and the extremities.[7] Equally as important is to protect the face, ears, hands, and feet. Boots should be waterproof and insulated. If possible and safe to do so, wear a hat though this should not unduly impact on vision and hearing. When working in extremely cold conditions, aim to take frequent short breaks in a warm and dry shelter. Drink warm beverages and eat warm, high calorie foods. If working for an extended time outside, use a 'buddy system'; this helps to avoid exhaustion and fatigue. In the worst situation, crew members working outside may begin to exhibit signs of hypothermia. This is the medical term for dangerously low body temperature. There are two phases to hypothermia. The early stage involves shivering, fatigue, loss of coordination, confusion, and disorientation. If not treated in the early stage, hypothermia can develop into a life-threatening condition. The second phase to hypothermia is the late stage. At this point the body stops shivering and the skin turns blue. The pupils dilate and the pulse slows. Breathing becomes harder and laboured. As the body diverts blood away from the extremities and inwards towards the vital organs, unconsciousness happens followed by cardiac arrest and death. Recognising the signs of hypothermia and treating them are critical for the short-term survival of the crew member. As soon as there is any indication of hypothermia developing, request immediate medical assistance. Remove the casualty into a warm room or shelter. Remove any wet clothing. Attempt to warm the centre of the casualty's body first (the chest, neck, head, and groin) as these are core locations of heat loss. If available, apply a loose dry layer of blankets, sheets, towels, or clothing. If the casualty is conscious, try to get them to sip a lukewarm drink but do not supply them with alcohol. Once the casualty's body temperature has begun to increase, keep them dry, warm, and wrapped in a blanket. If the casualty is unconscious, follow the same steps above but do not attempt to give the casualty any fluids or solids as they may choke.

CONFINED SPACES

Modern container ships are complex structures with numerous confined spaces such as cargo holds, chain lockers, cofferdams, water tanks, fuel tanks, void spaces, duct keels, engine crankcases, and exhaust and scavenge receivers, though in fact any area of the ship which has been left closed for any length of time without ventilation must be considered a confined space. This is because changes in the internal environment of a space which is not labelled unsafe can be rendered unsafe, for example by vapours from an adjacent space. To provide some context, the UK *Health and Safety Executive* (HSE) defines a confined space as any location on board the ship which is 'substantially enclosed and where serious injury can occur from hazardous substances or conditions within the space or nearby'. In effect, there are three defining features that make a compartment a confined space. First, the compartment must have limited openings for access and egress; second, the compartment must not be intended for continuous human occupancy; and third, the space is large enough to enter and work within. Many of the confined spaces on board are used for operational machinery, storing machine parts, or workshop equipment, and many more contain pipes, flutes, and other critical infrastructure. This presents a serious problem when it becomes necessary for crew members to enter confined spaces in the performance of their duties. This might include carrying out essential maintenance, repairing faults and eroded pipe-work, or cleaning out bilge and fuel tanks. Due to their awkward size and shapes, it is very easy for crew members to become stuck inside the confined space. Most confined spaces do not have natural or artificial lighting, which makes unaided visibility almost impossible. Furthermore, as most confined spaces are sealed shut, they tend to have little to no oxygen, which makes it impossible to breath without breathing apparatus. Breathing apparatus also prevent crew members from becoming overwhelmed by toxic fumes and gases. It cannot be stressed enough that confined spaces are inherently dangerous, and every possible precaution should be taken before attempting entry. Since 1 January 2015 it has been mandatory under SOLAS regulation III/19 for ship crews to carry out confined space entry and rescue drills at least once every two months.

36 The merchant mercantile

There are many hazards associated with confined spaces, many of which pose a serious threat to human health. As alluded above, the most serious threat is *oxygen deficiency*. The acceptable oxygen level where unassisted entry is permitted is between 19.5% and 23.55%. Any less than this and the compartment is too dangerous to enter without breathing apparatus. It is important to recognise that even if an oxygen sample at the place of entry shows safe levels of oxygen in the compartment, it is quite probable that further into the compartment the oxygen level will be much less. This is caused by a build-up of vapours and gases within the interior regions of the compartment. The most common reason is oxidation caused by rusting steel parts. As steel oxidises or rusts, it consumes the oxygen in the atmosphere. Oxygen depletion may also occur from hot work such as welding. Other causes are the ingress of inert gases as well as dust residues from sand and dry cargoes such as iron ore and coal. The latter is less likely to occur on container ships and more likely to occur on bulk carriers. When entering a confined space appropriate personal protective equipment and respiratory protective equipment[8] must be worn. This is because the presence of *toxic vapours* can make confined spaces lethal even if the oxygen level is between the 19.5% and 23.55% range. Even if the compartment is oxygen enriched (i.e., there is too much oxygen in the compartment), it is entirely possible for the person working in the compartment to succumb to oxygen poisoning. Common symptoms associated with toxic poisoning include eye irritation, headache, and unconsciousness. Medium to high concentrations of toxic vapours can cause suffocation and death. Inhospitable conditions within confined spaces are not solely caused by the ship. Leaking cargoes or tanks containing chemicals, ballast water, or even brown water can cause the atmosphere within a confined space to become lethal.

Although accidents should not happen, they commonly do, and the causes are usually related to human failings. Despite stringent checklists and permit to work (PTW) systems, seafarers remain their own worst enemy. This is partly down to inadequate training but also poor supervision. Complacency, laziness, and a general failure to appreciate the hazards on board ship are all common causes for accidents. To safeguard the safety and health of crew members, ships have systems that extensively use the *checklist*. Checklists are an important control measure and should never be treated as a simple box-ticking exercise. The SMS will clearly set out the procedures for preparing, entering, working within, and leaving confined spaces. These procedures and safeguards must be followed diligently and without exception. At the core of the SMS is the *risk assessment*. The risk assessment is the very first action that should be carried out when planning a confined space entry. The risk assessment should be completed by a competent officer and is designed to minimise the potential for accidents by assessing every aspect of the task, identifying the hazards, deciding the control measures, and finding alternatives or solutions to mitigate risks. A new risk assessment should be carried out every time a confined space entry is made. By doing so, the risk assessment can account for potential changes in the use of the confined space or changes in the internal environment.[9] Critical to the risk assessment is a list of the intended works and any known hazards. By identifying both, risk mitigation steps can be put in place to help safeguard the crew member against any hazards to their health.

Once the risk assessment has been completed and countersigned by the master, the point of entry to the confined space must be prepared. This might involve pressurising or depressurising the confined space to remove any toxic vapours that may be trapped in the compartment. All potential fire hazards should be removed at best, or at worst, reduced as low as reasonably possible (ALARP). This is especially important if hot work is to be carried out. Prior to entry, the confined space must be well ventilated. Sufficient time should be given to set up a ventilation system. This may involve the use of natural or mechanical ventilation using blowers. Once the compartment has been thoroughly ventilated, it should be tested for oxygen and the presence of toxic vapours using an oxygen analyser and gas detector.

Atmospheric testing instruments should also be used to detect the presence of carbon monoxide and hydrogen sulphide. These tests should be carried out at different heights within the compartment and ideally towards the top, middle, and bottom thirds. This is because gases behave in different ways; for example, methane rises to the top as it is lighter than air, carbon monoxide stays in the middle as it weighs the same as air, and carbon dioxide sinks to the bottom as it is heavier than air. Where possible, always wear a facemask or respirator, as exposure to even small amounts of toxic vapour can cause serious health issues. For example, as little as two to five ppm of hydrogen sulphide can cause blinding headaches, nausea, and eye irritation. Sadly, accidents happen with irregular frequency when crew members slip, trip, fall, or succumb to irrespirable air. Unlike on deck or in accommodation areas, even innocuous accidents that occur in confined spaces have the potential to escalate quickly.

PERMITS TO WORK

One of the main safeguards used on board ships to prevent accidents and injuries is the permit to work (PTW). Each permit to work is valid only for the specific task. The permit to work is an official document and contains important information such as the location of the confined space, the type of work to be performed and any limitations associated to the work activity, details of the work team and the tools to be used during the work, any potential hazards or risks, any necessary and specific precautions to be taken, required personal or respiratory protective equipment to be worn, agreed communication methods and intervals, the duration that crew members are authorised to carry out the work – usually in minutes; the time the permit to work was issued and the time the permit to work will expire. To be valid, the permit to work must bear the signature of the person authorising the permit to work at the time of issue, the signature of the person undertaking the work activity, and the signature of the person who authorised the permit upon completion of the work activity. A permit to work can only be issued for a specific amount of time. If the time expires and the task is not yet complete, then a new permit to work must be issued. Every permit to work must be reviewed and authorised by the master; failure to acquire the master's signature invalidates the permit to work meaning the work activity must not happen. Before starting the work activities, certain precautions must be taken. These include posting warning signs around the work area alerting other crew members to work activity. A general announcement should be made over the public address system advising whether specific plant, machinery, or systems will be switched off or isolated. If the works are likely to impact on the operation of the ship's main systems, the chief engineer and EOW should also be advised accordingly. Once the works are complete, the permit to work must be signed and closed off by the authorising officer and retained on the bridge for future inspection.

Seafaring has always been a dangerous occupation. It involves physically demanding work, long hours, and constant fluctuations in temperatures and environments. These can all take their toll on crew health and wellbeing. As well as the environmental factors that affect seafarers, the psychological demands of being at sea can be equally difficult to manage.

GENERAL HEALTH AND WELLBEING

Many of the health and safety risks faced by seafarers are immediate, but there are also many long-term onset health risks. Some of the major injuries and health complaints reported by seafarers over the course of their careers have included tennis elbow, hand arm vibration syndrome (HAVS), cardio-vascular disease (CVD), musculoskeletal disorder (MSD), various types of cancer including lung cancer, renal cancer, leukaemia and lymphoma, sexually transmitted diseases (STDs), and pandemic and epidemic diseases contracted from bacteria and viruses. Whilst it is impossible to completely eradicate these health issues, fostering a safety-first culture is a positive way of reducing the potential for long-term health-related issues. First and foremost, keeping mentally and physically active is the best way of maintaining a good standard of health. In recent years health and safety has come to cover a much broader spectrum than simply trying to avoid workplace-related accidents. Today, officers and crew members are expected to be aware of the significance of their safety and wellbeing and to apply it to their daily routine and work practices. It is widely accepted by most seafarers and maritime occupational health professionals that the deck is by far the most accident-prone area on board. That is not necessarily the same as saying the deck is the most dangerous; rather, it means more accidents and injuries are sustained on deck than anywhere else on the ship. The best way to avoid accidents is to be conscious of the risks, recognise the hazards, and to act accordingly. Operating equipment properly, avoiding danger zones, keeping a watchful eye over each other, and using PPE are recognised ways of preventing entirely avoidable accidents. Accidents are generally categorised into one of seven types: (1) slips, trips and falls; (2) incorrect manual handling and lifting; (3) compressed air incidents; (4) exposure to chemicals; (5) electrical incidents; (6) crane and lifting gear incidents; and (7) man-overboard incidents. In addition, injuries such as cuts, abrasions, and burns are a common occurrence on board, and more so when operating deck tools and machinery.

Slips, trips, and falls are three of the most common types of accidents that occur on the ship's deck. These accidents are not as trivial as they may sound, as slips and trips can cause severe physical injuries. The main causes for slips and trips are slippery deck surfaces, the improper use of catwalks, missing gratings, railings, and stanchions, missing warning signs, improper use of PPE (especially safety shoes and safety harnesses), lack of situational awareness, lack of awareness of the job, and absence of safe systems of work. Falls mostly happen when working at height such as on the masts, lashing bridges, and hatch covers, working in or around cargo holds, and working aloft or outboard. Most slips, trips, and falls are avoidable by keeping the deck clean and dry, following designated catwalks and correct passages, avoiding shortcuts, using proper non-skid safety shoes, using appropriate safety harnesses when working aloft, maintaining situational awareness, and regularly analysing the hazards and risks associated with the task. *Manually handling, lifting, and carrying* is an activity performed every day by seafarers the world over. Yet incorrect manual handling techniques are one of the primary causes for accidents and injuries. The correct method for lifting a heavy load is to bend the knees and squat down to the load. Keep the back as perpendicular to the ground as possible. Use the leg and arm muscles to lift the load instead of the back muscles. By doing so, the weight of the load is put on the arms and legs, and not the back. Distribute the weight evenly. If the load is too heavy to lift by one person, ask for help and avoid lifting alone. Try to avoid sharp edges wherever possible. When walking with the load, take small steps. Regularly stop and rest wherever it is safe but avoid creating hazards for other crew members. Try to ensure the load does not prevent clear vision of the way forward. When changing direction, use the feet and do not twist the body. When laying the load down, bend the knees to squat. Never bend the back. *Compressed air* is often used on board by pneumatic power tools and cleaning equipment. Mishandling compressed air is extremely dangerous and can cause severe injuries. When compressed air is applied to an open cut or wound the compressed air can force its way into the blood stream causing blood clots. These are difficult to diagnose and can cause death. When using compressed air, never point or blow the compressed air in the direction of someone. Avoid using compressed air to dust down clothing such as boiler suits. This prevents dust and other sharp foreign object debris from being lodged into the fabric. Air cylinders containing compressed air and pressurised gases should be secured in a vertical position and far away from sources of heat such as vents and ducts. Before using compressed air equipment, make sure to depressurise the line after use to prevent pressure clogs from developing.

Chemical exposure is another cause of serious injury. Before working with chemicals, always take note of the nearest emergency eye wash station. Wear the correct PPE such as safety goggles and a splash apron. Any spills and drips must be cleaned immediately using the correct cleaning fluid or sand. Chemical contact with the eyes can lead to partial or complete loss of eyesight, and contact with naked skin can cause burns and dermatitis. Direct and constant skin exposure to chemicals such as paints, thinners, and metal polish should be avoided as much as possible. Any splashes or drips into the eyes, on to naked skin, or if ingested must be reported to the Medical Officer immediately. Any kind of *oil spill or leak* must be prevented to avoid polluting the marine environment. This is a serious offence under the MARPOL regulations, and all steps should be taken to avoid oil or oily water from washing overboard. *Electrical equipment* is used extensively on deck. Without the right precautions in place, these can be potentially lethal. Contact with live wires, poorly insulated tools, and defective equipment can all cause electric shock. Electric arcs, flashes, and fires caused by overheated electrical equipment can lead to severe burns and electrocution. Before using any electrical equipment always check for signs of frayed or damaged contacts. If required, isolate and quarantine the equipment for repair or destruction. Keep wires and leads away from sources of heat or conductive fluids such as seawater. Never leave cables lying across the deck plate, as this presents a trip hazard. Always wear appropriate PPE such as rubber soled shoes or safety boots and rubberised electrical gloves.

Refrigerated holds and reefer containers present a novel hazard. Before entering a refrigerated hold, reefer container, or chilled store, always ensure the point of entry and exit is free from obstruction. Where possible, assign a lookout to remain outside the compartment and maintain constant contact. Agree some form of emergency signal in case it becomes impossible to vacate the compartment. If working for an extended period, it may be necessary to request a permit to work. *Cranes and lifting gear* operations pose many hazards and are often the cause of very severe injuries. Cranes and lifting gear should only ever be used by SQEP operators. When loads are in suspension, all crew members must maintain a safe distance from the drop hazard zone. Standard signalling systems and two-way radios should be used to facilitate communication between the crane operator and ground crew. Slings, hooks, and chains should be approved and certified. Never exceed the crane's Safe Working Load (SWL) limit. *Man-overboard* or MOB incidents are discussed in more detail later but suffice it to say that incidents involving man-overboard are most likely to occur on deck. This is due to the heightened risk of slips, trips, and falls.

Incidents involving dangerous goods must be reported immediately by the master to the appropriate authorities of the nearest coastal State. The report must follow the reporting procedures set out in the *Supplement to the International Maritime Dangerous Goods Code. Boiler hazards* are a perennial issue for the engine room crew. On earlier ships, the marine boiler was primarily used for the propulsion plant, which ran on steam. Today, the steam generated by the boiler is utilised in various systems throughout the engine room including heating the fuel for the main engine. Despite advances in marine technology, the boiler remains a dangerous fitment. Boiler explosions are an infrequent but extremely dangerous occurrence that has the potential to maim and kill anyone within the vicinity of the explosion and to cause severe structural damage to the vessel. Boiler explosions can happen when the fuel system within the boiler is mishandled or when the steam pressure inside the boiler drum is improperly regulated. *Boiler fires* and *boiler meltdowns* are just as hazardous

40 The merchant mercantile

as they can destroy the internal tubing of the boiler. This can lead to a boiler explosion and engine room fire. *Scalding* is a common consequence of failing to take appropriate precautions when operating and maintaining the boiler system. Scalding is a burn caused by high-temperature steam. By some industry standards, eight out of every ten marine engineers have sustained scalding at least once in their careers. The boiler and associated pipework, valves, and auxiliaries have very hot surfaces as they carry steam to different parts of the ship. Direct skin contact with any of these exposed surfaces will cause severe skin burns. Therefore, safety is critical when operating marine boilers.

Asbestos is a natural material that was used extensively in shipbuilding up to the mid-1980s. A cheap and abundant resource, asbestos is fire resistant and has excellent heat resilient properties. This made it ideal for fire proofing insulation. Unfortunately, asbestos can also be hazardous to health. When left in an undisturbed condition, asbestos is a benign material. But when it disintegrates it forms small-hooked particles that when inhaled get stuck in the lungs. Asbestos particles have been linked to all manner of cancers including Mesothelioma and lung cancer. Though asbestos is no longer used in the construction of new vessels, there is still a considerable quantity of asbestos in ships typically over 40 years old. For that reason, SOLAS chapter II-1 regulation 3-5 sets out specific provisions where asbestos may remain such as in the vanes of rotary vane air compressors and rotary vane vacuum pumps; in insulation and watertight joints where the temperature of circulating fluids exceeds 350°C (662°F) and the pressure exceeds 70 bar; in locations where there is a heightened risk of fire, corrosion, or toxicity; and in locations where there is a requirement for supple and flexible thermal insulation on equipment or machinery that regularly operates at temperatures above 1,000°C (1,832°F). *Toxic substances* that are known to cause cancer are referred to as carcinogens. In every life on board it is quite normal to unwittingly interact with many carcinogenic substances. This is because many of the materials on board ships contain carcinogenic agents. In this instance 'materials' includes not only cargo but other essential substances such as paints, greases, lubes, and oils. These substances contain toxic chemicals such as *benzene* and other organic compounds. Benzene has low solubility in water but can mix in air. This means it is very easy to inhale benzene fumes. Benzene causes body cells to mutate, preventing them from functioning properly. This in turn can lead to cancer and other associated health-related complications. Organic compounds such as *butadiene* and *trichloroethylene* are also widely used carcinogenic agents as are variants of *turpentine*.

Physical contaminants such as silica dust or quartz particles are also dangerous when inhaled. Silicosis affects the lungs causing pneumonia, Potter's Rot, and tuberculosis (TB). Silica dust and quartz particles are often more pronounced when sanding and grinding or sailing in areas affected by sandstorms. When carrying perishable cargoes, certain foods can turn toxic during transit. *Aflatoxins* are carcinogenic and are caused by the presence of fungi. The development of aflatoxins is almost impossible to prevent, as ship's holds are generally warm and moist – ideal conditions for breeding many strains of harmful bacteria. Before and after handling food cargoes, always exercise good personal hygiene to avoid infection and spreading bacteria throughout the ship. One of the major attractions of working at sea is the opportunity to travel the world. Often this means stopping at ports not frequented by tourists. This also means it is much easier to contract *contagious diseases and pathogens*. It is vital that crew members exercise extreme caution when going ashore for any reason. As the Covid-19 pandemic has demonstrated, it is all too easy to be infected and to then spread that infection to others. In a small, closely knit community like a ship, that can be a disaster. The risk of contracting contagious diseases is not limited to crew members going ashore. Equally, it is just as important to prevent anyone who is infected with localised diseases from boarding the ship. Many different officials from the port authority, stevedores, superintendents, Port State Control (PSC), pilots, agents, and company representatives may come aboard whilst the ship is alongside. Every one of these is a potential source of infection. Before arriving in port, it is good practice to liaise with the local health authorities to establish whether there are any health concerns the ship should be aware of. If so, avoid going ashore and limit the number of people coming on board to the bare minimum. Anyone who does not have an essential reason to board the vessel should be refused access at the gangway.

Humans are not the only source of disease transmission. Mosquitoes are one of the worst causes of infection and disease amongst seafarers. *Malaria* and *Dengue Fever* are both deadly if not treated. Luckily, it is quite easy to prepare the ship for entering regions where mosquitoes are prevalent. Anti-malarial medication should be taken before, during, and after any port visit or when transiting through a mosquito-infected area. Always wear appropriate clothing when outdoors, for example long-sleeved shirts, long trousers tucked into socks, and headwear. Shut all exterior doors and bulkheads and fit mosquito nets across open windows. Fitting a mosquito net above and around the bed can help prevent mosquito bites when asleep and wear plenty of insect repellent. Aside from airborne contaminants, bloodborne contaminants also pose a somewhat less significant risk for seafarers. In 2014 the IMO issued *Circular Letter No.3484* providing information and guidance, based on recommendations developed by the *World Health Organisation* (WHO), on the precautions to be taken to minimise the risks to seafarers of *Ebola* and other related bloodborne infections. This circular was issued following the outbreak of Ebola in Equatorial Guinea in December 2013. Despite the Ebola outbreak in West Africa waning (as of June 2021), the spread of the Ebola virus has continued to infect other West African countries. It is therefore important that seafarers exercise discretion and common sense when visiting infected regions. Some container ships are fitted with swimming pools which are filled with untreated seawater. Though it is unusual for bacteria to survive in open water, the effluence from bays, rivers, and estuaries are perfect bacterial breeding grounds and can spread bacteria into open water where concentrations are high enough to sustain bacterial colonies. Avoid swimming in coastal water areas and always wash thoroughly afterwards.

THE MUSTER LIST AND MUSTER CARD

The *Muster List* (ML) is a legal document mandated under SOLAS chapter III, regulation 8 and 37, and applies to all ships. The ML must conform to set standards of presentation and information. It states what actions must be taken in the event of an emergency; lists the various types of alarms and whether they are audible, visual, or both; and states where individual crew members are required to assemble in different emergency situations. The ML must be written in English and any other language stipulated by the Flag State. It must also be prominently displayed in conspicuous locations throughout the ship. The ML further specifies how the order to abandon ship must be given.[10]

Accordingly, each crew member when joining the vessel is assigned specific emergency duties. These might include closing watertight doors and hatches; assembling and carrying equipment and supplies to the lifeboats; or performing fire response and emergency team duties. The ML also provides for alternates. On most ships, this follows the standard chain of command. If the master is incapacitated, the chief officer takes command. If the master and chief officer are both incapacitated, the second officer takes charge and so on. Where a vessel has more than one lifeboat, the ML will display an annex called the *Lifeboat Crew Assignment List* (LCAL). Each crew member has their name annotated against an assigned lifeboat. The list displays the name of each officer assigned to command the lifeboat and the

42 The merchant mercantile

duties of each crew member. All crew members are assigned specific duties in the event of abandoning the ship. These might include carrying lifesaving appliances such as the EPIRB or SART, readying the lifeboats or life rafts for launch, and launching the lifeboats or life rafts. The *muster card* is a summary of the muster list and must be available in every cabin and office on board. The muster card specifies each crew member's muster station and their assigned emergency duties. Like the ML, the muster card must be written in English and any other language stipulated by the Flag State. It must also include clear and unambiguous safety instructions supported by illustrations.[11]

FIRE AND EMERGENCY DRILLS

Fire and emergency drills are designed to acquaint new crew members with the onboard emergency response procedures and to maintain procedural currency for experienced crew members. Drills provide an opportunity to train the crew in the use of firefighting appliances such as Self-Contained Breathing Apparatus (SCBA), different types of fire extinguishers, the CO_2 flooding systems, casualty evacuation equipment, donning and doffing PPE, donning life jackets and immersion suits, operating the sprinkler system, and so on. It is imperative that drills are carried out as realistically as possible. In accordance with the *Merchant Shipping Act 1995*, muster and fire drills must be carried out at specific points in time and at regular intervals thereafter. The act specifically mandates that fire drills must be carried out within 24 hours of leaving port where more than 25% of the crew have not taken part in a muster or fire drill within the previous month. The Muster List for the drill must be conspicuously displayed. The list must also be available on the bridge, in the engine control room, and throughout the crew accommodation. A *Fire Control Plan* (FCP) should also be displayed at strategic locations around the ship. Every crew member should be provided with clear instructions on how to respond in the event of an emergency. The timings of drills should be regularly changed to allow those crew members who did not attend the previous drill to participate (for example, watchkeepers). The location of the drill should also be changed regularly. Muster stations must be positioned such that they are readily accessible from the accommodation block and as close as possible to the disembarkation station.

All ships must have assigned emergency response teams (ERT) whose members are SQEP in specific duties. Most ships follow a generic response framework consisting of the Command Team, Emergency Team, Engine Room Team, a Roving Commission, and a Medical Team. The Command Team consists of the master and the third officer, whose duties include coordinating and overseeing the incident from the bridge. Members of the *Emergency Team* operate at the incident location and are led by the chief officer or second engineer. The *Engine Room Team* is led by the chief engineer and ensures all critical propulsion, steering, and power distribution systems remain operable. The *Roving Commission* is usually led by the bosun and, as the name implies, rove about the vessel looking for any secondary incidents or signs of damage that may not have been identified earlier. The Medical Team consists of the Chief Cook and the stewards, who are on standby to render any emergency first aid as may be required. Of all the causes of accidents and casualties on board ship, fire remains at the very top. Even small fires have the potential to ground and sink ships. Most fires on board are caused by crew member negligence. The accommodation and galley are particularly vulnerable. Maintaining good standards of housekeeping is key to preventing accommodation fires. This includes resisting the temptation to smoke in bed. Disposing of lit cigarette butts into wastepaper baskets is an excellent way of starting fires. Lighting incense sticks and candles are also common causes for cabin fires and should be strongly – but sensitivity – discouraged.[12] Under no circumstances should crew members be permitted

Health and safety 43

to use hot plates or heaters for cooking inside their cabin, nor should any personal equipment with loose or open wires be permitted on board. Drying clothes over portable heaters is strictly forbidden as it can cause the appliance to overheat and spark. When in the laundry room, it is important to ensure irons are never left on and unattended. Last of all, oily rags should be left in the engine room or work areas and never brought into accommodation spaces and cabins. Galley and mess fires are just as likely to occur as general accommodation fires if the galley staff do not pay sufficient attention to what they are doing. Therefore, they should always ensure the galley is attended when the hot plate is switched on and hot oil is never left unsupervised.

Lifeboat drills, sometimes referred to simply as boat drills or muster drills, are an exercise that is conducted regularly when the ship is at sea and every time new personnel join the crew. The lifeboat drill, as the name infers, is designed to prepare the crew for the worst possible eventuality – abandoning ship. The drill requires the crew to don lifejackets and make way towards the muster point. Depending on the aim of the drill, the lifeboats may be manned and deployed. The planning and preparation, attendance, performance, and any lessons learnt from the drill must be recorded and kept on board for Port State Control inspection. In some maritime jurisdictions, local laws hold crew members liable for civil charges if they do not attend lifeboat drills without good reason. For example, on US flagged ships, crew members who do not attend lifeboat drills may receive substantial fines directly linked to their rank. Lifeboat drills are not typically carried out on short sea voyages such as cross channel ferries, dinner cruises, and river boats. Instead, a safety briefing is usually delivered by a senior deck officer. On container ships, the lifeboat drill is performed in accordance with the procedures set out in the Muster List.

The 'women and children first' concept

Perhaps one of the most famous aspects of ship emergencies is the concept of *women and children first*. Made famous by the tragic sinking of the *RMS Titanic* in 1912, the concept of *women and children first* actually originates from the untimely demise of the *HMS Birkenhead*. This gave rise to what would become known as the 'Birkenhead Drill'. Whilst there is no provision in maritime law that states women and children should be evacuated from a sinking vessel first, the Birkenhead Drill is a persistent code of conduct that dates from 1852. The *HMS Birkenhead* was on route from Cape Town to Algoa Bay in South Africa when it struck rocks in rough weather and swiftly sank. As there were insufficient lifeboats on board, the crew and soldiers famously stood firm allowing the women and children to evacuate. Of the estimated 643 lives on board, only 193 survived. The *Birkenhead Drill* later became the subject of a poem by the English poet and author Rudyard Kipling and would become synonymous with extreme acts of courage and chivalry in the face of hopeless circumstances.

EXAMPLE: SAUNA FIRE

A large shrimp-processing ship was engaged in fishing. At approximately 1515hrs, the bosun awoke to the smell of smoke. On leaving his cabin, he saw flames through the window of the closed sauna door and smoke venting from the top of the door. He went to the messroom and alerted the crew members there. One crew member took a fire extinguisher and accompanied the bosun back to the sauna while another crew member went to the bridge. The bosun opened the sauna door and the other crew member emptied the fire extinguisher in the direction of the flames. The door was then closed and the two lefts for the muster station on deck 3. Meanwhile, the OOW had activated the fire alarm and announced over the PA system that there was a fire on board; this was not a drill. Some crew members mustered with their lifejackets at the muster station and began preparing the ship's fire hoses while other crew members waited for instructions from the chief officer, who had remained on the bridge. One person was still unaccounted for. The second officer donned breathing apparatus and went to deck 3 to check the cabins. After confirming that the deck had been evacuated, he returned to the bridge, donned a fire suit, exchanged the air cylinder on his breathing apparatus, and left the bridge for the forward deck.

The chief engineer, second engineer, and maintenance man were working in the shrimp-processing factory when the alarm sounded. The chief engineer sent the second engineer and maintenance man to the muster station, and then went to the engine control room, where he met the missing person from the muster. He sent the person to the muster station then confirmed with the bridge that the missing crew member had been located and instructed to attend the muster station. Approximately ten minutes after the fire alarm sounded, everyone on board was now accounted for. At the muster station, one person was now dressing in a fire suit but was encountering difficulties. The boots did not fit, the suspenders broke, and the helmet visor was cracked. Once the fire hoses were ready, he proceeded to the forward deck. When he reached the forward deck, neither he nor the other crew members there received direction on how to fight the fire. He took the initiative to enter deck 3 with a fire hose, alone and without a safety line, as the line had broken.

Another crew member remained on deck to assist with the firehose and open the forward hatch. Dense smoke limited visibility as the firefighter descended the ladder and arrived on deck 3. When he entered the tanning room within which the sauna was located, he stumbled and fell over boxes that were stored there. Recovering, he used the fire hose to spray in and around the sauna, inside the tanning room, and the adjacent changing room. Before returning to the forward deck, he tried to close the sauna door but was unable to do so and left it open. When the second officer arrived on the forward deck, he proceeded down the hatch with a prepared firehose and a makeshift safety line. He was unable to see through the dense smoke, and inadvertently blocked the way of the firefighter leaving the sauna who was ascending the ladder. The low-pressure alarm was sounding on his breathing apparatus. The crew on deck now decided to fight the fire with two teams of two, but air in the breathing apparatus was low for team one and soon the alarms sounded. They returned to the muster station. As there were no spare air cylinders on board, they re-entered deck 3 with a firehose, employing dust masks as a rudimentary form of airway protection. Team one could see another firefighter in front of the tanning room door but could not progress further as the firehose was not long enough to reach the sauna door.

They sprayed the entrance to the tanning room with water while the other firefighter sprayed the inside of the tanning room and the sauna door. At approximately 1630hrs, the three crew members retreated from the tanning room area and closed access to deck 3 to contain the fire. Crew members on the forward deck then closed the accommodation fire dampers in the vents to suffocate the fire. By approximately 1745hrs, the heat and smoke from the fire was dissipating. It was considered likely that the fire was contained within the sauna and smouldering. Once the fire was fully extinguished, burned pieces of a wooden footrest were found below the sauna's electric heater, indicating that the footrest may have been on the heater when it was turned on. With the heater left unattended, the heat likely ignited the footrest, starting the fire. Among other things, the investigation found that past fire drills conducted on the ship had been repetitive and did not include realistic emergency scenarios. The crew would start the main and emergency fire pumps, inspect, and pressurise the fire hoses, and then simulate a fire on deck by spraying the trawl doors with water. The crew did not perform post-drill evaluations.

LESSONS LEARNED

Regular fire drills using varied and realistic scenarios are critical to confirm that firefighting equipment is in working order and to reinforce the crew's knowledge of how to use the equipment and of their assigned emergency duties. Post-drill evaluations in a round-table discussion with all involved are a valuable tool for quality assurance and continued improvement. While hindsight can be said to be 20/20, in this case it remains debatable whether the first intervention of opening the door and emptying a fire extinguisher in the general direction of the fire was effective or only gave the fire more air. Normal procedures would have put boundary cooling in effect, followed by properly dressed and equipped firefighters attacking the fire in an organised manner with a pressurised hose for full effect and safety. It was over an hour after the fire had been discovered and after the attempted re-suppression with hoses before ventilation dampers were closed to starve the fire of oxygen. This is yet another indicator of lack of practice and familiarity with fire suppression procedures. Attacking the fire with dust masks was unnecessarily foolhardy.

As we have already discussed, drills play an important role in preparing the crew for emergency situations, and the ship's engine room is no exception. Engine room personnel are required to carry out drills and training procedures on a regular basis to ensure they are fully familiar and competent in responding to emergencies. On most container ships, there are ten specific training regimes that marine engineers and engine room ratings must be familiar with. These are:

1. *Engine room fire drill*. Fire drills, which include firefighters from both the deck and engine departments, must be carried out frequently to ensure the ship's crew are well versed in tackling engine room fires. Fire drills should be carried out at various levels and on different machinery fixtures within the engine room including the boiler, generator, purifier, main engines, scavenger, and so on
2. *Flooding drill*. A delayed action during engine room flooding can lead to the loss of critical machinery such as the generators and the main engines. This in turn can lead to blackout situations. Engine room flooding response training and immediate repair actions must be carried out regularly. Flood training should include response actions to grounding and collisions
3. *Enclosed space drill*. Engine rooms and machinery spaces typically comprise several tanks and confined spaces. These are unsafe to enter without authorisation and preparation. Therefore, enclosed space training, together with risk assessment and dedicated checklist familiarisation, should be carried out regularly
4. *Scavenge fire drill*. All engine room personnel must be competent in scavenge firefighting procedures

5. *Crankcase explosion drill*. Crankcase explosions can lead to fatal situations and loss of the ship's power infrastructure. The engine crew should always be prepared for the event that the engine's oil mist detector alarm sounds and respond accordingly.
6. *Uptake fire drill*. The engine crew should be trained on how to respond to boiler uptake fires. This should include the various stages of uptake fire development and the correct procedures for responding to uptake fire incidents
7. *Oil spill drill*. The oil carried on board as cargo or for use by the ship is managed and handled by the engine department. It is therefore critical for the marine engineers to be familiar with the correct oil transfer procedures and to know how to respond to oil spills
8. *Bunker training*. Bunkering is one of the most dangerous operations carried out on board ships. At least 24 hours before the bunkering operation is due to commence, the ship's crew should be invited to attend a mandatory briefing where the bunkering operation is outlined, specific duties are assigned, and safety considerations such as signals, stopping, and oil spill reporting procedures are highlighted
9. *Pollution prevention appliance training*. Port State Control have become increasingly strict when it comes to complying with the MARPOL regulations. It is therefore important for the ship's crew to know and apply pollution preventative measures when at sea and in port. This includes knowledge of and competence in the operation of pollution prevention equipment such as the oily water separator (OWS), incinerator, sewage treatment plant, gash disposal, and so forth
10. *Blackout training*. When a ship loses power, it becomes entirely dependent on sea and wind conditions. This is known as being *dead in the water*. Blackout training is therefore one of the most important training regimes the engine department must prepare for

EXAMPLE: UNATTENDED INCINERATOR

A ship underway started its incinerator to dispose of oily rags and sludge. About five hours later, after the job was completed, the incinerator was stopped. All specifications appeared normal, and the furnace temperature was noted to be 950°C. Following company procedure, the crew continued to monitor the incinerator during the cooling-off period. By 1900hrs, five hours after the incinerator had been turned off, the temperature of the furnace was noted to be 280°C and the blower fan was still running. At 2032 hrs, the EOW noticed smoke coming from the outer body of the incinerator. On closer inspection, he could see paint peeling off the body of the incinerator. The temperature of the incinerator body was between 250–350° C. He informed the chief engineer, and an emergency response was initiated. The crew mustered and fire parties began boundary cooling. Boundary cooling continued for about four hours until heat indications suggested that the fire was extinguished. During the investigation, it was found that the fire had started in the air-cooled incinerator chamber jacket. Later, it was found that refractory and outside body plates were intact. Traces of oil were found between the sludge dosing door and the combustion chamber, which was an indication that oil had accumulated in the double-shell refractory lining.

LESSONS LEARNED

Even during the cool-off period, an incinerator must be attended to and regularly checked. Boundary cooling and cool heads are a great asset when fighting a shipboard fire.

So far in this chapter we have discussed some of the key themes around health, safety, and crew welfare. We will continue to touch on some of these issues and other issues as we carry on through this book. But for now, we can turn our attention to that moment all seafarers look forward to the most. The day of *signing off*. Signing off usually happens when a seafarer has fulfilled their contractual obligation on board. For most people, it is a bittersweet experience, with mixed emotions ranging from happiness and sadness. For the past few months, the ship has been a home from home. Leaving the ship means an end to routine, uncertainty, and saying goodbyes to colleagues and perhaps even friends. At the same time, going home means seeing family again. In the rush to pack up and sign off, it is easy to forget there are essential tasks that must be completed before leaving the ship. First and foremost is collecting identification and other personal documents from the master's safe. When joining a ship, it is customary to hand over any passports, discharge book, STCW certificates, and medical records for safe keeping. During crew changes, it is normal for the incoming crew to shadow the outgoing crew for a few days. This ensures any important information can be passed over in good time. Before leaving the ship, it is good practice to provide the oncoming crew member with a handover report. This does not need to be expansive; a short precis of the day-to-day duties and any tips are usually well received by the incomer. When leaving the cabin for the last time, it is always good practice to double check for any missed personal property. Always aim to hand over the cabin in a clean and tidy condition. For the last few months, it has been home; now, it will be someone else's. Ending a stint at sea by leaving a dirty and damaged cabin will not endear the seafarer to the new incumbent, the master, or the seafarer's employer. When signing off, it is quite usual for crew members to ask if small packages and personal effects can be carried home on their behalf. Whilst this is not in itself illegal, it is best practice (and safer) to politely refuse. Being caught by customs and immigration with pirate videos and music, narcotics, or other prohibited items will not end well. It is very rare for seafarers to sign off in their home country; knowing a little about local laws and customs will make the travel home that little bit easier. On occasion the master may ask that a package be delivered to the company's offices ashore. In this situation, the seafarer has the right to refuse the request pending their personal judgment.

In the next chapter, we will begin to explore some of the technical attributes that define container ships.

NOTES

1. Reid, Marc. 'The Piper Alpha Disaster: A Personal Perspective with Transferrable Lessons on the Long-Term Moral Impact of Safety Failures' in *ACS Chemical Health & Safety*. 2020 27(2), 88–95.
2. The senior management team usually consists of the master, the chief officer, and the chief engineer. The third officer, being responsible for the maintenance of safety equipment, may be invited to attend SMT meetings on an ad hoc basis.
3. SSOs serving on oil tankers require an additional six month's consecutive seagoing service.
4. I.e., a seven-day period.
5. If we remember from the previous chapter, OOW stand four-hour watches, twice in any 24-hour period. This leaves eight hours between each watch, which is usually sufficient to perform whatever duties the officer is required to carry out as well as leaving sufficient time for rest and relaxation.
6. The human body has a normal core temperature between 97°F and 99°F, but on average, a normal body temperature is 98.6°F (37°C). To maintain this temperature without the help of warming or cooling devices, the surrounding environment needs to be at about 82°F (28°C). Clothes

aren't just for looks – they're necessary to keep warm. You can usually bundle up in more layers during colder months, and you can use fans or air conditioners in warmer months to maintain a healthy core temperature.

7. Vital organs include the brain, heart, lungs, kidneys, and liver. Extremities are any regions of the body that protrude outwards, such as the fingers, toes, ears, and nose.
8. Personal protective equipment (PPE) includes overalls, boots, gloves, hardhat, and goggles. Respiratory protective equipment (RPE) includes breathing apparatus and facemask.
9. For example: after hot work, drydocking, repairs, changes in use, etc.
10. This is usually by the master's verbal command over the ship's public address system (PAS).
11. For example, how to don the lifejacket, interpret emergency alarms, and how to recognise the abandon ship signal.
12. Some religions and cultures use incense and candles, therefore senior officers should be sensitive to individual crew member needs, whilst simultaneously maintaining high standards of safety.

Chapter 5

Container and RORO ships

As the name suggests, container ships are large vessels designed to carry vast quantities of cargoes compacted into metal boxes called containers. The process of shipping cargo in containers is known as containerisation. Container shipping is one of the most efficient ways of transporting dry and bulk goods around the world. In fact, over 90% of products are carried onboard container ships at one point in their lifecycle. The reason why containerisation has proven so successful is the ease with which container shipping operates. The containers themselves come in standardised shapes and sizes, and with their dimensions set by the ISO. This has led to some people referring to containers as ISO containers or ISO boxes. We will cover the types and dimensions of shipping containers later in this book, so we need not concern ourselves with this too much now. Suffice it to say that containers are designed to be transferred from one mode of transport to another without emptying and refilling the container. The intermodal nature of the container means it can be filled with goods at the factory, hoisted onto a flatbed lorry, driven to the terminal, loaded onto a ship, unloaded at the next terminal, loaded onto a flatbed train, and taken to the end customer. As we can imagine, this marked a major development for the transport and logistics industry. This intermodal capability is only possible because of the simple and standard design of the container. Almost anything can be shipped worldwide in an ISO container from computer equipment to racing cars, gaseous chemicals to champagne. Ever-increasing demand in the global consumer market has led to corresponding growth in cargo-carrying capacity. As a result, the container ships of today are truly behemoths of the sea. To put this into context, the largest container ships in operation today have increased in size by more than 1,200% compared to 1968.

The first ships designed to carry standardised load units were built in England towards the end of the 18th century. In 1766 the English engineer James Brindley designed the first box boat, *Starvationer*, which could carry ten wooden crates of coal from Worsley Delph in Lancashire to the port city of Manchester via the Bridgewater Canal. Over the course of the next hundred or so years, engineers and shipwrights continued to develop rudimentary designs for vessels to carry loose cargo in wooden crates and boxes. In February 1931 the first purpose-built container ship was launched by the *Southern Railway Company* of England. This vessel, *Autocarrier*, was designed with 21 slots on the main deck into which railway boxes could be secured. During the Second World War (1939–1945) development of container ships stalled as attention was drawn towards building ships cheaply and quickly for the British Convoys. By the end of the war, a surplus of US built Type 2 oil tankers had amassed. These were relatively small ships with a flat open weather deck. A small number of these ships were repurposed after the war to carry boxes and crates much in the same way as the *Autocarrier*. In 1955 the American trucking entrepreneur Malcolm McLean, founder of the McLean Trucking Co., realised that the T2 could be cheaply reconfigured to carry large sealed boxes instead of individual crates. In that same year he purchased his first

DOI: 10.1201/9781003244615-6

49

ship, the *Ideal X*. On 26 April 1956, the *Ideal X* left the Port of Newark (New Jersey) with 58 metal containers onboard. Owing to the success of the *Ideal X*, McLean purchased the small *Pan American Steamship Company* from *Waterman Steamship*. He adapted all their ships to carry cargo in metal containers. By the beginning of 1957 McLean had built up one the largest and most successful transport companies in America. Built off the back of James Brindley's early construction, and Southern Railway's *Autocarrier*, McLean had introduced the world to the age of containerisation.

Despite the success of the *Ideal X* and her repurposed T2 sister ships, it would not be until 29 February 1964 that the world's first fully cellular purpose-built container ship – the *MV Kooringa* – would be built at Yard 72, New South Wales State Dockyard in Newcastle, Australia. The *MV Kooringa*[1] was designed and built for *Associated Steamships Pty. Ltd* and *McIlwraith, McEarchen & Co*. The ship was completed on 17 May 1964. The unique design of the MV Kooringa meant 10,000 tonnes of containerised cargo could be simultaneously loaded and unloaded in as little as 36 hours. For the time, this was record breaking. The ship entered the Melbourne to Freemantle route arriving at the Port of Freemantle on 19 June 1964. By 1969 two more fully cellular ships – the *MV Kanimbia* and the *MV Manoora* – were added to the *Associated Steamships Pty. Ltd* fleet. All three vessels remained in operation until 1975 when competition from onshore rail freight made the sea service unviable. Despite the three sister ships falling out of service due to competition from rail freight, ship designers, and owners were quick to realise the benefits of eliminating the individual hatches, holds, and dividers that were common to general cargo ships. Subsequently, from the mid-1960s onwards, shipping companies continued to invest vast sums of capital in developing container ship technology. By the late 1970s and early 1980s a new development in container ship design started to emerge. Throughout the 1960s car ownership was increasing. Consumers were finding they liked buying imported electronics from Japan. Young Americans liked the idea of driving German-made *VW Beetles*. This meant that ships were no longer required to only carry containers, but also rolling cargoes such as cars, lorries, and machinery. What if the two could be combined? A ship that carries containers on its deck and cars in its hold! In the late 1970s that is exactly what happened. A new type of container ship emerged; one with an open flat weather deck and a large ramp on the stern. Unlike conventional container ships where the hold is compartmentalised, this new breed of vessel would have long open internal decks where rows and rows of rolling cargo could be driven straight on and off. By dint of genius, these new ships would become known as *Roll-On, Roll-Off* ships or *ROROs*.

As mentioned above, the hull of a typical container or 'box' ship is a huge warehouse divided into compartments or *cells* by vertical guide rails. These cells are designed to hold the containers. Shipping containers are usually made of a special type of steel, but other materials such as aluminium, fibreglass, or even plywood may be used. Containers are designed to be intermodal, which means they are easily transferred from one mode of transport to another. Today, about 90% of all non-bulk consumer cargo worldwide is shipped by container. The largest container ships in service (as of July 2021) can carry in excess of 23,000 20 ft^2 containers. As a class, container ships now rival crude oil tankers and bulk carriers as the largest commercial vessels in service. Although containerisation caused a revolution in the world of shipping, its introduction was not universally accepted. Port authorities, railway companies, and individual shipping companies were all initially concerned by the huge costs needed to redevelop new port facilities and the road and railway infrastructure needed to handle the containers to and from the port. Trades unions were concerned by the imminent loss of jobs among port and dock workers, as containers were sure to eliminate the manual job of cargo handling. In fact, it took ten long years of legal battles before international container shipping would start in earnest. In 1966, a container liner service from the US to the Dutch city of Rotterdam commenced. By revolutionising the way goods could be packed and shipped around the world, containerisation changed not only the face of shipping, but also revolutionised global trade.

In the 60-odd years since the first container ships began plying the world's oceans, the global economy and consumerism has continued to grow. Whereas in the 1950s it was common for ships to lie alongside for days on end as gangs of stevedores would manually unload sacks and crates in small bundles, today vast quantities of containers can be loaded and unloaded in a matter of hours. This has drastically cut labour costs, reduced port times, improved shore-based logistics, and given rise to increasingly efficient manufacturing processes. As the container is locked at the point of collection and is opened only on delivery or by customs officials, the risk of theft has greatly diminished. Cargo that once arrived in cartons, crates, bales, barrels, or bags now comes in factory sealed containers, with no indication to the human eye of their contents, except for a product code that machines scan and computers trace. This system of tracking is so exact that a two-week voyage can be timed for arrival with an accuracy of under 15 minutes. Raw materials and parts arrive in containers less than an hour before they are needed for production, resulting in reduced inventory and storage costs. The advantages and benefits of containerisation are myriad and whilst some jobs have literally fallen by the quayside, others have developed in their place. The container shipping industry is truly fascinating, and we have the 17th-century engineer James Brindley to thank for it.

Container ships have undergone a process of evolution that has happened over many decades and through several phases. Each phase has culminated in the design of a new generation of container ship, with each new generation more efficient and equipped than the one before. As we have already seen, the first container ships were repurposed World War Two oil tankers. In the 1960s a new breed of purpose-built container ships appeared. In the absence of specially designed terminals, these ships were fitted with their own gears. These ships would become known as *geared ships*.[3] These continued in service until the early 1970s, when cargo terminals started installing their own gantry cranes. Throughout the 1970s container ships continued to expand in size and stature. By the late-1970s and into the 1980s container ships capable of carrying rolling stock were introduced. These dual container/roll-on roll-off ships or RORO[4] ships would remain popular until the mid-1990s when specialised car carriers would take over. From 1989 onwards container ships would continue to expand exponentially. Whereas earlier container vessels had their superstructure[5] situated as far back as possible to maximise cargo carrying capacity, the newer classes had the accommodation block located somewhere within the stern third. This meant containers could be stowed behind the superstructure as well as along the forward length of the ship. These ships would become known as *Panamax* ships. Between 2001 and 2015 the *Panamax* ship was replaced by the *Post Panamax* ship. Too long and too wide to safely navigate the Panama Canal, this new generation of ship led to the Panama Canal Authority deciding to deepen and widen the canal in a multi-billion-dollar project. In 2015 the container ship would enter another evolutionary phase with the introduction of the *Maersk Triple E* class. The E class, starting with the *Emma Maersk*, were so long and carried so many containers at once that a revolutionary new design was needed. Unlike standard ships where the superstructure is situated within the stern third, the Triple E class had the superstructure situated amidships, providing the master and OOW with a clear view of the bow, with the smokestacks situated by themselves in the stern third. Though loosely reminiscent of the old-style merchant ships built in the 1920s to 1950s, there the resemblance ends. The technology on these fifth-generation ships far outmatches anything previously employed. See Table 5.1.

52 The merchant mercantile

Table 5.1 Generations of container ship design and development

Time Span	Generation
1956–1970	First generation
1971–1980	Second generation
1981–1988	Third generation
1989–2000	Fourth generation
2001–2005	Fifth generation
2006–Present	Sixth generation

Box ships are by far the most common type of container ship in operation today. Unlike ROROs they can only be loaded with containers. Cargo handling is carried out by quayside cranes that belong to the port authorities. Box ships generally trade between major ports that have the requisite container terminal infrastructure such as gantry cranes, container stowage bays, and railway loading facilities. ROROs have the added advantage of being able to carry both containers and rolling cargoes. ROROs are extremely flexible vessels, as containers can be stowed both above the main deck and in the internal decks by virtue of heavy lift vehicles and forklift trucks. Lift On/Lift Off, LOLO, or *geared* container ships are much less common as they are both expensive to purchase and costly to maintain. These ships are fitted with their own deck mounted crane which autonomously loads and unloads containers without needing shore side facilities. This provides two obvious advantages: it means the ship is not dependent on port authorities providing cranage, which in turn means the ship can visit ports lacking quayside facilities. Admittedly, this is an advantage partially shared with ROROs. Ships that are not fitted with an onboard crane are called *ungeared* ships as they are not fitted with gear systems.

In the first chapter we discussed how ships are categorised according to their size. If we recall, there are seven size categories: small feeder, feeder, Feedermax, Panamax, Post-Panamax, New Panamax, and Ultra-Large Container Ships (ULCS). Small feeders generally carry up to 1,000 TEUs with feeders able to carry between 1,001 and 2,000 TEUs. Feedermax ships can carry up to 3,000 TEUs. These are small ships that typically operate between smaller container ports. They tend to collect their cargo from smaller regional ports and discharge it at larger international ports for transhipment on larger ships. Feeder ships are most likely to be fitted with a geared crane. As noted above, the size of *Panamax* ships was limited by the original lock chambers of the Panama Canal, which were able to accommodate ships with a maximum beam of 32.31 m (106 ft), a maximum LOA of 294.13 m (965 ft), and a maximum draught of up to 12.04 m (39.5 ft). The largest *Panamax* ships to enter service were the *Bay* class operated by the former company *P&O Nedlloyd*.[6] These ships had a LOA of 292.15 m (958.49 ft), a beam of 32.2 m (105.64 ft), a draught of 13.3 m (43.63 ft), and a maximum carrying capacity of 5,100 TEUs. The *Post-Panamax* category has historically been used to describe ships with a moulded breadth over 32.31 m, however the Panama Canal expansion project has led to changes in terminology. The *New Panamax* category is based on the maximum vessel-size that can transit a third set of locks which opened in June 2016. The third set of locks were built to accommodate container ships with LOA of 366 m (1,201 ft), a maximum breadth of 49 m (161 ft), and a tropical fresh-water draught of 15.2 m (50 ft). These vessels, often referred to as the *New Panamax* class, are wide enough to carry nine columns of containers, have a maximum capacity of 12,000 TEUs, and are comparable in size to a *Capesize* bulk carrier or a *Suezmax* tanker. The largest container ships in service are the *Ultra-Large* class of container ship (ULCS). Ships of this class have a minimum carrying capacity of 14,501 TEUs and a maximum of

22,000 TEUs. These behemoths measure LOA 366 m (1,200 ft), have a beam wider than 49 m (160.7 ft), and a draught over 15.2 m (49.9 ft).

There are several key points that distinguish container ships from other categories of cargo ships. The ship's frame or *hull*, like that of bulk carriers and general cargo ships, is built around a strong *keel*. The keel is the bottom most frame that runs the length of the ship. Into this frame are set one or more cargo holds, numerous tanks, and, of course, the engine room. The holds are topped by hatch covers, onto which more containers are stacked. The hull construction of modern cargo ships is a complex arrangement of ribs, strengthening beams, and steel plates. The ribs are fastened at right angles to the keel and provide the square shape of the hull. The steel plates that cover the ribs and the beams are called the shell. The metal plates that cover the top of the hull are referred to as the main deck or *weather deck*. The weather deck is supported by the beams that are attached to the tops of the frames and run the full breadth of the ship. These beams not only support the deck, but along with the deck, frames, and transverse bulkheads, strengthen, and reinforce the shell. Most container ships built over the past few decades have an additional feature not often found in other ships. This is the *double-bottom hull*. The double-bottom hull essentially consists of the keel, a series of tanks, then a second watertight shell that runs the entire length of the ship. The tanks hold liquids such as fuel oil, ballast water, or fresh water. The benefit of having tanks situated along the bottom of the ship – as opposed to along the sides on conventional ships – is that it provides greater stowage potential. Having tanks situated along the sides of the ship reduces the amount of space available for cargo.

The engine room accommodates the main engines and auxiliary machinery such as the fresh water and sewage systems, electrical generators, fire pumps, and air conditioners. In all ships, the engine room is always located in the stern third, and as far aft as possible. This not only maximises the amount of space available for cargo stowage, but also reduces the length of the propeller shafts. As we said earlier, container ships typically have the superstructure positioned towards the aft of the ship. In newer build, the superstructure itself may be located forward of the engine room, which means a separate smokestack must be provided above the engine compartment. One of the defining characteristics of container ships is whether they are fitted with gears. We already know that ships which have cargo cranes are called *geared* ships, and those that do not are called *ungeared* or *gearless* ships. The earliest purpose-built container ships dating from the 1970s were all gearless. Since then, the percentage of geared newbuilds has fluctuated widely, but has decreased overall, with only 6.9% of container ship capacity in 2021 being equipped with gears. Whilst geared container ships are more flexible than ungeared ships, they suffer from several drawbacks. Geared ships cost more to purchase and are more expensive to maintain. The added weight of the gear also increases fuel and operation costs. Furthermore, ship mounted gears generally load and discharge containers much slower than quayside gantry cranes. The United Nations Conference on Trade and Development (UNCTAD) goes so far as to characterise geared ships as a 'niche market only appropriate for those ports where low cargo volumes do not justify investment in port cranes or where the public sector does not have the financial resources for such investment'. Despite this, there is a small demand for geared container ships albeit usually on coastal and inter-port routes. The gear generally comes in one of two forms. The first is the stationary rotary crane that swivels around on its own axis. The second type is a ship mounted gantry crane. These cranes are specialised for container work and roll forward and aft on rails. Vessels in the 1,500–2,499 TEU class are the most likely to be fitted with cranes, with more than 60% of this class being geared. Slightly less than a third of the very smallest class ships (100–499 TEU) are geared, and almost no ships with a capacity over 4,000 TEU are geared.

54 The merchant mercantile

The introduction and improvement of quayside gantry cranes have been key to the success of containerisation. The first crane specifically designed for container work was installed at the Port of Alameda in California in 1959. Originally slow and cumbersome, by the 1980s, quayside gantry cranes were shifting containers on a 3-minute-cycle, roughly equivalent to 400 tonnes per hour. By the 2000s crane technology had improved so much that in March 2010 a world record was set when 734 container moves were made in a single hour at the Port of Klang, Malaysia. This record beating achievement was made possible by simultaneously using nine cranes to load and unload the 9,600 TEU vessel *MV CSCL Pusan*. Efficiency has always been a key consideration to the design of container ships. While containers may be carried on conventional break-bulk ships, the cargo holds on dedicated container ships are specially designed for speed loading and unloading and to keep containers secure at sea. One of the key aspects of container ship design is the use of hatches. These are the openings on the main deck which provide access to the cargo holds beneath. The hatch openings stretch the entire breadth of the cargo hold and are surrounded by a raised steel structure called the *hatch coaming*. Positioned on top of the hatch coaming are the hatch covers. Until the 1950s, hatches were typically secured with wooden boards and tarpaulins. These would be held down with battens. On modern container ships, the hatch covers are either solid metal plates that are lifted on and off the ship by cranes or opened and closed using powerful hydraulic rams. Inside the cargo hold itself, *cell guides* keep the containers in straight rows and columns. Cell guides are strong vertical structures made of steel. These structures guide containers into each row during the loading process. They also provide some support for containers against rolling. Cell guides are so fundamental to container ship design that UNCTAD uses their presence to distinguish dedicated container ships from general break-bulk cargo ships.

When planning where to stow containers, the ship's officers develop a loading plan. This plan sets out the location of each container in terms of its cargo, port of loading, port of discharge, weight, and any other relevant information. Containers are then stowed using a system of three-dimensional coordinates. The first coordinate is the *bay*, which starts at the front of the ship and increases aft. The second coordinate is the *row*. Rows on the starboard side[7] are given odd numbers and those on the port side are given even numbers. The rows nearest the centreline are given low numbers, with the numbers increasing as the slots move further away from the centreline. The third coordinate is the *tier*, with the first tier being at the bottom of the cargo hold, the second tier on top, and so forth. Container ships generally carry TEU and FEU sized containers though 45 ft containers are becomingly increasingly popular. The FEU is the most common container size and makes up approximately 90% of all containers in service. As container shipping moves around 90% of all global freight, over 80% of goods are shipped in FEU containers. Despite the terminology, 20 ft and 40 ft containers are not actually 20 ft and 40 ft long. There is a small discrepancy which we will look at later. Because of this, two TEU containers can be stowed below or above one FEU container, but it is not permitted to stow an FEU container above two TEUs. Due to their irregular size, 45 ft containers can only be stowed on deck.

Various systems are used to secure containers once they have been loaded onboard. The system used depends on many factors such as the type of ship, type of container and the location of the container. Hold stowage inside fully cellular ships is by far the simplest as the cell guides guide the container into place. Locating cones and anti-rack spacers then lock the containers into place. Containers stowed above deck do not have the benefit of cell guides so additional securing mechanisms must be used. These include lashing, locking, and buttress systems. Lashing systems secure containers to the ship using devices made from wire rope, rigid rods, or chains. These are then held in place using tension and turnbuckles. The effectiveness of the lashing is increased by securing each container to another. This is done by using a stacking cone or a twist-lock. The twist-lock is inserted into the casting hole of one container and rotated to hold it in place. Another container is lowered on top of the lower container. The two containers are then locked together by twisting the twist-lock handle. The typical twist-lock has a shear strength of 48 tonnes. Alternatively, larger container ships may use a *buttress system*. This consists of a series of towers attached to the ship at both ends of each cargo hold. As the ship is loaded, a rigid removable stacking frame is added which secures each tier of containers together.

ROROs are an interesting development in the history of the container industry. Although ROROs were first introduced into service in the late 1970s, it wasn't until November 1995 that they were formally recognised as a separate class of ship under chapter II-1 of SOLAS. The 1995 amendment classified ROROs as a 'passenger ship with RORO cargo spaces or special category spaces'. This distinction is important as RORO ships are structurally different to conventional box ships as they are fitted with a stern ramp. The first RORO to come into service was across the Firth of Forth in Scotland in 1851. Rails were laid along the length of the ship to enable locomotives and wagons to roll directly onto and off the ship. Today, there are many different types of ROROs in service ranging from car ferries, cruise ferries, cargo ships, and barges. The type we are most interested in here is the CONRO, a hybrid container, and rolling stock vessel. This type of vessel uses the area below the main deck for vehicle storage with containers stowed on the main deck. Some CONROs are divided into two sections: the underdeck of one side has cell guides for containers; and the other side has arrangements for carrying vehicles and out of gauge cargoes. Similar to the CONRO is the ROLO, which is the acronym for *Roll-On and Lift-Off*. ROLOs are also a hybrid type vessel where the ramp serves the vehicle decks, but the other decks are accessible only by crane. These vessels can carry both vehicles and general cargo. Since the weight of the general may exceed the payload of the ramp, shore cranes must be used to load and discharge the cargo directly into the hold.

RORO ships were immensely popular in the 1980s and early 1990s as they had the benefit of carrying consumer goods as well as consumer vehicles. By the late 1980s however a new type of ship was beginning to emerge. With global car ownership increasing, it became readily apparent that current capacity was insufficient. This would lead to the development of the *car carrier* and the demise of the RORO. Car carriers are huge box like structures that either carry only cars[8] or a combination of cars and trucks.[9] They do not ordinarily carry containers. Ships that carry both rolling cargoes (including containers on flatbed trailers) and passengers are referred to as ROPAX ships. These generally include cross channel and cruise ferries. Unlike static cargoes which are measured in metric tonnes, RORO cargo is measured using a unit called *Lanes in Metres* or LIMs. A LIM is calculated by multiplying the cargo length in metres by the number of decks and by the width of lanes. The lane width will differ from vessel to vessel. For context, the largest ROPAX is the Norwegian cruise ferry *MS Color Magic*. She weighs in at a hefty 75,100 gross tonnes DWT. Built by Aker Finnyards of Finland, the ferry has a LOA of 223.70 m (733,92 ft), a beam of 35 m (114.82 ft), and a capacity to carry 550 cars with a maximum LIM of 1,270 m (4,166 ft). By comparison, the ROPAX with the largest car-carrying capacity is the *MS Ulysses*, operated by Irish Ferries, and named after the novel by the Irish poet James Joyce. She has a deadweight of 50,938 gross tonnes, a LOA of 209.02 m (685.76 ft), a beam of 31.84 m (104.46 ft) and a maximum capacity of 1,342 cars with a LIM of 4,101 (13,454 ft). The first cargo ships to be built specifically for rolling cargo came into service in the early 1960s. These early designs of RORO had their own gear and a 'hanging deck' with the first car carrier chartered by *Volkswagen AG* of Germany to transport vehicles from Europe to the US and Canada. During the 1970s the market for exporting and importing cars increased dramatically, resulting in a similar increase in RORO capacity. In 1970 Japan's K Line built

56 The merchant mercantile

the *Toyota Maru No.10*, Japan's first dedicated car carrier. In 1973, this was followed by the *European Highway*, which was the largest PCC at that time with a maximum capacity of 4,200 vehicles. In 2008 the Norwegian/Swedish company *Wallenius Wilhelmsen* took ownership of the 8,000 capacity *Faust* and as of June 2021, the largest PCC in service are the six *Horizon* class vessels operated by the Norwegian company *Höegh Autoliners*, each with a maximum carrying capacity of 8,500 units.

THE CONTAINER SHIP INDUSTRY

As of July 2021, there were 6,226 registered container ships in service of which 5,451 were fully cellular with a total global capacity of 24,781,400 TEU and a total deadweight of 297,811,295 gross tonnes. This is a significant increase from the industry's 11 million gross tonnes in 1980. The combined deadweight tonnage of container ships and general cargo ships, which may also carry containers, represents 21.8% overall of the global merchant fleet. In terms of age, as of July 2021, the average container ship was 10.6 years old, making them comparatively the youngest vessel class, followed by bulk carriers at 16.6 years, oil tankers at 17 years, general cargo ships at 24.6 years, and other classes of ships at 25.3 years. The majority of carrying capacity using fully cellular container ships is the liner service, where ships trade on scheduled routes. As of January 2021, the top 20 liner companies controlled 67.5% of the world's fully cellular container ship capacity, with a fleet of 2,673 vessels, with each vessel averaging 3,774 TEU. Of these, a clear majority are owned and operated by German shipowners, with Hamburg based brokers controlling 75% of that market. When demand for container space is high, it is common practice for large container lines to supplement their own tonnage with chartered ships. In 2020 alone, 48.9% of tonnage of the top 20 lines consisted of chartered vessels. The container sector is dominated by 10 shipowner/operators: *Maersk Line*; *Mediterranean Shipping Company*; *CMA CGA*; *COSCO*; *Hapag-Lloyd*; *Ocean Network Express*; *Evergreen*; *Hyundai Merchant Marine*; and *ZIM Integrated Shipping*.

Modern developments in marine engine technology mean that newly built container ships powered by significantly smaller main engines. In fact, the engine types fitted to ships with a capacity of 14,000 TEUs are sufficiently powerful enough to propel vessels with a capacity of 20,000 TEUs. Despite the development of modern technology, shipping companies tend to be quite traditional. For example, *Maersk Line*, the world's largest container ship operator, opted for twin engines (two smaller engines powering two separate propellers) when it ordered a series of ten 18,000 TEU vessels from *Daewoo Shipbuilding* in February 2011. These ships were delivered between 2013 and 2014. In March 2017, the first ship with an official capacity over 20,000 TEU – the *MOL Triumph* – was launched by *Samsung Heavy Industries*. This maritime mammoth has a maximum capacity of 20,150 TEU though it only took a meagre three years for this record to be smashed by the *HMM Algeciras*, which boasts a record-breaking deadweight of 228,283 gross tonnes, a LOA of 399.9 m (1,312 ft), a draught of 33.2 m (61 ft) and a maximum carrying capacity of 23,964 TEU.

Partly due to the increasing demand for larger container ships, oversupply of container ship capacity has caused prices for new and existing ships to fall. From 2008 to 2009, new build prices dropped by as much as 19–33%, while the price for container ships over ten years old dropped by as much as 47–69%. In March 2010, the average price for a geared 500 TEU container ship was $10 million, while a gearless ship of between 6,500 and 12,000 TEU averaged at $74 million and $105 million, respectively. At the same time, second-hand prices for geared ships over 10 years old with a capacity of 500, 2,500, and 3,500 TEU capacity averaged at $4.0 million, $15 million, and US $18 million respectively.

Container and RORO ships 57

Table 5.2 Largest container ships by class and TEU capacity (2021)[a,b,c,d,e,f,g,h]

Year Built	Vessel	Class size	Max TEU capacity
2020	HMM Algeciras	7	23,964
2020	HMM Oslo	5	23,820
2019	MSC Gülsün	6	23,756
2019	MSC Mina	5	23,656
2020	CMA CGM Jacques Saadé	9	23,112
2017	OOCL Hong Kong	6	21,413
2018	COSCO Shipping Universe	6	20,954
2018	CMA CGM Antoine de Saint Exupery	3	20,954
2017	Madrid Maersk	11	20,568
2018	Ever Golden	2	20,388
2017	MOL Truth	2	20,182
2017	MOL Triumph	4	20,170
2019	Ever Glory	4	20,160
2018	Ever Goods	5	20.124
2018	COSCO Shipping Taurus	5	20,119

[a] www.hmm21.com/cms/company/engn/introduce/prcenter/news/index.jsp. Accessed 2 June 2021.
[b] www.msc.com/gbr/about-us/our-fleet. Accessed 2 June 2021.
[c] www.cmacgm-group.com/en/group/at-a-glance/fleet. Accessed 2 June 2021.
[d] lines.coscoshipping.com/home/Services/ship/0. Accessed 2 June 2021.
[e] www.oocl.com/eng/ourservices/vessels/Pages/default.aspx. Accessed 2 June 2021.
[f] www.maersk.com/transportation-services/ocean-transport. Accessed 2 June 2021.
[g] www.shipmentlink.com/tvi1/jsp/TVII_VesselParticulars.jsp. Accessed 2 June 2021.
[h] www.mol.co.jp/en/services/index.html. Accessed 21 June 2021.

Over the past 20 years, 85% of new builds were built in South Korea, China, and Japan, with South Korea alone accounting for over 57% of the world's total. On average, new container ships accounted for less than 15% of total new tonnage, with oil tankers averaging at 22.6% and bulk carriers at 28.9%. When a ship reaches the end of its useful life, it is removed from the active fleet through a process known as scrapping. Scrapping is rare for ships under 18 years of age and most common for ships over 40. Shipowners and scrap metal buyers negotiate scrapping costs based on factors such as the ship's empty weight (called *light tonne displacement* (LTD)) and the prevailing cost of scrap metal on the open market. Scrapping rates are volatile with the price per LTD swinging from a high of $650 in mid-2008 to less than $200 in early 2009 and rising again to $400 in March 2010. Incidentally, this period also happened to be the worst global economic recession since the Wall Street Crash in 1932. In 2009 alone over 364,300 TEU worth of container ship capacity was scrapped, up from 99,900 TEU in 2008. This equals roughly 22.6% of the total container ship tonnage for 2009.

All commercial ships must be registered by a national authority, called the *Flag State*. The Flag State is the country to which the ship is registered. This is important as Flag States exercise regulatory control over the vessels in their registry. This includes carrying out seaworthiness inspections, certifying the ship's equipment and crew, and issuing safety and pollution control standards. Although a ship must be registered in one country, that does not necessarily mean that the ship belongs to that country. This is because many countries offer a *Flag of Convenience*. Flags of convenience are often used by shipping companies to reduce the financial and regulatory burden on their fleets. As each Flag State sets their own criteria and regulatory frameworks, standards and requirements between Flag States can differ quite substantially, especially in terms of enforcement. Panama has consistently been

58   The merchant mercantile

Table 5.3 Six largest ship registries by number of ships registered (2021)[a]

Liberia	415	Cyprus	139
Germany	248	Marshall Islands	118
Singapore	177	United Kingdom	104

[a] UNCTAD (2020a). UNCTADstat. https://unctadstat.unctad.org. Accessed 1 June 2021.

the leading ship registry, owing to the relatively low cost of the registry and lax enforcement by Panamanian Ship Registry authorities.

When a ship is operated by a company, but it is not owned by the operator, the ship is said to be *chartered*. This is akin to a shipping company renting the ship. Ship *charters* are usually one of three kinds. With a *voyage charter*, the vessel is leased from the port of loading to the port of discharge. In this instance, it is common for the vessel to come complete with officers and crew. The company leasing the vessel is not responsible for operation and maintenance of the vessel as this responsibility is retained by the vessel owner. A *time charter* is similar to a *voyage charter* except that the vessel is leased for a period of time instead of a set voyage. The vessel is chartered to carry out as many voyages as the charterer directs within the period of the charter. The last type of charter is the *bareboat charter*. In this situation, the vessel owner provides the vessel only to the operator for a set period. The vessel and its crew become the responsibility of the operator, including the maintenance of the ship, bunkering, and its compliance with maritime regulations.

Shipping costs are highly volatile and often change daily. In 2010 the United Nations Conference on Trade and Development noted in its annual report that there are two primary factors that determine container shipping costs. The first factor is the *chartering price* which is the cost to time-charter one TEU slot weighing an average of 14 tonnes. The second factor is the freight or *comprehensive daily cost* of delivering one 14 tonne TEU on any given route. In other words, the charge to ship one container weighing in at 14 tonnes is determined by the fixed price of the route, and the variable cost of shipping the container from port to another. To collate its annual figures on container shipping costs, the United Nations Conference on Trade and Development the *Hamburg Shipbrokers' Association* or the *Vereinigung Hamburger Schiffsmakler unter Schiffsagenten e.V* (VHSS) as its main industry source of information. The VHSS maintains numerous indices of container ship charter prices. The oldest, which dates as far back as 1998, is called the *Hamburg Index*. This index considers time-charters on fully cellular container ships that are controlled by Hamburg brokers. It is limited to charters of three months or more and is presented as the average daily cost in US dollars for one 14 tonne TEU slot. The *Hamburg Index* data is divided into ten categories based on vessel carrying capacity. Two additional categories exist for smaller vessels under 500 TEU, and those that carry their own gears. In 2007, the VHSS started a second indices called the *New ConTex Index*. This index tracks similar data obtained from a global basket of shipbrokers. The *Hamburg Index* shows clear trends over recent years in the charter market. First, it shows that rates generally increased from 2000 to 2005. From 2005 to 2008 the rates slowly decreased, and in mid-2008 began a 'dramatic decline' of approximately 75%. This fall in rates did not stabilise until April 2009. In the years since then, rates have consistently increased to pre-2008 levels though the Covid-19 pandemic, which struck in late 2019, has caused a similar drop in charter rates. The United Nations Conference on Trade and Development also tracks container freight rates. Freight rates are expressed as the total price in US dollars for a shipper to transport one 14 tonne TEU on a specific route. The data is collated for the three main container liner routes, i.e., US to Asia, US to Europe, and Europe to Asia. Freight prices often differ between the two

Table 5.4 Average container freight market rates (2009–2014)[a]

USD per TEU from Shanghai to	2009	2010	2011
United States West Coast	$1,372	$2,308	$1,667
United States East Coast	$2,367	$3,499	$3,008
Northern Europe	$1,395	$1,789	$881
Mediterranean	$1,397	$1,739	$973
South America (Santos)	$2,429	$2,236	$1,483
South Africa (Durban)	$1,495	$1,481	$991
Singapore	-	$318	$210
East Japan	-	$316	$337
USD per TEU from Shanghai to	2009	2010	2011
United States West Coast	$1,372	$2,308	$1,667
United States East Coast	$2,367	$3,499	$3,008
Northern Europe	$1,395	$1,789	$881
Mediterranean	$1,397	$1,739	$973
South America (Santos)	$2,429	$2,236	$1,483
South Africa (Durban)	$1,495	$1,481	$991
Singapore	-	$318	$210
East Japan	-	$316	$337

[a] https://unctad.org/system/files/official-document/rmt2017ch3_en.pdf. Accessed 1 June 2021.

legs of the voyage, for example Asia-US rates are usually significantly higher than the US to Asia route. This is primarily down to the higher operating costs of Asian terminals and higher bunkerage costs.

When capacity exceeds demand liner companies often respond one of several ways: for example, in early 2009 during the global economic recession, some container lines took drastic actions by dropping their freight rates to zero on the Asia to Europe route, and only charging shippers a surcharge to cover their operating costs. This measure is extremely rare as most shipping companies tend to respond to overcapacity by either laying ships up or reducing their fleet operating costs. The easiest way to reduce a ship's outlay is to reduce its speed. This is called *slow steaming*. Whilst slow steaming benefits the shipping company by reducing the amount of fuel burnt, it obviously impacts on cargo delivery times. Slow steaming from Asia to Europe can easily take as long as 40 days. Another strategy used by some companies is to manipulate the market by publishing notices of rate increases. When a notice of rate increase is issued by one carrier, it is common for other carriers to follow suit. Whilst this is not itself strictly illegal, market manipulation is, and any company caught trying to unduly influence market rates is likely to face difficult questions. As if economic downturns and global pandemics are not enough, competition from land-based transportation routes have also made maritime shipping more competitive. The Trans-Siberian Railroad (TSR) has become a viable alternative to maritime transport on the Asia to Europe route. The TSR can potentially deliver a container in as much as ⅓ to ½ of the time it takes to ship the same container by sea. Add the benefit of intermodal exchange, and the allure of land-based transportation is quite attractive. To compete in an increasingly competitive business environment, in 2015 sixteen of the largest container shipping lines consolidated their routes and services into three *alliances*, accounting for 95% of container volumes moving in the dominant East to West trade routes.

In this chapter we were introduced to some of the main design factors of container ships, as well as the differences between box ships and RORO ships. We have also looked briefly at

60   The merchant mercantile

Table 5.5 Container industry alliances (2021)[a]

Alliance	Partners	Ships	Weekly services
Ocean Alliance	CMA CGM COSCO, Evergreen[b]	323	40
THE Alliance	Hapag-Lloyd HMM ONE Yang Ming[c]	241	32
2M Alliance	Mærsk Line MSC[d]	223	25

[a] https://container-xchange.com/blog/shipping-alliances/. Accessed 1 June 2021.
[b] France, China, and Taiwan respectively.
[c] Germany, South Korea, Japan, and China respectively.
[d] Denmark and Switzerland respectively.

how the container industry works and the many factors that influence shipping costs. Some of these subjects we will return to later but in the next chapter, we will turn our attention to maritime regulatory framework that governs the shipping industry, how ships are operated, and how the ship, her crew and her cargo are kept safe.

NOTES

1. 6,753 gross tonnes DWT; LOA 126.2m (414ft); beam 19.1m (63ft).
2. Containers are categorised according to their length. A 20 ft container is referred to as a TEU or 20-foot equivalent unit, whereas a 40 ft container is referred to as an FEU or 40-foot equivalent unit. Container sizes are set by the ISO.
3. A geared ship is a ship with a deck mounted crane than can load and discharge cargoes. Geared ships can operate without the need for a shore-based crane.
4. Sometimes referred to as ConRo ships.
5. The accommodation block, officer's day rooms, galley and mess, the bridge, and smokestack.
6. *P&O Nedlloyd* was formed as a joint merger between *P&O Containers Limited* and the Dutch container company *Royal Nedlloyd Lines* in December 1996. In 2005 the company was acquired by Mærsk and ceased to trade as an independent company in 2006.
7. When looking forward, toward the bow of a ship, port and starboard refer to the left and right sides, respectively.
8. Pure Car Carrier or PCC.
9. Pure Car and Truck Carrier or PCTC.

Chapter 6

Maritime regulatory framework

The shipping industry is one of the most regulated industries in the world. The framework of regulations, guidance, and standards extends as far back as the 18th century when the British Parliament implemented laws governing the welfare of Royal Navy sailors. It was not until 1974 that SOLAS, the most important maritime convention was adopted. Since then, various conventions and regulations have been introduced over the years including the *International Prevention of Pollution from Ships* (MARPOL) in 1973, ISM in 1998, amended 2002, and the ISPS Code in 2004. Central to the management and supervision of the maritime regulatory framework is the *International Maritime Organisation* or IMO, which has its headquarters in London, UK. In addition to the IMO, numerous other organisations and authorities work together to improve the maritime industry through the development and adoption of legislation including Flag States, classification societies (administrations), and Port State Control authorities. This chapter will introduce us to some of the more important conventions and regulations. But first, we will find out a little about the IMO. The IMO was established in 1958, and formally met for the first time in 1959. At first, the IMO was called the *Inter-Governmental Maritime Consultative Organisation* (IMCO), a title it held until 1982 when the present name was adopted. The purpose of the IMO is to act as a central technical body for the facilitation and promotion of international standards in shipping. Within its broad remit are responsibilities that include maritime safety, the prevention and control of marine pollution and environmental protection, safe navigation, and maritime security. Since its formation, the IMO has been instrumental in turning the shipping industry into a safe and environmentally conscious industry.

The IMO is a relatively small organisation consisting of an Assembly, a Council, and five main operational committees. These are the *Maritime Safety Committee* (MSC), the *Marine Environment Protection Committee* (MEPC), the *Legal Committee*, the *Technical Cooperation Committee*, and the *Facilitation Committee*. In addition, there are several sub-committees which assist and support the main committees in their work. The Assembly is the governing body of the IMO and consists of representatives from all IMO member states. The member states are the governments of countries that have shipping interests. The Assembly is the highest authority within the IMO. The Assembly meets every two years and elects the IMO Council. The Council is responsible for ensuring the programme of work set by the Assembly is carried through to completion and for supervising the work of the individual committees. The Council is responsible for submitting proposals from the committees to the Assembly for consideration and for advising the Assembly. The first committee is the Maritime Safety Committee (MSC), which consists of representatives from all member states, conducts work related to navigation and collision avoidance, ship construction, ship equipment, safe manning requirements, and cargo operations. In addition, the MSC is also responsible for all marine casualty investigations, salvage, and worldwide search and rescue operations. The Technical Cooperation Committee (TCC) is responsible

DOI: 10.1201/9781003244615-7

61

62 The merchant mercantile

Table 6.1 Summary of the shipping industry regulatory framework

International Maritime Organisation	Develops and adopts legislation
Flag State Authority	Implements and enforces legislation (administration)
Classification Society	Inspects, certifies, and verifies
Port State Control	Inspects, certifies, and verifies

for conducting technical research and facilitating cooperation projects with other technical bodies and organisations. The Legal Committee is responsible for all legal matters relating to the work of the IMO. The Legal Committee was established in 1967 following the *MV Torrey Canyon* incident. On Saturday 18 March 1967, at about 0850hrs, the Torrey Canyon, en route from Kuwait to Wales, ran aground on Pollard's Rock between Land's End and the Scilly Isles. She was a first generation Capesize super tanker with a LOA of 297 metres. Her grounding was the world's first major oil tanker disaster. The incident led to a major reconsideration of how the maritime industry is regulated and the impact of the marine industry on the environment. The Maritime Environment Protection Committee or MEPC is responsible for all matters relating to the prevention and control of pollution from ships including the adoption and oversight of the MARPOL regulations. Last of all, the Facilitation Committee works with the other committees, as well as relevant bodies and organisations, to eliminate unnecessary formalities and bureaucracy from within the shipping industry. The aim of the committee is to strike a balance between safety and security, and enhance maritime trade.

CODES AND CONVENTIONS

The development and implementation of SOLAS predates the establishment of the IMO as do several other key conventions such as the Load Line Convention and *International Regulations for Preventing Collisions at Sea* (COLREG), 1972. However, the responsibilities for maintaining, updating, and developing the maritime conventions – including those already in existence – passed to the IMO upon its creation in 1982. The following is a summary[1] of the main maritime conventions in force as of July 2021: the *International Maritime Dangerous Goods Code* (IMDG), which is the main regulatory code for carrying dangerous goods by sea transport; the *International Maritime Solid Bulk Cargo Code* (IMSBC), which is a mandatory regulation for ships carrying solid cargo in bulk form – this replaced the *Bulk Cargo Code* (BCC) and ensures the safe stowage and shipment of solid bulk cargoes; the *International Code for the Construction and Equipment of Ships carrying Liquefied Gases in Bulk* (IGC), which provides guidance for gas carrier operators and ship's crews regarding the construction, operation, and safety of ships carrying liquified gas cargoes. As with the other forms of cargo and their respective codes, this code is specific to the carriage of LPG; the *International Code for the Construction and Equipment of Ships carrying Dangerous Chemicals in Bulk* (IBC) relates to the carriage of chemicals in bulk in addition to the design, construction, and operation of equipment with respect to the ship and its cargo; the *International Ship and Port Facility Security Code* (ISPS) arose from the terrorist attacks New York on 11 September 2001. The code sets out minimum level security measures to be enforced by ships and port facilities; the *International Safety Management Code* (ISM) is perhaps one of the most important codes and governs day-to-day safety on board. It also provides regulatory protection against maritime pollution; the International *Code for the Safe Carriage of Packaged Irradiated Nuclear Fuel* (INF) sets the minimum standards required for ships involved in the transportation and shipment of plutonium and radioactive waste. It is a complete guideline for all ships of 500 gross tonnes and above carrying INF cargo; the *International Code for Intact Stability* (IS) provides construction guidelines for ships for maintaining ship stability in all working conditions; the *Casualty Investigation Code* is a point of reference for resolving and investigating incidents on board ships involving casualties; the *Code of Safe Practices for Ships carrying Timber Deck Cargo* (TDC) provides complete guidance for the design and construction of ships and the loading, stowage, and discharging of timber deck cargo. The TDC was implemented as a revision to the original code adopted in 1991; the *Code of Safe Practice for Cargo Stowage and Securing* (CSS), which provides guidelines for ships' personnel regarding the secure stowage of cargoes; the *International Convention of the Safety, Training, Certification and Watchkeeping* (STCW) is the primary reference for seafarers. The STCW was amended in 2010 with the revised version entering into force on 1 January 2012;[2] the *Code of Safe Working Practices for Merchant Mariners* (COSWP) provides guidance for the provision and management of health and safety on board ships, and is intended primarily for merchant mariners though all seafarers will find its guidance of great help; the *Code of Conduct for the Merchant Navy* provides a system of protocols and expected behaviours for all merchant mariners; the *Code of safe practices for Offshore Supply Vessels* (COSV) provides a complete guideline for offshore vessels supplying cargo and personnel in littoral coastal regions; the *International Life Saving Appliances Code* falls under SOLAS and deals with onboard safety equipment in terms of construction, operation, and all other requirements for the wellbeing of crew members; the *Polar Code* came into force on 1 January 2017 as a mandatory requirement of SOLAS and MARPOL. The Polar Code provides guidance and information for ships operating in the north and south polar regions; the *International Fire Safety System Code* (FSS) also falls under SOLAS. FSS deals with all the firefighting appliances, safety measures, and systems used on board to detect, alert and extinguish onboard fires; last of all, the *Fire Test Procedure Code* (FTP) provides guidelines for manufacturers and shipbuilders involved in the design and construction of ships. It also provides important information for officers involved in performing fire drills.

International Convention for the Safety of Life at Sea

Of all the regulations and conventions governing the maritime industry, SOLAS is by a nautical mile the most important. SOLAS established the minimum safety requirements for the construction, equipment, and operation of merchant ships. Originally implemented in 1974, IMCO revised the SOLAS Convention in 1978 to incorporate major changes in maritime safety procedures. Since 1978, the Convention has undergone several updates to meet the changing needs of safety in the modern shipping industry. SOLAS 1974 comprises 14 chapters, with each chapter containing its own distinct set of regulations. Each SOLAS chapter has the same basic structure and applies to all ships, regardless of individual Flag State or location of operation. Given that it may not be possible for every regulation to be fulfilled in every maritime jurisdiction, alternative 'equivalency' rules are provided where appropriate. The 14 chapters that comprise the SOLAS 1974 regulations are: *Chapter I General Provisions:* this includes the survey and certification of all maritime safety equipment and infrastructure; *Chapter II-1 Construction: Subdivision and Stability, Machinery and Electrical Installations:* this includes the systems and equipment used for watertight integrity; Chapter II-2 Construction: Fire Detection and Fire Extinction: this includes all means and measures relating to onboard fire protection in the ship's accommodation, cargo spaces and engine compartments; *Chapter III Lifesaving Appliances and Arrangements:* this includes all lifesaving appliances, equipment, and their use in emergency situations; *Chapter IV Radio Communications:* this includes GMDSS, SART and EPRIB; *Chapter V*

64 The merchant mercantile

Safety of Navigation: this chapter deals with all seagoing ships of all sizes and covers passage planning, navigation, and distress signals; *Chapter VI Carriage of Cargoes:* this chapter sets the requirements for the loading, stowage, and securing of different types of cargo such as containers but excludes oil and gas cargoes; *Chapter VII Carriage of Dangerous Goods:* this chapter sets the requirements for the loading, stowage, and securing of dangerous cargoes as defined by the *International Maritime Code for the Storage and Transportation of Dangerous Goods* (IMCSTDG). This covers dangerous cargoes not covered in either the preceding or following chapters; *Chapter VIII Nuclear Ships:* this chapter includes the Code of Safety for Nuclear Propelled Ships

Chapter IX Management for the Safe Operation of Ships: this chapter incorporates the International Safety Management Code for Shipowners and Ship Operators; *Chapter X Safety Measures for High-Speed Craft:* this chapter sets out the safety code for high-speed craft; *Chapter XI-1 and 2 Special Measures to Enhance Maritime Safety:* these chapters provide information and guidance on enhanced surveys for safe ship operation, other operational requirements and the ISPS Code; *Chapter XII Additional Safety Measures for Bulk Carriers:* this chapter relates specifically to bulk carriers in excess 150m in length; *Chapter XIII Verification of Compliance:* this chapter came into force in 2016 and incorporates the Instrument Implementation Code; *Chapter XIV Safety Measures for Ships Operating in Polar Waters:* this chapter came into force in 2017 and incorporates the Polar Code.

Regulation for the Prevention of Pollution by Oil

In the same way that the SOLAS regulations safeguard the safety of seafarers, MARPOL safeguards the marine environment from maritime pollution. MARPOL came into force at the same time as SOLAS in 1973 and was similarly amended in 1978. MARPOL consist of six annexes for controlling and eliminating maritime pollution: *Annex I: Regulation for the Prevention of Pollution by Oil* (entered into force 2 October 1983); *Annex II: Regulation for the Control of Pollution by Noxious Liquid Substances in Bulk* (entered into force April 1987); *Annex III: Regulation for the Prevention of Pollution by Harmful Substances carried by Sea in Packaged Form* (entered into force 1 July 1992); *Annex IV: Regulation for the Prevention of Pollution by Sewage from Ships* (entered into force 27 September 2003); *Annex V: Regulation for the Prevention of Pollution by Garbage from Ships* (entered into force 31 December 1988); *Annex VI: Regulation for the Prevention of Air Pollution from Ships* (entered into force 19 May 2005).

International Ship and Port Facility Security Code

The ISPS Code is one of the cornerstone maritime regulations. It sets out the framework for the safety and security of ships, ports and terminals, cargo, and crew. Following the terrorist attacks on New York on 11 September 2001 international terrorism has become one the biggest challenges the world has faced. Even before the attacks on New York maritime security was a serious issue. On 26 February 2000 two bombs exploded on the Philippine ferry *Our Lady of Mediatrix*, killing 45 passengers. Before the implementation of the ISPS Code, the primary focus of SOLAS was on the safety of the ship and seafarers. As safety and security are two very different regulatory areas, SOLAS was amended to incorporate a revised chapter XI where chapter XI-1 would focus on maritime safety and chapter XI-2 would focus on maritime security. The new SOLAS chapter XI-2 would become known as the ISPS Code. The ISPS Code was implemented by the IMO on 1 July 2004. The provisions of the ISPS Code apply to all ships over 500 gross tonnes and engaged in international voyages. This encompasses passenger and cargo ships. As the ISPS Code also covers passenger vessels, it is worth mentioning the provisions only concern the security of the ship, its crew, port, or terminal facilities and port workers. By extension this covers passengers though the provisions do not relate to passenger security directly. The ISPS Code sets out the preventative measures that should be taken in the event a security threat is identified.

This includes monitoring the activity of people and cargo operations; detecting security threats on board and in port, and implementing appropriate security measures; providing an appropriate security level for the ship and setting various duties and functions appropriate to the security level assigned; establishing respective roles and responsibilities of contracting governments, agencies, local administrations, and the shipping and port industries; defining and implementing the roles and responsibilities for port state officials and shipboard officers to tackle maritime security threats at the international level; collecting data from the maritime industry concerning threats to security and establishing ways to protect the industry from those threats; facilitating the global exchange of security-related information and data with port authorities, shipowners, and ship operators; providing a methodology for carrying out security assessments and putting in place plans and procedures for reacting to changing security levels; and establishing shortcomings in ship security and port security plans and implementing measures for improvement. The ISPS Code incorporates various functional requirements to enable it to achieve certain objectives. Some of these critical requirements include gathering security-related information from contracting government agencies; assessing the information received; distributing security-related information to appropriate contracting government agencies; defining proper communication protocols for ships and port facilities to encourage efficient information exchange; preventing unauthorised entry into port facilities and onto ships, or any other restricted areas, even if the unauthorised entry does not pose a threat; preventing the carriage of unauthorised weapons, incendiary devices, or explosives on ships and through port facilities; providing alternative means for raising security alarms should an incident occur; implementing security plans for port and ship-based activities based on security risk assessments and analysis; and plan and implement training, drills, and exercises for the ship's crew and shore-based personnel.

Merchant ships are particularly vulnerable to security threats as they do not ordinarily carry any means of defence. Piracy, terrorism, and stowaways are all very real threats that present acute security concerns for the shipping industry. The ISPS Code recognised that improved ship security is required to identify and take preventive measures against these security incidents. Subsequently, administrations were provided additional responsibilities for reviewing and approving ship security plans, including making recommendations and amendments for improvements. Central to the ISPS Code is the formation of several key appointments. Under the provisions of the ISPS Code, ships must appoint a fully qualified and certified onboard Ship Security Officer (SSO). The SSO is responsible for the continuous review of the Ship Security Plan (SSP) and for ensuring the measures within the SSP are followed. A copy of the SSP must be retained by the company and approved by the administration. In addition to the appointment of the SSO, is the Company Security Officer (CSO). The CSO is a company appointed person whose duties include carrying out the ship security assessment and onboard survey. These are both designed to confirm the development and implementation of the SSP as per the ISPS Code. Should any deficiencies be found, the CSO is responsible for making the appropriate amendments and for overseeing the relevant changes to bring the SSP in line with the requirements of the ISPS Code. The SSP is a document that must always be retained on board as it provides in detail the duties of the SSO and each member of the ship's crew in accordance with the different ISPS security levels. The SSP also sets out the actions that crew members must take in the event of a security threat. The SSO is responsible to the CSO for implementing and overseeing the SSO on board.

It is the responsibility of the SSO to implement the appropriate measures on board in accordance with the security level set by local government and port authorities. The security levels under the ISPS Code describe the current security conditions as related to the security threat to the country in question and its coastal regions. This encompasses all ships operating within their territorial waters and exclusive economic zones (EEZ). As soon as the security level has been confirmed, it must be displayed prominently at each point of entry to the ship. There are three Maritime Security (MARSEC) levels under the ISPS Code: MARSEC Level 1; MARSEC Level 2; and MARSEC Level 3. The security level for the ship must always be the same or higher than that set by the port authority. MARSEC Level 1 is the normal operating level for ships and port facilities under normal circumstances. This means those liable for boarding the ship must be searched in accordance with the protocols set out in the SSP. It is important that searches of persons are coordinated with the port authority to avoid violations of local laws or customs. MARSEC Level 2 is the second security level available under the ISPS Code and indicates there is a heightened and realistic security threat to the ship or the port facility. In addition to the measures contained under MARSEC Level 1, additional security measures must be implemented, including but not limited to assigning additional personnel for patrolling ship access areas; deterring waterside access to the ship; establishing a restricted area on the shoreside of the ship; increasing the search frequency of personnel boarding and disembarking the ship; escorting all visitors on board including port and company officials; arranging additional security briefings for the ship's crew; and carrying out partial or full ship searches.

MARSEC Level 3 is the highest security level available under the ISPS Code and is used only when a security threat is actively taking place. Unlike MARSEC Levels 1 and 2, Level 3 may only be enforced for a limited timeframe, although there is no limit on the number of times the security level can be raised and lowered. This provides a degree of flexibility as the specific target may not yet be known but intelligence suggests there is a heightened security risk. Throughout a Level 3 imposition, the ship must maintain regular contact with the port facility and exercise the highest degree of vigilance possible. The SSP must identify areas of the ship that are restricted. The purpose of identifying restricted areas is to prevent unauthorised access to sensitive parts of the ship, to protect the personnel on board, and to protect cargo from pilferage or tampering. Restricted areas will be specific to each vessel but usually include the bridge, machinery spaces, spaces with security-related equipment, ventilation spaces, spaces containing IMDG cargo, the crew accommodation areas, and any other areas specified in the SSP. In addition to preventing unauthorised access to the ship, the SSP must implement measures to prevent the pilferage and tampering of cargo. These measures must also prevent the onboarding of cargo that has not been authorised. When bringing stores and victuals on board, these should be inspected against the manifest (date of expiry, weights, and so on) as well as for integrity including random sample checks. Unless a valid order for stores has been authorised, any delivery should be refused. No stores should be accepted without a stringent inspection *before* the stores are brought on board the ship. There may be occasions when baggage is brought on board. This might include mail sacks, equipment and parts, crew luggage, or other items purchased by the crew for delivery home. All baggage must be screened before it is brought on board. Wherever possible, advanced screening methods such as x-ray should be used.

Port authorities must ensure that the facilities under their responsibility are protected from any sort of threat that may arise from air, land, and water. Port authorities must also monitor ships coming into their waters for any security risk. It is the port facility that sets the security level to be followed by ships whilst the ship is in the port facility's territorial waters. The master has sole discretion whether they apply the security level set by the port or enact a higher security level. In any case, the security level of the ship cannot be less than the port security level. The port authority is responsible for preparing the *Port Facility Security Plan* (PFSP). The PFSP must also include a port facility security assessment, which is forms an integral part of the process of drafting and updating the PFSP. The assessment is usually assessed and reviewed by the Flag State or by the government organisation responsible for shipping and port development for that country. Like the ISPS Code provisions for ships port facilities are also mandated to assign security-related roles and responsibilities. First and foremost is the Port Facility Security Officer (PFSO). The PFSO is a government-appointed official responsible for implementing the PFSP and for setting the security levels for the port facility and all ships within its area of authority. The PFSO is responsible for carrying out the port facility security assessment. The PFSP includes the strategies and actions to be taken during each of the three security levels. The PFSP also sets out the roles and responsibilities for personnel involved in port security as well as the actions to be taken in the event a security breach occurs. Port facilities must ensure minimum security equipment such as scanners and metal detectors are always available and operational. This includes ensuring appropriately trained personnel are available to operate the equipment. Finally, security levels are set and enforced by the port authorities following consultation with local and national government. The security level adopted for the port facility must be communicated to every ship that enters the port's waters.

As might be expected, every regulation comes with its own unique set of challenges, and the ISPS Code is no exception. Since its implementation in 2004, several concerns with the ISPS Code have been mooted. One of the major concerns relates to seafarer health and mental wellbeing. It is argued that the ISPS Code places unnecessary stress on seafarers by restricting access to shore leave and potentially extending working hour durations beyond those permitted in SOLAS. A second concern arises from the implementation of the ISPS Code. There are vast variances in the level and quality of training for crew members who are assigned ship security duties. Carrying out additional ISPS measures places extra strain on crew members; this is particularly acute for crew members assigned security watch duties. Implementing security measures in accordance with heightened security levels is often a time-consuming task that impinges on normal operational duties. It often requires crew members who are due downtime to participate in security briefings or to help set up and man security cordons, or to carry out ship searches. Moreover, port activities are negatively affected when the security level rises resulting in slower cargo operations. When the security level is at its highest, all cargo operations cease resulting in longer port stays and delays in the ship's schedule.

International Safety Management Code

The ISM Code was adopted in 1993 by resolution A.741(18) and was made mandatory on 1 July 1998. The 1994 amendments to SOLAS incorporated the ISM Code as a new chapter IX. Since 1998, several additional amendments have been added to the IMS Code including in the 2000 resolution MSC.104(73) which came into force on 1 July 2002; followed by resolution MSC.179(79) in 2004, which came into force on 1 July 2006; the 2005 resolution MSC.273(85) which came into force on 1 July 2010; and the 2013 resolution MSC.353(92) which came into force on 1 July 2015. The purpose of the ISM Code is to provide an international standard for the safe management and operation of ships and to prevent maritime pollution of the marine environment. Although the IMO had already invited the international community to implement steps necessary to ensure the maritime industry promoted standards in maritime safety and environmental protection (resolution A.443(XI)) it was widely recognised that the existing system needed a codified mechanism which could enforce the agreed standards. This mechanism was formed through resolution

A.680(17); which later became the ISM Code. Recognising the intrinsic differences in the way shipowners and crews operate, the ISM Code was built on a foundation of general principles and objectives. These include provisions for the identification and mitigation of risks to ships, ship personnel, and the environment as well as the establishment and implementation of appropriate safeguards. The provisions of the ISM Code are designed to be as broad as possible to ensure the widest application. Fundamental to the ISM Code is the acceptance and adoption of good top-down safety management. Clearly different levels of management – shore-based or shipboard – require varying levels of knowledge, competence, and awareness of safety management. In answer to this, the ISM Code sets out the requirement for each respective level of application.

In addition to chapter IX of the SOLAS Convention, which incorporated the IMS Code, further provisions have been brought into effect including the Revised Guidelines for the Operational Implementation of the ISM Code by Companies (MSC-MEPC.7/Circ.8); Guidance on the Qualifications, Training and Experience necessary for undertaking the role of the Designated Person under the ISM Code by Companies (MSC-FAL.7/Circ.6); Guidance on Near-Miss Reporting (MSC-MEPC.7/Circ.7); Guidelines on Maritime Cyber Risk Management (MSC-FAL.1/Circ.3); and Maritime Cyber Risk Management in Safety Management Systems (MSC.428(98). The provisions of the ISM Code provide a common platform that must be followed by all ships of all nationalities. This removes the potential for discrepancies arising from poorly implemented safety and environmental protection standards across different jurisdictions. In most cases, the ISM is supported by the ship's SMS, which in turn details the various requirements stipulated under the Code, including the establishment of a managerial committee to oversee the implementation and governance of maritime security and environmental protection. It also sets forth the assignment of responsibility for managerial officers to carry out their duties appropriately; the establishment of protocols for identifying and resolving deficiencies in maritime security and environmental protection; and the establishment of a ship safety management auditing system (SMAS).

Safety management auditing is carried out as both an internal and external activity. Internal auditing forms part of the Planned Maintenance Schedule and is performed by the shipowner or ship operator. External auditing is carried out every two to three years by officials assigned by the Flag State. If after external audit the ship has successfully incorporated all of the safety requirements mandated under the ISM and SMS, the company is issued with a *Document of Compliance* (DOC) and the ship is issued with a *Safety Management Certificate* (SMC). The DOC is only issued once the Flag State has confirmed the company has a robust SMS in place and that all ships under the company's control are managed in accordance with the SMS. The DOC is issued to a company based on the type of ships they operate; this means that a company which operates more than one type of vessel will be issued separate DOCs for each ship type. For example, companies that operate oil tankers and container ships will be issued one DOC for their tanker fleet and another DOC for their container fleet. The DOC is issued under the authority of the Flag State and only after an external audit has taken place. There are three different types of DOCs which may be issued.

The first is the *interim DOC*. An interim DOC is issued to newly established companies or to companies receiving a new class of ship to their existing fleet. Where an interim DOC is issued, the company is required to submit an *SMS Implementation Plan* and is given 12 months to comply with the ISM requirements. The interim DOC has a validity of 12 months and is contingent upon the successful completion of an initial audit. Further audits are carried out each time the company adds a new class of ship to their fleet within the first 12 months of operation. For newly established companies, further reviews may be carried out prior to the Flag State audit. The second type of DOC is the *short-term DOC*. A short-term

DOC is issued on the day of the audit by the Flag State, and confirms the satisfactory completion of the initial, annual, or renewed audit. The validity of a short-term DOC is five months. The *full DOC* is issued only after the successful completion of the initial audit or when the requirements of an interim DOC have been fully met. The DOC is usually issued three months following the implementation of the SMS and must cover at least one ship in the fleet. The validity of the DOC is five years and is subject to annual audit. If during the annual audit, a major nonconformity is found, the DOC may be withdrawn by the Flag State. The original copy of the certificate is held by the company with copies circulated to all ships in the company's fleet. As mentioned above, when a company is issued a DOC, the ships within the company's fleet are issued with a *Safety Management Certificate* (SMC). Every individual ship must have an SMC which documents (a) the ship's compliance with the onboard *Safety Management Manual* (SMM) and (b) that the SMM complies with the provisions of the ISM. The SMC is issued only after a successful audit confirms the ship's compliance with the SMM and by extension the ISM. Like the DOC, there are three types of SMC that can be issued. The *interim SMC* has a validity of six months and may be issued in accordance with any one of the following provisions: (a) when a company holds either a full, short-term, or interim DOC; or (b) the company is in receipt of a newbuild into their existing fleet; or (c) the company has changed the country registry of their ship resulting in a change of Flag State; or (d) where an existing ship is transferred from one company to another. For the ship to be issued an interim SMC, it must first undergo an initial audit which provides sufficient evidence of compliance with the SMM. This is necessary for the interim SMC to be exchanged for a full SMC.

A *short-term SMC* may be issued on the day of the Flag State audit as evidence of having successfully completed the initial, annual, or renewal audit process. The short-term SMC a validity period of five months. Last of all, the *full SMC* is issued by the Flag State following successful completion of an initial audit or the fulfilment of interim SMC requirements. The validity of a full SMC is five years and is subject to intermediate audit. The intermediate audit is carried out between the second and third anniversary of the ship's registration. If a major nonconformity is found during the audit process, the SMC and DOC may be withdrawn. Unlike the DOC, the original SMC is kept on board the ship and a copy is sent to the company.

Casualty Investigation Code

The rules concerning the investigation of casualties at sea form a significant body of regulations contained in several regulatory instruments. SOLAS regulation I/21 and MARPOL articles 8 and 12 stipulate that every Flag State must carry out an investigation into any casualty occurring on board ships under the supervision of their Flag. Casualty investigation is further mandated under article 23 of the *Load Lines Convention* and article 94 of the *United Nations Convention on the Law of the Sea* (UNCLOS), which declares that

> each State shall cause an inquiry to be held by or before a suitably qualified person or persons into every marine casualty or incident of navigation on the high seas involving a ship flying its flag and causing loss of life or serious injury to nationals of another State or serious damage to ships or installations of another State or to the marine environment. The Flag State and the other State shall co-operate in the conduct of any inquiry held by that other State into any such marine casualty or incident of navigation.

In May 2008, the IMO adopted a new *Code of International Standards and Recommended Practices for a Safety Investigation into a Marine Casualty*, otherwise known as the *Marine*

Incident Code or the *Casualty Investigation Code*. In addition, amendments to SOLAS chapter XI-1 were also adopted making parts I and II of the Code mandatory, with an additional part III containing related guidance and explanatory notes. The new regulations entered into force on 1 January 2010 and expanded on the original provisions set out in SOLAS regulation I/21. This is because the original provisions only required Flag State administrations to undertake an investigation 'when it [the administration] judges that such an investigation may assist in determining what changes in the present regulations might be desirable'. The Code now requires a marine safety investigation to be conducted into every 'serious marine casualty', which is defined by the Code as the 'total loss of the ship, a death or severe damage to the environment'. The Code also recommends Flag State investigations into non-serious marine casualty incidents, especially where the investigation might provide useful information that could prevent further such accidents from occurring in future. To further enhance the framework around casualty investigation, the IMO passed several resolutions aimed at securing international cooperation and recognition of mutual interest. The first such resolution was A.173(IV) on the *Participation in Official Inquiries into Maritime Incidents* and was adopted in November 1968. Since then, further resolutions have been passed including resolution A.322(IX) on the *Conduct of Investigations into Casualties* (November 1975), resolution A.440(XI) on the *Exchange of Information for Investigations into Maritime Casualties*, resolution A.442(XI) on *Personnel and Material Resource Needs of Administrations for the Investigation of Casualties and the Contravention of Conventions* (November 1979), and resolution A.637(16) on the *Cooperation in Maritime Casualty Investigations* (October 1989).

These individual resolutions have been amalgamated by the IMO into the *Code for the Investigation of Marine Casualties and Incidents* and further developed with the adoption of resolution A.884(21) or amendments to the *Code for the Investigation of Marine Casualties and Incidents*; and resolution A.849(20), adopted in November 1999, which provides *Guidelines for the Investigation of Human Factors*; the December 2013 resolution 1075(28) on the *Guidelines to Assist Investigators in the Implementation of the Casualty Investigation Code* (which included resolution MSC.255(84) which revoked the previous resolutions A.849(20) and A.884(21). Under the amended regime, reporting maritime casualties and incidents to the IMO is mandatory as per the *Code of International Standards and Recommended Practices for a Safety Investigation into a Marine Casualty or Marine Incident* (Casualty Investigation Code), 2008 edition (resolution MSC.255(84)), §14.1, chapter 14 of Part II; *Guidelines to Assist Investigators in the Implementation of the Casualty Investigation Code* (resolution MSC.255(84) (resolution A. 1075(28)); *Safety of Fishermen at Sea*, resolution A.646(16), §3; *Reports on Casualty Statistics concerning Fishing Ships and Fishermen at Sea*, MSC/Circ.539/Add.2, §2; *Report on Fishing Ships and Fishermen Statistics*, MSC/Circ.753, §3; *Provision of Preliminary Information on Serious and Very Serious Casualties by Rescue Coordination Centres*, MSC/Circ.802, §3; *Guidance on Near-Miss Reporting*, MSC-MEPC.7/Circ.7, §4; and *Casualty-Related Matters, Reports on Marine Casualties and Incidents*, MSC MEPC.3/Circ.4/Rev.1, §6 and §8. To avoid unnecessary duplication and facilitate the harmonisation of reporting procedures, the IMO coordinates maritime casualty and incident investigation with the *European Maritime Safety Agency* (EMSA), who in turn manage their own *European Marine Casualty Information Platform* (EMCIP).

Code of Safe Practice for Cargo Stowage and Securing

Cargoes on board ships are subject to significant acceleration and centrifugal forces resulting from a combination of longitudinal, vertical, and transverse motions. These forces are the single most common cause for incidents arising from poor cargo stowage. To this end, in November 1991, the IMO adopted through resolution A.714(17) the *Code of Safe Practice for Cargo Stowage and Securing* (CSS Code). The CSS Code has undergone several revisions since its implementation including MSC/Circ.664, MSC/Circ.691, MSC/Circ.740, MSC/Circ.812, MSC/Circ.1026, MSC.1/Circ.1352, MSC.1/Circ.1352/Rev.1. The purpose of the CSS Code is to provide an internationally recognised and adopted standard for the promotion of safe cargo stowage. It does this by drawing the attention of shipowners and ship operators to the need to ensure that the ship is suitable for its intended purpose; by providing advice to ensure ships are appropriately equipped with proper means of lashing and securing cargo; by providing general advice concerning the proper stowage and securing of cargoes to minimise risks to the ship and her crew; by providing specific advice on those cargoes which are known to be hazardous; by providing advice on actions to be taken in heavy seas; and by providing advice on the actions to be taken to remedy shifting cargo.

All cargoes must be stowed and secured in a way that does not impact or interfere with the safety of the ship and the people on board. The master is absolutely responsibility for the safe conduct of the voyage and for the safety of the ship, her crew, and her cargo. This encompasses the safe stowage and securing of cargoes, which is dependent on proper planning, execution, and supervision. All personnel involved in the loading, securing, and lashing of cargo must be SQEP and sufficiently informed of the *Cargo Securing Manual*. This is because any cargo not properly stowed and secured poses a hazard and risks affecting the stability and integrity of the ship. The measures for stowing and securing cargo should be based on the worst weather scenarios expected during the intended passage.

International Maritime Dangerous Goods Code

The IMDG Code was adopted in 1965 as per the SOLAS Convention of 1960 under falls under the oversight of the IMO. The IMDG Code was developed as a means of preventing incidents resulting in maritime pollution. The IMDG code also ensures that goods shipped by sea are packaged in such a way that they are safe during transport. The IMDG Code is a uniform code. This means it applies to all cargo-carrying ships anywhere in the world without exception. The original IMDG Code proposal was drafted in accordance with the recommendations made by the *UN Panel of Experts on the Transportation of Hazardous Goods*, in conjunction with advice provided by IMCO. The initial proposal was presented as a report to the UN General Assembly in 1956; following further work and amendments, the IMDG Code was published in 1961. Since 1961, the Code has undergone regular review every two years which helps ensure it remains current. It really goes without saying that shipping dangerous cargo is a risky business. To maximise safety and minimise risk, a system was devised to categorise cargo in accordance with their hazard potential. The IMDG Code classifies products in one of nine categories:

- *Classification 1* is for explosives. The same classification has six sub-divisions for materials which pose a high, medium, and low explosive risk, etc.
- *Classification 2* is for gases. This clause has three sub-categories that classify gases as highly inflammable, not inflammable, and neither inflammable nor toxic
- *Classification 3* is for liquids and has no sub-divisions
- *Classification 4* is for solids. There are three sub-categories that deal with highly combustible solids, self-reactive solids, and solids that react with water to emit toxic gases
- *Classification 5* is for substances that have a risk of oxidisation
- *Classification 6* is for all kinds of substances that are toxic and that could pose a biohazard

72 The merchant mercantile

- *Classification 7* is specifically for materials that are radioactive
- *Classification 8* is for materials that are corrosive
- *Classification 9* is for those substances that cannot be classified under any of the above categories but are still considered dangerous goods

At present, the IMDG Code is recognised by 150 countries with around 98% of ships following the Code's requirements. For ships that do comply with the Code, all crew members must – whether involved directly or not with dangerous cargoes – be fully trained in dangerous cargo handling procedures, including being able to classify specific dangerous goods and identifying their shipping names; knowing how particular IMDG cargoes should be packed; understanding the different types of markings, labels, or placards used to identify various dangerous goods; knowing safe practices for loading and unloading dangerous cargoes; understanding the transport documents required when transporting dangerous goods; knowing how to handle dangerous goods when the ship is under voyage; knowing the right of inspectors to conduct surveys; knowing the best procedures for fighting and containing fires involving dangerous goods; knowing how to prepare dangerous goods loading and stowage plans taking into consideration ship stability, safety, and emergency preparedness; and understanding the importance of correct dangerous goods declarations for port authorities and onward land transit.

International Regulations for Preventing Collisions at Sea

The *International Regulations for Preventing Collisions at Sea* or COLREGs were developed by the IMO and set out, amongst other things, the *rules of the road*. These are effectively the navigational rules ships must follow to prevent and avoid collisions between two or more vessels. The COLREGs may also refer to the specific political line that divides inland waterways, which are subject to their own navigation rules, and coastal waterways which are subject to international navigation rules. The COLREGs are derived from a multilateral treaty called the *Convention on the International Regulations for Preventing Collisions at Sea*. The rules for navigating vessels inland are generally different to oceangoing vessels though the rules specify the COLREGs should be followed as closely as possible. In any event, in most of continental Europe, the *Code Européen des Voies de la Navigation Intérieure* (CEVNI, or the *European Code for Navigation on Inland Waters*) applies whereas in the US, the rules for vessels navigating inland waterways are firmly in line with the international rules. Prior to the development of the COLREGs, each individual nation was responsible for drawing up their own rules and conventions. As expected, this created a patchwork situation where inconsistent and sometimes contradictory rules would lead to collisions. Furthermore, there was no standardised approach to the use of navigational lights during the hours of darkness nor was there any consistency in the use and placement of navigation landmarks.

The advent of steam-powered ships in the mid-19th century led to the adoption of conventions for sailing vessel navigation. This was considered necessary as sailing vessels lacked the manoeuvrability enjoyed by steamships. In London in 1840, Trinity House[3] drew up a set of regulations which were adopted by an Act of Parliament in 1846. The *Trinity House Rules* were adopted through the *Steam Navigation Act 1846*. Admiralty Regulations regarding the use of navigation lights for steamships were added in the 1848 amendments. The following year in 1849 the US Congress extended the light requirements to sailing vessels in US waters. In the UK in 1858, coloured sidelights were recommended for sailing vessels, and fog signals became mandatory. On steamships this was the ship's whistle and on sailing vessels either the foghorn or ship's bell. A separate but similar requirement was adopted by the US shortly after. In 1850, English maritime law was adopted wholesale by the US. That same year, courts in England and the United States developed a common law approach pertaining to reasonable speeds within the *Assured Clear Distance Ahead*. In 1863 a new set of rules were drawn up by the British Board of Trade, in consultation with the French Government. By 1864, these regulations (or Articles as they were called) had been adopted by more than 30 maritime nations including Germany and the United States. In 1867, Thomas Gray, assistant secretary to the British Department of the Board of Trade published his treatise *The Rule of the Road*. In 1878, the US codified its common law rules for preventing collisions at sea. In 1880, the 1863 Articles were supplemented with whistle signals, and in 1884 a new set of international regulations was adopted by Congress. In 1889 the US convened the first International Maritime Conference in Washington, D.C. Following the conference, new rules were implemented 1890 and brought into effect in 1897. Some minor changes were made during the 1910 Brussels Maritime Conference, and at the International Conference on Safety of Life at Sea in 1929 further rule changes were proposed but never ratified. In 1935, the recommendation that the direction of a turn be referenced by the rudder instead of the helm or tiller was informally agreed. At the 1948 SOLAS International Conference it was proposed that radar should be recognised as an approved means of navigation. This proposal was eventually ratified in 1952 and came into effect in 1954. Further recommendations were made at the SOLAS Conference in London in 1960, which were later came into effect in 1965.

The COLREGs, as they stand today, were formally adopted on 20 October 1972, and entered into force on 15 July 1977. These new regulations were designed to update and replace the *Collision Regulations* of 1960, and particularly the *Traffic Separation Scheme* (TSS) which was introduced in the Strait of Dover in 1967. As of July 2021, the COLREGs have been ratified by 155 countries representing 98.7% of global merchant marine tonnage. The COLREGs have been amended several times since their first adoption in 1977. In 1981 Rule 10 was amended regarding the dredging or surveying in areas subject to traffic separation schemes. In 1987 amendments were made to several rules, including rule 1(e) for vessels of special construction; rule 3(h) pertaining to vessels constrained by their draught and rule 10(c), regarding crossing traffic lanes. In 1989 rule 10 was altered to stop the unnecessary use of inshore traffic zones associated with TSS. In 1993 amendments were made regarding the positioning of lights on vessels. In 2001 new rules were added relating to wing-in-ground-effect (WIG) craft and in 2007 the text of Annex IV (Distress Signals) was redrafted. The UK version of the COLREGs is provided by the MCA and is published in the *Merchant Shipping (Distress Signals and Prevention of Collisions) Regulations, 1996*. They are distributed in the form of a Merchant Shipping Notice (MSN).

FLAG STATE AUTHORITIES

Despite its role in developing conventions, the IMO has no powers to enforce the conventions it implements. This enforcement responsibility rests with individual Flag State administrations. Flag States are the national authorities that maintain the registry of all merchant vessels that operate under their national flag. under their flag. As we touched on earlier, some Flag States offer their registries as *flags of convenience*, wherein a ship owned by a company in one country sails under the flag of another country, usually for financial or regulatory reasons. The enforcement of applicable legislation is the responsibility of each Flag State. In practicality, this means a ship registered in Liberia is subject to the rules, regulations, and enforcement of the Liberian maritime authorities. Under the provisions of international maritime law, Flag States have statutory responsibilities which include ensuring the seaworthiness of ships registered under their flag and for ensuring all structures, systems, and equipment are maintained in a satisfactory condition. This is normally enforced through regular surveys, inspections, and certification regimes; ensuring ships registered under their flag are designed and operated in accordance with the relevant legislation and standards including general IMO and specific Flag State requirements; issuing certificates including the Certificate of Registry and Safe Manning Certificate;[4] ensuring that minimum manning levels are maintained at all times and that all crew members comply with minimum crew competence and training requirements under STCW; ensuring that ships registered their flag are fitted with appropriate navigation systems, equipment, and publications – including charts – to facilitate safe navigation and conduct; and the investigation of incidents and accidents on ships registered under their flag and on ships operating within the territorial jurisdiction of the Flag State authority.

PORT STATE CONTROL

All ships, when entering sovereign coastal state waters, place themselves under the direct jurisdiction of that coastal state. In the UK, for example, any ship entering the 12-mile offshore limit falls under the authority of the MCA, which is the UK's Port State Control authority. Port State Control has the jurisdiction to enforce international obligations such as SOLAS and MARPOL. To fulfil this obligation, every Port State Control has the authority to conduct summary inspections on board all ships within their jurisdiction, irrespective of the vessel's Flag State. Port State Control inspections are primarily concerned with verifying the seaworthiness of the ship, and for checking the condition of the equipment on board and confirming crew competence. Noncompliance with the regulations and conventions can result in the ship being summarily detained by Port State Control. If an accident occurs within the jurisdiction overseen by the Port State Control authority, then Port State Control has the legal competence to initiate action against the ship and its owners. A common example is when a ship runs aground causing oil spills and damage to the marine environment. It should be noted, however, that the responsibility for ensuring ships comply with international regulations lies with the Flag State authority in the first instance. The role of the Port State Control is merely to verify ship and crew compliance. That said, Port State Control officials cannot overrule judgements made by the Flag State authority.

CLASSIFICATION SOCIETIES

Classification societies are independent, non-governmental organisations that work with shipping companies and shipowners to develop the technical standards to which all ships must be designed, constructed, and operated. These are then published as *Classification Rules*. When a ship conforms to classification rules, it is said to be *in class*. Classification societies inspect ships throughout their lifetime to ensure the vessel is maintained in accordance with class rules. If the ship is deemed compliant, the classification society will issue the ship with a Certificate of Class. The ship will continue in class provided she is regularly inspected in accordance with the Classification Rules. Classification societies may also be delegated as approved authorities to act on behalf of the Flag State. In this function, the classification society is employed to carry out impartial ship inspections with the intent of verifying compliance with international and Flag State requirements. In this instance, the classification society may inspect a ship for compliance with SOLAS, and if found compliant, will issue the appropriate certificate on behalf of the Flag State authority. Classification societies are usually contracted to inspect and issue 'standard' certificates such as the Cargo Ship Safety Equipment Certificate, Cargo Ship Safety Construction Certificate, the Safety Management Certificate (SMC), the International Ship Security (ISS) Certificate, International Oil Pollution Prevention (IOPP) Certificate, International Air Pollution Prevention (IAPP) Certificate, and the International Sewage Pollution Prevention (ISPP) Certificate. Worldwide there are over 50 different classification societies though the main societies are members of the International Association of Classification Societies (IACS).[5]

In summary, the maritime regulatory framework is an extremely complex area of law. Fortunately, officers need only have a functional understanding of the different conventions, regulations, and statutory requirements rather than an in-depth understanding of the legal aspects of each regulation. In Part 2 of this book, we will explore the architectural and engineering design of container ships and the impact of intact and damaged stability.

NOTES

1. Indicative only and not exhaustive.
2. The revised STCW is referred to as the Manila Amendments.
3. The Corporation of Trinity House of Deptford Strond, also known as Trinity House, is the official authority for lighthouses in England, Wales, the Channel Islands, and Gibraltar. Trinity House is also responsible for the provision and maintenance of other navigational aids, such as lightvessels, buoys, and maritime radio/satellite communication systems. It is also an official deep sea pilotage authority, providing expert navigators for ships trading in Northern European waters.
4. Most statutory certificates are issued by classification societies on behalf of the Flag State authority.
5. American Bureau of Shipping (ABS); Bureau Veritas (BV); China Classification Society (CSS); Det Norske Veritas (DNV); Germinischer Lloyd (GL); Korean Registry of Shipping (KRS); Lloyds Register (LR); Nippon Kaiji Kyokai; Registro Italiano Navale (RINA); Russian Maritime Register of Shipping.

Part II

Principles of ship architecture and engineering

Chapter 7

Basic container ship architecture

In this chapter, we will discuss some of the main design aspects that define the modern container ship. We have already examined many of the distinguishing features of box ships and ROROs in previous chapters, but as we noted then, box ships and ROROs share many of the same features. The design and construction of container ships are quite unique though they do share some similarities with bulk carriers and general cargo ships. Every ship regardless of type or purpose shares certain structural forms. These include decks, the keel and hull, and watertight doors and bulkheads. The single defining factor for both container ships and bulk carriers is that they are built around a firm *keel*. This means the lower portion of the ship has a significant influence on the design and construction of the entire ship literally from the bottom up. Like most modern vessels, container ships have their engine and steering compartments situated towards the aft. Forward of the engine compartment are compartmentalised holds. Inside these holds are cell guides, which help the crane operator to slide each container into a preassigned slot. When loading containers into the hold, crane operators must exercise caution as any damage to the guides can cause an entire block of containers to be misaligned. Once the loading operation for that hold is complete, the top is covered with a hatch cover, onto which more containers may be stacked. Most modern container ships have a *lift away type* hatch cover. This means to access the hold the hatch cover must be lifted away by a crane. Once the loading and unloading operation is complete, the hatch cover is lowered back into place. Hatch covers perform two important functions. First, they increase the carrying capacity of the ship, and second, they prevent water ingress into the holds. To ensure this watertight integrity, the hatch covers have cleats, which must be closed after every cargo operation and before the vessel leaves port.

As we have already mentioned, the keel is one of the most important sections of the ship. From the keel, the rest of the hull is built upwards. It is designed to provide not only the required strength to withstand the weight of the cargo but also to withstand the external *hydrostatic loads* that act on the lower sections of the hull. The ship's hull essentially consists of metal plates that are welded together. These metal plates are bent into shape and stiffened. If the plates are not stiffened then the bending moments felt by the plates, which is caused by the hydrostatic load, can exceed the stress value of the metal, leading to structural failure. To prevent this from happening, the metal plates are stiffened by adding stiffeners. There are two ways to stiffen a ship: the first is through *transverse stiffening*, and the second is through *longitudinal stiffening*. Transverse stiffening or transverse framing is used on ships that are less than 120 m in length. With transverse stiffening, the stiffeners run along the entire breadth of the ship. We will cover this in more detail a little later. By comparison, longitudinal stiffening, or longitudinal framing (also called the *Isherwood system* after the British naval architect Joseph Isherwood who patented the system in 1906) uses stiffeners that run longitudinally, that is along the length of the ship, and is used on all seagoing ships with a length of more than 120 m. The frames are spaced out at equal distances to form a

DOI: 10.1201/9781003244615-9

80 Principles of ship architecture and engineering

rib-like structure. In between the frames, strengthening members are fitted to provide additional strength and to provide fixtures for the metal plating. Now that we have an idea of the two types of framing used on ships, we can begin to explore the two types of hull bottom.

HULL STRUCTURE

Typically, smaller ships have single bottomed hulls as they do not require a double bottom to withstand cargo loading. In these ships, the deck floor acts as the stiffening members for the bottom shell plating. Deck plate floors transversely run through every frame space. When hydrostatic pressure from under the bottom shell exerts a bending moment on the bottom shell, the deck plate floor takes up the bending stress. Subsequently, naval architects and ship designers must treat all members that take up bending stress as *beams*. The bending moment in the beam increases with the increasing span (length) of the beam. To counterbalance this, ships have smaller span plate floors, as this reduces the stress load on each member. To help reduce and balance the stress load on each member, *intercostal girders* are fitted. The number of intercostal girders increases with the widening beam of the ship. On top of the deck plate a wood ceiling is fitted. This provides a flat area for the stowage of cargo. It should be noted the wood ceiling does not constitute a double bottom as the wood has no capacity for absorbing bottom structure stresses. Wood is used as it is easily repairable and replaceable. By comparison, most container ships are *double bottomed*. A double bottom is a ship hull design and construction method where the bottom and sides of the ship have two watertight layers. The first outer layer forms the external hull of the ship, and the second inner layer provides a redundant barrier to seawater in the event the outer hull surface is breached. The empty space between the two layers is mostly used for the storage of ballast water. Unlike oil tankers, container ships are rarely *double hulled*. Double hulls are a more extensive safety feature than double bottoms, which have two layers in the bottom of the hull only and not along the sides of the vessel. In low energy collisions, the double hulls can prevent flooding beyond the penetrated compartment. In high energy collisions, the distance between the outer and inner hull is insufficient to provide much protection. In addition to providing limited protection against flooding, double bottoms and double hulls provide a stiff and strong girder or beam structure with the two hull plate layers forming lower and upper plates for a composite beam. This adds significant strength to the hull.

With such structural arrangements, a tank top is provided above the plate and bracket floors. Bracket floors are a little different from plate floors, in as much as they are not comprised of one single plate running athwartship, but only brackets at the port and starboard ends, with struts that support the tank top with the bottom shell. Bracket floors are mostly placed at each frame, and plate floors are generally placed at every three to four frame spaces. The space within the double bottom (that is, between the tank top, and outer bottom shell) is used for storing ballast, fuel oil, dirty oil, fresh water, and other consumables. One of the most important factors in designing the double bottom of a ship is deciding the height of the double bottom. This is governed by the height of the keel required by the ship. When estimating the scantling[1] of a ship, the naval architect must first calculate (using the rules specified by the relevant classification society, which is covered later) the height of the centre girder. This must always be accommodated within the double bottom. Hence, this factor now decides the double bottom height. Double bottom heights often increase around the engine spaces. This is because they need to absorb higher stresses caused by the heavy machinery that operates in those areas. Within the engine space, the frames are provided with plate floors; bracket floors are not used. Moreover, there is an additional factor the naval architect must consider when designing increased double bottom heights in high stress areas. The height of the double bottom must ease upwards gradually and not abruptly as this would result in the formation of a *discontinuity*. Discontinuities lead to concentrations of stress and eventual structural failure. The increase in height should taper up and down. The taper should start a few frames forward of the engine room bulkhead and continue three or four frames aft of the engine room to allow for proper stress flow through a structural continuity.

When a ship's bottom is designed, the naval architect must take into consideration the type of ship, the length of the ship, the types of cargoes the ship is likely to carry, and the maritime conditions the ship is likely to operate in. We have already discussed how ship hulls are built from the keel upwards using a combination of beams and girders; we have also discussed how container ships are predominantly built with double bottoms. Now that we understand these basic principles, we can begin to look at the design and construction of ship hulls in greater detail. As we know, vessels under 120 m typically have transversely framed, single bottom hulls. This is because they rarely need the extra strength and redundancy provided by double bottom hulls though it is not unheard of for some ships to have transversely framed, double bottoms. Ships longer than 120 m almost always have longitudinally framed, double bottoms, as this is a requirement mandated by SOLAS. We might ask why longitudinal framing is used when it would be perfectly reasonable to use transversal frames in longer ships. The answer lies in the fact that ships longer than 120 m are subject to high global longitudinal bending stresses such as hogging and sagging. Smaller ships do not suffer these stress loads in the same way. This means if longer ships are stiffened transversely, the transverse stiffeners would not be able to absorb the longitudinal bending stresses. This would result in structural failure. Hence, stiffeners are aligned longitudinally in longer ships. In the same way the longitudinal stiffeners provide the ship with longitudinal strength, the double bottom provides transversal strength. It is for this reason that longitudinal single bottom hulls are never used.

With transversely framed, single bottom hulls, the key defining feature are the deck plates, as they act as the transverse stiffeners. Their span is reduced using intercostal side girders that run longitudinally. Most single bottom ships are provided with a bar keel that extends along the length of the ship up to a certain waterline at the stem. The bar is slightly protruded outside the outer bottom shell. The outer bottom shell plating located just adjacent to the bar keel is called the *garboard strake*; the thickness of the garboard strake is greater than the thickness of the remaining bottom shell. The deck plates are flanged at the top. This increases their bending strength. To enable crew access, manholes are provided in the deck plates. The manholes are also flanged to reduce the concentration of stress. Today, most vessels under 120 m in length have transversely framed, double bottomed hulls. The bracket floor forms the transverse stiffener at each frame, with deck plates provided at every three to four frame spaces, or approximately at 1.8 m intervals. To reduce the span of the plates, intercostal side girders called a *keelson* are used. These run longitudinally to the hull. An important factor to note is that the side girders are continuous members, that is, where there is an intersection between a plate floor and a side girder, the plate floor is cut and welded onto both the sides of the girder, and not the other way round. This is done to reduce the span of the deck plate. Hence the girders act as supporting members to the deck plate. Flat deck plate keels are used with these structures. The keel plate thickness is very important in determining the strength of the ship. This is calculated using a formula provided by the classification society. Intercostal girders or side girders, and deck plates have lightening holes installed at regular intervals to reduce the structural weight, together with flanged manholes to provide crew access. The deck plates are further stiffened by way of flat bar stiffeners; and the bracket floors are strengthened by angle struts which help prevent warping. Lastly, drain holes are provided in the deck plates to help facilitate the drainage of fluids.

82 Principles of ship architecture and engineering

With longitudinally framed, double bottom hulls the prime stiffening members are formed from longitudinal running bulb sections or angle sections. The stiffeners located on the bottom plating are called *outer bottom longitudinals*, and those that stiffen the tank top plating are called *tank top longitudinals*. The span of each longitudinal is equal to three or four frame spaces. That means, at every three to four frames, there is a plate floor to support the longitudinal. A bracket floor is placed at every frame, though this does not support the longitudinal. Intercostal girders are used, as usual, to reduce the span of the plate floors. The longitudinals run across the plate floors through holes called *scallops*. Where a frame is required to support the span of a longitudinal using a plate floor, the longitudinal is welded with a small plate to the plate floor. The scallop then forms a support end. In bracket floors, the tank top and bottom shell longitudinal are supported to each other by angle struts. With plate floors, the longitudinal of the tank top and the bottom shell are supported to each other by flat bar stiffeners. These help to restrict bending, torsion, and buckling. As with transverse single and transverse double bottoms, drainage holes are used to drain fluids, and air holes are used for the free flow of air. Margin plates are sometimes fitted to enable the flow of bilge waste towards the bilge wells located on either side of the ship. A continuous centre girder runs the entire length of the ship. This supports the entire bottom structure, the keel plate, and the garboard strake.

Hull shape and geometry

The first and most prominent design aspect of any type of ship is the geometry of its hull. A visual comparison of the hull of a container ship with a bulk carrier or an oil tanker will clearly show the container ship has a *fine form* hull when compared to the other types of vessels. The term fine form is used to describe a hull where the forward and aft sections are streamlined and incline inwards and upwards unlike the fuller form that is characteristic of bulk carriers and oil tankers. The reason why container ships have fine form hulls lies in the nature of the cargo they carry. Goods shipped in containers are often high value and high priority. This means container ships must operate to tight schedules. As well as spending as little time in port as possible the resistance of the hull must be minimised insofar as is practicably possible. The obvious way to achieve this is by having a fine form hull. To put this into a technical perspective, container ship hulls have a *low buoyancy coefficient* that ranges from 0.6 to 0.7. Furthermore, container ship hulls have a *high prismatic coefficient*. This means the midship section for the most part is rectangular. This is done to accommodate the maximum number of containers within the hull. The ballast, bilge, and fuel tanks are located within the double bottom, which maximises the transverse cargo stowage area within the hull. As we discussed above, container ships are longitudinally framed as the variable stress load conditions they experience often result in substantial hogging and sagging movements. These movements result in longitudinal bending stresses which can affect the structural integrity of the hull. Because the shape of the midship section is rectangular and box-like, it allows for a high midship area coefficient, typically within the range between 0.75 and 0.85. Older ships had an angular plate that was used to join the inner side shell of the hull to the tank top plate. This angular plate was called the *bilge strake*, and due to its position and shape, prevented containers from being stowed perpendicular to the bottom of the hull. Modern ships have done away with the bilge strake to allow for greater stowage capacity.

As we know, box ships are equipped with deck hatches. Whilst these make loading and unloading containers much easier, it also means the ship has no continuous main deck running the full breadth of the ship. In fact, the only internal decks or *stringers* are located within the double bottom. The stringers provide additional strength to the hull. When a ship is at sea, the hull and keel are subjected to variable wave loads. These wave loads force the hull to react in different ways. For example, when the direction of the wave is at 45 degrees to the position of the ship, the port side forward section and the starboard aft section will simultaneously experience the wave crest. This results in a type of periodic loading that causes the hull to *twist*. This twisting effect is called *torsion*. Torsion causes extreme stress on the hull and in the worst cases can rupture or even break the keel. To prevent this from happening, the topmost edges of the port and starboard sides of a container ship are strengthened with high scantling web sections. This creates a box-like structure along the entire length of the hull frame. This box structure is called the *torsion box* and is unique to container ships. The torsion box is such an important factor in container ship design that it is worth dwelling a little on the design and physics that makes the torsion box so important to container ship design.

Since the 1950s the maritime industry has seen rapid growth in the container transport sector. This has inevitably led to an exponential increase in the length and breadth of container ships. Today, the longest container ships are 399.9 m (1,312 ft) long and carry in the region of 23,964 containers. As these ships have increased in size, the physical effects, and stresses they endure, have also intensified. This has caused ship designers and naval architects to revisit the design and construction of the hull girder and its behaviour under torsional and wave bending loads. The twisting or torsion of the ship is caused by competing forces that do not pass through the sheer centre line axis of the ship's hull cross section. This means, in simple terms, that the torsion effect twists the vessel in the same way a dish cloth is twisted to drain it of water. Technically, torsional momentum has two fundamental characteristics: static torsion or still water torsion, and dynamic torsion or wave-induced torsion. Moreover, other forms of torsional momentum may arise from the vibration of the propeller shaft, the vibrations stemming from twin screw propellers, and a variety of other sources.

As the name suggests, wave-induced torsion is caused by unsymmetrical hydrodynamic wave loading on the port and the starboard sides of the ship. Oppositely, still water loading is caused by the unsymmetrical loading of cargo over the port and starboard sides. A ship heading obliquely into a wave will be subject to righting moments of opposite direction at both ends. This twists the hull and causes a state of torsion. With most ships, these torsional moments are negligible, but with container ships, which have extremely wide and long deck openings, the effects are significant. Naturally, ships are designed to withstand the maximum torsional loads caused by static and dynamic (or a combination of both) torsional moments acting together. However, in cases where there are large deck openings, it is only possible to strengthen the ship with hull girders and stiffeners. To counterbalance the effect of torsion, container ship hulls are designed with a *torsion box*. The strengthening benefit of the torsion box is perhaps best demonstrated by using the example of a bucket of water. Most household buckets are made from plastic, which is relatively malleable. This means the bucket can flex and wane as pressure is increased and decreased. Buckets also have a curl on the uppermost periphery. This curl performs a similar function to the torsion box found on container ships. If we remove the curl from the periphery of the bucket, we see that the strength of the bucket decreases rapidly. The bucket bends easily even if we apply light pressure about its edge. The curl therefore increases the structural integrity of the bucket. This prevents the bucket from splitting and spilling its contents. We can apply the same principle to the torsion box. Obviously, the design and structure of the torsion box are very different to that of the curl on a bucket, but the principles are much the same.

The torsion box is a continuous structure formed between the top part of the longitudinal bulkhead, the freeboard deck, and the sheer strake. It runs from the collision bulkhead in the forward third of the ship and extends aft to the stern peak bulkhead. It is heavily stiffened – usually by bulb angles – which provide sufficient strength against the torsional moments

84 Principles of ship architecture and engineering

and other bending loads. As mentioned earlier, container ships are particularly susceptible to torsional moments because of their large hatch openings. This leads to increased warping stresses developing at the corners of the openings due to a lack of structural rigidity. Because of this, the torsion box is fitted to the upper part of the double hull. As it is not always possible to have large cross-sectional areas, the thickness of the plate increases to provide the required torsional rigidity. The marginal distance between the hatch end and the side shell is approximately one metre or 1.5 feet. This is done to maximise stowing space. As it is common for the main deck to experience most of the torsional moments, this concentration of stress can lead to cracking at the corners of the hatches or for cracks to develop on the deck plate itself. To prevent this from happening, the torsion box is fitted with welded joints on the side shell and the deck plating. This configuration works to prevent the torsion produced by the ship twisting.

BULBOUS BOW

In addition to the hull, the second key element that defines the design of container ships – and in fact almost all high-speed vessels such as ferries and cruise ships – is the unique shape of the forward-most section, or the *bow*. Although the shipping industry on whole has increasingly erred towards slow steaming as a way of reducing operating costs, container ships have several unique advantages. Larger diameter and low rpm propellers, combined with refined hull structures, means container ships can cruise at slower speeds but still operate with maximum efficiency. The key design feature here is the *bulbous bow* or the bulb-like projection at the forward end of the keel. The bulbous bow is one of the most important characteristics of modern container ships. Bulbous bows first appeared in 1928 with the sisterships *SS Bremen* and *SS Europa*; two German-built ocean liners designed to operate in the North Atlantic. Partly due to her unique bow design, the *SS Bremen* won the Blue Riband Award for crossing the Atlantic Ocean at a top speed of 27.9 knots.[2] Prior to the invention of the bulbous bow, the bow simply tapered down towards the keel line at an inverse angle. The purpose of the bulbous bow is to streamline the ship's hull as it passes through the water. When a ship surges forwards, it creates a form of positive energy called *Kelvin waves*.[3] This energy converts into the waves that form around a ship when it sails. The energy is created by the moving mass of the ship. Note the word 'moving'. As the ship is powered by its own propulsion system, part of the energy delivered by the engine goes into rotating the propeller. This pushes the ship forward causing *thrust*. However, only a fraction of the *force* generated by the propellers is used by the propellers. The rest of the energy is absorbed by the water immediately surrounding the ship. It is this excess energy that creates the waves. Technically, this is called *Wave Making Resistance*. As the ship surges forward, water is pushed down towards the stern, and along the length of the ship. Water particles located at the centreline of the keel stem have an instantaneous velocity of zero, which in scientific terms, is referred to as the *Stagnation Point*. According to Bernoulli's principle,[4] the pressure at the stagnation point is higher than the pressure in the surrounding area. Therefore, the pressure of the water at the bow is higher than the water around the hull. It is this that creates the crest of a wave. This wave is called the *bow wave* as it is generated by the movement of the bow through the water. With a straight bow, there will always be a continuous wave form, with its crest at the bow. This results in a vast amount of energy loss. This equates to wasting valuable engine power. As engines run on fuel, and fuel is expensive, wasting fuel means wasting money. By introducing a discontinuity (any structure in the ship below the waterline which disturbs the laminar flow of water) below the waterline at the bow, and in front of the stem of the ship, the discontinuity will create another wave at its forward most point.

The shape of the bulbous bow results in destructive interference. This reduces wave formation and decreases drag. Wave formation is a significant characteristic of finer hull forms and is why we notice prominent *Kelvin waveforms* on cruise ships, liners, yachts, and naval vessels. Bulk carriers and oil tankers (which have fuller hull forms) do not produce prominent Kelvin waveforms. This is because the waterline width at the stem is so large (or the discontinuity in flow is higher) that the pressure rises to a level that the bow wave height exceeds the threshold up to which a wave can retain its properties. In this instance, the wave breaks right at the point of the bow travelling down along the keel length of the ship. Given this adversely affects the efficiency of bulk carriers and oil tankers, it is common for bulbous bows to be either retrofitted to existing builds or for bulbous bows to be a design feature on new builds. The position of the bulb significantly affects the phase difference between the bow wave and the bulb wave. The bulb's spatial volume is a deciding factor of the wave amplitude that is formed. Another advantage of the bulb is that it reduces the dynamic pitch motion of the ship. On most ships, the interior of the bulb is used as the fore-peak ballast tank. In the event of high pitching, the forepeak tank is ballasted to reduce pitching. This is because the period of pitching is directly proportional to the longitudinal distance of weight from the ship's longitudinal *centre of gravity* (LCG). When the forepeak is ballasted, it increases weight at a larger distance from the LCG of the ship (which in most ideal cases is abaft the midship). This means the pitch radius of gyration increases, therefore increasing the pitch period of the ship. An increased period of pitch translates into a lower dynamic effect of pitch motion.

We can visualise the benefit of the bulbous bow by using the example of a ship navigating through sheet ice. The bulb forces the broken ice to glide past the ship with the wet aspect of each ice shard up against the hull. As the wet aspect of the ice has a lower friction coefficient, this reduces the overall drag on the ship's hull. The bulbous bow also provides ample accommodation for bow thrusters. We can clearly see these on most modern ships fitted bow thruster units. On naval ships that use high frequency underwater acoustics like *sonar*, the bulbous bow offers protective housing, in addition to the positive effect of reducing drag. Interesting though, studies of ships fitted with bulbous bows have shown that the addition of the bow structure does not always translate to increased efficiency. This is mainly down to different speed variables. The explanation as to why this happens is complex and requires an understanding of the *Froude number*. In *continuum mechanics*, the Froude number (*Fr*) is a dimensionless number defined as the ratio of the flow inertia to the external field. Named after the English engineer, hydrodynamicist and naval architect William Froude (1810–1879) the Froude number is based on the speed–length ratio which he defined as:

$$Fr = \frac{u}{\sqrt{gL}}$$

where u is the relative flow velocity between the sea and ship, g is the acceleration due to gravity, and L is the length of the ship at the waterline level, or L_{wl} in some notations. It is an important parameter with respect to the ship's drag, or resistance, especially in terms of wave-making resistance. With a very low Froude number, the bulbous bow was found to increase drag. This is because the bulb is only effective when it makes its own wave, along with the bow wave. With a very low Froude number, wave making hardly occurs. But, as the bulb is below the waterline, this increases the total wetted surface area of the ship, therefore contributing to an increase in skin friction resistance. This helps compensate for the low Froude number, although the speed of the vessel is still negatively affected. Rolling and pitching is a natural but unfortunate occurrence that affects every ship. As container

86 Principles of ship architecture and engineering

ships have continued to expand, they have gained increasingly larger *bow flare* and wider beams. This helps to deflect some of the frictional resistance that is generated when the ship's bow passes through water. As the wave crest travels along the side of the hull, it causes flare immersion in the wave crest as the bow falls. The stability (*GM*) of the ship varies as per the pitching and rolling of the ship. The combination of buoyancy and wave excitation force pushes the ship to the opposite side. A similar action takes place as the bow falls again on the next wave cycle. This causes a synchronous motion which leads to heavy rolling. In the worst cases, this can be as much as 30 degrees in just a few cycles. This phenomenon is known as *parametric rolling* and is unique to container ships.

Parametric rolling only occurs when the sea condition is at the head or stern or within very near proximity of either. There are two pitch cycles associated with parametric rolling: maximum and minimum. The period of roll is half the natural rolling period that coincides with the large phase angle. This means the maximum roll always occurs when the ship is forward pitching, i.e., when the bow is down in the water. Other than being extremely uncomfortable for the crew, parametric rolling can result in heavy stresses against the ship's structure, especially in the fore and aft thirds. Parametric rolling exerts extreme stresses on containers and their lashings. If these are not properly installed the force of the rolling motion can cause the lashings to fail. This will result in the overboard loss of topside containers. It may also cause the bottom level containers in one or more stacks to collapse. Moreover, the lack of equilibrium forces variations on the load of the ship's engines and propulsion system leading to propulsion failure. Subsequently, if parametric rolling is not corrected quickly, it can result in the ship capsizing. When parametric rolling starts, it is important for the OOW and helmsman to remain calm, as rash and panicked reactions can often lead to panicked responses. If rolling and pitching occur simultaneously, it is best to avoid a head-on sea by changing the ship's course accordingly. Maintaining the correct *GM* is paramount as the ship should never be too tender or too stiff. Where installed, roll damping measures can help to maintain a balanced keel.

EXAMPLE: PARAMETRIC ROLLING

A large container ship was underway in the open ocean when the weather began to deteriorate. The wind was force 6 and the ship was rolling between 7 degrees and 12 degrees in a three-metre swell. The deck crew began daily lashing checks as usual, but the weather conditions meant that they were only able to inspect the bays forward of the bridge. Later that day the swell increased to 4.5 metres (14.76 feet). That evening, the ship experienced a sudden large roll of approximately 16 degrees. Later that evening, it started to roll routinely to 15 degrees. The master reviewed the data provided by the ship's electronic motion monitoring and forecasting system and instructed the OOW to switch to hand-steering and alter course from 088 degrees to 082 degrees. Following the alteration of course the ship's rolling reduced to less than 10 degrees.

Later, the master told the OOW to return to automatic steering as he was now confident that the autopilot was up to the task. About an hour later the ship unexpectedly rolled 20 degrees to starboard, paused for a few seconds, then made a similar roll to port. The deck lights were turned on after the large roll, but no damage was seen from the bridge and the container stows appeared to be intact. At daylight, an officer went to the weather deck with the bosun to investigate. They found that bays 18, 54, and 58 had collapsed. It was later determined that 137 containers had been lost overboard and 85 damaged. The official investigation found, among other things, that it is likely that the forces generated when the ship rolled 20 degrees to port and starboard initiated the collapse of the container stows at bays 18, 54, and 58. The amplitude of the ship's rolling exceeded the limits set by the company for the class of ship. It is almost certain that the ship experienced parametric rolling prior to and at the time of the container collapse. The master and his bridge team were familiar with but did not fully understand, the functionality of the ship's motion monitoring, forecasting, and decision support tool. As a result, they did not appreciate the imminent risk of a parametric roll. The cause of the collapse at bay 18 could not be determined. It is most likely that this collapse was initiated following the structural failure of one of its containers, brought about by a combination of factors including excessive stack loads because of mis-stowed or overweight containers; excessive racking loads or contact between containers due to loose lashings and/or existing damage or poor material condition of a container.

LESSONS LEARNED

Parametric rolling is where a ship experiences larger than expected roll behaviour when the primary sea wavelength is like the ship's length with either:

1. The wave crest amidships and the bow and stern in wave troughs
2. The ship is supported by a crest at the bow and stern with the trough amidships

IMO guidance suggests that parametric rolling may occur when either the period of roll equals the period of encounter or the period of encounter is approximately half the roll period. The risk of parametric roll in the following sea is very sensitive to minor changes in the relative direction of the sea. Large container ships are particularly vulnerable to parametric rolling due to their length and fine hull form. If you work on a ship equipped with a motion monitoring, forecasting, and decision support tool, ensure you are fully conversant with its functionalities.

HOLDS AND HATCH COVERS

The third most important design feature of the hull is the manner in which containers are stowed within the ship's holds. The stowage of containers on a container ship is one of the key critical aspects naval architects must consider when designing a newbuild. Containers are always orientated with the longer dimension positioned forward to aft. This is because the ship is more prone to rolling motions than pitching or yawing. The stowage of containers in this orientation ensures there is less potential for cargo to shift within the container. Below the main deck, containers are restrained against lateral or longitudinal motion by cell guides. These are angle sections that also serve as guides for crane operators when loading containers into the hold. Cell guides are not formally part of the ship's hull as they do not absorb stress. Above the main deck, containers are stowed longitudinally, with their motion restricted by a series of lashings. Twist locks fitted at each quadrant of the containers prevent vertical motion, and lashing prevents longitudinal and transverse motions. The lashings are usually fitted from lashing bridges which are positioned at height intervals of one or two container tiers. Lashing rods are secured at the ends by turnbuckles. This maintains the tension in the lashings.

88 Principles of ship architecture and engineering

We will cover container loading and lashing in more detail later, but it is worth mentioning here that containers are loaded and stowed according to a container loading plan. This plan sets out the maximum quantity of containers the ship can carry at any one time. It also determines the required weight distribution for each container. The loading plan accounts for the anticipated programme of loading and discharge. This means containers are planned according to the sequence of ports of call. This provides a logical and systematic approach to container loading. There is no sense in placing one container below another container if the first container is to be discharged first. Whilst it is perfectly rational to stow containers according to their port of discharge (i.e., A before B, and B before C, etc.) there is a fatal flaw in the logic. This is because not all containers are of a uniform weight. Heavier containers should never be placed above lighter containers as the weight distribution of the load will be top heavy. This will increase the centre of gravity of the ship and decrease the margin of stability. This problem is solved in part by specialised computer programmes that automatically calculate the weight distribution of different containers and works out the optimal location to stow them in relation to the ships schedule and other defining factors such as the ship's structural integrity and intact stability. Of course, the final factor that must be considered in the loading plan is the visibility from the bridge. Containers loaded above deck and forward of the bridge must be stowed in such a way that the line of sight from the bridge is not affected. Therefore, the stack of containers in front of the bridge reduces in height as the stacks move closer to the forward-most stack. This of course reduces the total quantity of containers that may be carried by the ship at any one time. To solve this problem, many ultra-large container ships (starting with the *Maersk Triple E* class) have their superstructures towards the midship section, which means containers can be stowed at full height aft of the superstructure.

The primary objective of hatch covers and their coamings is to prevent the ingress of water into the cargo hold and to protect the goods from being dampened and damaged. Hatch covers also act as a barrier to the ship's internal structure by enduring green water loads in extreme weather. Green water can damage the internal structure of the ship through corrosion and must be prevented from getting inside the internal structure of the vessel. There are various types of hatches and covers including lift types, rolling types, folding types, sliding types, and roll stowing types. Lift or lift away type covers are predominantly found on container ships, whereas rolling types are more frequently used on bulk carriers. Folding type hatch covers are used on general cargo ships. The lift-type hatch cover can be categorised according to two types: the first is the *single panel cover*. These consist of a single cover for each opening and are used mainly on bulk carriers. The second type is the *multi-panel cover*. Where multi-panel covers are used, a single hold is covered by more than one hatch cover. These are commonly found on cellular container ships with longitudinal joints and on multipurpose cargo ships with transverse joints. On smaller container ships, a *stacking cover type* may be used. This type of cover is used on ships that require a relatively small hatch cover. It consists of a hydraulically powered lifting crane mechanism that lifts the covers longitudinally and stacks them one over the other.

Hatch covers are a far more complex facility than just the cover and its coaming. There are many key components involved that ensure the hatch cover stays intact and is effective for long periods of time and in all weather conditions. These typically include bearing pads, securing devices such as cleats and wedges, pontoons and panels, the operating mechanism, stoppers, drains and non-return valves, and compression bars. For effective operation, maintenance of the above-mentioned components must be carried out regularly. When designing hatch covers for a new build, naval architects must take into consideration a number of factors, the most important being the *deck opening*. The strength of the hull is dependent on the size of the deck opening. High tensile steel must be used to provide adequate longitudinal strength in ships where the hatch width is more than 70% of the beam. Stress concentration points are usually located at the corners of the openings. These can be reduced or eliminated entirely by providing thick elliptical or parabolic plates. The coaming height is measured from the main deck to the top of the coaming. The hatch is then closed with steel covers fitted with direct securing arrangements. Most container ships have a coaming height of about 1–1.8 m as this allows a greater volume of cargo. The coaming may be designed to slope inwards, creating a larger opening at the deck level. The hatch corner construction is an element of design that the naval architect must pay particular attention to. This is necessary to avoid sudden discontinuities of longitudinal strength at the ends of the side coaming. This is achieved by extending the girders to a suitable point beyond the hatch end to create a structural continuity. Usually, taper brackets are used to extend the hatch coaming which reduces stress concentrations. As mentioned above elliptical or parabolic plates at the corners also help to reduce stress concentrations, which would otherwise lead to metal fatigue followed by fracture. Drainage is provided by a channel situated around the peripheral seal of the hatch cover. The water is discharged onto the weather deck through a hole in the coaming. This prevents the ingress of green water into the cargo hold.

BULKHEADS

Collision bulkheads

All ships are designed with watertight integrity in mind. We have already discussed in detail the difference between single and double-bottomed hulls, and how the double bottom can help prevent the ingress of water into the ship's hull in the event of a breach. But what happens if the ship is involved in a collision and both layers of the hull are penetrated? In this situation, the ship is almost always dependant on the integrity of her collision bulkheads. A bulkhead is nothing more than an upright wall within the hull of the ship. The term originates from the Old Norse word *bulki* which means cargo. In the 15th century, ship builders began to realise that internal walls within the ship's hull would prevent cargo from shifting in rough weather. In shipbuilding, any vertical panel is called a *head*. This led to the adoption of the term *bulkhead*, which refers to any vertical wall within a ship except for the hull itself. Returning to the original point, modern ships are fitted with collision bulkheads to prevent the spread of water throughout the should the outer and inner skins be penetrated. Each hold is separated by a bulkhead which stretches the entire beam of the ship. These bulkheads are in themselves designed to prevent flooding from one hold to another. At the bow and stern, however, are extra strengthened bulkheads. These bulkheads are specially designed to withstand the force of a head-on collision at slow speed with another vessel. The stern collision bulkhead serves the same purpose but at the aft of the ship. There are three factors that determine the design and position of the forward collision bulkhead. The first factor is the position of the bulkhead based on floodable length calculations. The second factor is based on the position dictated by class rules. Most classification society rules have an allowable range for the distance at which the collision bulkhead can be located from the forward-most point of the ship's hull. This distance is usually a function of the length of the ship and factors related to the shape of its bow. The third factor is based on the SOLAS regulations which state that the collision bulkhead should be located aft of the forward perpendicular and at a distance not less than 5% of the ship's length or 10 m (whichever is less). Whichever is used, the distance must not exceed 8% of the ship's total length.

For maximum strength, the collision bulkhead is usually stiffened with vertical sections of scantlings, located higher than those on the surrounding structures. They are also stiffened by triangular-shaped stringers of higher scantling, called *panting stringers*. Panting stringers are usually provided every two metres from the bottom, and forward, of the collision bulkhead. As per the SOLAS regulations, the collision bulkhead must be watertight up to the bulkhead deck. The bulkhead deck is the deck level at which all watertight bulkheads terminate. For providing access to the chain locker room and the forward part of the bulkhead, steps may be provided though these must not violate SOLAS factor three. Furthermore, there must be no doors, manholes, access hatches, ventilation ducts or any type of openings on the collision bulkhead below the bulkhead deck. That said, the bulkhead may be allowed one piercing below the bulkhead deck for the passage of one pipe which caters for the forepeak ballast tank. The passage of the pipe must be flanged and must be fitted with a screw-down valve which can be remotely operated from above the bulkhead deck. For added security, this valve is usually located forward of the collision bulkhead. The classification society certifying the ship may authorise a valve aft of the bulkhead provided it is easily serviceable at any condition and is not located in the cargo area. For ships having superstructures in the forward third, the collision bulkhead is not terminated at the bulkhead deck. Instead, the bulkhead must extend upwards to the deck level adjacent to the weather deck. This ensures there is sufficient structural continuity to keep shear forces within safe and acceptable limits.

Watertight bulkheads

Most watertight bulkheads are transverse in orientation, though some ships may also be designed to have longitudinal watertight bulkheads within a compartment to provide sectionalisation within the compartment. Other than watertightness, transverse bulkheads also add to the transverse strength of the ship. We will investigate this a little later. On small ships, a transverse bulkhead may be constructed from a single plate. However, for larger container ships, the transverse bulkhead usually consists of a series of horizontal strakes welded together. The thickness of these strakes increases with depth. This strengthens the bulkhead against the maximum hydrostatic pressure should the compartment become fully flooded. When a compartment is constructed, two-dimensional strakes are cut out from plates with different thicknesses. The bulkhead plate itself is not resistant enough against large scale transverse forces like shear forces, so they are vertically stiffened. This is because horizontal stiffening in ships with a wide beam requires stiffeners with a long span. This in turn increases the scantling and the weight of the stiffener. This adversely impacts on the available cargo stowage space. With vertical stiffening, the span and the scantling of the stiffener are kept low by introducing a stringer at the midpoint. The stringer acts as a fixed end, therefore reducing the span of the stiffener. The sections used for stiffening the bulkheads are usually flat bars, angles, or bulb bars, depending on the required section modulus. An important aspect of the design of bulkhead stiffeners is the boundary conditions. To meet the boundary conditions, in such a way that the stiffeners behave as per the naval architect's theoretical calculations, the end supports must be designed accordingly. At the upper end, they are attached to the underside of the deck plating with brackets, providing a hinged boundary condition. To achieve fixed ends, they are welded directly to the deck plate and the stringer. Most modern container ships use advanced technology to provide the required strength of the bulkhead plates such as using corrugated bulkheads instead of stiffened bulkheads. The corrugations flow vertically, except when the breadth of the bulkhead is significantly low, in which case the corrugations may flow horizontally. However, there is one trade-off that needs to be recognised. Corrugated bulkheads are made of plates with uniform thickness. This thickness is equal to the lowermost strake of a conventional bulkhead. This means corrugated bulkheads are substantially heavier compared to straked bulkheads.

Despite this, corrugated bulkheads are more popular as they are easier to fabricate and reduce the quantity of welded joints in the bulkhead construction. The bulkheads found in container ships are much the same design and construction as those found in bulk carriers, but with one distinct difference. On container ships, the bulkhead rises flush from the floor at a 90-degree angle. This provides maximum space for stowing containers within the hold. After installation, the bulkheads are tested for their strength integrity and watertightness. Since it is not feasible to fill each of the cargo holds or compartments with water, the test is done with a pressure hose. In this process, the bulkhead is subjected to water pressure from a hose for a fixed period after which the structural integrity of the bulkhead is inspected. The inspection looks for signs of buckling and other deformations. Leak tests can also be done by sealing the hold and pressurising the air within the compartment. Any air leaks in adjacent compartments will indicate there are deficiencies in the construction of the bulkhead.

Fire class bulkheads

To prevent of fire from one compartment to another, ships are fitted with special fire-resistant panels called *fire class bulkheads*. There are three main types of fire class panels, each capable of withstanding different heat loads. The strongest type is the Class A type. There are three Class A type fire class bulkhead. The first is the Class A-60 panel which can withstand a fire load of 160°C (320°F) for 60 minutes, whilst maintaining an average temperature of 120°C (248°F) on the unaffected side of the bulkhead. The second type of Class A bulkhead is the A-30 panel, which can withstand the same heat load for 30 minutes; the A-15 type can withstand the same heat load for 15 minutes. Class-B bulkheads are constructed from incombustible materials that are approved by SOLAS and class. These must pass standard fire testing by preventing the spread of fire or smoke to an unaffected compartment for a minimum period of 30 minutes. Like Class A bulkheads, Class B bulkheads must be capable of maintaining an average temperature on the unaffected side of 120°C (248°F) but are rated up to and including a maximum heat load of 206°C (402°F). The Class B-15 bulkhead is designed to withstand this heat load for a minimum of 15 minutes. The third type of fire class bulkhead is the Class C. These are constructed from incombustible materials approved by SOLAS and class. Unlike the Class A and Class bulkheads, Class C bulkheads are not required to meet any requirements related to temperature or the spread of smoke from the affected compartment to adjacent compartments. Class A and Class B bulkheads are usually situated adjacent to the enclosed spaces within the ship. This typically includes the cargo holds, control stations, stairways, lifeboat stations, galley, machinery spaces, tanks, public spaces, and accommodation areas. Class C panels are used mostly in open deck areas and promenades, where the need for fire safety is minimal. Class C bulkheads may also be used between two adjacent spaces within the hull structure but where there is no requirement for a Class A or Class B panel.

WATERTIGHT DOORS

Watertight integrity is paramount on every ship yet there are situations where access from one compartment to another is necessary.[5] As access requires some form of opening in the bulkhead, this obviously undermines the watertight integrity of the vessel. This problem is solved using watertight doors. Where a watertight door is required, a rectangular aperture is cut into the bulkhead panel. To maintain stress levels at safe and acceptable limits, the aperture is strengthened with doubler plates that increase the thickness of the bulkhead plate around the opening. If a vertical bulkhead stiffener is in the way of the opening, the stiffener is terminated

92 Principles of ship architecture and engineering

at the upper and lower edges of the opening. To avoid this, naval architects generally tend to increase the stiffener spacing to accommodate the aperture. Where this is done, the scantling of the stiffeners adjacent to the opening is increased from the remaining stiffeners. Watertight doors are either hydraulically or electrically operated and slide either horizontally or vertically. They never swing open and close as it would be impossible to close the door should the compartment be flooded. Watertight doors must operate even when the ship has is at a list of 15 degrees to either side. The control system is designed so that the door can be operated from the vicinity as well as from a remote location. On all ships, visual indicators are provided at the remote operation site to denote whether the door is open or closed. Like bulkheads, watertight doors are subjected to pressure tests following installation. This confirms their structural integrity against the hydrostatic pressure of a fully flooded compartment.

Because watertight doors are necessary to (a) provide access from one compartment to another, and (b) must be structurally able to withstand extreme hydrostatic pressure, their design and performance parameters are mandated by SOLAS in chapter II-1, regulation 14 to 25. The main considerations that SOLAS sets out for watertight door design and construction are (a) the number of openings for pipes and access should be kept to a minimum to retain the strength of the bulkhead. In case such openings are provided, proper reinforcement must be provided to prevent stress concentration and retain watertightness of the structure. Also, proper flanging must be incorporated into the openings for pipelines and cables; (b) not more than one watertight door is permitted per watertight bulkhead. However, where ships have twin shafts, it is permitted to have two separate watertight doors, each providing access to each individual shaft tunnel. The mechanical gears required for manual operation of these doors must be located outside the machinery space; (c) the time required to close or open any watertight door when triggered from the engine control room or the bridge must not exceed 60 seconds when the ship is in an upright condition; (d) the transverse location of watertight doors should be such that they are easily operated even if one-fifth of the bulkhead is damaged from the ship's side; (e) every watertight door should be equipped with an audible alarm that is distinct from all other alarms in the immediate area. When the door is operated remotely, the alarm should sound at least five seconds prior to the door sliding either way and must continue until the door is completely open or closed. However, if the door is operated on location, the alarm must sound only when the door is moving. On passenger ships, the audible alarm must be accompanied by a visual alarm; (f) all watertight doors must be lockable; (g) access doors and hatches on watertight bulkheads must remain closed when the ship is at sea. Visual indicators must be provided at the door location and on the bridge.

Although the term '*watertight*' is used as a general reference for any hatchway that prevents the ingress of water, technically SOLAS defines two types of access: *watertight* and *weathertight*. Whilst both serve similar functions in that they prevent water ingress they are in fact quite distinct. SOLAS defines watertight doors as being able to prevent the free flow of water from one side of the door to the other under a head of water likely to occur in intact and damaged conditions. By comparison, SOLAS defines weathertight doors as preventing seawater from penetrating the ship in any sea condition. In other words, a watertight door stops water from flooding the ship and are usually found at or below the waterline; and weathertight doors stop seawater from getting into the ship and are usually found above the waterline. Watertight doors are rated according to one of four categories: the first are *Type A* category watertight doors. These may be left open at sea but must be closed during emergencies. The second are *Type B* category watertight doors that should always be closed unless personnel are working in the adjacent compartment. The third are *Type C* watertight doors. These must always be kept closed and are opened only to allow personnel to pass through to an adjacent compartment. The fourth type are *Type D* watertight doors. These are not rated by SOLAS as compliant and must therefore be closed before the passage starts and must remain closed when at sea. Type D doors cannot be upgraded to any other category. Type A watertight doors may remain open when the ship is at sea unless there is an emergency, or during any of the following conditions: (a) when there is restricted visibility; (b) in ports where the port limits are further than the compulsory pilotage limits; (c) when the depth of water is less than three times the draught of the ship; (d) when navigating in high-density traffic; and (e) any other conditions where the master feels that the conditions are dangerous. Watertight doors can be further classified according to their method of operation. For example, hinged type doors have a pivoting motion about one vertical or horizontal edge. Sliding watertight doors operate by a horizontal or vertical motion that is parallel to the plane of the door and are powered by hydraulic cylinders or electric motors. Powered watertight doors are extremely heavy but are more likely to malfunction or stop operating in the event of a blackout or other power-related incident. Moreover, if used incorrectly, they can easily maim or crush. It is imperative that watertight doors are closed when the ship is underway. This is because in addition to preventing the free flow of water from one compartment to another, watertight doors also help prevent the spread of smoke and fire. As with most systems and equipment on board ship, there are specific drills for the operation of watertight doors in emergency situations. These drills must take place every week. Watertight doors must also be checked before leaving port. All watertight doors, whether hinged or power operated, should be checked daily during the officer's rounds. The officer should be able to operate the watertight door from both a local and remote position such as on the bridge or in the engine control room.

BALLAST TANKS, VOID SPACES, AND COFFERDAMS

During the design and construction phases of a ship, ballast tanks are incorporated at various locations throughout the lower structure of the vessel. These are designed to help maintain the stability of the ship during passage. The concept of ballast is not new and, in fact, has been around since ancient times. In early maritime history, ships used solid ballast such as sandbags, rocks, and iron blocks. These were packed and unpacked according to whether the ship was loaded or unloaded with cargo. This method was relatively helpful in maintaining the ship's stability. Today, ships use liquid ballast, which may include freshwater, saltwater, or brackish water. The water is pumped on board and stored in vast ballast tanks. This ballast is used for maintaining the trim and stability of the ship. If the ship does not ballast correctly, then several things may happen. First, the propeller may not fully immerse in water. This will affect propulsion. Second, the ship may list or trim (more on this later). Third, shear, and torsion moments may increase the stress loads on the ship structure, leading to bending and slamming. And fourth, the vessel may face issues concerning dynamic transversal and longitudinal instability. To compensate for these conditions, ballast is pumped on board. The chief officer is responsible for calculating how much ballast must be added or removed according to the ship's condition. There are three conditions where ballast is calculated. (1) *Light Ballast*. When the ship is heavily loaded and does not require additional ballast for stability, the ballast tanks are emptied. This condition is known as a light ballast. (2) *Heavy Ballast*. In a seagoing state, if the ship is not fully loaded, the ballast tanks are filled accordingly. This condition is known as heavy ballast. (3) *Port Ballast*. Many ports have restrictions regarding the discharge of ballast water within the port vicinity. Subsequently, dedicated port ballast tanks are provided for correcting the trim and list of the ship during cargo loading or discharging operations.

The ballast tanks are positioned at different locations depending on the type of ship. Container ships tend to have double bottom tanks. Double bottom tanks are found in the double bottom of the ship and are a safety feature that help to avoid the ingress of water in the event of grounding or collision. These void spaces are also used to store ballast water for stabilising the ship. The double bottom tanks are located between the forward part (till the collision bulkhead) and the aft peak bulkhead. This divides the engine room. On some ships, the double bottom space is divided transversely into three sections instead of two. This is done to provide a cofferdam in the centre known as the 'duct keel', which is used to carry ballast and bunker tank valves, and piping for the ship's ballast tank and bunkering systems. The construction of the double bottom tanks is directly related to the length of the ship. A vessel more than 120 m in length will have longitudinal framing compared to vessels less than 120 m which will have transverse framing. Unlike upper topside tanks, double bottom ballast tanks are situated adjacent to the fuel oil tanks. Hence, they are usually kept separate from the ballast system to avoid oil contamination. Fore and aft peak ballast tanks are provided for precise trimming. To achieve the required trim, these tanks are only partially filled to avoid free surface effect. The construction of the fore and aft peak tanks is different from the ship's other ballast tanks as their shape is irregular due to their location. The shape of the tank is proportional to the shape of the bow and the stern. Subsequently, the tanks are narrow at the base and as the tank moves upward, the width of the tank increases. The breadth at the top of the tank is relational to the ship's beam. The valve which controls the flow of water into and out of the ballast tank is either manually controlled using a butterfly valve or hydraulically operated using a remote valve. Fore and aft peak tanks are only remote control (hydraulic) operated using valves.

The ballast tank is filled with seawater, which is highly corrosive. When the tank is empty, the damp atmosphere increases the effect of corrosion on the ballast tank surface. This means corrosion is a major problem for ships. Fortunately, the crew do have several techniques available to them to combat the effect of saltwater corrosion. *Tank coatings* are the most common protection system used in ballast tanks. The advantage of coatings is that they protect the entire tank. Some coatings consist of a dry film whose thickness can be as thin as 300 microns. Such thin coatings are on the one hand extremely expensive, but they do save considerable weight. The most common type of coating is heavy-duty dual-component epoxy. The second type of anti-corrosion method is the use of *sacrificial anodes*. These are metallic elements such as zinc and aluminium alloys. They help to reduce the corrosion of the steel tank by sacrificing themselves instead. The third type of corrosion prevention is the *controlled atmosphere*. If the atmosphere of the ballast tank is controlled to reduce the oxygen content, the corrosion rate decreases. This system is known as oxygen stripping and is done by introducing an inert gas into the tank. The inert gas helps to maintain the oxygen level to below 4%. This system is used in tanks with protective coatings and sometimes tanks fitted with sacrificial anodes. Using the controlled atmosphere technique can reduce corrosion by as much as 84%. This improves coating maintenance and decreases the need for steel renewal. Because corrosion is such a serious problem, the ship's officers must know the conditions inside the ballast tanks. When inspecting the ballast tank, the extent of corrosion should be noted, and localised corrosion should be marked appropriately. If tank corrosion exceeds 75% of the allowable margin, then corrective repairs such as hull structure renewal may be needed. The inspection also needs to determine the state of the *coating condition*. Coatings play an important role in ballast tank surface protection. Any visible failure of the coating must be noted along with rusting of the tank surface, especially along weld lines and at the edges of the tank. The tank structure itself should be inspected for signs of cracks or buckling. Finally, the strengthening arrangement should be checked for bends or cracks. Where any deformity is identified, these must be repaired at the earliest possible opportunity. If not, it is quite possible for structural failures and fractures to develop.

In addition to ballast tanks, ships also have various other types of liquid containment tanks: (1) heavy fuel or diesel oil tanks; (2) lube oil tanks; (3) freshwater tanks; (4) seawater tanks; (5) oily bilge water tanks; and (6) sludge tanks. These tanks are situated around the ship. Container ships generally have fewer tanks compared to oil tankers and chemical carriers as they carry products that need to be kept separate. As the functions and properties of each of the tanks listed above are all different, care must be taken not to mix them even when there is a leak or failure in the tank structure. This separation is achieved by way of a *cofferdam*. A cofferdam is essentially an empty or void space that is provided in a ship so that compartments on each side of the partition have no common boundary. Cofferdams may be located vertically or horizontally. As a rule, cofferdams are kept airtight and must be ventilated and of sufficient size to allow inspection and maintenance. The purpose of the cofferdam is to prevent two or more different fluids from mixing with each other. This means if there is a leak or structural failure in one tank, the fluid will flow into the cofferdam as opposed to the adjoining tank. Cofferdams must provide a minimum space of 600 millimetres from the face of each bulkhead. The cofferdam is provided with sealed manholes for entry and inspection. The size of the cofferdam should be sufficiently large for crew access and should cover the entire adjacent tank bulkhead. Though manholes and lighting holes are provided, the lighting holes must not be cut into the bottom or top third of the vertical web diaphragm plates as this may lead to the plate buckling. They are also provided with a sounding pipe to check for leaks from any of the subordinate tanks. To be effective, the cofferdam must be maintained and kept dry to allow early detection of leaks. Some cofferdams are provided with bilge suction pumps so that any accumulated water, oil, or oily water can be pumped out. Cofferdams are constructed with stiffeners and girders to withstand the hydrostatic effect of fluids sloshing around (in case of leakage), vibratory loads from the propellers, and other stress loads. Due to their location and propensity to hold oil discharge and explosive vapours, cofferdams are constructed from materials that are not flammable or likely to cause sparks.

Cofferdams are present on all ships irrespective of the size or type of vessel and are usually found between fuel oil tanks which are installed inside the engine room (i.e., the diesel oil and heavy fuel oil tanks); between the freshwater tank and other engine room tanks adjacent to them; between the lube oil tanks including the auxiliary engine, main engine, and cylinder oil and lube oil storage tanks; between two oil tanks carrying different grades of fuel such as low sulphur fuel oil (LSFO) and high sulphur fuel oil (HSFO). Cofferdams are also installed around the main engine lube oil drain or sump tank. This is mainly to separate them from other double bottom tanks. The main engine is located on the bed plate which carries the oil sump. The bedplate is mounted and secured to the engine foundation plate using chocks and holding down bolts. The cofferdam helps engineers to access and inspect the holding down bolts and chalks for the engine. In oil tankers, apart from the locations mentioned above, cofferdams are also fitted between the bulkheads of the first cargo hold which is adjacent to the machinery space and accommodation of the ship. The pump room is also separated from the adjacent tanks using a cofferdam. The pump rooms and ballast tanks may be accepted as cofferdams; however, a ballast tank may not be categorised as a cofferdam if it is a protected slop tank.

TYPES OF DECKS

If there is one thing every seafarer ought to know, it is the different types and functions of decks. In simple terms, the deck forms a singular central construction, which acts as a ceiling of sorts to the hull of the vessel. It also refers to each of the levels or storeys within

96 Principles of ship architecture and engineering

a ship's structure. Most ships have several types of decks which are located at different levels and locations within the ship. The first deck we will examine is the *poop deck*. Originating from the Latin term for a ship's stern side – *Puppis* – the poop deck is located on the vessel's stern. The poop deck was traditionally used by the vessel's commander for navigation and for observing the vessel as she made way. Technically speaking, the poop deck forms the roof of a cabin built in the far aft quarter of the ship's superstructure. On sailing ships, this cabin was used by the master for their private quarters. Second is the *main deck*. This deck forms the primary deck of the ship, often extending from the bow to the stern. The main deck may be situated at any point in the ship's hull and provides longitudinal rigidity. The third type of deck is the *upper deck*. This covers the hull from its fore to its aft. The upper deck is the largest deck and is where containers are stowed above the holds. The fourth type of deck is the *lower deck* which is located below the main deck. The lower deck comprises more than one level and is usually next to the *orlop deck*. The fifth deck is the *promenade deck*. On container ships, the promenade deck is the area around the superstructure and provides exterior access for the crew. The promenade deck may or may not be a *weather deck*. The weather deck is any type of exterior deck which is uncovered and therefore open to the elements. This includes the poop deck, the fore deck, and the *Monkey Island*.

The monkey island refers to the location on a ship that is located at the uppermost accessible height. Technically, it denotes the location directly above the bridge. Some people refer to the monkey island as the *flying bridge* the ship's *upper bridge*. Pre-radar and modern navigational technology, deck officers would use this location to perform solar and stellar observations. On modern-day container ships, the monkey island is an integral part of the ship where most of the bridge's external equipment is located. While the bridge accommodates the display interfaces, the monkey island holds the physical hardware contained in the VDR capsule, the AIS Tx/Rx antennae, the radar scanner(s) attached to the radar mast, Sat C/F77 Tx/Rx antennae, various components of communications equipment, the ship's weathervane, and the halyards that connect to the yardarm for hoisting flags. The monkey island also holds the mast leading up to the '*Christmas Tree*' (i.e., the navigation lights) and the mast leading up to the ship's aft whistle. Moreover, the monkey island also houses the magnetic compass. The magnetic compass is an essential piece of equipment. The SOLAS regulations state that 'all ships irrespective of size shall have a properly adjusted standard magnetic compass or other means, independent of any power supply to determine the ship's heading and display the reading at the main steering position'. A periscope leads from the compass to the bridge which allows the OOW to read the magnetic heading. Maintenance of the monkey island is critical. The monkey island must be rust free, painted, and cleaned to prevent the build-up of salt particles and dust and to reduce the potential damage caused by exposure to the elements.

More often found on ROROs are *tween* or '*tween*' decks. Tween is a colloquial abridgement of the word 'between.' In ship design, the tween deck is an empty space that separates or is between (tween) two other decks. Tween decks are also often found on ferries as they provide additional car stowage capacity. The flush deck is any deck that extends without any constructional breaks from the frontal part of the ship to the aft. On ships with a flush deck, there is no raised fo'c'sle or lowered quarterdeck. At the top of the ship's superstructure is the bridge deck. This is where the ship's navigation and communication equipment are held. The bridge serves as the command station for the master and the OOW. It is where the helmsman steers the ship and where cargo loading and discharging operations are managed from. On either side of the bridge deck are protrusions called the *bridge wings*. These protrusions extend lengthways on the port and starboard sides and allow the master and the OOW to see the full length of the ship without obstruction. The bridge wings are especially important when the ship is manoeuvring alongside. At the far stern is the *quarter deck*. The quarter deck forms part of the upper deck and is inclusive of the poop deck.

SUPERSTRUCTURE

The ship's superstructure is the large rising construction that is usually found towards the aft of the vessel on conventional ships, or towards the midship section on larger container ships. Some types of vessels have their superstructure located at the fore such as offshore support vessels and anchor handling tugs. Passenger ships such as cruise liners and ferries have superstructures that extend the full length of the main deck, as this provides maximum space for passenger cabins, entertainment and hospitality facilities, and crew quarters. The term superstructure is derived from the Latin prefix 'super', which means *in addition*, *above* or *more than*, and the stem word *structure*, which means to 'build' or to 'heap up'. Thus, *superstructure* means to add a construction to an already existing structure. On container ships, the superstructure houses the master's cabin and day room, the officer's cabins, crew's living quarters, the galley and mess, stores, the sickbay or hospital, and the bridge. An increasing number of merchant ships are also being retrofitted with a *citadel* or strong room. The size of a ship's superstructure can heavily influence the performance of the ship. This is because the superstructure impacts on the structure, the displacement, and the stability of the vessel. The height and weight of the superstructure shape the amount of freeboard that is needed, right down to the waterline. As mentioned above, the superstructure is effectively the part of the ship where the crew live and work the most. For that reason, it is worth spending a little describing the various compartments found in the ship's superstructure. First and foremost are the *officer's cabins*. On most ships, officers are afforded the privilege of their own cabins. These are self-contained quarters with a bunk, a small deck and chair, storage racks, and an ensuite toilet/shower. The senior officers tend to have plusher cabin fittings including private refrigerators. Ratings, on the other hand, tend to share berths. These are also self-contained cabins with the same fixtures as the officer cabins but are usually smaller and shared between two ratings. There has been a shift over the past couple of decades to provide ratings with their own cabins; this has largely evolved from the increasing numbers of females working on board merchant ships. It is also interesting to note that a similar approach for separate berths has been adopted on the latest Royal Navy warships. Given their senior position on board, and the need for additional privacy and security, the master and chief engineer are almost always provided with a main cabin, which contains their sleeping quarters, ensuite shower facilities, and a small day area usually consisting of a sofa, coffee table, and easy chair. Attached to the cabin is the day office, where they carry out their day-to-day administrative duties.

The *galley* is the food storage, preparation, and cooking compartment. It is usually laid out with longitudinal units and overhead cabinets. This makes best use of the limited space available. It helps counterbalance rolling and pitching. To prevent the spillage of hot liquids, galley stoves are often gimballed and surrounded by side bars which prevent the cook from falling against hot stoves. Attached to the galley is the *mess*. The mess is where the ship's crew eat and often socialise outside working hours. The *sickbay* is a compartment within the ship that contains the medicine chest. This is usually divided into separate cabinets for refrigerated medicines requiring cold storage and a locked cabinet for controlled substances such as morphine. In addition to the medicine chest, the sickbay also has a sink and potable water supply, first aid materials, a sickbed, and a logbook for recording incidents. The sickbay, and more importantly the medicine chest, must always remain locked when not in use. In most cases, access to the sickbay is restricted to the master and the ship's medical officer. Almost all container ships have a separate day room where the officers and crew can relax. The facilities will obviously differ from one ship to another though most have at least a television and VCR or DVD player, and a small library. Most ships today have computers with limited internet access for sending and receiving emails and checking news. Very lucky crews may even have access to a gym and an indoor or outdoor swimming pool. With the increase in piracy across many of the world's most important sea lanes, merchant ships are increasingly being fitted with a *citadel*. The citadel is a strong room where the officers and crew can retreat to in the event the ship is overwhelmed by pirates. For safety, the citadel is usually located within a concealed void which makes detection much harder. Most citadels simply consist of a fireproof room with bottled water and canned supplies. More advanced facilities allow the crew to remotely disable the ship's engines and electronic systems, making it impossible for the attackers to sail the ship to a different location. Although they are costly to install, citadels have proven their worth. In 2010 alone, 4,185 ships were attacked with 1,090 seafarers taken hostage. An estimated 342 seafarers managed to escape captivity by remaining hidden in their citadel.

By far the most important part of the superstructure is the bridge. When the ship is underway, the bridge is usually manned by the OOW. The OOW may be accompanied by an able seaman whose duties include manning the helm or being a lookout. When the ship is encountering foul weather, heavy seas, navigating busy sea lanes, or coming into or out port, it is customary for the master to also be on the bridge. This is not to detract responsibility from the OOW but rather to allow the master to promulgate urgent commands. The development of the bridge concept is quite interesting. Traditionally, sailing ships were commanded from the quarterdeck, which was located aft of the mainmast. This is where the ship's wheel was positioned to be near the rudder. With the arrival of paddle steamers, marine engineers realised the need for a platform from which they could inspect the paddle wheels and from where the master could have a clear view of the entire ship without his view being obstructed by the paddle houses. This led to the construction of a raised walkway – or literally a bridge – which connected the port and starboard paddle houses. Even after the screw propeller replaced the paddle wheel, the term *bridge* survived and is used in today's maritime lexicon. Though the term *bridge* is widely used, it generally refers to the topmost structure on large merchant and naval vessels. Smaller craft such as tugs have a wheelhouse as opposed to a bridge. The wheelhouse is a small enclosure around the ship's wheel and is most often located on the quarterdeck. On ships built before the mid to late 20th century, commands would be passed from the OOW on the bridge to stations dispersed throughout the ship. This is because the technology did not exist to remotely control the ship from one single location. Helm orders would be passed to an enclosed wheelhouse, where the coxswain or helmsman would operate the ship's wheel. Engine commands would be relayed to the engine officers in the engine room by an engine order telegraph that displayed the master's orders on a dial. The engine officer would then carry out the order to ensure the correct combination of steam pressure and engine revolutions were available. Weatherproof pilot houses supplanted open bridges so that the pilot, who was in most cases also the ship's navigation officer, could issue commands from under shelter. The advent of iron, and later steel, ships also required a compass platform. This usually consisted of a tower where a magnetic compass could be positioned far away from the ferrous interference of the ship's hull. Today, many naval vessels still have a flying bridge, which is a platform atop the pilot house and is open to the weather. The flying bridge contains a binnacle and voice tubes that allow the conning officer to direct the ship from a higher position during fair weather conditions.

Bridge layout and design

The bridge functions as the eyes and brain of the ship and, as such, must have a clear and unobstructed view of the entire ship and its surroundings. For this reason, it is customary for the bridge to be demarcated into two broad areas. The first is the area at the front of the bridge which provides the best position for observation, and the second is the area towards the rear which has the controls, communications equipment, and the chart room. The observation space is enclosed by large panes of strengthened glass, built to withstand storms and other adverse conditions such as hale. Shades that can be lowered are also fitted so that visibility is not reduced when the sun is bright and direct. The remaining area of the bridge houses the navigation, radar, steering, and communication equipment. Along with this, are numerous controls that operate various parts of the ship remotely. Several internal telephone lines connect the bridge directly to the chief engineer, the master, the chief officer, and the engine control room. On either side of the bridge are the bridge wings. These wing-like structures extend outwards and provide the OOW with an unobstructed view of the sides of the ship. They also house controls for the individual bow and stern thrusters. The thrusters are small propellers located deep within the hull that provide a higher degree of control for precise turns and adjustments. The bridge wings may be open-topped or closed depending on the design of the ship. In most cases, the wings are kept open to allow for maximum unobstructed visibility. The bridge is the most sensitive part of the vessel and entry is prohibited to anyone who does not have the necessary authorisation. This includes members of the crew. Normally, access to the bridge is restricted to the master, the officer coming on watch, the officer going off watch, and the helmsman/lookout.

To steer the ship, controls for the rudder, engines, and thrusters are located on the many bridge consoles. Although primary control of the engine rests with the chief engineer and the EOW in the engine room, it is typical for the OOW to issue commands to the engine room, who then carry out the action accordingly. To increase propulsion, an engine telegraph allows for a variety of speeds and even directs the propellers to go into reverse. There are also often different controls for the multiple engines. In addition to the engines and propellers, there are bow and stern thrusters. As mentioned previously, these are usually controlled from the bridge wings where there is better visibility. Vessel steering is controlled through the rudder and thrusters, and the controls for both are on the bridge. The rudder must be able to turn 45 degrees to both port and starboard without colliding with the propellers. Instead of conventional separate propellers and rudders, an increasing number of ships have started using *azipods*. These are large fully integrated propulsion and steering systems that can rotate 360 degrees. On smaller ships, or ships requiring dynamic positioning capability, the azipods may be fitted at the stern, or at the stern and the bow. This provides multidirectional steering and advanced position keeping. Due to their immense weight and size, container ships are generally not considered suitable for azipods, though the latest Cunard liners *Queen Mary 2* (2003) and *Queen Elizabeth* (2010) are both fitted with azipods instead of conventional propellers and rudders.

Safe navigation is a keystone task for every vessel. For this reason, the bridge is fitted out with a vast array of navigation and communications equipment. Although the equipment on board differs from one to another, all ships must have the basic systems mandated by SOLAS. This includes Global Positioning Systems (GPS), a Navtex receiver, Electronic Chart and Display Information System (ECDIS), radar systems, and maritime communications equipment. When underway, vessels must maintain strict compliance with the SOLAS and IMO regulations. As the bridge controls the whole ship, it is essential that the bridge layout and equipment is also compliant. For navigation purposes, the bridge must be located with a clear view both ahead and abeam. There must also be a minimum vision of 255 degrees for the OOW, with at least 112.5 degrees of visibility on both the port and starboard sides. For the bridge wings, the side of the vessel must be clearly visible to 180 degrees on the beam and 45 degrees to the opposite. For the helmsman, a minimum of 60 degrees is needed on both sides. Ships weighing more than 10,000 gross tonnes must carry a minimum of one X band–9 GHz radar. Should any of the bridge equipment malfunction, an alarm will sound. Furthermore, the bridge also has emergency alarm panels that sound an alarm in the event any machinery or systems malfunction anywhere around the ship. For critical alarm systems, if there is no response from the OOW, a backup alarm will sound for 30 seconds in the ship's offices, the mess, and the officer's cabins. If firearms are carried on board, these will also be located on the bridge in a fireproof lockable cabinet.

In this chapter, we have covered many of the structural elements of container ships. We have examined the basic design of the ship hull and the bulbous bow, the design and construction of the cargo holds and hatch covers, the provision of ballast tanks and cofferdams, the various types of decks found on board, and the main compartments that make up the ship's superstructure including the bridge. In the next chapter, we will look at the engineering side of container ship design including power generation, propulsion, and ancillary systems.

NOTES

1. Scantling is a measurement of prescribed size, dimensions, or cross-sectional areas. In shipbuilding, the scantling refers to the collective dimensions of the framing (apart from the keel) to which the deck plates are attached to form the hull.
2. For reference, 1 mph = 0.86 knots; therefore, the *SS Bremen*'s record-breaking speed was 32.10 mph. By comparison, the top speed of the *RMS Titanic* (1912), which had a standard tapered bow, was 23 knots or 26.46 mph.
3. Named after Willian Thomson, 1st Baron Kelvin (26 June 1824–17 December 1907).
4. The principle is named after *Daniel Bernoulli* who published it in his book *Hydrodynamica* in 1738. In fluid dynamics, Bernoulli's principle states that an increase in the speed of a fluid occurs simultaneously with a decrease in static pressure or a decrease in the fluid's potential energy. Although Bernoulli deduced that pressure decreases when the flow speed increases, it was *Leonhard Euler* who derived Bernoulli's equation in its usual form in 1752. The principle is only applicable to isentropic flows: i.e., when the effects of irreversible processes (such as turbulence) and non-adiabatic processes (heat radiation) are small and can be ignored.
5. For example, under-deck access from one cargo hold to another. On most ships, access to the shaft tunnel is necessary to monitor shaft oil temperatures or to effect repairs on the shift drive.

Chapter 8

Primary ship engineering systems

If the eyes and brain of a ship are the bridge, then the heart lies in the engine room. In this chapter will briefly look at the main engineering systems on board including the main engines, propulsion systems, generators, and ancillary systems. As we might expect, marine engineering is a very in-depth and complicated subject as is therefore beyond the scope of this book. As such, this chapter aims to provide a high-level overview only. Container ships are powered by enormous marine engines which run off *high sulphur fuel oil* (HSFO). In optimal conditions, container ships can reach speeds as high as 21 knots or 24 miles per hour. The machinery responsible for propelling the massive steel bulk is the large multi-blade propeller located at the far aft of the ship. The propulsion system works in much the same way as the driveshaft works in a car. The main engines provide power which is transferred along the propeller shaft as rotational energy. The propellers then convert this rotational energy into translational energy, which pushes the ship forward. Although modern marine engines and propulsion systems are highly advanced, the principle behind the concept is remarkably simple. Modern propulsion systems work off the fundamental principle of the screw. This was first discovered by the Greek mathematician, Archimedes, circa 234 BC. Applying the principle of Archimedes' screw, rotational energy is provided by two to four marine engines located in the engine compartment of the ship. Depending on the vessel size, the engine may be of two- or four-stroke design. Marine engines typically burn HSFO or heavy diesel oil.[1] Inside the engine, pistons force the fuel to combust through alternating compression and expansion cycles. Compression is achieved by igniting the fuel. This compresses the air and vapours within the compression chamber forcing the crankshaft to make a half rotation. As the hot and vapours expand, they force the crankshaft to complete the second half of the rotation. The most common type of marine engine is the reciprocating diesel engine. These engine models offer a higher efficiency when compared to other engine models. Reciprocating engines are categorised into three types based on the number of revolutions per minute (rpm): slow, medium, and high speed. Each of these engine types has its own benefits. For instance, large and heavy ships, such as container ships, require low speed but high torque propulsion systems. This is because moving the dead weight of the vessel is more important than moving at speed. The problem with slow-speed engines is that they consume a huge amount of space. To circumvent this problem, container ships are fitted with high-speed engines and then an adjustable gearbox which is attached to the propeller shaft. The gearbox works by reducing the rotational torque before it is transferred to the propellers.

PROPULSION SYSTEM

The propeller and shaft are divided into three main sections: (1) the thrust shaft; (2) the intermediate shaft(s); and (3) the tail shaft. The *thrust shaft* is the primary shaft that emerges out of the engine. It directly receives the rotational motion from the crankshaft, which rotates

DOI: 10.1201/9781003244615-10

102   Principles of ship architecture and engineering

at maximum velocity. For high rpm engines, the thrust shaft is connected to other components that lie further aft. The next component is the *intermediate shaft*. There is no specific restriction on the number of intermediary shafts that a ship may have. That said, beyond two shafts, it can be difficult to properly service and maintain. The reason for this is the large catenary force that acts on the propeller shaft. This force tends to deform and damage the parts due to their substantial weight. When coupled with the large vibrational shocks that act on the shafts, this can lead to permanent propeller shaft damage. Subsequently, ship designers try to keep the number of intermediary shafts as low as possible. In any case, the only legitimate reason to have multiple intermediary shafts is if the engine is located far away from the propellers. On container ships, this is almost never the case. The last component is the *tail shaft*. This is directly connected to the propeller and lies mainly encased in the stern tube. The tail shaft is connected to the intermediate shaft via a gearbox that manipulates the torque transfer. The tail shaft is built to withstand the variety of forces that act on the stern. In addition to the thrust, intermediate, and tail shafts, are the coupled bearings that connect two adjacent shafts. The coupling is achieved by a series of joints that are usually rigid. The coupling units are bolted to each other using high strength fasteners that can withstand large vibrational stresses. The shaft bearings are components that are used to support and bear the load of the shafts. They run along the length of the shaft and ensure smooth rotation. These bearings are constructed from different materials based on their location. The last part of the marine propeller shaft system are the thrust blocks. These blocks support the propeller shafts at regular intervals. The blocks transfer excess power from the shafts into the hull of the ship. As the shafts rotate at very high speeds, some vibration inevitably occurs. This leads to jarring shocks that may compromise the structural integrity of the vessel. Thus, using specialised bearings, the shocks can be dispersed throughout the hull of the ship. To anchor these thrust blocks to the bed of the ship, a reinforced frame is needed. The primary thrust block is placed aft of the engine crankshaft. This disperses most of the shock into the hull girders and structures.

The design and construction of the propulsion system is important as it directly impacts on the structural integrity of the ship. With shaft speeds reaching anywhere between 300 and 1,200 rpm, care must be taken to manage material fatigue and to prevent damage being caused to the main components of the ship's propulsion and power generation systems. The construction of the shaft bearings is also important, as these hold the complete weight of the propeller shafts. There are two main types of shaft bearings: the full case bearing, which is located at the stern, and the half case bearing which is located elsewhere. The full casing forms an integral part of the propulsion system and provides a complete bearing for the weight of the shaft. The reason it is located at the stern is to account for both catenary weight forces and to counteract any buckling or reverse thrust forces felt at the aft caused by the motion of the propellers. This bearing is also known as the '*aftmost tunnel bearing*', as it encases the shaft like a tunnel. The other shafts only account for weight, and hence do not require an upward casing unit. These bearings must be constructed from high strength metals that do not easily buckle or deform under high-stress loads. In addition, low-level tolerances are expected during the manufacturing process. Special bearing pads are fitted into slots on the connecting inner face of the bearing, which allow for smooth rotation. To lubricate the shaft bearing, an oil dip arrangement is provided. By coating the rotating surface with oil at regular intervals from an oil thrower ring, a consistent coat of lube oil is maintained.

The coolant used to prevent overheating and damage to the shaft and its components is water circulated about the shaft bearing. This is stored in specialised tubes that run along the bearing and the shaft. Tanks stored above the engine platform accommodate the coolant. This is then fed and circulated around the propulsion machinery. Thrust blocks are used to dampen and absorb the vibrational energy emanating from the rotating propeller shafts. This energy is redirected into frames that make up the bed of the engine compartment. Once the energy is distributed about the frames, it is further dispersed into the hull surface through the hull girders. The hull girders serve as the framework upon which the hull of the ship is built. The thrust blocks are rigidly mounted in place to absorb vibration. Moreover, the primary thrust block may either be an independent unit that is built separately to the engine, or it can be integrated into the engine block itself. By integrating the block directly into the engine, space requirements and maintenance costs are reduced. That said, carrying out maintenance while berthed can be problematic as the engine block casing must be opened. The casing that makes up the thrust block is constructed in two parts – an upper half that is detachable and a lower half that supports the shaft. The shaft is laid onto the lower block, and the upper half is then bolted into place using shock-absorbing fasteners. To lubricate the rotating shaft, a regular coating of lube oil is applied to the rotating surface. This is achieved in the same manner as the shaft bearings. An oil thrower and deflector are installed to maintain a constant supply of lube oil from a storage unit located on the lower half of the thrust block. The operating temperature is controlled using cooling coils that circulate coolant throughout the block. It also draws coolant from the central propulsion cooling system. To absorb the vibrations and shocks, bearing pads are attached to the blocks. These are generally of two types – tilt pads or pivotal pads – both of which are held in place by holders integrated into the thrust block. The thrust pads transfer energy to the lower half of the casing. This enables the engine block to withstand large amounts of shock. A thrust collar is used to absorb thrust from the propeller shaft. The thrust blocks incorporate integral flanges that bolt the block into place. Additional flanges may be used to connect the gearbox to the engine. Where the thrust block is integrated into the engine block, both are manufactured from the same casing material as the engine base plates. This provides the added benefit of using the same lubrication and coolant channels as the engine itself.

The integrated block is the same in almost every other feature as the normal thrust block. The shafts themselves are built from robust materials with high yield strength, which provides a lower probability of buckling. Each shaft, starting from the thrust shaft, is built into small sectionswhich can be easily disassembled as required. In addition, seals and stuffing boxes are manufactured from materials that can seal the inner machinery from the external marine environment. High-grade metals and alloys are used for the propeller shaft manufacturing process, as they must be able to withstand large mechanical stress forces. In ships fitted with a high-speed engine, the gearbox forms an integral component that is attached between the tail shaft and the intermediary shaft. It is mainly used to manipulate the torque that is transferred from the engine crankshaft to the stern-mounted propellers. The stern tube arrangement refers to the way in which the tail shaft is borne by the stern tube that is attached to the stern frame. The stern tube is a hollow, horizontal metal tube that provides the primary connection between the propeller and the rest of the vessel. The stern frame is the primary structural member that supports the stern overhang that lies above the propeller and rudder arrangement. The stern tube accommodates the tail shaft of the marine drive shaft system and serves two main purposes: (a) withstanding load and (b) sealing the entire vessel at the aft portion. Since the stern tube serves as the primary link between the vessel and the propeller, it must be able to withstand the tremendous forces exerted by the suspended propeller. In addition, the stern tube should provide sufficient room for the propeller hub to move without creating friction. To handle the load, white metal[2] is commonly used. Lubrication is provided within the stern tube to ensure the smooth functioning of the propulsion system. Along with supporting the structural weight and forces of the propeller, the stern tube also serves as a plug to seal the vessel. It prevents seawater from entering the vessel through the stern. The plug is achieved by using a combination of seals along the length of the tube. There are two main seals located at the bottom and head of the tube. This provides dual protection against any potential leaks that may occur over long periods of time.

The seals consist of three main types: (a) stuffing boxes; (b) lip seals; and (c) radial face seals. Stuffing boxes are made from a variety of packing materials that are used to plug the stern tube. Lip seals are a type of gland seal which prevents lubricant from seeping out of the stern and into the surrounding water. They also prevent water from entering the stern tube. Radial face seals extend out from any point of ingress and use a spring system to seal the structure. Radial face seals are composed of two main components that join to completely seal the stern portion. Without doubt, the propeller shafts are an integral part of the ship. Various factors must be considered when designing and building the shafts and the stern tube. Properly aligning the shafts is extremely important, especially when there are more than one propeller arrangement. By having just one shaft off alignment by even a fraction of a millimetre can cause rapid oscillation. This would cause extreme stresses to develop on the shaft bearings which would permanently deform and damage the entire shaft.

The machinery systems on board ships are designed to work for long periods without stopping. This inevitably means energy is lost resulting in reduced efficiency. The most common form of energy loss is through heat. Heat energy must be reduced or transferred away from the machinery to prevent heat damage. This is achieved by using a cooling media. The cooling media is provided through a central cooling system. There are two types of central cooling system available. The first uses seawater as the cooling media. Seawater is pumped directly into the cooling system and circulated around the machinery before flowing back out again. As the cold seawater moves around the cooling ducts, it safely absorbs and removes the heat. The second type is the freshwater system. In this instance, freshwater is pumped around a closed circuit. As the freshwater returns from the heat exchanger, it is rechilled using seawater in a seawater cooler. This system comprises three different circuits. The first is the *seawater circuit*. With seawater circuits, seawater is pumped through heat exchangers to cool the freshwater. These form the central cooling facility of the system and are normally installed as a duplex. The second is the *low temperature* (LT) *circuit*. The low temperature circuit is used for LT zone machinery and is directly connected to the main seawater central cooler. This means the temperature is lower than in the high temperature (HT) circuits. The LT circuit comprises all auxiliary systems. The quantity of LT freshwater in the system is maintained in balance with the HT freshwater cooling system. This is done with an expansion tank which is shared by both systems. The expansion tank is filled from the hydrophore system or from a distilled water tank using a freshwater refilling pump. The third is the *high temperature* (HT) *circuit*. The high temperature circuit comprises a jacket water system where the HT water level is maintained by LT freshwater. This system normally comprises the main engine, freshwater generator, diesel generator (DG) during standby conditions, and the lube oil filter for the stuffing box drain tank. The high temperature water is circulated by electrical cooling water pumps, with one in service and one on standby. When in standby mode, the DG is kept warm by the circulating system from the DG in service. When the main engine is stopped, this too is kept warm by HT cooling water from the DG. If there is insufficient HT water to service both the DG and the main engine, additional water may be steam heated using the freshwater heater.

The loss of energy in the closed-circuit central cooling freshwater system is continuously compensated by the expansion tank. This also absorbs the increase in pressure caused by thermal expansion. The heat absorbed by the HT circuit is transferred to the LT circuit by a temperature control valve junction. The outlet temperature of the main engine cooling water is kept constant at between 85 and 95°C (185–203°F) by means of *temperature control valves*. These mix the water from the two central cooling systems to create a balanced temperature.

Primary ship engineering systems   105

MAIN ENGINES

Almost all marine engines are internal combustion (IC) type engines. These burn fuel to generate heat energy. The heat energy is then converted into mechanical energy. It is this mechanical energy that turns the propellers which propel the ship. Depending on the size and type of ship, the engine may be either a two-stroke or four-stroke type engine. Marine engines work by injecting a controlled amount of fuel at high pressure into the engine cylinder. A mixture of fuel and air is compressed inside the cylinder with the help of a piston. This results in the combustion of the mixture, which due to the compression, becomes pressurised. The resulting heat increases the pressure of the burning vapours. The sudden increase in pressure drives the piston downwards, which in turn transmits a transverse motion into the rotary motion of the crankshaft using a connecting rod arrangement. The combustion is repeated continuously to maintain power output. The crankshaft is connected via a flywheel to the alternator or the propeller arrangement. To obtain a regular rotation of the crankshaft, the combustion process must be continuous. Before the next combustion can take place, the used vapours in the combustion chamber are drawn out through an exhaust valve, promptly replaced by fresh air. The introduction of fresh air has two functions: first, it helps to push the used vapours out of the combustion chamber; and second, it provides new air for the next combustion phase.

As mentioned above there are two types of marine engine currently in service: the two-stroke and the four-stroke. Four-stroke engines are installed on ships to produce both electrical power as well as propulsion. The engine takes four cycles to complete the transfer of power from the combustion chamber to the crankshaft. Because of this, four-stroke engines are normally found on smaller vessels. By comparison, two-stroke engines only require two cycles to provide sufficient energy to power the propulsion system. For that reason, two-stroke engines are more commonly found on larger vessels such as container ships. With a two-stroke engine, the process starts with a suction and compression stroke. This is an upward movement of the piston which draws fresh air inside the combustion chamber and compresses the air-fuel mixture. The second cycle provides the power and exhaust, which involves the downward movement of the piston caused by the explosion inside the chamber. This is then followed by the removal of the exhaust gases. These exhaust gases are sucked out through the exhaust valve which is fitted to the top of the cylinder. A stuffing box is used to separate and seal the crankcase which holds the pistons from the combustion chamber. There are four dominant manufacturers of marine grade ship engines: MAN Diesel & Turbo (formerly B&W Engines) of Germany; Wärtsilä (formerly Sulzer Engines) of Finland; Mitsubishi Heavy Engineering of Japan; and Rolls Royce of the United Kingdom. As a point in fact (as of July 2021) Wärtsilä holds the *Guinness Book of Records* achievement for building the largest marine engine ever installed – the Wärtsilä RT-Flex96C two-stroke engine with turbochargers. This powerhouse was installed in September 2006 on the lead ship of the *Maersk Triple E class, Emma Mærsk*. Boasting a massive 14-cylinder capacity, this engine has a colossal height of 13.5 m (44 ft), a length of 26.59 m (87 ft) and weighs a hefty 2,300 metric tonnes producing 80,080 kW or 107,390 bhp. The crankshaft alone weighs 300 tonnes, while the 6 metre high pistons each weigh 5.5 tonnes.

Due to their size, marine engines are usually built in three sections. Depending on the size of the engine room and the availability of access for installation, the engine may be fitted in the shipyard as sections or as an entire assembly. The main components of the engine are the *bedplate*, the 'A-frame', and the *entablature*. The *bedplate* is the lowermost portion of the engine and forms the base. The bedplate accommodates the crankshaft bearings and the 'A-frame'. For small engines, a single iron casting is used but for larger two-stroke engines, prefabricated cast steel transverse sections with longitudinal girders are used. The '*A-frame*', as the name suggests, is similar in shape to the letter 'A' and is installed above the bedplate. It is built to separately carry the crosshead guide and the top acts as a support for the base of the entablature. The bottom surface of the 'A-frame' is machined to provide a mating surface for the top of the bedplate. The *entablature*, also known as the *cylinder block*, is made from cast iron and accommodates the cooling water and scavenge airspace. Depending on the size of the engine, the casting may be either single cylinder or multicylinder (i.e., bolted together). The lower portion of the cylinder block is machined to provide a mating surface and is fastened to the 'A-frame' using bolts. In addition to the main components listed above, marine engines also have a vast array of subsidiary parts including the exhaust valve, fuel valve pipe, servo oil rail, fuel rail, oil sump, gear drive, high pressure fuel pump and servo oil pump, water cooling system, air cooler, common rail platform, and the turbo charger.

Marine engines are extremely complex units that require constant maintenance. To ensure the engine is kept at peak condition, a planned or scheduled maintenance regime, which includes the overhauling of important moving and static parts of the combustion chamber, must be followed. The most common maintenance tasks to be completed include the overhaul and measurement of the piston, rings and piston rod, cylinder liner, exhaust valve, stuffing box, connecting rod and crosshead bearings, and the main bearings; measurement of crankshaft deflection; checks and measurement of the fuel pump timings; and checks and overhaul of the starter air system. The time between overhauling the different parts of the engine is provided by the manufacturer in the *Engine Operations Manual*. As well as planned or scheduled maintenance, ongoing maintenance needs to be carried out between any two overhauling periods. This includes checking the engine ratings and power circuits using a digital power indicator; carrying out scavenge space inspections to check the condition of the piston ring and checking the lubrication of the cylinder liner.

Basic operation of the engine order telegraph

On sea-going vessels, the navigation officers control the ship's navigation system from the bridge and the engineering officers control the propulsion plant from the engine room. The bridge is situated at the top of the superstructure. This means it is impossible for the OOW to know the condition of the engines and the EOW has no way of knowing where the ship is heading as the engine room is situated below the waterline. This means a fail-safe communication system is needed between the OOW and EOW. As the name suggests, the *engine order telegraph* is used as a way of communicating orders from the bridge to engine control room and vice versa. On ships with a manual style engine order telegraph, a lever is moved over different speed positions for setting ahead and astern directions. The telegraph and its bell, also known as the *telegraph bell*, are located both on the bridge and in the engine control room. A responsible officer from each department handles the telegraph from either location. One further telegraph is located on the emergency manoeuvring or local manoeuvring station of the main engine. There is a changeover switch located in the engine control room for telegraph selection which can be manually or automatically changed between the local control and engine control room telegraph. The telegraph dial is split into two sections – *ahead* and *astern*.

The ahead section has six different settings: *navigation full, full ahead, half ahead, slow ahead, dead slow ahead*, and *stop*. The astern directions have five settings: *dead slow astern, slow astern, half astern, full astern*, and *emergency astern*. To operate the telegraph, the initial movement is always initiated from the bridge and is done by moving the lever in the required direction. This rings the telegraph bell in both locations. After hearing the bell, the engineer acknowledges the command by adjusting the telegraph in the engine room to the same position as that of the bridge. Only when the two settings match does the bell stop ringing. This ensures that the correct movement is acknowledged, and the engine speed and direction is controlled accordingly. On modern ships with automated controls, the bridge telegraph is directly connected to the engine controls. This means no intervention from the engine crew is required. These types of telegraph are called remote-controlled telegraphs. A provision is provided which links both telegraphs so that they can be manually operated in case the automation fails.

GAS EXHAUST SYSTEM

Marine engines work by burning fuel. This process is not entirely efficient, resulting in a substantial loss of energy. Some of this energy is lost through heat and some through exhaust gases. Modern exhaust systems are designed so that the unused gases expelled by the cylinders are redirected to the turbocharger and the exhaust gas boiler for recovery and reuse. To maximise the energy extracted from the exhaust gases, the exhaust system comprises various components such as the exhaust gas pipes, exhaust gas boiler, silencer, spark arrester, and expansion joints. The *Exhaust Gas-Piping System* conveys the exhaust gas from the outlet of the turbocharger to the atmosphere. The exhaust gas from the cylinder unit is sent to the exhaust gas receiver where the fluctuating pressure generated from the different cylinders is equalised. From here, the gases – which are maintained at a constant pressure – are sent to the turbocharger where waste heat is recovered. This then provides additional scavenge air for the engine. One of the most important factors naval architects need to consider when designing the exhaust piping system is the *back pressure* on the turbocharger. The back pressure of the exhaust gas system at a specified *Maximum Continuous Rating (MCR)* depends on the gas velocity and is inversely proportional to the pipe diameter to the power of four. It is best practice to avoid developing incurring excessive pressure loss within the exhaust pipes. Therefore, the exhaust gas velocity is usually maintained at about 35$^\text{m}$/s to 50 $^\text{m}$/s at the specified MCR. The *Exhaust Gas Boiler (EGB)* is one of the most efficient waste heat recovery systems available on board. When the ship's propulsion plant is running at its rated load, the auxiliary boiler can be switched off to allow the EGB to generate the steam required for the ship's systems. The exhaust gases pass through the EGB, which is either located near the engine top or in the funnel space. The efficiency of the EGB is directly affected by the pressure loss as the gases cross the boiler. The parameters governing this pressure loss (such as the exhaust gas temperature and flow rate) are affected by ambient conditions. Therefore, the recommended exhaust pressure loss across the EGB should be maintained at no more than 150 mm at the specified MCR.

The engine room is a major source of noise, which can often be heard throughout the ship's superstructure. Noise levels are regulated under the *International Maritime Labour Convention* and must be kept to the absolute minimum possible. To measure noise levels, soundings are recorded one metre from the exhaust gas pipe outlet edge at an angle of 30 degrees, provided the exhaust gas system is without an EGB or silencer. Silencers are used to reduce the noise level in the exhaust gas manifold and are typically located after the EGB. Conventional silencers consist of absorptive and reactive chambers. They are constructed with a gas velocity of 35$^\text{m}$/s. The reactive chamber is only effective at one frequency. Subsequently, the latest design of silencers consists of three chambers to overcome the one frequency limitation. The three chambers are composed of a reactive element for attenuation of lower frequencies, a resistive element-absorptive silencer to tackle higher frequencies, and a combination element for both reactive and resistive elements. This reduces the noise level without increasing the back pressure on the turbocharger. It does this by tuning the elements to the same frequencies as the engine.

108 Principles of ship architecture and engineering

The low load operation of marine engines tends to produce partially burnt carbon and soot deposits within the exhaust gas piping system. As the exhaust gases produced after combustion are oxygen-rich, these partially burnt carbon particles are liable to spark as they are discharged from the exhaust manifold. To prevent this, a spark arrester is installed at the top end of the exhaust piping system to prevent sparks from spreading over the top tier decks. The latest design of spark arresters forces the exhaust gases to create rotatory movements by forcing them through angled positioned blades. The heavy carbon particles are then collected in the soot box, which can be cleaned or drained as required. The spark arrester can be combined with the silencer as one unit to economise space and installation costs. Although spark arresters are beneficial in that they prevent the emission of combustible sparks, they have the disadvantage of causing considerable pressure loss. The exhaust gas system undergoes vast temperature variations. As it is not possible to construct the entire exhaust piping system in one piece, multiple sections must be joined together. When the engine is at standstill, the temperature of the exhaust pipe can vary from as much as 10 to 40°C (10–104°F) depending on the climatic condition of the ship. When the engine is running the exhaust system temperature can reach 200°C (392°F). This variation in temperature requires special joints that can safely absorb the heat-induced expansions and contractions of the exhaust pipes. For this purpose, bellows and expansion joints are used.

AIR COMPRESSOR

The air compressor is a device whose primary function is to compress air to reduce its volume. There are typically four different types of air compressors used on board. These are the main air compressor, the deck air compressor, the air conditioning (AC) compressor, and the refrigeration compressor. Air compressors are devices that are used extensively in industrial, commercial, and household appliances. In the maritime sector, air compressors are a vital piece of equipment as they can be used in processes ranging from cleaning filters to starting the main and auxiliary engines. The air compressor produces pressurised air by decreasing the volume of air and increasing its pressure. Air compressors found on ships are generally categorised as main air compressors or service air compressors. The *main air compressor* is a high-pressure compressor with a minimum pressure value of 30 bars and is used to run the main engine. The *service air compressor* compresses air to a low pressure of only 7 bars and is used in service and control air lines. On board ships, the reciprocating air compressor is the type most widely used. A reciprocating air compressor consists of a piston, connecting rod, crankshaft, wrist pin, suction valve, and discharge valves. The piston is connected to the low and high side of the suction and discharge line. The crankshaft rotates which in turn rotates the piston. The downward moving piston reduces the pressure in the main cylinder, with the pressure differential opening the suction valve. The piston is drawn down by the rotating crankshaft. Low-pressure air then fills the cylinder. Afterwards, the piston reciprocates upwards. This upward movement starts rebuilding the pressure, closing the suction valve. When the air is pressurised to its specific value, a discharge valve opens, and the pressurised air starts moving through the discharge line towards a storage bottle. This stored pressurised air is used to run the main and auxiliary engines.

On most ships, there are four types of main air compressor. These are the main air compressor, the topping up compressor, the deck air compressor, and the emergency air compressor. The main air compressor is used to supply high-pressure air to start the main and auxiliary engines. To start the main engines, the air pressure must be at 30 bars. A pressure valve is provided which reduces the pressure and supplies controlled air from the storage bottle. The control air filter controls the input and output of compressed air. The *topping up compressor* is used to counteract any leakages in the system. If there is a leak from the main air compressor, the top-up compressor automatically jumps in and replaces the main compressor. This means there is no discontinuity in the supply of pressurised air to the main engines. The *deck air compressor* is used solely for deck operations and as a service air compressor. These are lower capacity pressure compressors as the pressure required for service air is within the range of six to eight bar. The last type of main air compressor is the *emergency air compressor.* The emergency air compressor is used for starting the auxiliary engine in times of emergency or when the main air compressor has failed to fill up the main air receiver. This type of compressor can be motor driven or engine driven. Where motor driven, it is supplied from an emergency source of power. Air compressors work efficiently when installed and maintained properly. Air compressor efficiency can be monitored using pressure bars or pressure gauges and safety devices. The pressure bar or pressure gauge is installed on all compressors to ensure the pressure and discharge are at the specified requirement. Without this device, it would be almost impossible to confirm whether the air is pressurised above, at, or below the requisite value. Safety devices are used to reduce the loss of energy from the air compressor and in so doing increase overall efficiency. Safety devices automatically shut down the input and output air when adequate compression is reached and save the device from building overpressure.

Although there are various types of air compressor systems used on board, there are several components that are shared by all of them. This makes the maintenance and replacement of faulty parts much easier. The first such component is *electricity or power source.* This is the key component of all compressors and is essential for running the compressor. The power source or electric motor is used to run the compressor with a constant unfluctuating speed. The second component is *cooling water.* Cooling water is used to keep the compressor from overheating. The third component is *lubricating oil* (LO). LO is necessary to keep the mobile parts of the compressor working smoothly. The lubrication reduces the friction of the compressor parts leading to reduced wear out. The fourth component is *air.* Without air the compressor simply cannot function. The fifth component is the *suction valve.* The suction valve is provided with a suction filter which pulls in the air to be compressed. The sixth and final component is the *discharge valve.* This valve removes the output air and discharges it at a suitable location. In addition to starting the main engines, compressed air is needed for various ancillary uses including control valves, throttle controls, and other monitoring systems and pneumatic tools. Some vessels also use compressed air to initiate the propellers from a cold start.

Every ship is equipped with a set of two air reservoirs. These may be vertical or horizontal. The air reservoirs are hydraulically pressure tested to 1.5 times their working pressure. As per SOLAS regulations, the total capacity of the air reservoir must be sufficient to provide at least 12 consecutive main engine starts for a reversible engine, and a minimum of six consecutive starts for a non-reversible engine, without refilling the reservoirs. There must also be two identical main air receivers and one emergency air bottle. Each air reservoir must be equipped with mountings. The first type is the *fusible plug*, which has a composition of bismuth (50%), tin (30%), and lead (20%), and a melting point of 104.4°C (220°F). The fusible plug is fitted at the reservoir bottom or on the reservoir wherever a relief valve is not fitted. The purpose of the fusible plug is to release compressed air in the event of an abnormally high build-up of compressed air temperature. The second type of mounting is the *atmospheric relief valve.* This is provided as over-pressure protection and as a back-up to the fusible plug. In the event of engine room fire when CO^2 flooding is required, the valve must be opened before evacuating the engine room. The air receiver relief valve may be situated either outside the engine room through the ship's funnel or inside the engine room itself. In the latter case, CO^2 bottle calculations for engine room firefighting must be carried out accordingly. The third type of mounting is the *spring-loaded safety valve*. This sets the pressure at 32 bar (for a 30 bar working pressure) with an equal to or greater than 10% rise in pressure accumulation. The fourth type of mounting is the compensation ring. When a hole is cut or machined into the pressure vessel, higher stresses act on the material around the hole. To reduce this, compensation rings are fitted. The ring is a flange onto which a valve or fitting is mounted. The compensation ring provides structural integrity to the air pressure vessel.

The compressed air is stored in large cylindrical air bottles that usually have one longitudinal welded seam. The longitudinal and circumferential seam is machine welded using full penetration welds. The welding detail is determined by the air pressure to be stored in accordance with class regulations. All welded air receivers must be stress relieved or annealed at a temperature of ~600°C (~1,112°F). The weld must be radiographed for signs of defect. Receivers are subject to statutory surveys and inspections during which they are periodically hydraulic tested at 1.5 times the working pressure. The air receivers must be inspected as per the planned maintenance schedule and checked for indications of corrosion. Any moisture in the air receivers can cause corrosion leading to structural failure. Despite proper operation of the compressor cooler drains, it is common for moisture to collect within the receiver. This is particularly so in humid conditions. Therefore, it is good practice to check the air reservoir drains regularly to assess the volume of ullage. In extremely humid conditions, the drains may have to be emptied 2–3 times daily to remove any accumulated emulsion. Where corrosion has occurred, this is commonly found around the air receiver drain. After carrying out a thorough visual inspection, it may be necessary to perform thickness measurements using an ultrasonic thickness gauge. If the thickness of the air receiver is compromised, the air pressure within the bottle must be reduced to a safe level. This can be done by calculating the pressure parameter and changing the cut-in, cut-off settings of the air compressor when the receiver is used. The relief valve settings must also be readjusted.

Furthermore, the air receiver can be isolated and kept on standby and if needed, may be manually filled. When performing preventative maintenance on the air bottle, all internal welds or small changes in cross-sectional integrity need to be investigated. If the air bottle is too small to enter, then internal inspection can be carried out using a probe mounted camera. The internal surface coating of the air bottle should be either a graphite suspension in water, linseed oil, copal varnish or epoxy coating. Whichever surface coating is used, it must be anti-corrosive, antitoxic, and antioxidant. Given the importance of the air bottle, they are fitted with various safety devices that are designed to operate in the event of malfunction. These safety devices include the fusible plug, the pressure relief valve, an atmospheric relief valve, a low-pressure alarm, and an automatic or remote-controlled moisture drain valve.

CONTROL AIR SYSTEM

The *control air system* consists of a branched air line through which a pressure-reducing valve can deliver controlled air. This is necessary as pneumatic control equipment is sensitive to contaminants, which may be present in compressed air. Viscous oil and water emulsions can cause moving parts in the control equipment and control valves to stick causing deterioration of the diaphragms, spools, and other rubber parts. The ingress of water can cause corrosion and rust. Metallic wear and other small particles can lead to abrasion damage. Solids mixed with oil and water emulsions can block small orifices. This means clean and dry control air is required for the operation of the control air system. When the source of control and instrument air is the main air compressors and the main air reservoir itself, special provision is needed to ensure the air quality is at the required standard. The pressure-reducing valve which brings the main air pressure to the 7–8 bar required by the control air system may be affected by emulsion carry over and often requires frequent cleaning to prevent cross-contamination. Automatic drain traps may be fitted in the control air system, though the majority have traps that require manual daily draining. Large amounts of free moisture and oil emulsion carry over in the air can be removed by special control-air membrane filters installed in the control air line. A typical control air filter arrangement consists of an oil- and moisture-collecting filter followed by a membrane air dryer filter. The treatment of air through these membrane filters results in air filtration and the removal of virtually all traces of oil, moisture, and airborne impurities. A simple line air filter is provided with a small plastic float and auto drain arrangement. The filter may also be drained manually if the vessel enters a humid climate. The filter dryer unit consists of a primary filter, secondary filter, and membrane hollow fibre elements. The control air enters the dryer chamber through the line filter located in the lower part of the dryer unit. In the dryer unit, the primary filter removes coarse rust particles, dust, and other large impurities. The secondary filter acts as a coalescer separating water droplets and oil mists up to 0.3 microns. A differential pressure gauge indicates the condition of the primary and secondary filters.

A higher differential pressure indicates a dirty membrane filter. The membrane elements must be renewed as per the ship's preventative maintenance schedule. The high-pressure air piping from the air compressor to the receiver should ideally be maintained as smooth as possible without any bends in the pipeline. This allows the control air to flow freely to the receiver without restriction. Bends in the piping can create backpressure in the line, especially where there is accumulated moisture or oil emulsion. The emergency air compressor is a small independent air compressor that can be driven by an independent prime mover like an engine, or a power supply from the emergency switchboard. It is used to fill up the emergency air bottle, which is designed to contain a sufficient volume of air to start the auxiliary engine of a dead ship. The control air is also used by the *Emergency Shut-Off Valve System*. This system consists of an air bottle of 7 bar pressure. This is used to operate the emergency quick closing valves and the fire and funnel dampers. In the event of an uncontrollable engine room fire, the quick closing valves are operated. This channels control air to shut specific outlet valves of the fuel oil and lube oil tanks and the engine room funnel and blower dampers, thereby cutting off all fuel and air supplies to fire.

STARTING AIR SYSTEM

Different methods are employed for starting the marine diesel engines on board ships depending on the type and kind of engine. Some of the most common methods used on board ships are manual, electrical, and mechanical systems. In the ship's main propulsion or auxiliary engines, considerable torque is required to overcome the inertia of large reciprocating masses. For this purpose, energy stored as compressed air is used. There are a number of important points the engineers must consider when operating the starting air system. First, the engineers must ascertain the required range of starting air pressure. The starting air pressure should be such that it provides sufficient speed to the piston during its compression stroke to quickly compress the charge air and reach the temperature required to initiate the combustion of the injected fuel. The starting air pressure is generally the same range for both the main propulsion engines and the auxiliary engines, i.e., between 25 and 42 bars. If the air pressure goes higher than this, the components of the engine must be robust enough to handle the excess pressure. SOLAS states that the starting air reservoirs should be able

112 Principles of ship architecture and engineering

to provide a minimum of 12 consecutive starts without needing replenishment. For non-reversible engines, six consecutive starts are considered sufficient.

Second is the time allowed for the induction of starting air to the injection chamber. It is with the expansion stroke that the starting air valves open to provide positive torque to the engine. For two-stroke engines, the starting air valves are opened when the piston just passes the top dead centre and close again when the exhaust valves are about to open. The starting air valve opens approximately 10 degrees before the piston reaches dead centre (this is provided for the valve to open fully when the piston passes dead centre) and around five degrees before the exhaust valve opens. In a pulse turbocharged two-stroke engine the maximum starting air angle is 115 degrees. In four-stroke engines, the exhaust valves open for a similar phase when the piston passes dead centre and closes before the exhaust valve opens in the expansion stroke. The starting air valve begins to open four degrees before dead centre and begins to close 130 degrees after dead centre. Third is the overlap period. Overlap is the simultaneous opening of two starting air valves during the starting air sequence. It is necessary to start the engine in any crank position; this ensures that at least one valve will open when the starting air is inducted. If there is no overlap provided, then the engine could stop in any position with all the starting air valves closed. There should be a minimum overlap of 15 degrees provided though the ideal condition should be between 20 and 90 degrees. For a 4-cylinder two-stroke engine the firing interval is 90 degrees (360/4), and if the starting air period is 115 degrees, then the total overlap period would be the difference between the two, i.e., $115 - 90 = 25$ degrees.

The fourth consideration is whether there are any indications of leaking starting air valves, and the cause of their leakage. The leakage of starting air valves is indicated by the overheating of line between the starting air valve and the starting air manifold when the engine is in operation. This heating generally occurs due to the passage of hot gases from the engine cylinder to the starting air line. Thus, during manoeuvring, each starting air line should be felt for abnormal temperatures close to the starting air valves. The common cause of leakage includes the deposit of foreign particles between the valve and the valve seat from the starting air supply system. Debris prevents the valve from closing fully or causes the valve to operate sluggishly. This is caused by an incorrect clearance between the operating parts. To determine the extent of the leakage in the starting air valve when the engine is at standstill, the automatic starting air valve is kept in an open position and the air to the distributor is kept shut. The indicator cocks for all of the units must be kept open. The air is now opened from the starting air receiver. By engaging the turning gear and bringing each unit's piston to dead centre, any air leakage can be checked from the indicator cocks of the corresponding unit. This will show which starting air valve is leaking and from which particular unit. If overheating of a particular line is felt and a starting air valve leak is detected, then the starting air branch on the starting air manifold will have to be blanked off. If two or more starting air valves are removed from the engine, then this raises the possibility of engine failure in a particular crank position during manoeuvring. Subsequently, the reversing control should be operated and the engine given a small amount of starting air in the reverse direction to obtain a different crank position. Alternatively, the turning gear may be engaged and one of the pistons moved in position just after top dead centre to provide the positive torque to turn the engine. If during manoeuvring, the starting air is not inducted for 30 minutes while the engine is on bridge control, this will trigger an automatic activation of the slow turning mode in which the engine is turned very slowly at 8–10 rpm and the air is restricted by a slow turning valve. This is done as a precautionary measure to prevent damage to the engine while starting, especially if there is an oil or water leak.

The fifth point is the running direction of the interlock. Interlocks are the blocking devices that ensure that the engine is started or reversed only when specific conditions are fulfilled

Primary ship engineering systems 113

or satisfied. Running direction interlock is an essential trait that prevents the injection of fuel to the engine when the telegraph is not synchronised with the running direction of the engine. It is also an important application for crash manoeuvring when starting air is used as a brake on the engine by reversing the operation. The turning gear interlock is another important function that prevents the admission of starting air to the engine cylinders when the turning gear is engaged. If the starting air is admitted with the turning gear engaged, then the turning gear along with the motor will fly off, puncturing the bulkhead. Thus, the interlock is necessary to prevent this from happening. These are just some of the important points marine engineers need to know about the air starting system on ships. Engine room fires have led to massive devastation in the past and are some of the biggest causes of causalities on ships. If a fire starts in the main engine, then the ship could easily lose control, leading to severe damage and loss. One of the causes of engine room fire is starting air line explosions.

For a fire to become self-sustaining, it needs four elements: heat, fuel, air, and a chemical reaction. This was previously known as the fire triangle but is now technically referred to as the *fire tetrahedron*. In an air starting system, fuel may be present in the form of lube oil carried over from the air compressor. Moreover, there is an abundant presence of oxygen in the system. The heat source may come from a leaking starting air valve fitted on the cylinder head. The combination of these three in a proper ratio (the chemical reaction) can lead to an air line explosion. As a precaution against starting air line explosions, different safety features are fitted. These include the *relief valve*. This is fitted on the common air manifold which supplies air to the cylinder head. Normally fitted at the end of the manifold, it lifts the valve in the event of excess pressure inside the manifold. The advantage of the relief valve is that it will sit back after removing the excess pressure. Thus, a continuous supply of air is fed to the engine. A *bursting disc* is fitted in the starting air pipe and consists of a perforated disc protected by a sheet of material that bursts in the event of excessive pressure caused by air line explosion. It also consists of a protective cap. If the engine is required to run even after the disc has ruptured, the cap will cover the holes when it is turned. This ensures that during manoeuvring or traffic, air is continuously fed to the engine. The *non-return valve* is unidirectional valve positioned between the air manifold and the air receiver. This prevents the explosion from reaching the air bottle. A *flame arrestor* is a small unit consisting of several tubes which arrest flames coming out of the cylinder through any leaking starter air valves. It is attached to every cylinder before the starter air valve.

To prevent starting air line explosions from happening, the following measures should be performed: (a) ensure all safety devices are fitted and working correctly; (b) always drain the air bottle during every watch; (c) the auto drain should be checked for proper functioning; (d) the air compressor should be well maintained to avoid oil carryover; (e) the oil separation discharger should be checked; (f) the starting air manifold pipe should be cleaned and checked for paint deformation, this will indicate overheating of the pipe; (g) the starting air valve should be overhauled regularly to avoid leakage; and (h) the starting air valve seat should be inspected and lapped.

OILY WATER SEPARATOR

One of the biggest problems that ships face is oil pollution. Ships produce oily water mixtures every day. This oily water needs to be separated before it can be discharged. MARPOL, adopted in November 1973, regulates the management of oil pollution from ships at Annex I. Annex I restricts the acceptable oil content in bilge water that a vessel can legally discharge at sea. It is now a requirement for all vessels to carry an oil discharge monitoring

114   Principles of ship architecture and engineering

and control system along with an oil filtering system commonly referred to as *Oily Water Separator* (OWS). As the name suggests, the function of the OWS is to separate oil particles from the discharge water. Discharge water may come from any number of sources including the engine room, cargo hold bilges, oil tanks, and oil-contaminated spaces. As per the MARPOL regulations, the oil content in water processed by the OWS must be less than 15 parts per million of oil. Furthermore, MARPOL Annex I, regulation 4, paragraphs 2, 3, and 6, states any direct discharge of oil or oily water mixture into the open sea is strictly prohibited. The regulation further stipulates that oily water mixtures should be treated before they can be discharged. Moreover, MARPOL Annex I further state that for ships over 400 gross tonnes, oily water discharge may only be performed in accordance with the following procedures: (a) the ship is en route; (b) the oily mixture is processed through an OWS filter meeting the requirements of regulation 14 of MARPOL Annex I; (c) after passing through the OWS, the oil content of the effluent without dilution must not exceed 15 parts per million. If the vessel is located around the polar regions, any discharge of oil or oily mixtures is strictly prohibited. Furthermore, MEPC 107(49) mandates that the bilge alarm or Oil Content Monitor (OCM), which provides internal recording of alarm conditions, must be certified by an approved authority. To be certified, certain criteria must be met. These are (a) the OCM and the OWS must be tamper-proof; (b) it must activate and sound an alarm whenever freshwater is used for cleaning or zeroing purposes; and (c) the OWS must be capable of achieving 15 parts per million using type C emulsion.

The OWS consists of three main components: a *separator unit*, a filter unit, and the *oil content monitor and control unit*. The *separator unit (SU)* consists of catch plates which are located inside a coarse separating compartment and an oil-collecting chamber. Oil, having a lower density than water, passes between the catch plates and rises into the oil collecting chamber. The rest of the non-flowing oil mixture settles down into the fine settling compartment. After a short period, more oil separates and collects in the oil-collecting chamber. The oil content of the water which passes through this unit contains around 100 parts per million. A control valve, which may be pneumatic or electronic, releases the separated oil into the designated OWS sludge tank. A heater may be incorporated into the unit for the smooth flow and separation of the oil and water. Where fitted, the heater is usually located either in the middle or the bottom part of the unit (depending on the area of operation and the capacity of the separator equipment). This first stage helps remove physical impurities to achieve a finer standard of purification. The *filter unit* (FU) consists of a separate unit whose input comes from the discharge of the first unit. The FU consists of three stages: (a) the filter stage; (b) the coalescer stage; and (c) the collecting chamber. In the first stage, the impurities and particles are separated by the filter and settle at the bottom of the chamber for removal. At the second stage, the coalescer induces a coalescence process in which the oil droplets join to increase their size. This happens by breaking down the surface tension between the oil droplets within the mixture. These larger oil molecules rise above the mixture in the collecting chamber and are then removed. The output from this unit should be less than 15 parts per million to meet the legal discharge criteria. If the oil content in the water is more than 15 parts per million then maintenance work such as filter cleaning or the renewal of the filters is required. A freshwater inlet connection is also provided to the FU to clean and flush the filter. This is usually done before and after the operation of the SU.

The *Oil Content Monitor* (OCM) *and Control Unit* (CU) function as two parts for monitoring and controlling. The parts per million of oil is continuously monitored by the OCM; if the parts per million are too high the OCM will sound an alarm and feed data to the CU. The CU continuously monitors the output signal of the OCM and, if the alarm sounds, will prevent the discharge of oily water by operating a three-way solenoid valve. There are normally three solenoid valves commanded by the CU located in the first unit oil collecting

Primary ship engineering systems 115

chamber, the second unit oil collecting chamber, and on the discharge side of the OWS. When the OCM alarm sounds, the three-way valve discharges the oily mixture into a sludge tank. A small freshwater pipe is fitted to the OCM for flushing. Whenever this line is used, an alarm is sounded and recorded in the OCM log. This ensures there is an accurate record to confirm the discharge valve was shut during the flushing operation. The OWS is usually operated by the chief engineer only, therefore training levels on the OWS system for subordinate crew members are usually negligible.

LUBRICATION SYSTEMS

Main engine lubrication

Lubrication of the main engine is necessary to maintain the various components in good working condition. Lubrication prevents the parts that touch from overheating caused by friction. It also removes debris and impurities. There are several types of lubrication systems used on ships. The first is *hydrodynamic lubrication* where a thin layer of oil is formed between the moving surfaces. The film is formed by the motion of the moving parts and the self-generated pressure. One component where hydrodynamic lubrication is used is around the main bearing and the journal of the crankshaft. The second system uses *hydrostatic lubrication*. This is where the oil film cannot be formed due to the motion of the moving parts, which means the oil pressure has to be supplied externally. For slow-moving heavy parts, the relative motion is not sufficient to provide self-generated pressure for lubrication hence pressure is provided externally with the help of a pump. In *boundary Lubrication*, a thin film of oil is placed between two rubbing surfaces, which otherwise might make surface contact. Boundary lubrication is used in relatively slow-speed, high-contact pressure and rough surfaces. With e*lastohydrodynamic lubrication*, the lubricating film thickness changes considerably in accordance with the elastic deformation of the part's surfaces. This is seen in line or at the point of contact between rolling or sliding surfaces; for instance, between rolling contact bearings and meshing gear teeth.

In addition to the above, the main engine has three separate lubricating oil (LO) systems. These are (a) the main LO system; (b) the cylinder oil system; and (c) the turbocharger LO system.

The main or crankcase lubrication system is supplied by one of two pumps: one which continuously operates and the other which is on standby. The standby pump is set to automatically start should there be a reduction in the lubricating oil pressure or primary pump failure. The main LO pumps take their suction from the main engine sump tank and discharge oil via the main LO cooler, which takes away the heat. An automatic backflushing filter unit with a magnetic core helps to remove metal debris. The plate-type LO cooler is cooled from the low temperature central cooling freshwater system. The supply pressure in the main lubrication system depends on design and requirement, and is generally around 4.5 kg/cm². LO supply to the cooler is via a three-way valve which enables some oil to bypass the cooler. The three-way valve maintains a temperature of 45°C (113°F) at the LO inlet to the engine. The main LO system supplies oil to the main bearings, camshaft, and camshaft drive. A branch of lube oil goes to an articulated arm or a telescopic pipe to the crosshead from where it performs three functions: (a) some oil travels up the piston rod to cool the piston and then comes down; (b) some oil lubricates the crosshead bearing and the shoe guides; and (c) the remaining oil passes through a hole drilled in the rod connecting to the bottom end bearing. A branch of LO is led to the hydraulic power supply unit for actuation of exhaust valves, to the thrust bearings, to the moment compensator, and the torsional vibration damper. The cooling effect of the oil at the vibration dampers is very important.

Two-stroke main engine lubrication

In this situation, we must assume the engine is stopped and is being prepared for start-up. First, check the level of oil in the main engine sump tank and replenish if necessary. Ensure that the low temperature central cooling system is operating and that freshwater is circulating through the main lube oil cooler. Ensure the pressure gauges and instrumentation valves are open and that the instruments are reading correctly. Ensure that steam heating is applied to the main LO sump tank if the temperature of the LO is low. Set the line and make sure the correct valves are open.[3] Select one main LO pump as the master (duty) pump and the other as the standby pump.[4] Keep the LO system circulating and allow the temperature of the system to gradually increase to normal operating temperature. Check the outlet flows from the individual units. Check that the temperatures are similar and that all pressure gauges are reading correctly. When the lubricating system temperatures and pressures are stable, the engine may be started. At this point, the main engine lubrication system is replenished from the main LO storage tank. The main engine LO purifier takes suction from the main engine LO sump and purifies the oil. Its feed temperature is maintained around 90°C (194°F) (as this allows maximum density) to allow efficient separation. The engine LO must be tested frequently to determine whether it is fit for further service. Samples should be taken from the circulating oil and not directly from the sump tank.

Some main engine lubrication systems also have a subsystem depending on whether the main engine is cam-less or has a camshaft. In cam-less engines, a branch from the LO inlet to the main engine is provided to the hydraulic power supply unit. The function of HPSU is to hydraulically control the fuel injection and exhaust valve actuators and to drive the cylinder lubrication units. In main engines with a camshaft, the lubrication system feeds the camshaft roller guides and bearings, which actuates the exhaust valves and the fuel pump. The main engine LO sump tank is located under the engine in the double bottom and is surrounded by cofferdams. A sounding pipe is used to determine the level of LO in the sump. A sounding pipe is used for the cofferdam to indicate if there is any leakage. The cofferdam needs to be inspected on a regular basis to determine whether there are any leaks. The main engine LO sump consists of a level gauge, sounding pipe, air vent pipe, heating steam coil, manholes, suction pipe and valves for the LO pump, and LO purifiers.

Turbocharger-bearing lubricating system

The turbocharger bearing lubricating system can be completely separate from the main engine lubricating system or it can be fed through the main engine lubricating system, depending on the design. It is essential to have a separate filter for turbocharger lubrication, which is generally a duplex filter. From the duplex filter outlet, the turbocharger LO flows to the inlet manifold supplying the turbochargers. The outlet of LO from the turbochargers have a sight glass to ensure the flow is continuous. Under normal circumstances, the LO supply is maintained to the turbochargers to ensure that they are always available for service and to prevent damage. An LO supply must be maintained when the engine is stopped, as natural draught through the turbocharger will cause the rotor to turn. Hence, the bearings must be continuously lubricated.

Cylinder lubrication system

The load-dependent lubrication of the cylinders is performed by a separate cylinder lubrication system. Cylinder lubrication is required to lubricate the piston rings to reduce friction between the rings and the liner, to provide a seal between the rings and the liner, and to reduce corrosive wear by neutralising the acidity of the combustion products. The alkalinity of the cylinder lubricating oil should match the sulphur content of the HFO supplied to the engine. If the engine is run on LSFO for prolonged periods, advice must be sought from the cylinder oil supplier and the engine manufacturer as to which is the most suitable cylinder oil to use. The ability of an oil to react with an acidic reagent, which indicates its alkalinity, is expressed as TBN; this stands for Total Base Number. The TBN should correspond to the sulphur percentage of the fuel oil to neutralise the acidic effect of combustion. If the engine runs off HSFO, then high TBN grade cylinder oils must be used. When the main engine is 'changed over' to LSFO or LSMGO, then low TBN cylinder oil should be used. There are two important subsystems used in modern lubrication systems. The first is the *Accumulation and Quill System* designed by *Sulzer Engines (Wärtsilä)* and the second is the *Cylinder Lubricating Unit Pump to Orifices in the Liner* as designed by *MAN B&W*.

The cylinder LO is pumped from the cylinder oil storage tank to the cylinder oil measuring tank. This should contain sufficient LO for two days' cylinder LO consumption. Cylinder LO is fed to the cylinder lubrication system by gravity from the measuring tank; a heater is located in the gravity line and pipe. The pipes are electrically 'trace heated' where the outer surface of the pipe is maintained at a steady 45°C (113°F) temperature. Before starting the main engine, it is necessary to pre-lubricate the liners. Pre-lubrication before the start can be done manually or by following a sequence in the bridge manoeuvring system. This is determined by two criteria: (a) the cylinder oil dosage must be proportional to the sulphur content of the fuel; and (b) the cylinder oil dosage must be proportional to the engine load, i.e., the cylinder fuel supply. The quantity of cylinder oil injected at the individual injection points is controlled by the cylinder lubrication control system. Each cylinder LO injector (quill) serves as a non-return valve which is opened by the pressure directed at it by the lubricator control system. The cylinder oil feed rates can be adjusted, but these adjustments must be made by authorised personnel only. Correct cylinder lubrication is essential for efficient engine operation as it helps to minimise lubricating oil costs and maintenance costs. It is essential that the cylinder lubricators are correctly set and that the correct cylinder LO is used for the fuel being burned. No adjustment should be made to the engine cylinder lubrication system without the authorisation of the chief engineer.

The cylinder oil measuring tank is replenished from the cylinder oil storage tank using the cylinder oil shifting pump. In the event the electrically driven cylinder oil shifting pump should fail, a hand-operated pump may be used. The electrically driven cylinder oil shifting pump is started manually, though a high-level switch in the cylinder oil measuring tank stops the pump when the tank level reaches the correct value. In addition, the tank is fitted with a low-level alarm. A separate cylinder oil storage tank is provided for when LSHO is used. The cylinder oil from this tank must be used when the main engine is changed to LSHFO operation. The cylinder oil measuring tank has an overflow system via a sight glass; the overflow line has a three-way valve which must be set to direct the overflow oil to whichever cylinder oil storage tank is in operation.

Piston rod gland and scavenge space drain system

The piston rod gland or stuffing box provides a seal for the piston rod as it passes through the separating plate between the crankcase and the scavenge airspace. The stuffing box has two sets of segmented rings that are in contact with the piston rod; the upper set of rings scrape crankcase oil from the piston rod, and the lower set of rings prevents oily deposits in the scavenge space from entering the crankcase. In the middle of the stuffing box, there is a 'dead space' which should normally be dry if the rings are working effectively. Any oil or scavenge space material that enters this space is drained directly to the oily bilge drain tank.

NOTES

1. It should be mentioned that the shipping industry has invested heavily in renewable and alternative energies, such as wind and solar power generation.
2. White metal alloys include antimony, tin, lead, cadmium, bismuth, and zinc.
3. It is normally assumed that main engine lubricating valves are open.
4. The main LO pumps have large motors and are generally fitted for auto transformer starting; after a start, the auto transformer must be allowed to cool down for 20 minutes before another start is attempted. Never attempt to restart before 20 minutes has elapsed between starts.

Chapter 9

Auxiliary ship engineering systems

Marine auxiliary engines are designed to maintain continuity of operation to provide an uninterrupted power supply to various ship systems. Shipboard power is generated using a prime mover and an alternator which work together. For this, an alternating current generator is used. The generator works on the principle that when the magnetic field around a conductor varies, a current is induced. The generator consists of a stationary set of conductors wound in coils on an iron core. This is known as the stator. A rotating magnet called the rotor turns inside the stator producing the magnetic field. This field cuts across the conductor, generating an induced electromagnetic force (EMF) as the mechanical input causes the rotor to turn. The magnetic field is generated by induction (in a brushless alternator) and by an energised rotor, winding by DC current through a series of slip rings and brushes.

POWER DISTRIBUTION

Onboard power distribution needs to be supplied efficiently throughout the ship. For this, a power distribution system is used. The distribution system consists of different components. These include the *ship generator*, which consists of the prime mover and alternator; the *main switch board*, which is a metal enclosure taking power from the diesel generator and supplying it to different machinery systems; *bus bars* which act as a carrier and allow the transfer of load from one point to another; circuit breakers which act as a switch and in unsafe condition can be tripped to avoid breakdown and accidents; fuses, which are a safety device for machinery; transformers to step up or step down the voltage.[1] Power is supplied through circuit breakers to large auxiliary machinery at high voltage; for smaller supplies a fuse and miniature circuit breaker are used. The distribution system uses three wires which can be neutrally insulated or earthed; an insulated system is preferred over earthed systems, as during an earth fault, essential machinery such as steering gear can be lost.

Synchronising the ship generators

Synchronising an incoming generator or alternator is very important before paralleling it with another generator. The synchronisation of the generator is done with the help of a synchroscope or with the three-bulb method in case of emergency. It is of paramount importance that before paralleling the generators the frequency and voltage of the generators are matched. There are two methods for synchronising the generators on a ship. One is the normal method, and the other is the emergency method.

DOI: 10.1201/9781003244615-11

119

120 Principles of ship architecture and engineering

Synchroscope method

The synchroscope consists of a small motor with coils on two poles connected across two phases. This is connected to the red and yellow phases of the incoming machine. The armature windings are supplied from the red and yellow phases of the switchboard bus bars. The bus bar circuit consists of inductance and resistance connected in parallel. The inductor circuit has the effect of delaying the current by 90 degrees relative to the current in resistance. These dual currents are fed into the synchroscope by way of slip rings to the armature windings. This produces a rotating magnetic field. The polarity of the poles changes alternatively in a north/south direction with changes in the red and yellow phases of the incoming machine. The rotating field reacts with the poles by turning the rotor in a clockwise or anti-clockwise direction. If the rotor is moving in a clockwise direction, this means the incoming machine is running faster than the bus bar and slower when running in an anticlockwise direction. Generally, it is preferred to adjust the alternator speed to slightly higher, which will move the pointer on the synchroscope in a clockwise direction. The breaker is closed just before the pointer reaches the noon position, at which point the incoming machine is in phase with the bus bar.

Emergency synchronising lamps or three bulb method

This method is generally used when there is a failure of the synchroscope. In case of failure, a standby method should be available to synchronise the alternator. In this method, three lamps are connected between three phases of the bus bar and the incoming generator. The lamps are connected in this manner because if they were connected across, the same phase lamps would go on and off together when the incoming machine is out of phase with the switchboard. In this method, two lamps will illuminate, and one lamp will remain unlit when the incoming machine is phased with the bus bar. The movement of the illuminated and unlit lamps indicates whether the incoming machine is running fast or slow. In other words, there will be a moment when lamp A will be unlit and lamp B and C will be illuminated; similarly there will be an instance when B is unlit, and A and C illuminated. This example indicates that the machine is running fast and the movement of the lamps from unlit to illuminated indicates a clockwise movement. A clockwise movement indicates fast and an anti-clockwise direction indicates slow running of the incoming generator. The lamps must be connected in this fashion, as otherwise the same phase lamps will go on and off together when the incoming generator is out of phase with the switchboard.

BLACKOUT SITUATIONS

Blackout is one condition every seafarer is familiar with. It is also the one situation everyone on board is terrified of as brings the ship to a complete standstill. The ship effectively becomes dead in the water. A blackout condition is caused when the main propulsion plant and associate machinery such as the boiler, purifier, and other auxiliaries stop operating due to the malfunction of the generator and alternator. With technologies and automation, measures are provided to avoid blackout situations by means of auto-load sharing and auto-standby systems. These provide redundancy by having the generators run in parallel or the standby comes on load automatically if the running diesel generator fails. In the event of blackout, the following precautions and actions should be taken. The EOW must immediately inform the OOW about the condition; they should also call for additional manpower and inform the chief engineer. If the main propulsion plant is running, then bring the fuel lever to zero position. Close the feed of the running purifier to avoid the overflow and waste of fuel. If the auxiliary boiler is running, shut the main steam stop valve to maintain the steam pressure. Investigate and rectify the malfunction. Before starting the generator set, start the pre-lubrication priming pump (if the supply is given from the emergency generator) otherwise use the manual priming handle. Start the generator and take it on load. Immediately start the main engine lube oil pump and main engine jacket water pump. Reset the breakers and start the other machinery and systems. Reset the breakers that are included in the preferential tripping sequence.

FUEL OIL PURIFIER

Every engine room machinery system needs systematic step-by-step starting and stopping procedures to ensure smooth running. Starting the fuel oil purifier also involves several important steps and checks. These include: (a) *checking the oil level in the Purifier Gear Case*. If the oil is not at the required level, the insufficient lubrication will damage the gears and other rotating parts (shaft, bearings etc.) in the purifier gear case; (b) *ensure the break is in the release position*. The purifier break, which is provided near the gear at the bottom of the purifier, must be in the release position. If the break is not released, the purifier will fail to reach its required speed and the motor current will increase. Moreover, this will cause the brakes to wear down; (c) *open the inlet and outlet valves*. Always ensure the inlet and outlet valves of the purifier are in the open position. If the discharge valve is not open, the purifier will overflow resulting in oil in the sludge side. Similarly, if the suction valve is not open, the purifier will not get the necessary oil supply; (d) *open the tank valves*. Check the valves of the specific tank (service or settling) where the discharge from the purifier is to be sent. If the tank valve is not open, the back pressure in the line will increase leading to overflow in the purifier; (e) *check the level of operating water*. If there is a separate operating water tank provided, check the water level. If the operating water is not sufficient, the purifier ball will not lift, resulting in the sludge ports remaining in the open position; (f) *check the feed pump*. Check that the purifier feed pump is running properly, together with the oil pressure and temperature. Some purifiers are provided with attached gear pumps for supplying fuel to the purifier. In such cases, ensure that the oil temperature is sufficient to ensure smooth running of the gear pump (via shaft and key). If the temperature is low, the oil viscosity will be high, which may lead to the breaking of the key that connects the shaft and the gear pump, thus stopping the oil supply; (g) *ensure the heater valves are open*. Ensure the fuel oil valves to the steam heater are open before opening the steam line valve near the heater. If the steam valve is opened first, the tubes can get damaged, leading to the ingress of water into the oil; (h) *increase the temperature*. Increase the temperature of the fuel oil to the limit provided on the purifier's digital control panel. In all automated purifiers, the control panel is provided with a pre-set minimum temperature limit. The purifier will not start until the fuel oil reaches this temperature; (i) *check for any abnormal sounds or vibrations*. Check to see or hear if there are any abnormal sounds or vibrations during start-up. If there are, shut down the purifier immediately and rectify the fault completely before attempting to restart; (k) *check the solenoid valves*. The solenoid valves should be operating properly; confirm this by checking the lights on the solenoid valves. If the lights are not working, take a screwdriver and bring it near to the top surface of the solenoid valve. When the solenoid starts working, the magnetic force will attract the screwdriver to the valve body. If the solenoid valves are not working properly, the purifier will also stop operating. For example, if the operating water line solenoid valve is not working properly, the ball will not lift; or if the high-pressure water line solenoid is not working, then the purifier will not de-sludge.

ENGINE ROOM DRAINS

Within the engine room, there are several drains provided to prevent water build-up and damage to machinery. These drains must be closely monitored by officers when carrying out their watchkeeping rounds. There are four drains that are of especial importance as their maloperation can have serious consequences in the engine room. The type of drain we need to be mindful of is the *air cooler condensate drain*. The air cooler condensate drain is one of the most important drains in the engine room. The charge air, when cooled, passes its dew point temperature, which generates a substantial volume of condensate. The volume of condensate generated depends on the humidity and ambient air temperature of the engine room and on the pressure and temperature of the charge air itself. It also depends on the temperature of the cooling water by which the air is cooled. This means proper condensate drainage is needed for the safe operation of the engine. This is because condensate consists of sediments such as dust which can damage the internal mechanisms of the engines. If the drain lines are not cleaned properly, water and sediment can find their way into the combustion chamber of the engine. Over time, this mixture may peel off paint and corrode the surface of the charge air chamber and the flange. It can cause the failure of the intake valve. Peeled paint is often the main reason why drain lines get choked. Furthermore, as the condensate is incompressible, over time, it may break the piston and even bend the connecting rod, causing the engine to breakdown.

To prevent this from happening, it is generally recommended by marine engine manufacturers to remove the condensate regularly by installing a float chamber from the air cooler drain. When the water level rises in the float chamber the float rises causing the valve to open. This allows the condensate to harmlessly drain away. It is quite common for newbuilds (and existing builds) to have an orifice of three millimetres (0.11 in) installed on the drain line. This tends to clog quite often by the build-up of sediments present in the condensate drain. It is advisable to replace this with a five-millimetre (0.19 in) orifice instead. Several engine manufacturers have removed the ball float from inside the chamber or the condensate drain tank to get rid of the clogging problem. Instead, they have recommended the installation of a ball valve which may be opened partially to allow the removal of condensate. Whilst this is more effective, there is the risk the ball valve may be closed accidentally. There is also the possibility of the air cooler drain line getting choked from within due to condensate and sediment resting for prolonged periods. For this reason, the intake air chamber should also be inspected as well. If the countermeasures mentioned above are followed, then the possibility of problems generated by the clogging of the air cooler condensate drains can be largely avoided. That said, the regular opening of the float chamber is recommended by most engine manufacturers as an ongoing precautionary measure. The interval for opening the drains and intake air chamber should be adjusted according to the engine running hours. This is best undertaken as part of the ship's planned maintenance schedule.

The second drain of note is the *auxiliary engine turbocharger drain*. Auxiliary engine turbochargers are installed with a drain which must be regularly checked every day during morning and evening rounds. There is a faint probability that the drain might become clogged by particles of combustion from the exhaust gases being carried over. Supercharging is one method that is employed by the auxiliary engines to increase their efficiency. This is achieved by increasing the weight of the air that is supplied to the engine. This helps to burn more fuel per stroke of the engine, which increases the power output. Turbochargers are used to increase the weight of the air. The turbocharger is driven by the exhaust gas from the engine, which in turn drives a compressor wheel to compress the ambient air and hence supply charge air to the engine. Several types of fuel oil may be used including HSFO, VLSFO, LSMGO and ULSFO.[2] From 2020 new marine fuels have been introduced following the global sulphur cap or IMO 2020.[3] Existing ships fitted with scrubber systems may still use HSFO, whereas ships without a scrubber must use VLSFO, which apparently is something very similar to HSFO as it is blended with LSMGO. Turbochargers that use HSFO and VLSFO are frequently subject to fouling. This originates in the fuel burn process and is most often caused by low load operation of the engine. This causes incomplete combustion and the build-up of carbon soot in the exhaust gas. One way to prevent this from happening is to use good quality fuel and by maintaining the correct viscosity. This is generally recommended by engine manufacturers to be between 12 and 18 Cst. Fouling reduces the turbocharger's efficiency which may increase exhaust temperatures and fuel consumption. Therefore, turbine side cleaning is necessary to ensure the efficient operation of the turbochargers. This will further help in increasing overall engine performance.

The washing system installed on all the auxiliary engines allows the cleaning of the turbine side while the engine is operated on a certain load. There are two methods used for turbocharger washing: for older turbochargers, three x30-second injections of high-pressure water; or for newer models, one single injection of high-pressure water for 10 minutes. Whichever method is used, it is strongly recommended the turbocharger is washed every 100 operating hours. During the washing, the drain must be opened for clear water to pass at a load of about 20 to 40% of the maximum rated value. There have been some cases of water accumulating in the turbine casing after the washing of the turbine side. This can have deleterious effects on the turbocharger. One noticeable effect is the development of holes in the turbocharger gas outlet casing. This has mainly happened due to the incomplete drainage of water during the periodical cleaning of the turbocharger turbine and the ingress of rainwater from the funnel. This water causes corrosion of the turbocharger outlet casing eventually leading to a hole in the casing. In severe cases, the drain may clog resulting in water collecting inside the casing. This has been known to mix with the exhaust gases from the combustion chamber to form dry soot. If not cleaned, this soot can stick to the turbine wheel and nozzle ring. If this happens, there is the potential for the turbocharger to lose its bearing and stop rotating. This will cause the generator to seize during operation. The likely consequence is the vessel losing turbocharged power and hence the loss of an important ancillary operation.

To prevent this happening, the drain should be checked every day during rounds for the accumulation of water. Furthermore, during and after washing the turbocharger the drain must be left open for at least 30 minutes so that all water can drain from the casing. During heavy rainfall, it is strongly advised to open the drain connected to the gas outlet casing. If the turbocharger is losing rpm, then it must be opened immediately and checked for possible traces of soot inside the casing.

The third type of drains of note are the *fuel oil settling and service tank drains*. These two drains are the most important drains in the engine room. The fuel oil settling and service tank drains are used to remove water from the tanks which is carried over when fuel oil is transferred from the bunker tank to the settling tank. Fuel oil is the post-refining product that is generated after blending the distillate and the residual fuel oil. During this process, water and various sediments develop in the blended product which arise due to the cleaning of the tanks. These unwanted sediments and water are unavoidable and need to be removed. The water present in fuel oil (in small quantities) is generally removed by a fuel oil centrifugal separator, commonly known as the purifier. The purifier may fail to remove the water if it is present in large quantities letting it carry over to the fuel oil supply pumps. Once the fuel oil has passed through the fuel oil purifiers, there are no other steps for the removal of water from the fuel oil line which is fed to the main and auxiliary engines. This means a failure in the purifier can lead to large water deposits entering the engines. If water finds its way to the auxiliary engines, then this will most certainly result in a vessel-wide blackout. Worst still, it will be extremely difficult to revive the engines until all the water is removed. If auxiliary engines cannot start, then the main engine will not either. In effect, the ship will be dead in the water.

Similarly, if water finds its way into the boiler, then the boiler will be very difficult to fire and there will be no steam generated to heat up the tanks and the fuel oil. Once water gets into the system, draining it becomes a very difficult and onerous task. The fuel oil settling and service drains should be opened once every watch and in so doing, it should be made certain that any water is removed completely from the system. This is because the system is a closed cycle and hence the water removed from the settling and service drains goes back to the fuel oil drain tank, which again is transferred to the settling tank. Without physically removing the water, it will just recirculate. Fuel oil settling and service tanks are often provided with two suction valves. These are mainly low suction and high suction valves. The high suction valve is used to prevent the shut-down of the main engine, auxiliary engine and the boilers in case the tank is contaminated by large quantities of water. The low suction valve works continuously.

The fourth and final drain is the *air receiver drain*. This is used to drain water that has collected in the air bottle from the condensation passing over the compressor. The temperature of the air compressed by the compressor is in the range of 90–100°C. This air contains a considerable quantity of water and oil carried over in the form of mist, which generally condenses in the air bottle and is then collected in the bottom of the air receiver. Compressed air is used for starting the main engine and auxiliary engines and is also used for instrumentation and controls which are stored in a separate air bottle. This air is used to drive the various pneumatic tools on board. Furthermore, some ships are provided with air-driven soot blowers for the economisers. The compressed air on board a ship can be categorised as starting air, service air, and control air. Any water and oil present in small quantities can be drained by the two drain valves installed in the bottom of the compressor. This water and oil, if not drained, can find their way to the main engine (as starting air) and hence enter the combustion chamber of the relevant cylinder. As water is incompressible, this is disastrous for the engine. Similarly, if water mixed with oil enters the starter air line, it can cause an explosion. It is therefore important that the main and auxiliary engines are blown through to dislodge any water or oil particles before the engines are started. The air receiver drains must be emptied every day in the morning and at least once during every watch, if the engine room is manned.

To drain the air receiver, there is a specific method. Each air bottle is provided with two valves in the drain line; one connected directly to the pressure vessel and the other next to it. The one connected directly to the pressure vessel must be fully opened and the one next to it must be throttled. This is done to prevent leakage of the valve connected directly to the pressure vessel. An air bottle inspection must be carried out to ascertain the condition of the internal wall and the mountings connected therein. The *starting air line drain* is similar to the starting air receiver drain, as it is used to drain the moisture and sediments that collect in the starting air line after the engine is secured. This drain is supposed to be opened every time the engine is secured. Moisture and oil tend to condense in the starting air line as is the case with the air receivers. This must be drained regularly. Unlike the air receivers, however, these drains cannot be opened when the main engine is running and hence can only be opened when the main engine is stopped. Again, if water gets into the starting air system, it can lead to severe consequences for the engine. This drain should be opened after the main engine is secured and kept open to drain any residual oil or water that is present in the line. This should become standard practice by all engineers every time the main engine is secured.

Auxiliary ship engineering systems   125

SCRUBBER SYSTEMS

Scrubbers or Exhaust Gas Cleaning Systems (EGCS) are used to remove harmful particulate matter such as sulphur oxides (SOx) and nitrogen oxides (NOx) from the exhaust gasses generated from the fuel combustion process. These scrubbing systems have been developed to minimise the pollution given off by ships. Sulphur emissions to the atmosphere by seagoing vessels are limited by new and updated international regulations, which came into effect on 1 January 2020 under the MARPOL. IMO regulations mandate that the sulphur content in fuels carried by merchant vessels must be limited to 0.5% globally and 0.10% m/m in Emission Control Areas (ECA). These include the Baltic Sea, North Sea, US and Canada, and the Caribbean Sea. Prior to this, the maximum sulphur cap in fuels was 3.5% m/m. Compliance with the new regulations requires that vessels either use expensive fuels with low sulphur content or clean the exhaust gases using scrubbing systems. As fuel costs are highly volatile, the industry has seen a surge in the installation of exhaust gas scrubbers.

Operational principles of the scrubber system

Exhaust gas streams are passed inside the scrubber where an alkaline scrubbing material neutralises the acidic nature of the exhaust gases and removes any particulate matter from the exhaust. The used scrubbing material is then collected with wash water which may be stored or immediately disposed of as effluent. The cleaned exhaust is passed out of the system and into the atmosphere. The scrubbing material is designed to remove specific impurities such as SOx or NOx. For desulphurisation purposes, marine scrubbers use lime or caustic soda. These allow the sulphur-based salts which are produced after treatment to be easily discharged as they do not pose a threat to the marine environment. Scrubbers may use seawater, freshwater with added calcium, or sodium absorbents or pellets of hydrated lime as the scrubbing medium. To increase the contact time between the scrubbing material and the exhaust gas, packed beds consisting of gas-pollutant removal reagents (such as limestone) are used inside the scrubbers. These packed beds slow down the vertical flow of water inside the scrubbers and intensify the exhaust gas cooling and acidic water neutralisation process.

Classification of marine scrubbers

On the basis of their operation, marine scrubbers can be classified as dry and wet scrubbers. Dry scrubbers employ solid lime as the alkaline scrubbing material. This removes the sulphur dioxide from the exhaust gasses. Wet scrubbers use water that is sprayed into the exhaust gas for the same purpose. Wet scrubbers are further classified into closed-loop or open-loop scrubbers.

Wet scrubbers

In closed-loop scrubbers, freshwater or seawater may be used as the scrubbing fluid. When freshwater is used in closed-loop scrubbers, the quality of water surrounding the ship has no effect on scrubber performance. Open-looped scrubbers consume seawater. Hybrid scrubbers can utilise both closed and open running modes either at the same time or by switching between the two. Seawater hybrid scrubbers can be operated in both closed and open mode. Inside the wet scrubber, the scrubbing liquid may be seawater or freshwater with chemical additives. The most common additives are caustic soda (NaOH) and limestone (CaCO3). Scrubbing liquid is sprayed into the exhaust gas stream through nozzles to distribute it

126 Principles of ship architecture and engineering

effectively. In most scrubbers the design is such that the scrubbing liquid moves downstream, although some scrubbers use an upstream flow.

The exhaust inlet of the scrubber can be made in the form of a venturi in which the gas enters at the top and water is sprayed in the high exhaust gas speed areas at the neck or above the neck in the form of a spray. The exhaust intake is either on the side or the bottom of the tower. The design of the scrubber ensures that the sulphur oxides present in the exhaust are passed through the scrubbing liquid with reacts to form sulphuric acid. When diluted with alkaline seawater, the sulphuric acid, which is highly corrosive, is neutralised. The wash water is then discharged into the open sea after being treated in a separator to remove any sludge. Mist eliminators are used in the scrubbing towers to remove any acid mist that forms in the chamber by separating droplets that are present in the inlet gas from the outlet gas stream. MARPOL regulations require that the wash water must be monitored before being discharged to ensure that its $_pH$ value is not too low. Since the alkalinity of seawater varies (e.g., by distance from land, volcanic activity, marine life, etc.) wet scrubbers are divided into two types: open-looped and closed-looped systems. Both systems have been combined into a hybrid system, which can employ the most suitable scrubbing action depending on the conditions of the voyage.

With open-looped scrubber systems, the system uses seawater as the scrubbing and neutralising media. No other chemicals are required for desulphurisation. The exhaust stream from the engine or boiler passes into the scrubber and is treated with the alkaline seawater. The volume of this seawater depends on the size of the engine and its power output. The system is extremely effective but requires a large pumping capacity, as the volume of seawater required is high. An open-looped system works perfectly well when the seawater has sufficient alkalinity. However, seawater which is at a high ambient temperature, freshwater, and even brackish water, are not effective and cannot be used. Therefore, open-looped scrubbers are not recommended for sea areas where the water salinity is not high enough, such as the Baltic Sea. The reactions involved in the open-looped scrubber system are:

$$SO_2(gas) + H_2O + \tfrac{1}{2}O_2 \rightarrow SO_4^{2-} + 2H + (Sulphate\,Ion + Hydrogen\,Ion)$$

$$HCO_3 + H^+ \rightarrow CO_2 + H_2O\,(Carbon\,Dioxide + Water)$$

The advantages of using the open-looped scrubber system include very few moving parts which means the design is simple and easy to install. Apart from de-fouling and operational checks, the system requires very little maintenance, and the system does not require storage for waste materials. The disadvantages of the system include the cooling of the exhaust gas; a large volume of seawater is required for efficient cleaning therefore the system consumes excessive power; the operation of the system depends on the alkalinity of the seawater and is not suitable for all maritime areas, therefore in ECA zones and ports, expensive fuels must be used.

The closed-loop scrubber system works on similar principles as the open-looped system. It uses freshwater treated with a chemical (usually sodium hydroxide) instead of seawater as the scrubbing media. The SOx from the exhaust gas is converted into sodium sulphate. Before being recirculated for use, the wash water from the closed-loop scrubber system is passed through a process tank where it is cleaned. The process tank is also used for the operation of a circulation pump which prevents the pump suction pressure from sinking too low. Ships can either carry freshwater in tanks or generate the required water from freshwater generators. Small amounts of wash water are removed at regular intervals to holding tanks where freshwater can be added to avoid the build-up of sodium sulphate in the system.

A closed-loop system requires almost half the volume of wash water required by open-loop systems however more tanks are required. These include a process tank or buffer tank, a holding tank (as overboard discharge is prohibited) and a storage tank capable of regulating its temperature between 20–50°C (68–122°F) for the sodium hydroxide which is usually used as a 50% aqueous solution. The dry sodium hydroxide also requires large storage space. The hybrid system is a combination of both wet types that can operate as an open-loop system when water conditions and the discharge regulations allow and as a closed-loop system at all other times. Hybrid systems are proving to be the most popular because of their ability to cope with different marine and regulatory conditions. The chemical reactions involved in the closed-loop system are:

$$2NaOH + SO_2 \rightarrow Na_2SO_3 + H_2O \, (Sodium \, Sulphite)$$

$$Na_2SO_3 + SO_2 + H_2O \rightarrow 2NaHSO_3 \, (Sodium \, Hydrogen \, Sulphite)$$

$$SO_2 \, (gas) + H_2O + \tfrac{1}{2}O_2 \rightarrow SO_4^{2-} + 2H^+$$

$$NaOH + H_2SO_4 \rightarrow NaHSO_4 + H_2O \, (Sodium \, Hydrogen \, Sulphate)$$

$$2NaOH + H_2SO_4 \rightarrow Na_2SO_4 + 2H_2O \, (Sodium \, Sulphate)$$

The advantages of the closed-loop system include the need for minimal maintenance; independence of the operating environment of the vessel; and eradication of the exhaust gas cooling problems associated with the wet scrubbing system. On the other hand, the disadvantages include the need for storage space for the buffer tank which holds the wastewater until it can be discharged; selective catalytic reduction systems must operate before the wet scrubbers; and fitting the system together, especially for dual-fuel engines, can be quite complex and costly.

Hybrid scrubber systems offer a simple solution for retrofitting vessels with scrubbers that are capable of operation on both open-loop and closed-loop configurations. These systems run on open-loop mode at sea and closed-loop mode in ECA zones and ports. They can be switched over with ease. As the system runs on lower costing fuels for longer periods of time and can be used virtually anywhere around the world, they more than justify the initial outlay. The advantages of the hybrid system include being suitable for long and short voyages; ships with hybrid systems can spend more time in ECA zones and in port than those with open-loop systems; and they use less expensive HFO. The disadvantages are more structural modifications are needed for installing the system; they require large storage spaces for chemicals and additives; and the system is costly and time consuming to install.

Dry scrubbers

Dry scrubbers work without water. Instead, pellets of hydrated lime are used to remove the sulphur. The scrubbers work at higher temperatures than their wet counterparts, which has the added benefit of burning off any soot and oily residues in the system. The calcium in the caustic lime granulates reacts with the sulphur dioxide in the exhaust gas to form calcium sulphite. Calcium sulphite is then air-oxidised to form calcium sulphate dehydrate. When mixed with water, this forms gypsum. The used pellets are stored on board for discharge in port. This is not considered a waste product as gypsum is used in fertiliser and construction materials. Dry scrubber systems consume less power than wet systems as they do not

128 Principles of ship architecture and engineering

require circulation pumps. However, they weigh much more than wet systems. The chemical reaction involved is:

$$SO_2 + Ca(OH)_2 \rightarrow CaSO_3 + H_2O \, (calcium \, sulphite)$$

$$CaSO_3 + \frac{1}{2}O_2 \rightarrow CaSO_4 \, (calcium \, sulphate)$$

$$SO_3 + Ca(OH)_2 \rightarrow CaSO_4 + H_2O \, (gypsum)$$

The advantages of using the dry over the wet system include the efficient removal of nitrogen and sulphur oxides; there is no production of liquid effluent that must be disposed of overboard; and the gypsum obtained after the exhaust gas cleaning process can be sold for use in various industrial applications. The disadvantages are that the system requires significant onboard storage to handle the dry bulk reactants and products associated with the process; this means there must be a ready supply of the reactants; and the reactants are costly, especially the urea needed for NOx abatement and calcium hydroxide for SOx abatement.

Choice of scrubber system

For a shipping company to select the most suitable kind of scrubber system to install on board, there are many factors to be considered. These include the installation spaces available on board, the area of operation and the chartering schedule of the ship, the power and output of the engine and boiler, the availability of freshwater on board, and the availability of power to run the system in different conditions. It is a well established fact that whenever machinery is operated it is impossible to achieve 100% work efficiency due to various factors including friction, heat dissipation, etc.

Reducing NOx and SOx emissions

When it comes to the ship's engine, a massive mechanical structure with several moving parts, the work efficiency achieved is approximately 70–85% during optimal working conditions. The combustion of gases inside the engine emits harmful exhaust gases into the atmosphere which leads to loss in the system and pollution of the marine environment. MARPOL Annex VI deals with restricting harmful emissions from ship engines and provides guidelines for the management of SOx and NOx. Several technologies have been introduced to reduce the level of harmful emissions produced by the ship's exhaust system. The presence of NOx in the marine engine's exhaust emission is due to the high combustion temperature which reacts with nitrogen in the air supplied for combustion. Various methods can be used to reduce ship NOx emissions. The first is the *Humid Air Method*. In this method, water vapour is mixed with the combustion air before it is supplied to the cylinder. Air from the turbocharger blower is passed through a cell that humidifies and chills the hot air taking moisture from the cooling water until air saturation is achieved. Generally, saline seawater is utilised in this method by heating it with jacket water and turbocharger heat. The leftover brine is disposed of overboard. This method alone can achieve a reduction in NOx by 70–80%. Second is *Exhaust Gas Recirculation* (EGR). As the name suggests, an amount of engine exhaust is returned to the scavenge space to mix with the air supplied to the cylinder for combustion. This reduces the air oxygen content and hence reduces the formation of NOx. Third is *Water Injection and Water Emulsion*. In this method, water is added to reduce the temperature of combustion, leading to low NOx emissions. With water emulsion, fuel is blended with water. The water is injected using a separate freshwater injector mounted in the cylinder head. This method has the disadvantage of increasing the specific fuel oil combustion and offers a reduction in NOx by only 20–45%.

The fourth method is using a *High Scavenge Pressure and Compression Ratio*. With HSP/CR, a large amount of air is introduced inside the cylinder to lower the combustion temperature and NOx emissions. Fifth is *Selective Catalytic Reduction*. The SCR is the most efficient method for reducing NOx emissions from ships (>90–95%). In this method, LSFO is used with the exhaust temperature maintained above 300°C (572°F). The exhaust gas is mixed with a water/urea solution which is then passed through the catalytic reactor. The only problem with SCR is the high installation and operating costs. The sixth method is to use the *two-stage turbocharger*. Developed by ABB, the two-stage turbocharger reduces the exhaust temperature in the intercoolers thereby reducing the NOx content in the exhaust. The seventh and last method is through *engine component modification*. Clearly it is better to design an engine that has the properties to reduce NOx formation during the combustion process rather than investing in expensive secondary measures. Integration of slide valve type fuel injectors with zero sack volume eliminates fuel dripping and after burning. This provides optimal cylinder temperature operation and minimal NOx formations.

SOx or sulphur oxides are formed during the combustion process because of the presence of sulphur in the fuel. Like NOx, there are various ways of minimising SOx emissions. The first is the use of *LSFO*. Although expensive, it is the most common method for complying with MARPOL Annex VI. Second is the use of *Exhaust Gas Scrubber Technology*. The exhaust gas from the engine is passed through the scrubber tower where it is showered with a cleansing liquid. Freshwater blended with caustic soda (NaOH) is used as the scrubbing liquid, which reduces SOx by 95%. The scrubbing water is then sent to a water treatment effluent emulsion breaking plant after which it can be discharged overboard. The third method involves *Cylinder Lubrication*. Good quality cylinder lubrication along with efficient control systems such as Pulse or Alpha Lubrication Systems can neutralise the sulphur in the fuel and reduce SOx emissions from the engine.

PUMPS

Almost every type of major machinery plant on ships is supported by some form of pump. In fact, none of the main machinery such as the main engine or boiler can run without pumps. From supplying fuel to the engine to discharging cargo in port, every single procedure is backed by a certain type of pump. Understanding the different types and functions of pumps is central to the work of the marine engineer. Likewise, recognising common problems in pumps and their symptoms is extremely important for safe and smooth operation of the engine room. There are several key parameters that marine engineers must manage to ensure the pumps are kept in good working order: (1) *Temperature*. While making engine room rounds, it is vital to check the motor temperature using a thermal gun or by feeling the motor by hand. Any abnormality or increase in temperature may indicate a problem in the pump-motor assembly. (2) *Current*. Ensure to monitor the pump motor amperage regularly. Any variation or abnormal change in the current will indicate a malfunction. (3) *Vibration*. Continuous monitoring of pump vibrations is very important. Any sudden or gradual increase in vibrations indicates loose foundation, loose coupling, misalignment, or worn-out shaft-bearing. (4) *Sound*. Regularly monitoring the pump's sound will determine the normal working volume of the pump. Any variation in this will indicate a malfunction. (5) *Pressure*. The main function of pumps is to supply/transfer liquids or semi-liquids with pressure. This means the rated pressure must be maintained. If the pressure reduces, check the pump and any associated parts (e.g., filters and valves). (6) *Running Hours*. Every mechanical part is designed for set running hours. Once the running hour of the pump is

130 Principles of ship architecture and engineering

over, it will need to be renewed. Maintain a log of the pump's running hours and change them at the required interval. (7) *Planned Maintenance*. Always ensure the planned maintenance schedule for the pump is followed. Overhauling of the pumps should be carried out as dictated by the PSM. (8) *Gland Packing and Seals*. Ensure that the gland packing and the mechanical seals of the pumps are in good condition. Attend to any leakage immediately. (9) *Motor/Prime Mover Condition*. A pump is either driven by an electric motor or a prime mover engine. Always ensure that the prime mover engine or the motor winding and its insulation are in good working condition. (10) *Correct Operating Procedures*. There are several different types of pumps in the ship's engine room and each one has a SOP. Therefore, marine engineers should ensure they know the correct SOP for each type of pump.

MAIN FIRE PUMPS

For any seafarer, working on board means dealing with several challenges on a daily basis for which they need to be prepared for at all times. The fire pumps, also popularly known as Marine Fifi Pumps, are essential safety equipment that helps seafarers to tackle emergency situations involving fire. Typically, centrifugal pumps are used as marine fire pumps as they have high flow capabilities and can swiftly handle water and foam. In the event of a fire on board, it is very important that sufficient water is available at high pressure. An alternative arrangement is made in case one fire pump fails to operate or its controls are inaccessible. For this purpose, multiple marine firefighting pumps are required on board. The main fire pumps installed on ships are located inside the ship's engine room, usually at the bottom platform. They are electrically driven from the main supply. It is very common to find them installed near general service pumps and ballast pumps. The general service pump lines are interconnected with the fire main and at times are used to provide water to the fire system. In some settings, they may also be called general service fire pumps. These pumps should never be used for pumping oil. A changeover arrangement may be provided to use the main fire pump for general service, but only when approved by class. The general service and main fire pump supply water throughout the vessel to the following locations: (a) the fire hose connections in the engine room, main deck, accommodation, shaft tunnel, and steering gear room; (b) the anchor washer in the fo'c'sle; (c) as driving water for the ejector fitted in the cargo hold bilges; (d) as driving water for the ejector fitted in the dangerous cargo hold bilges; and (e) to the swimming pool, if installed.

Capacity and requirements for main fire pumps

The number of fire pumps and their capacity will depend on the type of ship and its gross tonnage. For cargo ships of more than 1,000 gross tonnes, at least two fire pumps should be installed with an independent driving arrangement. For cargo ships that are less than 1,000 gross tonnes, the number of fire pumps will be decided by class. The fire pumps should be capable of discharging a quantity of water at not less than $^4/_3$ of the quantity provided by bilge pumps provided the total required capacity of the pumps needed does not exceed 180 m³/hr. Each main fire pump must have a capacity of not less than 80% of the total required capacity divided by the minimum number of required fire pumps but not less than 25 m³/hr with a minimum discharge of two water jets. If centrifugal fire pumps are used, a non-return valve must be fitted to prevent loss of water back through the open line when the pump is not working. Where positive displacement pumps are used instead a relief valve must be fitted to counter the rise in pressure if the line valve is closed when the pump is operated. The safe line pressure will depend on the design of the fire line and the capacity of the pump. These parameters are also decided by class.

Auxiliary ship engineering systems   131

EMERGENCY FIRE PUMP

On ships, every machinery is provided with a backup system, i.e., one duplex or spare system or an emergency backup system. For firefighting systems, the fire pump is an important piece of equipment and if it fails the complete fire line will become inoperable. As per SOLAS chapter I-2, part A regulation 4, all cargo ships over 2,000 gross tonnes and passenger ships over 1,000 gross tonnes must have an emergency fire pump in a separate space other than the engine room where the main fire pumps are situated. Only in special cases does SOLAS allow for the suction of the emergency pump from the same sea chest as the main fire pumps. This means the suction pipe must penetrate the engine room. Class will only allow this if the piping is of A-60 fire prevention standard. The suction of the emergency fire pump may be left open or opened using a remotely operated valve. The specific arrangements will again depend on the requirements set by class. In any case the emergency fire pump is driven in two ways: (a) by using a diesel engine; and (b) by using an electrical motor supplied from the emergency generator.

In the event of fire, and the main Fifi pump malfunctions (due to blackout, fire in the engine room, a problem in the main fire pump or its line etc.) the emergency fire pump must be used instead. As the pump is located outside the engine room space, it can be used as a backup for the main fire pump. Each ship will be different, but the following locations are preferred for stowing the emergency fire pump when not in use: on any upper deck of the ship; in the steering flat; in the shaft tunnel; or in the forward part (e.g., the bow thruster room, etc).

Capacity and requirements for the emergency fire pump

An emergency fire pump provided on cargo ships over 2,000 gross tonnes. It must be driven by a self-cooled compression ignition engine or by an electric motor powered from an emergency generator. The emergency pump must be located outside the engine machinery space, and in a compartment not forming part of the engine room. The emergency pump must be provided with its own independent suction arrangement and the suction head must not exceed 4.5 m (14.7 ft) under all conditions of list or trim. The capacity should be at least 25 m^3/hr delivering two half-inch bore jets of water with a horizontal plane of not less than 12 m (40 ft). If the pump is located above water level, a priming arrangement must be provided to fill the pump casing with water prior to starting. In a motor-driven emergency fire pump arrangement, a heating element must be provided which is also powered from the emergency switchboard. For engine driven pumps, the fuel tank capacity should be sufficient to allow the engine to run at full load for at least three hours. A separate reserve fuel tank is to be provided outside the engine room machinery space. The prime mover engine should be of a manual, battery or hydraulic start type which can be started and operated by one person. The pipeline used for fire pump line is usually galvanised to avoid corrosion caused by seawater. The diameter of the pipe varies between 50 mm (1.9 in) and 180 mm (7 in) depending on the type and size of the ship.

BOW AND STERN THRUSTERS

The bow thrusters and stern thrusters are small transverse propellers located within a duct on either side of the ship's bow and stern. They are much smaller in size compared to the ship's main propeller and are used to improve the manoeuvrability of the vessel at low speeds. Bow thrusters are generally used for manoeuvring the ship within coastal waters,

132 Principles of ship architecture and engineering

channels or when entering or leaving port and coming alongside. They may also be used when in strong currents and winds. The presence of bow thrusters eradicates the need for tugboats when leaving and entering port. This saves considerable time for the vessel and money for the shipping company. Today, almost all container ships are fitted with both bow and stern thrusters. Despite this, many port and harbour authorities dictate tugboats must still be used. Ostensibly this is for safety reasons though in practicality, it is probably to generate higher port fees. The number of thrusters fitted to a ship depends on the ship's length and its volumetric weight. To be used effectively, the thruster compartment – also known as the thruster room – must be easily accessible from the open deck by the ship's crew. Most vessels use an electric motor to power the thrusters. This usually generates significant heat. The thruster controls and motor must therefore be positioned in a dry and well-ventilated compartment. The thruster room should never be used to store flammable products.

The installation of the tunnel or conduit containing the propeller should be positioned perpendicular to the axis of the ship and the thruster propeller must never protrude further than the outer rim of the conduit. To prevent detritus and sea life from getting stuck in the conduit, grid bars are often fitted over the propeller space. It is important that the positioning of the thruster tunnel should not interfere with the water flow under the hull and should not add to hull resistance. Thrusters are usually of a CPP[4] type, i.e., the blades on the propeller boss can be moved to change the direction of thrust. The *boss* – which carries the blades – is provided with a movable shaft that is operated by hydraulic oil. These are sometimes referred to as *Hydraulic Pod Motor-Driven Thrusters*. Once the signal is given to change pitch, the hydraulic oil is supplied which operates the internal shaft (within the boss) to change the blade angle of the thruster. The motor shaft drives the shaft of the thruster via a pinion gear arrangement. To maintain the water in the tunnel, a sealing gasket is provided in the motor casing. The thruster arrangement consists of an electric motor that is mounted directly over the thruster using a worm gear arrangement. The motor runs at a constant speed, and whenever there is a change required in the thrust or direction, the controllable pitch blades are adjusted. When the blades are moved, the pitch is changed by the hydraulic oil which moves the hub on which the blades are mounted. As the thruster is a CPP, it can run continuously, and when no thrust is required, the pitch can be set to zero. The thrusters are controlled from the bridge, with directions given remotely. In the event of remote failure, a manual method for changing the pitch is available in the thruster room. From there, the thrusters can be manually operated. Usually, the hydraulic valve block which controls the pitch of the blades is operated in the thruster room, where the blade angle can be changed in an emergency.

When the bow thruster is operated singularly, and the signal is given to operate the pitch on the port side, the thrust will result in the ship turning towards the starboard side from the bow. Similarly, when the bow thruster is operated singularly, and the signal is given to provide pitch on the starboard side, the thrust will result in turning the ship towards the port side from the bow. When the stern and bow thrusters are operated in unison, the ship will move in an opposite lateral transverse direction. As with all systems on board, constant preventative maintenance is needed to keep the bow and stern thrusters in good working condition. The insulation needs to be checked regularly and kept dry. This is important where the thrusters are used infrequently and thus there is an increased chance of damage caused by a build-up of moisture. Moreover, because of the frequent idling state of the thrusters, a reduction in insulation resistance, especially in colder regions, may develop. To prevent this from happening, the thruster room heater must be checked to ensure the insulation is kept in an optimal condition. The bearings on the motor and the links should be greased monthly. The condition of the hydraulic oil must be checked regularly with samples collected and sent for onshore lab analysis. The thruster rooms must be inspected for signs of water ingress; evidence of which may indicate worn or leaking seals. The flexible coupling between the motor and the thruster should be checked regularly together with the cable connections for cleanliness and tautness. Finally, the motor grid should be vacuumed, or at least blow cleaned, to remove any build-up of carbon as this can increase the temperature of the thruster room leading to the outbreak of fire. Major overhauling and maintenance of the BT and ST are done during drydock when the ship's hull is out of water and the thruster blades and tunnel can be accessed easily. Major maintenance on the thruster infrastructure usually includes the replacement of the 'O' rings and sealing rings; removal of the pinion shaft; inspection and maintenance or replacement of the gear set; replacement of the bearings; repairs, cleaning, and replacement of the blades; inspection and repair of the hub if needed; and inspection and overhauling of the oil distribution box which operates the propeller blades.

Using the thrusters to manoeuvre the vessel has many advantages over attempting to manoeuvre the vessel manually. These include improved manoeuvrability at low speeds, improved operation and safety of the ship when berthing in inclement weather, and improved operational efficiency through shorter port stays and reduced tugboat assistance. As with most things, though, there are several disadvantages to using thrusters. These include the need for substantial induction motors, which require a high current and load. This means extra generator capacity is required. Retrofitting thrusters to ships is expensive and requires vast investment in engineering and technical expertise. It also requires additional crew training. Lastly, maintenance and repairs can be costly if the thrusters are not maintained or become damaged. The thrust force produced by the thruster motors to move the ship largely depends on various parameters such as hull design, power source, the design of the tunnel, use of grids, vessel draught, and vessel load. Furthermore, prevailing weather conditions and the state of the water can also adversely impact thruster performance.

NOTES

1. When supply provided to the lighting system, a step-down transformer is used in the distribution system. In a power distribution system, the voltage is set to 440v though there are some installations where the voltage is as high as 6,600v.
2. High Sulphur Fuel Oil; Very Low Sulphur Fuel Oil; Low Sulphur Marine Gas Oil; Ultra-Low Sulphur Fuel Oil.
3. www.imo.org/en/MediaCentre/HotTopics/Pages/Sulphur-2020.aspx
4. Controllable Pitch Propeller.

Chapter 10

Principles of ship stability

So far, we have explored some of the key factors in container ship design and construction. We have looked at different hull forms and bottom structures, as well as vessel watertight integrity. We have also discussed some of the main engineering systems used on board. Now that we have a basic grasp of ship design, we can turn our attention to *ship stability*. Ship stability is an area of naval architecture and ship operation that is concerned with how a ship behaves at sea under different conditions. There are four conditions to consider when calculating ship stability: still water, open water, intact stability, and damaged condition. In this chapter, we will lightly touch on some of the main concepts of ship stability as it is an in-depth subject worthy of much greater consideration than can be afforded in this book. Historically, ship stability relied on rule of thumb calculations however modern ship stability is much more complex. It can trace its origins to the 1740s when the French mathematician, Pierre Bouguer (1698–1758) introduced the concept of metacentre.[1] Prior to Bouguer's concept of metacentre, master shipbuilders used a simple system of adaptive and variant design. Ships were often copied from one generation to the next with only minor changes being made where necessary. By replicating tried and tested designs, shipbuilders were usually able to avoid problems associated with instability. Today, modern ships replicate this process of adaptation and variation albeit using advanced computational fluid dynamics and ship model testing techniques. Advances in science and technology have led to improved understanding of fluid and ship motions, which in turn have enabled more scientifically grounded and analytical ship designs. Ironically, Bouguer's calculus-based methods of determining stable ship conditions were so accurate they are still taught to aspiring naval architects and deck officers today. When a ship's hull is designed, stability calculations are performed to establish the intact and damaged states of the vessel. Ships are generally designed to slightly exceed the required stability requirements set by class. This means a small degree of stability redundancy is built into the ship design.

CONCEPT OF INTACT AND DAMAGED STABILITY

The first parameter or condition we ought to explore is *intact stability*. Intact stability calculations are relatively straightforward and involve calculating the centre of mass of the objects on board the vessel. These are then computed to identify the ship's centre of gravity, and thereafter the centre of buoyancy. Cargo loading and stowage arrangements, crane assemblies and lifting operations, and various sea states are taken into account. Ships are designed so that the centre of gravity is placed well above the centre of buoyancy. This ensures the ship remains stable. In essence, the ship is stable because as it begins to heel, one side of the hull rises from the water, the other side of the hull begins to submerge into the water. This causes the centre of buoyancy to shift toward the side that is lower. This means

134   DOI: 10.1201/9781003244615-12

the centre of buoyancy shifts with the centre of gravity as the ship heels. If we imagine a ship cut out, we can draw a line directly down the centre point of the ship. In a stable condition, the line will intersect both the centre of buoyancy and the centre of gravity. This is because the ship is completely stable. Now, if we imagine the ship has heeled slightly, the vertical line will shift and intersect the centreline at a point called the metacentre. So long as the metacentre is above the keel – i.e., higher than the centre of gravity – then the ship will be stable when in an upright condition. Damaged stability calculations are much more complicated than intact stability. Specialist software, which can calculate complex computations based on different factors, are commonly used. Doing so ensures the damaged stability calculation is correct, and it saves the person doing the calculation a headache. Loss of stability from flooding may be caused by free surface effect. Water accumulating in the hull usually drains to the bilges. This lowers the centre of gravity and increases the metacentric height of the ship. This assumes the ship remains stationary and upright. However, once the ship is inclined to any degree (for example, if a wave strikes), the fluid in the bilge moves to the lower side. This results in the ship *listing*. Stability may also be lost to flooding when, for example, an empty tank is filled with seawater. The lost buoyancy of the tank causes that section of the ship to lower into the water. This will also result in the ship listing unless the tank is positioned directly on the centreline of the vessel.

Stability calculations are different for each type of vessel. For container ships, and increasingly passenger vessels, damaged stability calculations are used to determine the vessel's response to flooding. This involves calculating the impact of flooding not just of one compartment – as is the case for oil tankers due to their compartmentalisation – but multiple compartments as container ships tend to lack the same degree of bulkhead divisions found on oil tankers. To be approved by class the blueprints of the ship must be submitted for independent review by an appointed classification society. Intact and damaged calculations must be provided which follow a structure outlined in the regulations by the appropriate Flag State. Within this framework different countries have established requirements that must be met. For example, US-flagged vessel blueprints and stability calculations are checked against the US Code of Federal Regulations in addition to the SOLAS Convention 1974. To ensure parity, compliance is overseen by the US Coastguard (USCG). Ships are required to maintain intact stability for the conditions in which they are designed to operate in. For container ships, this means stability must be maintained during loading, unloading, in port, and at sea, in calm sea conditions and in rough sea conditions. To a lesser extent, the same degree of stability must be maintained when the ship is in a damaged state.

SHIP MOTIONS

Ship motions are defined by the six degrees of freedom that ships experience. These are measured according to three reference axes: (a) the vertical / Z axis or yaw axis, which is an imaginary line running vertically through the ship and through its centre of mass, and results in yaw motion. This is the side-to-side movement of the bow and stern; (b) the transverse, Y axis, lateral axis, or pitch axis, which is an imaginary line running horizontally across the ship and through the centre of mass. This relates to the pitch motion and is an up or down movement of the bow and stern of the ship; and (c) the longitudinal, X axis, or roll axis. This is an imaginary line that runs horizontally through the length of the ship, through its centre of mass, and parallel to the waterline. A roll motion is a side-to-side or port-to-starboard tilting motion of the superstructure around the X axis. As noted above, there are three imaginary axes present in a ship: the longitudinal, transverse, and vertical axes. The movements around each of these axes are referred to as roll, pitch, and yaw respectively.

136 Principles of ship architecture and engineering

The pitch is the up/down rotation of a vessel about its transverse/Y (side-to-side or port-starboard) axis. An offset or deviation from normal on this axis is referred to as trim or out of trim. Roll is defined as the tilting rotation of a vessel about its longitudinal/X (front-back or bow-stern) axis. An offset or deviation from normal on this axis is referred to as list or heel. Heel refers to an offset that is intentional or expected, and is caused by wind pressure, turning, or other crew related actions. The rolling motion towards a steady state (or list) angle due to the ship's own weight distribution is referred to as heel. List normally refers to an unintentional or unexpected offset, caused by flooding or shifting cargo. Yaw is the turning rotation of a vessel about its vertical/Z axis. An offset or deviation from normal on this axis is referred to as deviation or set. This is referred to as the heading of the vessel relative to north on a magnetic compass (or true heading if referenced to the true North Pole). Yaw also affects the ship's bearing.

Ships also experience *translational movements*. The first of which is *heave*. Heave is defined as a linear vertical (up/down) motion, where excessive downward heave can result in the ship swamping. *Sway* refers to linear transverse (side-to-side or port-to-starboard) motion. This motion is generated directly either by water actions or by wind currents exerting forces against the hull; or by the ship's own propulsion; or indirectly by inertia when the ship is turning. This movement can be compared to the vessel's drift from its course. *Surge* is the linear longitudinal (bow/stern) motion caused by sea conditions.

HYDROSTATICS AND SHIP STABILITY

Understanding the principles of hydrostatics, and its impact on ship stability is critical as it has a direct bearing on the safety of the ship. The main characteristic parameters used to calculate the nature of stability and ship behaviour are called *ship hydrostatics*. For the ship's officers to understand stability parameters, it is important to be able to understand the meaning and practical significance of each hydrostatic condition, of which there are ten: vertical, longitudinal, and transverse centre of gravity; vertical, longitudinal, and transverse centre of buoyancy; mass displacement (Δ); volume displacement (∇); longitudinal and transverse centre of floatation; metacentre; metacentric height; metacentric radius; moment to change trim 1 cm (*MCT*); and, tonnes per cm immersion (TPC). Without further explanation, it is understandable that these terms probably seem as comprehensible as gobbledegook. Therefore, we need to acquaint ourselves with a few basic ship terms that are used when calculating hydrostatic and stability parameters. These are (a) the *Forward Perpendicular* (FP), which is the perpendicular drawn at the point where the bow of the ship meets the waterline while it floats at design draught; (b) the *Aft perpendicular* (AP), which is the perpendicular drawn through the rudder stock; (c) the *Length between Perpendiculars* (LPP or LBP). This is the longitudinal distance between the forward and aft perpendiculars; (d) the *Length of Waterline* (LWL). This is the length of the ship's hull intersecting the water's surface; (e) the *Length Overall* (LOA). This is the maximum length from the forward most point of the ship's hull to the aft-most point of the ship's hull; (f) the *Keel* (K). The keel is the lowest most point of the ship at any point of its length; and (g) the *Baseline* (B). This is the longitudinal line that runs directly along the keel. Before we move on, another important parameter we need to know is the *station*. A ship's hull is longitudinally divided into segments called stations. These are specified positions along the length of the ship with reference to the aft perpendicular, which is referred to as the *zero station*. The distance between each station remains constant in the vicinity of the midship where a significant parallel mid-body shape exists. As we move aft or forward, the shape of the hull begins to acquire an increasingly complex geometry, and hence for better results of analysis, the distance between the stations is reduced.

Centre of gravity (CG)

The longitudinal position of the centre of gravity (CG) with respect to any reference point on the ship is called the longitudinal centre of gravity (LCG). Usually, the reference point for locating the LCG is either the forward or aft perpendiculars. The vertical distance (along the ship's centreline) between the keel and the centre of gravity is expressed as KG.

Centre of buoyancy (CB)

The longitudinal position of the centre of buoyancy with respect to any reference point on the ship is called the longitudinal centre of buoyancy (LCB). Usually, the reference point for locating the LCB is either the forward or aft perpendiculars. The vertical distance (along the ship's centreline) between the keel and the centre of buoyancy is expressed as KB. The *centre of buoyancy* is located at the centre of the mass of the volume of water that the hull displaces. This point is referred to as B. We know the centre of gravity of the ship is commonly denoted as G or CG. When a ship is at equilibrium, the centre of buoyancy is vertically in line with the centre of gravity of the ship. The *metacentre* is the point where the lines intersect (at angle φ) at the upward force of buoyancy of $\varphi \pm d\varphi$. When the ship is vertical, the metacentre lies above the centre of gravity and so moves in the opposite direction of heel as the ship rolls. This distance is also abbreviated to GM. As the ship heels over, the centre of gravity generally remains fixed with respect to the ship as it depends on the position of the ship's weight and cargo, though the surface area increases, increasing the BM φ. Work must be done to roll a stable hull. This is converted to potential energy by raising the centre of mass of the hull with respect to the water level or by lowering the centre of buoyancy or both. This potential energy is released to right the hull and the stable attitude will be where it has the least magnitude. It is the interplay of potential and kinetic energy that results in the ship having a natural rolling frequency. For small angles, the metacentre, $M\varphi$, moves with a lateral component so it is no longer directly over the centre of mass. The righting couple on the ship is proportional to the horizontal distance between two equal forces. These are gravity acting downwards at the centre of mass and the same magnitude force acting upwards through the centre of buoyancy, and through the metacentre above it. The righting couple is proportional to the metacentric height multiplied by the sine of the angle of heel, hence the importance of metacentric height to stability. As the hull rights, work is done either by its centre of mass falling or by water falling to accommodate a rising centre of buoyancy, or both.

For example, when a perfectly cylindrical hull rolls, the centre of buoyancy stays on the axis of the cylinder at the same depth. However, if the centre of mass is below the axis, it will move to one side and rise, creating potential energy. Conversely, if a hull having a perfectly rectangular cross-section has its centre of mass at the waterline, the centre of mass stays at the same height, but the centre of buoyancy goes down as the hull heels, again storing potential energy. When setting a common reference for the centres, the moulded (within the plate or planking) line of the keel (K) is generally chosen; thus, the reference heights are KB to Centre of Buoyancy; KG to Centre of Gravity; and KMT to the Transverse Metacentre.

Metacentre (M)

When a ship heels (rolls sideways), the centre of buoyancy of the ship moves laterally. It might also move up or down with respect to the waterline. The point at which a vertical line through

138 Principles of ship architecture and engineering

the heeled centre of buoyancy crosses the line through the original, vertical centre of buoyancy is the *metacentre*. The metacentre remains directly above the centre of buoyancy and is considered fixed relative to the ship for small angles of heel; however, at larger angles of heel, the metacentre can no longer be considered fixed, and its actual location must be found to calculate the ship's stability. The metacentre can be calculated using the formulae:

$$KM = KB + BM$$

$$BM = \frac{I}{V}$$

Where KB is the centre of buoyancy (i.e., the height above the keel), I is the second moment of area of the waterplane measured in metres and V is the volume of displacement in metres. KM is the distance from the keel to the metacentre. Stable floating objects have a natural rolling frequency, just like a weight on a spring, where the frequency is increased as the spring gets stiffer. On a ship, the equivalent of the spring stiffness is the distance called 'GM' or 'metacentric height', being the distance between two points: 'G' being the centre of gravity of the ship and 'M', which is the metacentre. Metacentre is determined by the ratio between the inertia resistance of the ship and the volume of the ship. The inertial resistance is a quantified description of how the waterline width of the ship resists overturning. Wide and shallow or narrow and deep hulls have high transverse metacentres (relative to the keel), and the opposite have low metacentres; the extreme opposite is shaped like a log or round-bottomed boat. Ignoring ballast, wide, and shallow or narrow and deep means that the ship is very quick to roll and very hard to overturn and is thus 'stiff'. A log-shaped round bottom means that it is slow to roll and easy to overturn and thus 'tender'.

Where 'G' is the centre of gravity, 'GM' is the stiffness parameter of the ship and can be lengthened by lowering the centre of gravity or changing the hull form and thus changing the volume displaced and second moment of area of the waterplane, or both. An ideal hull form strikes a balance. Very tender ships with very slow roll periods are at risk of overturning but are comfortable for the crew and passengers. Vessels with a higher metacentric height are excessively stable, with a short roll period resulting in high accelerations at deck level. When a ship heels (rolls sideways) to any angle, the centre of buoyancy of the ship moves laterally. In other words, a portion of the lower side of the ship becomes submerged, and a portion of the hull from the upper side rises out of the water. This can be defined using the reference points WL (without heel) and W_1L_1 (after heel). Due to this shift of submerged volume, there is a shift of the centre of buoyancy from the centreline to the side that is lower after the heel. If a vertical line is extended from the new centre of buoyancy, then the point at which this line meets the centreline of the ship is called the transverse metacentre.

Centre of floatation (LCF)

When the ship floats at a particular draught, any trimming moment on the ship would act about a particular point on the waterplane. This point is the centroid of the area of the waterplane and is called the centre of floatation. The distance of the centre of floatation is read with respect to either of the perpendiculars or the midship and is abbreviated to LCF.

Metacentric radius (BM)

The metacentric radius of a ship is the vertical distance between its centre of buoyancy and the metacentre. To visualise this, we can imagine a pendulum swinging on a length of string.

As we swing the pendulum, it rocks from side to side. The metacentric radius is the length of each swing from CG to the outermost point of the swing. The ship behaves in a similar fashion. Subsequently, the metacentre of the ship changes itself at every moment. This is because with every angle of heel, the transverse shift in the centre of buoyancy varies, creating a new metacentre. We can calculate the metacentric radius by applying the following mathematical expression:

$$\text{Transerve Metacentric Height}(BM) = \frac{\text{Transverse moment of Inertia of Waterplane}}{\text{Volume Displacement of the Ship}}$$

A ship floating at a particular draught (T) has a unique waterplane. When a ship rolls in a condition, looking from the top, the entire waterplane area seems to oscillate about its longitudinal centroidal axis. The area moment of inertia of this waterplane area about its centroidal axis is called the transverse moment of inertia of waterplane at the corresponding draught.

Metacentric height (GM)

The metacentric height (GM) is a measurement of the initial static stability of a ship. It is calculated as the vertical distance between the CG of a ship and its metacentre. A larger metacentric height implies greater initial stability against overturning. The metacentric height also influences the natural period of rolling of a hull, with very large metacentric heights being associated with shorter periods of roll. A sufficiently, but not excessively, high metacentric height is considered ideal for passenger ships. The *IMO Codes of Stability for Ships* have laid down stability criteria for ships that are based predominantly on this parameter. The value of GM needs to be obtained at various phases starting from the initial design stage to the hull design stage, during stability analysis of a newly designed hull, after the construction of a ship, and, importantly for us, during operations at sea. The methods used in these stages are different from each other because firstly, at each stage, the purpose behind the evaluation of GM is different; and secondly, the known parameters required to evaluate the GM are also different at each stage. For now, given the fact we know the parameters BM, KB, and KG, we can use these to calculate the metacentric height of a ship:

$$\text{Metacentric Height}(GM) = KB + BM - KG$$

Righting arm

The metacentric height is an approximation for the vessel stability at a small angle (0–15 degrees) of heel. Beyond that range, the stability of the vessel is dominated by what is known as a righting moment. Depending on the geometry of the hull, naval architects must calculate the centre of buoyancy at increasing angles of heel. They then calculate the righting moment at this angle, which is determined using the equation:

$$RM = GZ\Delta$$

Where RM is the righting moment, GZ is the righting arm, and Δ is the displacement. As the vessel displacement is constant, common practice is to simply graph the righting arm versus the angle of heel. The righting arm is the horizontal distance between the lines of buoyancy and gravity. There are several important factors that must be determined with

140   Principles of ship architecture and engineering

regards to righting arm/moment. These are known as the maximum righting arm/moment, the point of deck immersion, the down flooding angle, and the point of vanishing stability. The maximum righting moment is the maximum moment that could be applied to the vessel without causing it to capsize. The point of deck immersion is the angle at which the main deck will first encounter the sea. Similarly, the down flooding angle is the angle at which water will be able to flood deeper into the vessel. Finally, the point of vanishing stability is a point of unstable equilibrium. Any heel lesser than this angle will allow the vessel to right itself, while any heel greater than this angle will cause a negative righting moment (or heeling moment) and force the vessel to continue to roll over. When a vessel reaches a heel equal to its point of vanishing stability, any external force will cause the vessel to capsize.

Moment to change trim by one centimetre (MCT)

The moment to change trim or *MCT* is the longitudinal moment (about the *LCF*) required to bring about a trim of one centimetre for any given draught. This parameter plays a vital role especially when the ship is required to load cargo in only one hold, or when the ship is ballasting or de-ballasting. By calculating the *MCT*, it is possible to predict the trim caused by the action. Since the expression of this parameter does not play any significant role in understanding the concepts of ship stability, we do not need to go into any further detail but do remember that *MCT* is a very important hydrostatic parameter required by stability analysis software and officers during cargo loading and ballasting.

Tonnes per centimetre immersion (TPC)

For any given draught, the weight required for the ship to sink or rise by one centimetre is called the tonnes per centimetre or *TPC*. This is like the *MCT* and is used extensively by officers to predict the new draught of the vessel following any operation that involves the addition or removal of weight from the ship. The expression used to calculate the *TPC* of a ship at any given draught is as follows:

$$\text{TPC in seawater} = \frac{1.025 \times \text{Area of Waterplane}}{100}$$

$$\text{TPC in freshwater} = \frac{\text{Area of Waterplane}}{100}$$

The above expressions provide us with three important bits of information. First, the *TPC* of a ship floating in water of uniform density depends solely on the area of waterplane. Second, the sinkage resulting from loading in freshwater is *more* than if the same loading is done in seawater, where the amount of sinkage will be *less*. Third, the officers must recalculate the predicted new draughts after loading or unloading when the ship moves from freshwater to seawater or vice versa.

HYDROSTATIC CURVES

All hydrostatic parameters are calculated using stability analysis software, which is then plotted onto a graph set against different draughts. This graph is called the *hydrostatic curve*. The hydrostatic curve is used by officers to obtain the value of a hydrostatic parameter of the ship for a given draught. Using hydrostatic curves requires caution as the graph uses a multi-scale horizontal axis with multiple parameters using different measures of units. Important observations can be made when studying the nature of hydrostatic curves. First, the only hydrostatic parameters that decrease with an increase in draught is the height of metacentre from the keel (KM), and the longitudinal centre of buoyancy (LCB). If we recall that the LCB is calculated from the forward perpendicular (read horizontal axis on the graph), this means a decreasing LCB with increasing draught implies the LCB moves forward with an increase in draught. While the nature of KM is mostly constant, the nature of change of LCB with draught will vary according to the form of the hull. For instance, a fine stern means, with an increase in draught, the percentage of submerged volume towards the forward of the midship increases more rapidly than the submerged volume aft. Hence, at larger draughts, most of the submerged volume will be concentrated forward of the midship. If this had been a ship with a finer bow and fuller stern, an increase in draught would have caused the LCB to shift towards the aft, thereby showing an opposite nature on the hydrostatic curve. Ship designers can therefore predict the hull form of a ship just by looking at its LCB curve. The MCT of all surface ships usually increases with increases in draught. This means a surface ship is very sensitive to trimming moments when floating in low draught conditions. We have so far acquainted ourselves with the hydrostatics of ships, an understanding of which will enable us to study the stability of ships in further detail. We can recognise each hydrostatic parameter, its significance, and how it is represented in the stability book of a ship in the form of curves. Now, we will discuss the basic concepts of ship stability including an introduction to intact stability and damaged stability. At the end, we should have a basic understanding of how to evaluate the intact stability of a ship.

INTACT AND DAMAGED STABILITY

An understanding of the ship's stability can be divided into two parts. The first part concerns *intact stability*. This field of study deals with the stability of a surface ship when the intactness of its hull is maintained, and no compartment or watertight tank is damaged or flooded by seawater. The second part relates to *damaged stability*. The study of damaged stability of a surface ship includes the identification of compartments or tanks that are subjected to damage and flooding by seawater, followed by a prediction of the resulting trim and draught conditions. Damaged stability, however, cannot be understood without a clear understanding of intact stability. Hence, we will apply what we have just learnt about hydrostatics and focus first on intact stability.

Intact stability

The fundamental concept behind intact stability is *equilibrium*. There are three types of equilibrium conditions that occur for a ship, depending on the relationship between the CG and CB.

STABLE EQUILIBRIUM

A stable equilibrium is achieved when the vertical position of G is lower than the position of the transverse metacentre (M). This means when the ship heels to an angle of say, theta – Θ, the centre of buoyancy (B) shifts to B_1. The lateral distance or lever between the weight and buoyancy in this condition results in a moment that brings the ship back to its original upright position. The moment resulting in the uprighting of the ship to its original

142 Principles of ship architecture and engineering

orientation is called the *Righting Moment*. The lever that causes the righting of the ship is the separation between the vertical lines passing through G and B_1. This is called the *Righting Lever* and is abbreviated as GZ.

NEUTRAL EQUILIBRIUM

A state of neutral equilibrium is by far the most dangerous condition possible for any ship in terms of stability, and all precautions must be taken to avoid it. It occurs when the vertical position of CG coincides with the transverse metacentre (M). In such conditions, no righting lever is generated at any angle of heel. As a result, any heeling moment will not give rise to a righting moment, and the ship will remain in the heeled position for as long as the condition of neutral stability exists. The risk is, at a large angle of heel in a neutrally stable shift, an unwanted shift in weight – for example, caused by shifting cargo – that might give rise to a condition of unstable equilibrium.

UNSTABLE EQUILIBRIUM

An unstable equilibrium is caused when the vertical position of G is higher than the position of transverse metacentre (M). When the ship heels to an angle (say theta – Θ), the centre of buoyancy (B) now shifts to B_1. The righting lever is now negative, or in other words, the moment created will result in further heel until a condition of stable equilibrium is reached. If a condition of stable equilibrium is not reached by the time the deck is immersed, the ship is said to have capsized. If you recall from earlier, we said the metacentric height is one of the most vital parameters of ship stability. We are now able to appreciate just how important this is. A ship's stability, as seen above, is directly relational to the value of its metacentric height (GM). For ease, we can record the three states of stability as:

- GM > 0 means the ship is stable
- GM = 0 means the ship is neutrally stable
- GM < 0 means the ship is unstable

UPSETTING FORCES ON A SHIP

Analysis of static transverse stability arises from the effect of upsetting forces or heeling moments, which can be categorised as two types depending on their sources with respect to the ship. These are *external heeling moments* and *internal heeling moments*.

EXTERNAL HEELING MOMENTS

Beam winds: act on the portion of the ship above the waterline. The resistance acts as an opposing force on the submerged part of the hull. Now, there are two sets of force couples and corresponding moments generated. The moment (clockwise) created by the wind force and water pressure is the heeling moment, and the moment (anti-clockwise) created by the weight and buoyancy couple acts as the righting moment. So, when a ship experiences beam winds, it will till up to the angle at which the righting moment generated will cancel out the heeling moment.

Lifting of weight by the sides. Weights are usually loaded or unloaded by the sides of the ship when lifting operations are carried out by the deck top crane. In this case, a heeling moment is caused by a shift in the centre of gravity. To understand why, we need to understand that when a weight is lifted by a crane, its weight acts on the *fulcrum* – that is, the end of the derrick of the crane, irrespective of the height of the weight above the ground. This also means that once a weight (for example, a container) is lifted from the berth, the weight of the container acts through the end of the derrick (which is a fixed point with respect to the ship), irrespective of the swinging motion of the container. When a container of weight (w) is lifted by the port side, the centre of gravity of the weight (g) will not lie on the centre of mass of the container, but rather at the end of the derrick. The ship and the container can now be treated as a two-point mass system. The final centre of gravity of the system (G_1) will lie on the line joining the initial CG of the ship (G) and the centre of gravity of the weight (g). Since the final CG of the ship has shifted from the centreline, it will create a heeling moment towards the port side. The ship will heel till it reaches an equilibrium position where buoyancy and weight act along the same line.

Highspeed turning manoeuvres. When a ship executes a turn, a centrifugal force acts horizontally on the CG of the ship, in a direction opposite to that of the turn. This force is balanced off by the hydrodynamic pressure acting on the underwater part of the hull in the opposite direction. The ship will heel in the direction opposite to that of the turn until the righting moment generated due to the weight and buoyancy couple equalises the heeling moment generated by both the centrifugal force and hydrodynamic pressure. This means the sharper the turn, the more centrifugal force is generated, resulting in a greater angle of heel.

Grounding. When a ship runs aground in such a way that only one side of the submerged hull is hit, the upward reaction force at the point of contact between the hull and the seabed results in heeling. Part of the energy of the forward motion of the ship is absorbed by the upward reaction force (R), which also causes the ship to initially lift up. When the tide ebbs, the ship sits further down onto the seabed, whereby the magnitude of the reaction force increases. In such conditions, the buoyancy reduces as the weight of the ship (w) is being supported by a combination of the reaction force (R) and remaining buoyancy force (w-R). The ship will heel up to the point where the moments of the weight of the ship (w) and buoyancy (b) about the point of contact with the seabed are balanced. This is what happened with the *MV Costa Concordia* (2012) which became grounded, and as the tide ebbed, the ship capsized. However, the capsizing was not a result of grounding alone. The damage to the hull caused by running aground was a contributory effect, which is something we will cover in damaged stability. Subsequently, we can predict which side of a ship is grounded just by looking at the direction of its heel. To prove this, we know the *MV Costa Concordia* ran aground on its portside but capsized on its starboard side.

Mooring. Container ships are moored to bollards when berthed alongside and tankers are often moored to guyed buoys while loading oil from offshore loading sites. If the mooring lines are too tense, or in case the ship drifts away from the moored point, the increased tension on the mooring lines may cause the ship to heel. This, however, can be easily prevented by adopting proper mooring techniques.

INTERNAL HEELING MOMENTS

The previous examples relate to external heeling moments where phenomena outside the ship resulted in heeling but there are also numerous internal causes that may result in the same effect. Most of these can be prevented by taking proper operational measures, some

144 Principles of ship architecture and engineering

of which will be discussed throughout this book. We will now briefly focus on how heeling moments are caused due to internal phenomena.

Movement of weight athwartship. Movement of any weight athwartship (in a transverse direction) will alter the position of the CG of the ship (from G to G_1). The initial lever created between weight acting through G_1 and buoyancy acting through 'B' will create the heeling moment. The ship will heel to a point at which a new centre of buoyancy (B_1) occurs at such a position such that weight and buoyancy act through the same line. This also happens when ballast water is transferred from one side of the ship to another, or when ballast water is taken into only one side of a tank. In the case of container ships, disproportionate loading on one side will constitute a weight shift; and on passenger ships, passengers crowding on one side of the ship may also constitute a weight shift. It is important to understand that though this is an equilibrium condition, a heeled condition is not desirable for the operation of the ship. Hence, corrective measures must be taken to bring the ship back to an upright position.

Water trapped on deck. Seawater is frequently washed on deck in rough seas or heavy winds. If trapped on deck, the motions of the ship will result in periodic weight shift in both directions, creating cyclical heeling moments caused by the continuous change in the ship's CG. To prevent this, decks must provide adequate drainage for green water.

LONGITUDINAL STABILITY

In all that we have discussed up to now, we have dealt only with the heeling of a ship. In other words, we have been discussing the ship's transverse stability. Yet a ship's stability analysis is not just restricted to the transverse direction. Longitudinal shifts in weights on board, or any longitudinal trimming moment (i.e., a moment that would cause the ship to trim), are aspects that are discussed as part of the longitudinal stability of a ship. The effect of the shift of weight towards the aft of the ship results in trim by the stern. The centre of gravity of the ship (G) now shifts aft to a new position (G_1), which causes the trimming moment. The ship now trims by aft, which means more volume of the hull is submerged at the stern, and part of the submerged volume towards the forward now emerges. This causes a shift in the centre of buoyancy of the ship towards the aft (from 'B' to 'B_1'). The equilibrium trim angle is reached when the final centre of gravity (G_1) lies in line with the final centre of buoyancy (B_1). The metacentre of the ship in its longitudinal direction is called the longitudinal metacentre (ML), and the vertical distance between the centre of gravity and longitudinal metacentre is called the longitudinal metacentric height of the ship (GML). Like transverse stability, a positive longitudinal GM means the ship is longitudinally stable and will not plunge. The important thing to note here is that the values of longitudinal GM usually range from 100 to 110 times the value of the transverse GM. And since the values of transverse GM of all ship types vary from 0.2 to 0.5, it implies that GM in the longitudinal direction is usually as high as 100 m or above. It is because of this, that ships are inherently stable in the longitudinal direction, and hence, most studies of ship stability are focused on the transverse stability of the ship.

INCLINING TEST

An *inclining test* is a test performed on a ship to determine its stability, lightship weight, and the coordinates of its CG. The test is applied to newly constructed ships greater than 24 m in length, and to ships altered in ways that could affect its stability. Inclining test procedures are specified by the IMO, other relevant international associations, and Class. The weight of a vessel can be readily determined by reading the draught and comparing this with the known hydrostatic properties. The metacentric height (*GM*), which dominates stability, can be estimated from the ship's design, but an accurate value must be determined by an inclining test. The inclining test is usually done in perfect conditions – i.e., inshore, in calm weather, in still water, and free of mooring restraints. The *GM* position is determined by moving weights transversely to produce a known overturning moment in the range of 1–4 degrees. Knowing the restoring properties (buoyancy) of the vessel from its dimensions, the floating position, and by measuring the equilibrium angle of the weighted vessel, the *GM* can be accurately calculated. As in a new ship test, the weight shifts must be known, and the angles of tilt measured. To do this, a series of weight (ballast) movements are used to obtain an average and variance for *GM*.

LIST

The *angle of list* is defined as the degree to which a vessel heels (leans or tilts) to either the port or starboard side at equilibrium, with no external forces acting upon it. Listing is caused by the off-centreline distribution of weight due to uneven loading or flooding. By contrast, roll is the dynamic movement from side to side caused by waves. If a listing ship goes beyond the point where a righting moment will keep it afloat, it will capsize and sink.

ANGLE OF LOLL

Angle of loll is defined as the state of a ship which is unstable when in an upright condition (in order words, a vessel that has a negative metacentric height) and therefore takes on an angle of heel to either port or starboard. When a vessel has a negative metacentric height (*GM*) any external force applied to the vessel will cause it to start heeling. As the ship heels, the moment of inertia of the vessel's waterplane increases, which in turn increases the vessel's *BM* (the distance from the centre of *B*uoyancy to the *M*etacentre). Since there is relatively little change in *KB* (the distance from the *K*eel to the centre of *B*uoyancy), the KM (distance from *K*eel to the *M*etacentre) of the vessel increases. At some angles of heel (say 10 degrees), *KM* will increase sufficiently equal to *KG* (distance from the *K*eel to *CG*), thus making the *GM* of the vessel equal to zero. When this occurs, the vessel goes to neutral equilibrium, and the angle of heel at which it happens is called angle of loll. In simple terms, when an unstable vessel turns towards a progressively increasing angle of heel, at a certain point, the centre of buoyancy (*B*) will fall vertically below the centre of gravity (*G*). Importantly, the angle of list should not be confused with the angle of loll. The angle of list is caused by unequal loading on either side of the centre line of the vessel. Although a vessel at angle of loll does display features of stable equilibrium, this is a dangerous situation and rapid remedial action is required to prevent the vessel from capsizing. It is often caused by the influence of large free surface or the loss of stability due to damaged compartments. It is different from list in that the vessel is not induced to heel to one side or the other by the distribution of weight; it is merely incapable of maintaining a zero-heel attitude.

STABILITY

GM and rolling period

The metacentre has a direct relationship with a ship's rolling period. A ship with a small GM will be 'tender' or have a long roll period. An excessively low or negative *GM* increases

146 Principles of ship architecture and engineering

the risk of a ship capsizing in rough weather, for example the *Mary Rose* (1545) or the *Vasa* (1628). It also puts the vessel at risk of potential for large angles of heel if the cargo or ballast shifts, such as with the *MV Cougar Ace* (2020). A ship with low *GM* is less safe if damaged and partially flooded because the lower metacentric height leaves less safety margin. For this reason, maritime regulatory agencies such as the IMO specify minimum safety margins for seagoing vessels. A larger metacentric height on the other hand can cause a vessel to be too 'stiff'; excessive stability is uncomfortable for the crew and passengers. This is because the stiff vessel quickly responds to the sea as it attempts to assume the slope of the wave. An overly stiff vessel rolls with a short period and high amplitude, which results in high angular acceleration. This increases the risk of damage to the ship and to cargo and may cause excessive roll in special circumstances where the eigen period of wave coincides with the eigen period of ship roll. Roll damping by bilge keels of sufficient size will reduce this hazard. Criteria for this dynamic stability effect remain to be developed. In contrast, a 'tender' ship lags the motion of the waves and tends to roll at lesser amplitudes. A passenger ship will typically have a longer rolling period for comfort, perhaps 12 seconds, while a tanker or box ship might have a rolling period of six to eight seconds. The period of roll can be estimated using the following equation:

$$T = \frac{2\pi l a_{44} + K}{\sqrt{g\overline{GM}}}$$

where g is the gravitational acceleration, $a44$ is the added radius of gyration and k is the radius of gyration about the longitudinal axis through the centre of gravity and GM is the stability index.

EXAMPLE: CAR CARRIER GOES SIDEWAYS!

A car carrier had been loaded, in this instance not with cars but with bundles of timber. These were stowed on decks five and seven, the only decks allowing forklifts without height restrictions. The remaining decks would remain empty. This was just the second voyage for the chief officer on a Pure Car Carrier. A pre-sailing calculation was made on the stability computer, but the drafts as visually checked were found to be different from those calculated (actual forward draft 8.850 but calculated 8.256, actual aft draft 8.850 but calculated 8.460). The chief officer went back to the stability computer and adjusted the cargo weights to see if the drafts as seen would affect the final GM. He was satisfied all was safe and the ship sailed. During the sea passage, ballast tanks five port and starboard were being used as heeling tanks; there was no ballast exchange. During the voyage, a small heel developed. The chief officer decided to do a five-minute transfer between the heeling tanks. The next day, the swell was increasing and coming from the stern. Over the next few hours, the weather worsened with six to seven-metre swells from the port quarter. The master ordered a reduction in engine rpm and a switch to manual steering. In the afternoon of the same day, the ship rolled heavily to starboard, then back to port and again to starboard, a roll of about 30 degrees to 40 degrees. A loud noise was heard from the cargo decks. The helm was put hard to starboard, but the ship did not respond. The angle of list now made moving on the bridge almost impossible. A *MAYDAY* message was issued, the master activated the GMDSS distress signals, and then the abandon ship alarm. All crew were ordered to move to the port upper side deck.

Fire hoses were extended and attached to railings to help the crew move to the port side and don their immersion suits. Both the port life raft and the lifeboat were lowered but both were pushed to the ship side due to the heavy list, making it dangerous to embark through the vertical ladder. Finally, a helicopter evacuation was arranged, and the crew were disembarked by air. A few days later the ship was towed to safety. The official investigation found, among other things, that cargo weights were about 29% greater than those declared by the stevedores, contributing to a reduction in real GM. Also, more ballast was used than had been estimated, so GM was again less than calculated. Calculations were not efficiently supervised or followed up and no arrival calculations were considered. The chief officer and master appeared to pay little attention to the importance of stability calculations since they were confident of the stability of the ship based on similar conditions in the past. However, conditions on this trip were not in fact like those in the past because this time bunkers had been kept to a minimum in anticipation of dry dock.

LESSONS LEARNED

Sailing without a finalised and accurately calculated GM is never a good idea. Without proper training it is likely that unsafe practices will become the norm. When unsafe practices become the norm, it is only a matter of time before an accident occurs. If you are required to carry an unusual cargo or a cargo that is not necessarily adapted to your ship, it is always best to seek advice from Class or cargo experts before loading.

Damaged stability

If a ship floods, the loss of stability is caused by the increase in KB, the centre of buoyancy, and the loss of waterplane area – thus a loss of the waterplane moment of inertia – which decreases the metacentric height. This additional mass will also reduce freeboard (distance from water to the deck) and the ship's angle of down flooding (minimum angle of heel at which water will be able to flow into the hull). The range of positive stability will be reduced to the angle of down flooding resulting in a reduced righting lever. When the vessel is inclined, the fluid in the flooded volume will move to the lower side, shifting its centre of gravity toward the list, further extending the heeling force. This is known as the free surface effect.

FREE SURFACE EFFECT

In tanks or spaces that are partially filled with a fluid or semi-fluid (fish, ice, or grain, for example) as the tank is inclined the surface of the liquid, or semi-fluid, stays level. This results in a displacement of the centre of gravity of the tank or space relative to the overall centre of gravity. The effect is like that of carrying a large flat tray of water. When an edge is tipped, the water rushes to that side, which exacerbates the tip even further. The significance of this effect is proportional to the cube of the width of the tank or compartment, so two baffles separating the area into thirds will reduce the displacement of the centre of gravity of the fluid by a factor of nine. This is of significance in ship fuel tanks or ballast tanks, tanker cargo tanks, and in flooded or partially flooded compartments of damaged ships. Another worrying feature of free surface effect is that a positive feedback loop can be established,

148 Principles of ship architecture and engineering

in which the period of the roll is equal or almost equal to the period of the motion of the centre of gravity in the fluid, resulting in each roll increasing in magnitude until the loop is broken or the ship capsizes. This has been significant in historic capsizes, most notably the *MS Herald of Free Enterprise* (1987) and the *MS Estonia* (1994).

TRANSVERSE AND LONGITUDINAL METACENTRIC HEIGHTS

There is also a similar consideration in the movement of the metacentre forward and aft as the ship pitches. Metacentres are usually separately calculated for transverse (side to side) rolling motion and for lengthwise longitudinal pitching motion. These are variously known as $\overline{GM_T}$ and $\overline{GM_L}$, $GM(t)$ and $GM(L)$, or sometimes GM_t and GM_l. Technically, there are different metacentric heights for any combination of pitch and roll motion, depending on the moment of inertia of the waterplane area of the ship around the axis of rotation under consideration, but they are normally only calculated and stated as specific values for the limiting pure pitch and roll motion.

MEASUREMENT

The metacentric height is normally estimated during the design of a ship but can be determined by an inclining test once it has been built. This can also be done when a ship or offshore floating platform is in service. It can be calculated by theoretical formulas based on the shape of the structure. The angle(s) obtained during the inclining experiment are directly related to GM. By means of the inclining experiment, the 'as-built' centre of gravity can be found; obtaining GM and KM by experiment measurement (by means of pendulum swing measurements and draft readings), the centre of gravity KG can be found. So, KM and GM become the known variables during inclining and KG is the wanted calculated variable ($KG = KM - GM$).

STABILITY CALCULATIONS

The stability conditions of a ship are the various standard loading configurations to which the ship may be subjected and are recognised by Classification Societies. Classification Societies follow rules and guidelines laid down by SOLAS, the IMO, and specific laws of the country under which the vessel is flagged. Stability is normally divided into two distinct types: Intact and Damaged. Intact stability refers to a vessel that is in its normal operational configuration and the hull has not been breached in any compartment. The vessel is expected to meet various stability criteria such as GM_t (metacentric height), area under the GZ (righting lever) curve, range of stability, and trim computations. Intact stability includes several conditions that must be met. These include *lightship* or *light displacement*. This means the vessel is complete and ready for service in every respect including permanent ballast, spare parts, lubricating oil, and working stores but is without fuel, cargo, drinking or washing water, officers and crew, passengers, their effects, temporary ballast, or any other variable load. A *full load departure* or *full displacement* means all the conditions carried under lightship or light displacement are met but the vessel has all systems charged meaning that all freshwater, cooling, lubricating, hydraulic and fuel service header tanks, piping, and equipment systems are filled with their normal operating fluids. Crew and effects are at their normal values. Consumables such as provisions, potable water, and fuel are at 100%

capacity. For naval ships, this includes ammunition, and for merchant ships, cargo is loaded at maximum capacity. All in all, the vessel is at its limiting draft or legal load line. In addition to full load departure or full displacement, naval vessels must also conform to *standard conditions*. Along with all lightship loads, the vessel has all systems charged.

Crew and effects are at their normal values. Consumables such as provisions, potable water, and fuel are at 50% capacity though ammunition and or cargo is at 100% capacity. This condition is ordinarily used for calculating range and speed. The final displacement variable is *light arrival*. Along with the lightship loads, the vessel has all systems charged. Crew and effects are at their normal values though consumables such as provisions, potable water and fuel are only at 10% of their full load. Ammunition and or cargo is at 100% capacity. The vessel in the assessed 'Worst Intact Condition' is analytically damaged by opening various combinations of watertight compartments to the sea. The number of compartments and their location are dictated by IMO regulations, SOLAS conventions, or other rules that may be applicable. Typically, these conditions are identified by the compartments that are damaged, for example 'Hold Number 3 and Water Ballast Tank 4 Port'.

SHIP DISPLACEMENT

The displacement or displacement tonnage of a ship refers to its weight. As the term suggests, displacement is measured indirectly using *Archimedes' principle*. First, we calculate the volume of water displaced by the ship. We can then convert this value into weight. Traditionally, various measurement rules have been used. Initially, ship weights were calculated using long tons though today the standard measure is metric tonnes. Ship displacement varies by a vessel's degree of load, from its empty weight as designed (known as 'lightweight tonnage') to its maximum weight (known as 'deadweight'). Numerous terms are used to describe varying levels of load and trim. It is important not to confuse ship displacement with a ship's volume or capacity. Volume and capacity are generally measured in net and gross tonnage. Similar in principle to ship stability, ship displacement is calculated using different load-displacement conditions. For instance, *loaded displacement* is the weight of the ship including its cargo, passengers, fuel, water, stores, dunnage, and any other items necessary for the ship to use on its voyage. This brings the ship down to its 'load draft', also colloquially known as the 'waterline'. *Full load displacement* is defined as the displacement of a vessel when floating at its greatest allowable draught as established by a Classification Society and designated by its 'waterline'. *Light displacement (LDT)* is defined as the weight of the ship minus all cargo, fuel, water, ballast, stores, consumables, crew, and passengers, but with water at steaming level in the boilers. *Normal displacement* is the ship's displacement 'with all outfit, and two-thirds supply of stores' on board.

LOAD LINE MARKS

In the Middle Ages, the Venetian Republic, the city of Genoa, and the Hanseatic League required ships to show a load line. In the case of Venice this was a cross marked on the side of the ship, and of Genoa three horizontal lines. The first 19th-century loading recommendations were introduced by Lloyd's Register of London in 1835, following discussions among shipowners, shippers, and underwriters. Lloyd's recommended freeboards as a function of the depth of the hold (three inches per foot of depth [250 mm/m]). These recommendations were used extensively until 1880 and became known as the 'Lloyd's Rule'. In the 1860s, following increased loss of ships due to overloading, a British Member of Parliament,

150 Principles of ship architecture and engineering

Samuel Plimsoll, took up the load line cause against strong opposition. This resulted in the formation of a *Royal Commission on Unseaworthy Ships* was in 1872. By 1876 the *United Kingdom Merchant Shipping Act* made the load line mark compulsory, although the positioning of the mark was not fixed by law until 1894. In 1906, further laws were passed requiring foreign ships visiting British ports to be marked with a load line. It was not until 1930 (with the 1930 *Load Line Convention*) that international consensus for a universal application of load line regulations was agreed. In 1966 the *International Convention on Load Lines (ICLL)* was concluded in London. The ICLL re-examined and amended the 1930 rules with further amendments being made in 1971, 1975, 1979, 1983, 1995, and 2003, although none of these have been entered into force. The purpose of the load line is to indicate the draught of the ship and the legal limit to which the ship may be loaded for specific water types and temperatures, to safely maintain buoyancy regarding the hazard of waves. This is because varying water temperatures affect a ship's draught as warm water is less dense than cold water, thus providing less buoyancy.

In the same way, freshwater is less dense than salt or seawater, with the same lessening effect upon buoyancy. For vessels with displacement hulls, hull speed is determined by, among other things, the length of the waterline. The waterline may also refer to any line on a ship's hull that is parallel to the water's surface when the ship is afloat in a normal buoyant position. Hence, all waterlines are one class of 'ships lines' that are used to denote the shape of a hull in naval architecture designs. The purpose of the load line is to ensure that a ship has sufficient freeboard (the height from the waterline to the main deck) and thus sufficient reserve buoyancy. The freeboard on merchant vessels is measured between the lowest point of the uppermost continuous deck at the side and the waterline and this must not be less than the freeboard marked on the load line certificate issued to that ship. All merchant ships, other than in exceptional circumstances, have a load line symbol painted amidships on both sides of the ship's hull. This symbol is also permanently marked so that if the paint wears off it remains visible. The load line makes it easy for anyone to determine if a ship has been overloaded. The exact location of the load line is calculated and verified by a Classification Society, with that society issuing the relevant load line certificate. The original 'Plimsoll mark' was a circle with a horizontal line through it to show the maximum draught of the ship. Additional marks have been added over the years, allowing for different water densities, and anticipated sea conditions.

Letters may appear to the sides of the load line mark indicating the Classification Society that has surveyed the vessel's load line. The initials used include **AB** for the American Bureau of Shipping, **BV** for Bureau Veritas, **VL** for **DNV GL**, **IR** for the Indian Register of Shipping, **LR** for Lloyd's Register, **NK** for Nippon Kaiji Kyokai, and **RI** for the Registro Italiano Navale (RINA). These letters are approximately 115 millimetres in height and 75 millimetres in width or 4.5 by 3.0 inches. The load line length is referred to during and following load line calculations. The letters on the load line marks also have specific meanings: TF for *Tropical Fresh Water*; F for *Fresh Water*; T for *Tropical Seawater*; S for Summer Temperate Seawater; W for *Winter Temperate Seawater*; and WNA for *Winter North Atlantic*. For the purposes of load line marks, freshwater is considered to have a density of 1,000 kg/m^3 (or 62 lb/cu ft) and typical seawater 1,025 kg/m^3 (or 64 lb/cu ft). Freshwater marks make allowances for the fact that the ship will float deeper in freshwater than in saltwater. A ship loaded to her freshwater mark in freshwater will float at her summer mark once she has passed into seawater at the same displacement. Similarly, if loaded to her tropical freshwater mark, the ship will float at her tropical seawater mark once she passes into seawater. The summer load line is the primary load line, and it is from this mark that all other marks are derived. The position of the summer load line is calculated from the load line rules and depends on many factors such as the length of the ship, the type of ship, the type and number of superstructures, amount of sheer, and the bow height. The horizontal line through the circle of the Plimsoll Mark is the same level as the summer load line. The winter load line is one-forty-eighth of the summer load draft below the summer load line. The tropical load line is one-forty-eighth of the summer load draft above the summer load line. The freshwater load line is an amount equal to

$$\frac{\Delta}{AT}$$

millimetres above the summer load line where Δ is the displacement in tonnes at the summer load draft and T is the tonnes per centimetre immersion at that draft. In any case where Δ cannot be ascertained, the freshwater load line is at the same level as the tropical load line. The position of the tropical fresh load line relative to the tropical load line is found in the same way as the freshwater load line is to the summer load line. The winter North Atlantic load line is used by vessels not exceeding 100 m (330 ft) in length when in certain areas of the North Atlantic Ocean during the winter period. When assigned it is 50 mm (2.0 in) below the winter mark.

TIMBER LOAD LINE MARKS

Certain vessels are assigned timber freeboards, but before these can be assigned, certain additional conditions must be met. One of these conditions is that the vessel must have a fo'c'sle of at least 0.07 the length of the vessel and of not less than standard height, which is 1.8 m (5 ft 11 in) for a vessel 75 m (246 ft) or less in length and 2.3 m (7 ft 7 in) for a vessel 125 m (410 ft) or more in length with intermediate heights for intermediate lengths. A poop or raised quarter deck is also required if the length is less than 100 m (330 ft). The letter L prefixes the load line marks to indicate a timber load line. Except for the timber Winter North Atlantic freeboard, the other freeboards are less than the standard freeboards. This allows these ships to carry additional timber as deck cargo, but with the facility to jettison their cargo in emergencies. The letters on the timber load line marks, like standard vessel load line marks, have specific meanings: LTF for *Timber Tropical Fresh Water*; LF for *Timber Fresh Water*; LT for *Timber Tropical Seawater*; LS for *Timber Summer Seawater*; LW for *Timber Winter Seawater*; and LWNA for *Timber Winter North Atlantic*. The summer timber load line is arrived at from the appropriate tables in the load line rules. The winter timber load line is one-thirty-sixth of the summer timber load draft below the summer timber load line and the tropical timber load line is one-forty-eighth of the summer timber load draft above the summer timber load line. The timber fresh and the tropical timber fresh load lines are calculated in a similar way to the freshwater and tropical freshwater load lines, except that the displacement used in the formula is that of the vessel at her summer timber load draft. If this cannot be ascertained, then these marks are one-forty-eighth of the timber summer draft above the timber summer and timber tropical marks, respectively. The timber winter North Atlantic load line is at the same level as the winter North Atlantic load line.

SUBDIVISION LOAD LINE MARKS

Ships that have spaces which are adapted for the accommodation of passengers and the carriage of cargo alternatively may have one or more additional load line marks corresponding to the subdivision draughts approved for the alternative conditions. These marks show P_1 for the principal passenger condition, and P_2, P_3, etc., for the alternative conditions; however, in no case is any subdivision load line mark placed above the deepest load line in saltwater.

Hopefully we now have a basic understanding of ship stability and how to calculate for different water and load conditions. In Part 3, we will start to look at the different types of operations carried out on board starting with deck operations.

NOTE

1. Pierre Bouguer is widely considered the 'father of naval architecture'.

Part III

Ship operations

Chapter 11

Deck operations

Working on the ship's deck often involves carrying out routine tasks such as painting and chipping, operating deck machinery, and stowing cargo. Most of these tasks involve handling different types of deck tools and equipment. In this chapter, we will briefly look at some of the tasks carried out on deck such as mooring, slinging, and welding.

MOORING OPERATIONS

The term *mooring* means to bring a ship alongside its berth and to secure it in position using a collection of mooring lines or *hawsers*. The lines are fixed to deck fittings on the vessel at one end and to fittings such as bollards, rings, and cleats on the quayside. This prevents the ship from drifting. The term likely derives from the Dutch verb *meren* (meaning to moor) and has been used in English since at least the end of the 15th century. Where more than one bollard is lined in a row, these are called a *tier*. The mooring operation requires close cooperation between the dock workers on the quayside and the crew on board the vessel. Heavy mooring lines are often passed from larger vessels to the people on a mooring by smaller, weighted *heaving lines*. Once a mooring line is attached to a bollard, it is pulled tight. Large ships tighten their mooring lines using heavy machinery called *mooring winches* or *capstans*. The largest container ships can have as many as a dozen mooring lines employed at any one time. Smaller ships tend to be secured using four to six mooring lines. The mooring lines are made from manila rope or synthetic materials such as nylon. Nylon is easier to work with and lasts for many years, but it is extremely elastic. This elasticity has various advantages and disadvantages. The main advantage is that during mooring, when there are high winds or another ship is passing close, stress can be spread across several lines. However, should a highly stressed nylon line break the consequence this can be catastrophic. In the worst case the rope can *snapback*, which can fatally injure bystanders. The effect of snapback is analogous to stretching a rubber band to its breaking point then suffering a stinging blow from its flexing broken ends. Such a blow from a heavy mooring line can inflict severe injuries or even sever limbs. Mooring lines made from materials such as Dyneema and Kevlar are much less elastic and are therefore safer to use. However, such lines do not easily float and tend to sink. Furthermore, they are comparatively more expensive. Mooring lines and hawsers may also be made by combining wire rope and synthetic line. Such lines are more elastic and easier to handle than wire rope, but they are not as elastic as pure synthetic line.

Mooring operations are usually supervised by the chief officer (at the forward station) and the second officer (at the aft station) though this may vary from ship to ship. On some vessels the third officer may man the forward station. This allows the chief officer to support the master on the bridge. The mooring area on a ship comprises the forward and aft

DOI: 10.1201/9781003244615-14

155

156 Ship operations

sections. Most large container ships have six primary mooring stations: the headline, which keeps the forward part of the vessel against the dock; the forward breast line, which keeps the vessel close to the quay; the forward or head spring, which prevents forward drift; the back or aft spring, which prevents back drift; the aft breast line keeps the stern of the vessel close the quay; and the stern line which prevents forward drift. Most injuries and fatalities that occur during mooring are due to the rope or mooring wire parting. This causes the mooring line to snap back towards the mooring crew who are positioned in the 'snapback zone' of the mooring line. The tension and projection of the rope can easily generate sufficient force to severely injure, maim, or even kill. When the ropes are pulled straight the snapback zone is minimal but if the ropes are turned in towards the bollard, then the snapback area increases. On some ships, the snapback zone is clearly demarcated using bright paint or other markings. Whilst this helps the crew to stay outside the immediate danger zone, such markings do not take into account the complex behaviour that mooring ropes exhibit when great force is exerted. Subsequently, the 2015 version of COSWP revised its guidance on snapback zones and now dissuades ships from marking the snapback zones on the deck. Instead, COSWP recommends the *entire* mooring zone should be considered a potential snapback zone.

Mooring ropes are long and heavy and are stored in a coil. When these ropes are deployed, they tend to form a natural coil or ring shape. This is called the 'rope bight'. If a person involved in mooring becomes entangled in the rope bight, the pull of the rope can drag the person overboard or force them up against deck machinery. This can result in permanent injury. To avoid getting caught in the rope bight, mooring operators must be conscious of where they are standing when handling the mooring ropes and when standing within the vicinity of the mooring zone. Under no circumstances should any crew member stand on or within a rope bight. To help prevent accidents occurring during mooring, the mooring supervisor should concentrate on the actions of the mooring crew, and not get involved in the mooring operation itself. Inexperienced ratings and deck officer cadets should only be allowed to handle the ropes under the supervision of an experienced rating or officer. Moreover, as deck officer cadets and trainee deckhands are on board to learn and develop their seamanship skills, they should be expected to work as part of the mooring team but should be assigned duties where they stand to cause the least possible risk to themselves and others. When the mooring operation is especially difficult, for example in high winds or rain, they should only observe and not participate in the mooring operation. Handling the mooring lines is physically demanding under normal circumstances; add in variables such as hot or cold temperatures, wind and rain and the task becomes exponentially harder. Preparing the mooring ropes in advance is the best way to ensure the operation is efficient and the ship is berthed safely and without incident.

ANCHORING OPERATIONS

The anchor is a piece of marine equipment that is used to restrict the structural movement of the ship through water. Anchors achieve their purpose by using their weight to hold the vessel in place, by clamping onto the seabed, or by using a combination of both. In addition, anchors may also act as *drogues* (positive drag mechanism) for ships and other vessels during storms. Drogues provide a restoring drag that helps keep the vessel stable and steady and prevents the bow from slamming or flooding. This stops green water from washing over the bow. Bow slamming occurs when the forward section of the ship violently strikes the water surface. This is caused by large waves that can result in structural deformations and failure. Green water is the technical term for any water that is present on the upper decks, as a result of partial flooding caused by the natural motions of the sea. Anchoring is one of the many important operations that falls under the responsibility of the deck department. It involves the use of deck equipment and requires a high level of situational awareness. The key responsibility for the anchor supervisor positioned at the anchor station is to use the available anchoring machinery and manpower to perform the operation safely in accordance with the master's instructions. This requires clear and unambiguous communication between the bridge and the anchor station, and the anchor station and the deck crew. Prior to starting the anchor procedure, the anchor supervisor must first confirm the anchor to be used (i.e., the port or starboard anchor); the number of shackles that are to be lowered; and the method for lowering the anchor (i.e., 'letting go' or 'walking the gear'). Once the anchor supervisor receives the command to prepare for anchoring, they must first check and confirm the following: (a) are the crew members are in place and fully donned in PPE; (b) the correct anchor for the operation (port or starboard) is available and free from any defects; (c) the anchor lashings and bow stopper have been removed; (d) the hydraulic pumps have been tested prior to the operation (this applies to hydraulic windlasses only); (e) the condition of the windlass and its controls have been properly inspected and confirmed safe for use. Furthermore, if the bow thrusters are likely to be used during anchoring, the mooring supervisor must also ensure the required ventilations are open; above the bridge, the anchor day signal (ball) must be readied for hoisting once the anchor operation is complete; radio communications equipment must be set up and readied for use; and both sideboards must be checked for any obstructions.

There are two distinct types of anchoring operation: (1) 'Letting go', which involves dropping the anchor; and (2) 'Heaving up', which involves picking up the anchor. For both operations, the anchor supervisor has three responsibilities: first, to *oversee the safe operation of the windlass*. Normally, the operation of the windlass is done remotely from the anchor controls. The windlass operation is best carried out by the anchor supervisor, provided the controls are positioned near the ship's side or in such position that the anchor supervisor can maintain a visual check on the anchor and its chain whilst operating the controls. If this is not possible, then the anchor supervisor should be positioned where they can supervise the anchoring operation and assign control of the windlass to an experienced rating; second, to *maintain a visual check on the anchor and its chain*. As the anchor supervisor is responsible for reporting the position and stay of the anchor and its chain, it is recommended they keep a visual check on the anchor and chain themselves. This means any issues can be reported to the master immediately; and third, to *keep track of how many shackles are lowered*. Tracking the number of shackles lowered is done by visually observing the '*kender*' shackle of the chain. The kender shackle is bigger in size and is usually marked using different colour patterns or numbers for easy identification. On modern ships, the length of the chain below the hawse pipe is digitally displayed on the control panel, though it is strongly advised to always keep a visual check on the chain. If the anchor supervisor is operating the windlass, a crew member can be assigned to this duty. Remember, one shackle equals 27.5 m.

Reporting is a critical responsibility of the anchor supervisor. The anchor supervisor is in effect the eyes and ears of the master who, being on the bridge, will not have first-hand knowledge of how the operation is proceeding. Hence, the anchor supervisor must regularly report the progress of the operation to the master. It should be noted that each anchor supervisor will have their own way of reporting. This is perfectly acceptable so long as the master and the anchor crew are clear on what the anchor supervisor is saying. The important point to remember is that there can be no ambiguity between what the anchor supervisor is saying and what they mean. When the anchoring operation is underway, there are a number of points that need to be communicated between the anchor station and the bridge. These include the *anchor position*. Whilst anchoring operations are underway, the anchor-chain

158 Ship operations

position is a matter of critical importance. Positions are reported either in a clock format (for example, using the bulbous bow as the central focal point (i.e., 12 o'clock) the starboard anchor is reported from 1 o'clock to 6 o'clock; and the portside anchor is reported from 7 o'clock to 11 o'clock) or using cardinal points where every point equal 11.25 degrees (for example, 2 points off the starboard bow). The second important report is the *chain stay*. The chain stay refers to the tendency of anchor's chain movement. When reporting chain stay, the following terms are used to describe its movement: (a) short stay. This refers to a chain leading a short range from the ship's side; (b) *medium stay*. This refers to a chain leading a medium range from the ship's side; (c) *long stay*. This refers to a chain leading a longer range from the ship's side, extending from the hawse pipe; and (d) *up and down*. This refers to the position of the chain when it is vertically leading parallel to the ship's side. In this position, the chain will not extend and will lead vertically downwards from the hawse pipe to the seabed. When reporting the position and chain stay to the master, the anchor supervisor will say something along the lines of '*position 2 o'clock, long stay*'.

In normal situations, when letting go of the anchor, the chain needs to stretch out for the anchor to hold the vessel. After dropping anchor, the chain stay will extend. When the anchor is holding to the seabed and the chain has settled down, the stay gradually shortens, first with to a medium and then to a short range. Finally, the chain will go vertical from the bottom of the hawse pipe to the seabed. This means the anchor is holding and the chain has settled. Anchoring is a crucial and demanding operation. In most cases, theoretical guidelines are helpful but safe and efficient anchoring requires experience. This means having good knowledge of the ship's manoeuvrability and the limitations of the equipment involved. First and foremost, safety must be at the very heart of the operation. If the prevailing sea and weather conditions mean the operation cannot be carried out safely, it is the responsibility of the anchor supervisor to advise the master, who in turn will exercise their professional judgement on whether it is safe for the anchoring operation to continue.

OPERATING DECK MACHINERY

Container ships often have a vast array of deck-mounted machinery and equipment that are manually operated by the crew. Crew members must be properly trained in their operation, and appropriately supervised by a senior rating or officer. The most common types of machinery operated on deck include: (a) the *bow thruster* (BT). The officer operating the bow thruster joystick must never increase the pitch from minimum to maximum in one go as this can lead to a sudden jump in current. This will damage the motor as the bow thruster system uses a combination of high voltage and high current. The maximum pitch should never exceed 90% of the operating potential and operation at high pitch should not continue for longer than is needed to accomplish the desired manoeuvre; (b) the *mooring winch* (MW). When the ship is alongside, the berthing and securing operation of the ship is performed using mooring winches. It is important to avoid using the winch brakes in place of using the reduction gear to reduce or control the winch speed as this will damage the brake lining of the drum; (c) the *anchor winch* (AW). The chain stopper must always be used when the anchor winch is not in use. When greasing the anchor components, avoid applying grease to the friction washers or brake lining as this may lead to the anchor chain slipping; (d) the *deck crane*. Some ships are fitted with a small deck crane for loading stores and supplies. Every crane has a safe working limit (SWL) which is stencilled on the crane for easy reference. When operating the deck crane, never lift more than permitted by the SWL; (e) the *ballast system*. Although the ballast system is operated from the bridge, ballasting can affect the trim of the ship. When working on deck, a change in trim can lead to a loss of balance, especially when working at height or carrying heavy objects. Before ballasting, always check to ensure no one will be adversely affected. Furthermore, never start the ballast pump from the cargo control room without first checking the system valves and pump condition from the local position in the engine room; (f) the *hydro blaster*. For the safety of the ship's crew, a safety switch is provided on the hydro blaster. This is a 'dead man's switch' and must never be taped, tied, or otherwise altered so that the equipment stays in a permanent 'ON' position. Moreover, if the high-pressure pipe is mishandled or if the lance is dropped, it will whip about uncontrollably, which may cause serious injuries; (g) *welding and gas cutting*. We have briefly touched on the safety precautions required when welding or gas cutting, but it is appropriate to remind ourselves briefly here as well. Deck maintenance commonly involves hot work which requires using welding tools. Prior to starting hot work, always check the insulation of the welding cable and the condition of the gas cables before use. Inspect the surrounding area where the hot work will take place, accounting for any nearby fuel tank vents, oil tank sounding pipes, and so on; and (h) the *fire system*. The fire systems installed on ships consists of high-capacity fire pumps which provide water to the hydrants. These hydrants are located on deck and in the engine room. The pumps are used for emergency situations and should never be isolated except when carrying out essential maintenance on the waterline. After the maintenance is complete, close the fire line drain reinstate the pump to full operational mode.

DECK LOADING OPERATIONS

As mentioned above, ships are often fitted with deck loading equipment such as gantry cranes, general cargo cranes, provision cranes, and derricks. These help to lift heavy loads such as stores and cargo on board. As these lifting systems are subject to continuous loading stress, their parts are liable to wear down at a fast rate, thus requiring regular maintenance. Poor maintenance can lead to system failure, accidents, and in the worst case, loss of life and property. It is therefore important that deck loading equipment is inspected and maintained as part of the planned maintenance schedule. Operating deck loading equipment is a specialised job that requires extensive training and experience. It is important when operating deck loading equipment to keep the load weight below the SWL. The SWL is permanently marked on the load equipment. The only time the equipment may be permitted to exceed the SWL is during load testing. Due to the hazards associated with deck loading, and the dangers inherent in poor maintenance and equipment condition, loading equipment must have valid certificates that are certified by a competent inspection authority. These certificates certify that the loading equipment is in a safe and operational condition. Load operators must ensure that the load equipment is well lubricated. The wires must be checked and renewed at specified intervals. Wires must be checked for signs of deformation, corrosion, and stranding. Any defects found must be recorded and the defective wires removed from service and quarantined. These must then be repaired or destroyed by an approved contractor. Equally important is ensuring the *securing clamp* is fitted to the hook whenever a load is lifted. This avoids the load from slipping. The securing clamp should be provided with a spring-loaded system that will not open even when the load exerts positive pressure on the hook. It is the responsibility of the load operator to check and confirm the condition of the load before carrying out the lift. It is a general practice to self-estimate the load of an object with a visual check. This is done in conjunction with the specification list. When performing the lifting operation, always check the path of the load for any obstructions. The planned path of the cargo movement must be unimpeded before the load is hooked to the crane. If lifting is performed in poor weather or at night, ensure that the crane area, including the

160 Ship operations

load path, is well illuminated. Moreover, the rays from any of the light fittings in the vicinity should not impair the vision of the lift operator.

When objects are lifted by ship-mounted cranes, the load weight is transferred directly to the ship's structure via the crane's foundation. This places stress on the ship's hull. Always inspect the foundation of the lifting equipment for any signs of cracks or deformation before starting the lift operation and as part of the PMS. When the ship's crane is used for cargo loading and unloading, the chief officer will prepare a loading or unloading plan. This ensures the ship is at the correct parameters with ballast and load differentials duly calculated. The lift operator must follow the loading plan exactly as provided. When loads are lifted on a sling the general idea is to keep the load as secure in the air as it was on the ground. This can be achieved by ensuring the load is (a) completely contained within the sling (e.g., using bags in nets); (b) by using fixed lifting pendants or lugs; (c) using ropes or wire slings that are wrapped around the load – no loads should be left resting on loose bights of the line; (d) when using specialised components, these must be properly attached to the cargo. The sling must be attached to the lifting appliance with the load slung so that neither may collapse or change form when lifted. The load must not damage the sling or cause the slings to part. Using stuffing or padding at potential tension points or on sharp edges can prevent cuts and breaks.

WELDING

Welding is a maintenance task that involves joining two pieces of metal together to form an inseparable joint. On ships, this is most often achieved using oxyacetylene gas, though manual metal arc (MMA) welding may also be used. Like virtually every operation on board, welding has the potential to be extremely hazardous and requires extensive training and experience to be performed safely. Welding is a type of *hot work* that is carried out to replace worn out or fatigued metal components and deck plates. Because welding involves the use of extreme temperatures, there is the risk of injury to the equipment user and other crew members, as well as the risk of fire. In one incident investigated by the UK's *Maritime Accident Investigation Branch* (MAIB) a fire broke out on a cargo ship in the mast house where oxygen and acetylene cylinders were being stored. A member of the crew had arranged two gas torches in tandem for carrying out hot work on the windlass drum. Both torches were connected in parallel from the same pair of gas cylinders by temporarily fitting 'standard' t-joints at the regulator valves. At some point during the welding operation, it was decided to use one gas torch to carry out brazing repair work while the other torch was connected to the pressurised gas hose. The result was an intense *flashback*, which travelled from the torch being heated through the hose and up to the mast house, rupturing the hose at the regulator valve connection. This caused a gas fire to erupt. Fortunately for the crew members, the backfire arrestors on the regulators prevented the cylinders from exploding and no one was seriously injured. Accidents such as this can take place on any kind of ship if the proper precautions are not taken whilst handling gas welding equipment.

Compressed gas cylinders are frequently used in the engine room and on deck for various repair functions. When performing gas welding or gas cutting operations, there are important safety protocols and procedures that must be followed starting with *securing the cylinders in a vertical position*. Compressed gas cylinders must be handled with utmost care and always secured in a vertical position, even when empty. Full and empty cylinders must be marked and segregated. *Store cylinders in the correct spaces.* Never store oxygen and acetylene cylinders together in one space. *Keep the cylinders separated and stored in well-ventilated spaces.* Ensure that when they are not in use, the caps are firmly fitted and secured.

Keep the cylinders clean from grease and oil. The control valves and fittings should be clean and kept free from oil and grease. Under no circumstances should cylinder valves and parts be operated with oily and greasy hands. *Ensure the flame arresters are properly fitted.* It is important that the non-return valves and flame arresters are fitted to the acetylene and oxygen cylinder lines. It is normal to have one flame arrester fitted to the low-pressure side of the regulator near the cylinder and for another to be fitted near the torch. *Keep the oxygen pressure high.* When carrying out gas welding, always ensure the oxygen pressure is higher than the acetylene pressure to avoid the acetylene from backfilling the oxygen line. *Handle acetylene with care.* Acetylene should never be used for welding at a pressure exceeding 1 bar as it is liable to explode even in the absence of air. *Rectify any potential causes of backfire.* In the event of backfire, the priority is to close the oxygen valve and then immediately close the acetylene valve. The welding operation must not restart until the cause of the backfire is fully investigated and the cause rectified. *Respond to flashback immediately.* In the event of flashback, or gas pipe explosion, the first action to take is to isolate the valves for both cylinders. Once isolated, initiate the ship's fire drill procedures. *Ensure proper connections.* The connections between the hose and blowpipe, and between the hoses, should be securely fixed with fittings that comply with established safety standards. *Keep a steady watch.* A regular watch should be kept on the temperature of the acetylene cylinder. If the temperature starts to elevate, this is likely an indication of potential backfire or flashback. *Prevent the interchange of hoses.* Manifold hose connections including the inlet and outlet connections should be such that the hoses cannot be interchanged between fuel gases and oxygen manifolds and headers. *Replace old and faulty hoses.* Hoses are generally sold with a fixed lifespan. Before using the equipment, inspect the hoses and fittings and remove any that have signs of damage or deformity. Never use hoses that have exceeded the manufacturers stated lifespan. *Handle hoses properly.* When carrying out the welding operation, the hoses should be laid out properly and kept far away from moving machinery, sharp corners, and high temperature areas. Tangled hoses should be untangled and laid out straight. *Use only approved leak detection fluids.* Only approved leak detection fluids should be used for detecting hose leaks. If approved type fluids are not available, then use non-detergent soap. *Never use sealing tape.* Sealing tapes made from metallic joining materials should never be used as these can cause metal-oxygen induced fires. *Carry out proper maintenance.* Only ever use specialised tools to clean blow pipe clogs. Before carrying out any maintenance, the complete system must be isolated. Never attempt repairs on a pressurised oxyacetylene set or carry out unauthorised modifications on hot work equipment. *Use safe ignitors only.* The blowpipe should only be ignited with a friction ignitor or some other type of approved stable flame generator. Never use unapproved tools such as cigarette lighters as the flame may cause the blowpipe to hit the lighter body. This can then explode. *Never use oxygen.* When welding, oxygen should never be used for ventilation, cooling purposes, or for blowing dust off the weld surface or from clothes. *Discard hoses that have suffered flashback.* Any length of hose in which a flashback has occurred should be quarantined immediately and destroyed by an approved contractor.

By following these steps, hot work and welding operations can generally be completed safely and with minimum risk to the operator and the ship. Before carrying out any hot work or welding activities, always ensure the hot work checklist and risk assessment forms have been completed and signed. This may include a permit to work. Always follow the correct health and safety procedures when carrying out jobs in enclosed or confined spaces. Finally, remember that pressurised gas cylinders carrying highly flammable material are a major threat to the ship. Special care and attention must always be taken when handling this type of equipment. Always follow the manufacturer's instructions and if in doubt, stop the work and seek guidance from an experienced member of the crew. Taking shortcuts is never advisable and should in fact be discouraged. Safety procedures and protocols are in place for good reason. Officers and senior ratings should therefore encourage their subordinates by leading by example.

There are many operations and tasks which are carried out on deck. This chapter has highlighted some of the most common and dangerous. Safety should always be first and foremost in every crew member's mind, from the master down to the most junior rate. No member of the crew is exempt from working safely, unknowingly doing so is no defence. The deck is an extremely hazardous place. Mooring, anchoring, cargo loading and unloading, lifting stores and provisions, and carrying out maintenance with hot work tools: these are all essential duties performed by the deck department. It is the responsibility of the deck officers to ensure these duties are carried out safely. In the next chapter, we will turn our attention to some of the main operations carried out by the engine room crew.

Chapter 12

Engine room operations

On a ship, the engine room is the compartment where the machinery for marine propulsion is located. The engine room is usually located near the bottom, at the stern of the vessel, and comprises very few compartments. This design maximises the ship's cargo carrying capacity and situates the prime mover close to the propeller. The engine room typically contains several machinery plants, each serving a different purpose. The main, or propulsion, engine is used to turn the ship's propeller, which moves the ship forward. These typically burn diesel oil or heavy fuel oil. In some cases, they may even be able to switch over. Container ships have many propulsion arrangements including multiple engines, propellers, and gearboxes. Smaller engines drive the electrical generators that provide the power for the electrical systems. Larger container ships typically have three or more synchronised generators which ensure a smooth and uninterrupted power supply. The combined output of the ship's generators is well above the actual power needed. This provides redundancy during maintenance or if one generator is lost. Besides the propulsion and auxiliary engine systems, container ships also have a variety of generators, air compressors, feed pumps, and fuel pumps. These are usually powered by small diesel engines or electric motors, and some may even use low-pressure steam. Increasingly, modern container ships are moving away from the standard manned engine room and towards *unmanned machinery spaces* (UMS). These have the benefit of automation, which means the engine control room does not need to be occupied 24 hours a day. Whilst this is undoubtedly preferable from the marine engineer's perspective, it does present new challenges for engine room operations, and maintenance and fault rectification.

Engine room operations are governed by SOLAS 1974 and specifically chapter II-1, regulations 46–53. In summary, the regulations set out the provision, operation, and maintenance of the main and auxiliary propulsion and power generation systems including fire prevention and firefighting infrastructure, automatic fire detection, fire extinguishing systems, protection against compartmental flooding, control of propulsion machinery from the ship's bridge, centralised control and management of instrumentation alerts, emergency and non-emergency alarm systems, and automatic initiation of the emergency generator.

PREPARING TO START THE MAIN ENGINE

The step to starting the main engines is to initiate the air system. This involves several procedures, which are listed here.

Air systems

First, drain any water present in the starting air system then drain any water from the control air system at the receivers. Pressurise the air systems to the correct bar. Ensure compressed air is available at the exhaust valve 'air spring' closing cylinders.

DOI: 10.1201/9781003244615-15

Lubricating oil systems

Second, check the oil level in the main engine sump and replenish if necessary. Start the main engine and turbocharger LO pump. Ensure the oil pressures are correct. Ensure there is adequate oil flow for piston cooling and turbochargers. Check the oil level in the cylinder LO tank and confirm the supply to the lubricator is open. Ensure the cylinder oil flowmeter is properly functioning and note the counter of the flowmeter.

Cooling water systems

Third, ensure the main engine jackets are set to normal operating parameter and that the main engine jacket water is continuously circulating through the preheater. This should be operated continuously when in port and should never be allowed to cool down. Ensure the cooling water system pressures are correct and that the systems are not leaking. Check again when the engine is at its correct operating temperature. Check the level of the expansion tank. Any obvious decrease in the water level of the expansion tank will indicate leakage. Slow turn the engine with the turning gear.

Slow turn the engine

Slow turning of the engine must be carried out to prevent damage from fluid leaking into any of the cylinders. Always seek authorisation from the bridge before turning the engine. The slow turning operation should be done at the latest possible moment before the engine is started and only after pre-lubrication. Confirm the regulating handles are in the *Finished with Engines* position. Ensure the cylinder indicator cocks are open. Turn the engine one revolution with the turning gear. Check to see if fluid flows out of any of the indicator valves. Disengage the turning gear and ensure it is locked in the *out* position. Check that the indicator lamp for *Turning Gear Engaged* goes out.

Slow turning the engine on starting air (blow-through)

Permission must always be sought from the bridge before turning the engine, as they will need to provide propeller clearance. The slow turning procedure should be initiated no less than 30 minutes before the ship is due to depart. Before starting the slow turn procedure, bring the main engine to standby mode. Select *Slow Turning* on the main engine operating panel if present or momentarily move the regulating handle to dead slow. When operating the telegraph from engine control, liaise with the bridge, as they should follow your command on the bridge telegraph. As the engine turns, check to see if any fluid flows out of the indicator cocks. When the engine has turned one revolution, move the regulating handle back to the *Stop* position. Close the indicator cocks. Also, close the turbocharger drains.

FUEL OIL SYSTEM

Check the fuel oil supply pump and fuel oil circulating pump. If the engine was running on HFO when stopped, the circulating pump and fuel heaters should still be running. Check the fuel oil pressures and temperatures. Confirm the fuel oil flowmeters are properly functioning and note the counter of the flowmeter.

Miscellaneous

Check that the engine instrumentation panels are reading correctly. If not, investigate and replace as necessary. Confirm that all scavenge air receivers and box drains are open and that the test cocks are closed. Check that the engine top bracing system is in service. Confirm the thrust bearing temperature and LO pressure is in range. Confirm the axial vibration damper and torsional vibration damper LO pressure is in range. Check the fuel leak off alarm is functional. Test the level of the fuel leak off tank to see if there is any rise in level due to leakage. Check the level of the scavenge drain tank; the tank should be empty or else it may lead to the overflow of scavenge space in the main engine. Check the governor is responding as expected.

NORMAL OPERATION CHECKS

During normal running, regular checks have to be carried out to ensure the machinery and plant is working as expected. These involve checking the system, engine pressures, and operating temperatures against the values contained in the commissioning records. The main engine room checks are discussed here. (1) Compare temperatures by feeling the pipes. The essential readings are the load indicator position, turbocharger speed, charge air pressure, and exhaust gas temperature before the turbine. A valuable reading is also the daily fuel consumption. (2) Checking and comparing the cylinders against the mean indicated pressure, compression pressure, and maximum combustion pressures. (3) Check the operation of the oil mist detector. (4) Check all of the shut-off valves in the cooling and lubricating systems for correct position. The valves for the cooling inlets and outlets on each engine must always be fully open when in service. These serve only to cut off individual cylinders from the cooling water circuit during overhauls. When abnormally high or low temperatures are detected at the water outlet, the temperature must be gradually brought up/down to the normal value. Abrupt temperature changes can cause severe damage and should be avoided wherever possible. The maximum permissible exhaust gas temperature at the turbocharger inlet must not be exceeded. (5) Check the rate of combustion by observing the colour of the exhaust gases. (6) Maintain the correct charge air temperature after the air cooler with the normal water flow. In general, higher charge air temperatures will result in less oxygen in the cylinder, which in turn will result in higher fuel consumption and higher exhaust gas temperatures. (7) Check the charge air pressure drop across the air filters and air coolers. Excessive resistance will cause poor airflow to the engines. (8) The fuel oil must be carefully filtered before use. Open the drain cocks of the fuel tanks and fuel oil filters regularly for a short period to drain off any water or sludge which may have collected. (9) Maintain the correct fuel oil pressure at the inlet to the fuel injection pumps. Adjust the pressure at the injection pump supply manifold with the pressure-regulating valve in the fuel oil return pipe. This will allow the fuel oil to circulate within the system at the normal delivery capacity of the fuel oil circulating pump. (11) The HFO has to be sufficiently heated to ensure the correct viscosity.

(12) Determine the cylinder LO consumption. (13) The cooling freshwater pumps should be run at their normal operating value, i.e., that the actual delivery head corresponds with the designed value. If the pressure difference between the inlet and outlet exceeds the desired value, a pump overhaul should be considered. The vents at the uppermost points of the cooling water spaces must be kept closed. (14) Check the levels in the water and oil tanks as well as the drainage tanks. Any abnormalities should be investigated. (15) Observe the condition of the cooling freshwater and check for any signs of oil contamination. (16) Check the charge air receiver drain manifold's sight glass to see if any water is draining away and

166 Ship operations

if so, by how much. (17) Check the scavenge space test cocks to see if any liquid is flowing out with the charge air. (18) Check the pressure drop across the oil filters. Clean them if necessary. (19) The temperature of the running gear should be checked where possible by listening and observing the crankcase and by monitoring the oil mist detector readings. (20) Bearings, which have been overhauled or replaced, must be given special attention for some time after being returned to normal service. Listening to the noise of the engine will reveal any abnormalities. (21) The power developed by the cylinders should be checked regularly and adjustments made via the control system to preserve cylinder power balance. (22) Centrifuge the LO. Lube oil samples should be taken at frequent intervals and sent ashore for analysis. (23) Check the exhaust valves are rotating and operating smoothly. If not, the valve should be overhauled at the next opportunity.

SECURING THE MAIN ENGINE AFTER STOPPING

Once the bridge has finished with the engines, switch the engine control to the engine control room. Check that the auxiliary blowers switch off automatically at *Finish with Engines* if they are in AUTO mode otherwise switch off manually. Close the starting air valve of the main engine and vent control air system. A good practice is to lock the main starting valve in its lowest position by means of the locking plate. Close the valve for the starting air distribution system. Engage the turning gear and check the indicator lamp. After stopping the engine, wait a minimum of 15 minutes before stopping the main engine LO pump if work is to be undertaken in the crankcase. This prevents the overheating of cooled surfaces in the combustion chambers and counteracts the formation of carbon deposits in the piston crowns. Keep the engine preheated to a minimum of 50°C (122°F) or in accordance with the main engine operations manual. If the engine was operating on HFO, do not stop the FO circulator and supply pumps. If the engine was operating on MDO, the FO circulator and supply pumps may both be stopped. Switch off any equipment which is not required during the engine standstill period.

UNDERSTANDING MARINE ENGINE PERFORMANCE

It is important to check the performance of the marine engine from time to time to ascertain its working condition and to carry out fault finding and rectification. With earlier models, the diesel engine maintenance was undertaken manually, but with the advancement of technology, automatic monitoring systems are now widely used. With the help of these monitoring systems, monitoring of diesel engine performance can be performed easily. The new technology provides two types of monitoring systems. In the first system, the diesel performance is monitored continuously and is thus known as *online monitoring*. In the second system, the engineer must manually fix the monitoring instrument onto the cylinder head, connecting the wire to the rpm sensor before taking the readings manually. These are then transferring into the monitoring software. Most main engines have an online diesel performance system whereas diesel generators have a manual system. The type of system that is installed depends largely on the company and the type of ship and engine. This is because the online system is considerably more expensive when compared to the manual system. In the online system, diesel performance can be remotely monitored in the engine control room as well as in the chief engineer's cabin. The system also provides various graphs which analyse the condition of the engine. These graphs are like the indicator cards plotted by the manual system. From the graphs obtained, various characteristics such as engine timing, compression, cylinder output, and so on can be evaluated. They also indicate whether the engine is balanced or if some units are overloaded and whether the timing needs to be adjusted. Generally, the diesel performance of the main and auxiliary engines is taken once every month. The report is then analysed.

A copy of the report is sent to the company's technical department together with the chief engineer's observations. The technical department then checks and provides any relevant feedback. For emergency purposes, the manual method for checking diesel performance is used as a standby method. The diesel performance reports are kept on board as records so that they can be compared with previous and future trends. If the report indicates a downward trend, then maintenance is carried out and any necessary parts adjusted or replaced. Although costly to install, automatic diesel performance systems have several benefits. First, it ensures the efficient and reliable operation of the engine. Second, it reduces operational costs by saving fuel and optimising SFOC (Specific Fuel Oil Consumption). Third, the system predicts which parts will require repairs and replacement which helps to prevent engine failure. And fourth, it helps in reducing spare part inventory and increases the time between engine overhauls.

ENGINE COOLING SYSTEMS

The machinery systems on board ships are designed to work and run for long hours. The most common and maximum energy loss from machinery is in the form of heat energy. This loss of heat energy has to be reduced or carried away by a cooling media, such as the central cooling water system, to avoid the malfunction and breakdown of the machinery. There are two systems used on board for cooling. The first is the *seawater cooling system*, and the second is the *freshwater* or *central cooling system*. With the former, seawater is directly used by the machinery systems as a cooling media for the heat exchangers. In the latter, freshwater is used in a closed circuit to cool down the engine room machinery. The freshwater returning from the heat exchanger after cooling the machinery is further cooled by seawater in a seawater cooler.

Understanding the central cooling system

As discussed above, with the central cooling system, all working machinery on ships are cooled using circulating freshwater. This system comprises three different circuits: (1) *seawater circuit*. Seawater is used as a cooling media in large seawater cooled heat exchangers to cool the freshwater in the closed circuit. These are the central coolers of the system and are normally installed in a duplex. (2) *Low-temperature (LT) circuit*. The LT circuit is used for low-temperature zone machinery and this circuit is directly connected to the main seawater central cooler; hence its temperature is lower than that of the high temperature circuit. The LT circuit comprises all auxiliary systems. The total quantity of LT freshwater in the system is maintained in balance with the HT freshwater cooling system by an expansion tank which is common to both systems. The expansion tank used for these circuits is filled from the hydrophore system or from the distilled water tank using the freshwater refilling pump. (3) *High temperature (HT) circuit*. The HT circuit in the central cooling system mainly comprises a jacket water system of the main engine where the temperature is kept high. The HT is maintained by LT freshwater and normally comprises the jacket water system of the main engine, the freshwater generator, the DG in standby condition, and the LO filter for the stuffing box drain tank. The HT cooling water system is circulated by electrical cooling water pumps, with one in service and one on standby. During standby, the DG

168   Ship operations

is kept warm by the circulating system from the DG in service. When the main engine is stopped, it is kept warm by HT cooling water from the DG. If this is insufficient, the water may be heated by steam generated by the freshwater heater.

Heat loss in the closed circuit of the central cooling freshwater system is continuously compensated by the expansion tank which also absorbs the increase in pressure caused by thermal expansion. The heat absorbed by the HT circuit is transferred to LT circuit by the temperature control valve junction. The outlet temperature of the main engine cooling water is kept constant at 85–95°C (185–203°F) by means of temperature control valves by mixing water from the two central cooling systems.

FUEL OIL CALCULATIONS

Fuel oil consumption calculation and recordkeeping are one of the critical tasks that the chief engineer is responsible for. Fuel oil is provided by the charterers of the vessel and so the chief engineer must report every day with a fuel oil consumption report. The method for calculating the amount of fuel oil used, available, and required, is briefly discussed here. *Measuring and Reporting Fuel Oil Consumption.* Where a flowmeter is installed on the pipeline supplying fuel to an emission source (main engine, diesel generator, auxiliary boiler, etc.), the flowmeter readings are the principal means of determining fuel consumption. Flowmeter readings and fuel temperatures should be recorded daily at 1200 hrs ship's mean time, as well as at the time of arrival (as noted in the arrival report) and departure (as noted in the departure report). The formula for obtaining the corrected density at the recorded fuel temperature is as follows:

$$\text{Corrected Density} = \text{Density at } 150°C$$
$$\times \left[1 - \left\{ \text{Fuel Temperature } (0°C) - 150°C \times 0.00065 \right\} \right]$$

In addition to reporting fuel consumption each noon, on arrival, and at departure, it is also necessary to record flowmeter readings at each of the following stages: (a) at the end of sea passage; (b) at the start of sea passage; and (c) whenever a fuel change operation is completed. Fuel transferred from the fuel oil drain tank or fuel oil overflow tank back to the fuel/settling tank must be noted in the position, arrival, and departure reports. This amount is then automatically subtracted from the voyage fuel consumption calculation. For emission sources that are not fitted with flowmeters or when the flowmeter is not operational, bunker fuel tank monitoring is to be done instead. This method involves taking tank readings of all fuel tanks relevant to the emission source, using tank soundings/ullages or level gauge readings. These must be recorded in the Engine Room Sounding Log. In addition, fuel quantities in the fuel tanks should be inspected periodically and at least as per the following schedule: (a) upon arrival of the vessel at berth and at every departure from berth; (b) prior to bunkering/de-bunkering; (c) after bunkering/de-bunkering; and (d) as a minimum, once every seven days.

Position, arrival, and departure reports

Position, arrival, and departure reports are the ship's primary means of reporting MRV-related data including fuel consumption, transport work, and other voyage-related data. A *position report* must be submitted each day at 1200 hrs ship's time both when the ship is at sea or in port. There must not be a gap of more than 24 hours (ship's mean time) between any two position reports; between a position report and an arrival report; between a departure report and the next position report; or between departure and arrival reports. Generally, if the gap is more than 24 hours, the terminal operator will not be able to submit the report and will need to submit the missing report (with a gap of less than or equal to 24 hours) first. The *arrival report* must be submitted for the first arrival in Port. 'First arrival in port' means the first time (for a specific port/location) that the vessel is (a) all fast to a wharf/buoy moorings/SBM (if berthing directly, without anchoring); (b) anchored (i.e., 'brought up to anchor') within port limits; (c) anchored (i.e., 'brought up to anchor') outside port limits; (d) anchored at a lighterage area; (e) all fast to a lighter vessel (if berthing alongside lighter vessel directly, without anchoring); or (f) arrival at a lighterage area (if drifting, without anchoring, whilst awaiting lighter vessel). Alternatively, the *departure report* must be submitted for the final departure from port. 'Final departure from port' means a departure from the last: (a) wharf/buoy mooring/SBM (all lines cast off); (b) anchorage within port limits (anchor aweigh); (c) anchorage outside port limits (anchor aweigh at an offshore location); or (d) lighterage location (all lines cast off from lighter vessel/anchor aweigh).

An arrival report for a specific port or offshore location must be followed by a departure report from the same port or offshore location. It will not be possible to submit the departure report if the name of the port or offshore location is different from the arrival report. In addition to the position, arrival and departure reports, other relevant periodic reports including Noon Reports, Monthly Reports, and Quarterly Reports must also be submitted in accordance with the company's reporting procedures.

Determining fuel bunkered and fuel in tanks

The quantity of fuel bunkered as stated in the Bunker Delivery Note (BDN) must be checked by gauging the fuel tanks on board prior to and after the completion of bunkering. This means applying the appropriate correction factor to account for density allowances for temperature and obtaining quantities in metric tonnes before and after bunkering. The ship's figure of fuel bunkered is the difference between the fuel quantity before and after bunkering. The ship's figure is regarded as the authoritative quantity of fuel bunkered and is the quantity entered by ship's staff in the departure report. Written records showing the soundings before and after all fuel tanks and details of the calculations showing ship's figure in metric tonnes of the quantity bunkered must be retained on board. The temperature of the fuel in the tanks is to be obtained from tank temperature gauges if provided or by using portable temperature gauging devices if not. If no gauges are provided, the temperature of fuel in tanks may be determined by measuring the temperature of the tank sides using an infrared thermometer or by estimating the weighted average of the temperature of the fuel before bunkering and of the fuel bunkered in each tank. The density of fuel bunkered is obtained from the BDN. The density of comingled fuel in tanks is obtained by calculating the weighted average of the density of the fuel remaining in the tanks before bunkering and of the fuel bunkered in each tank. The density of fuel should be corrected using an appropriate temperature correction factor obtained from ASTM Petroleum Table 54B or equivalent or by using computer software. If neither are available, the following formula may be used:

$$\text{Corrected Density} = \text{Density (in air) at } 150^\circ\text{C}$$

$$\times\left[1 - \left\{(T\ 0^\circ\text{C}^* - 150^\circ\text{C}) \times 0.00065\right\}\right]$$

* Where T 0°C is the temperature of the fuel in °C

In case of bunkering from barge, all tanks on the barge are to be sounded before and after bunkering by a responsible officer. Barge tanks are also to be checked for the presence of

170 Ship operations

free water. A written record is to be made of the results of these soundings and free water checks. The chief engineer is responsible for checking the fuel quantity bunkered. The fuel quantity (in tonnes) in all bunkered tanks must be rechecked 24 hours after completion of bunkering or just prior to the use of the newly bunkered fuel. This accounts for the settling of the fuel due to air injection during bunkering. Prior to entering an ECA, fuel oil change-over to LSFO must be started. The time needed for starting depends on how much volume of fuel is used in the system. Logbook entries must be made accordingly recording the volume of LSFO in the tanks, as well as the date, time, and position of the ship when the fuel oil changeover was completed.

Measuring and reporting distance travelled

The distances travelled over land are measured between the departure and arrival point and are reported in the position and arrival reports. The distance may be taken from ECDIS or GPS, or by manual chart measurement. Distances travelled through water are also to be reported in the position and arrival reports and are to be taken from the (water) speed log. The distances travelled between the arrival and departure reports (such as during transit from anchorage to berth or when shifting between terminals within a port) are not required to be reported in the Voyage Reports but should be noted in the ship's Logbook. The *'hours underway'* from the last berth at the port of departure to the first berth at the port of arrival is calculated from the departure and arrival times (GMT) and the dates recorded in the departure and arrival reports. Times and dates must be recorded in GMT as well as SMT. The time spent between the first berth at the port of arrival to the last berth at the port of departure is considered time spent in port. This includes periods at berth, at anchor, and the periods spent manoeuvring within the port. Fuel flowmeters, fixed tank gauging devices, and temperature measuring devices/gauges should be checked and calibrated for accuracy at intervals stated in the PMS or as recommended by the manufacturer. Certificates of calibration are issued following calibration checks and are retained on board. These certificates are almost always checked during the annual internal audit.

Emission actor

CF is a non-dimensional conversion factor between fuel oil consumption and CO^2 emissions as per the 2014 Guidelines on the Method of Calculation of the Attained Energy Efficiency Design Index (EEDI) for New Ships. The annual total amount of CO^2 is calculated by multiplying the annual fuel oil consumption and CF for the type of fuel. From 2019, every ship above 5,000 gross tonnes must collect certain information about the ship and its fuel consumption and submit this to the IMO. This includes Ship Particulars, the period of the calendar year for which the data is being submitted, fuel oil consumption in metric tonnes, fuel oil type and the methods used for collecting fuel oil consumption data, the distance travelled, and hours underway. This data, as provided by the ship, helps the IMO to calculate the fuel oil consumption of all ships in the merchant fleet. These calculations are then used to research and establish ways for reducing marine emissions and maritime pollution.

BUNKERING OPERATIONS

Bunkering is one of the most hazardous operations that is carried out on any ship. The term *bunker* originates from the Scots for 'reserved seat' or 'bench'. Most people are probably more aware of the military use of the term, which refers to an area for storing and safeguarding personnel and supplies (such as fuel, ammunition, and food). In the shipping industry, the term *bunkering* or *bunker* is used to denote any fuel or LO which is used by the ship for the operation of its own machinery. This means if a ship is carrying fuel or LO for discharge as cargo in another port, this is not considered *bunker*. The operation for loading and discharging fuel and LO is called *bunkering*. Bunker fuel or bunker oil is stored on board in separate storage tanks called bunker tanks. These are fed directly to the ship's machinery. There are five main types of bunker that a ship typically carries depending on the plant and type of propulsion: HFO bunker, diesel oil bunker, marine gas oil bunker, LO bunker, and LNG fuel bunker. The bunker fuel can be supplied to the ship in different ways. The mode or method may vary depending on the grade or type of fuel being supplied. There can be different types of bunkering facilities which supply the required marine fuel or LO to the ship. A small barge or ship carrying bunker fuel may be used to transfer marine fuel oil (such as heavy fuel oil) to the vessel. If the quantity of oil is less (for example LO, MGO, or LNG) then this may be supplied by quayside lorries.

Bunkering procedure

In summary, the bunkering procedure can be divided into three important stages: preparation, performance, and closeout. The *preparation* stage involves the readiness of the bunkering equipment, storage tanks, and bunkering safety. *Performance* refers to carrying out the bunkering operation in real time as per procedures and receiving the marine fuel according to the bunker plan. The *closeout* of the bunkering operation means ensuring the correct amount and quality of bunker fuel has been received on board from the bunkering facilities. Before the bunkering operation starts, the chief engineer must calculate and check which bunker oil tanks are to be filled after they have received confirmation from the shore office about the amount of fuel to be accepted. This may require the emptying of some tanks and the transfer of oil from one tank to another. This avoids mixing the two oils and prevents any incompatibility between the existing oil and the incoming oil. The other fuel storage tanks (not to be bunkered) should be sounded to maintain an accurate record of the fuel already stored on board. This helps to ascertain if any valves are leaking during the bunker operation. Before the bunkering starts, a meeting should be called for the crew members who will participate in the bunkering operation. This allows important information to be shared including (a) which tanks are to be filled; (b) the sequence order of tanks to be filled; (c) how much bunker oil is to be taken; (d) bunkering safety procedures; (e) emergency procedures to be carried out in the event of an oil spill; and (f) the responsibilities of each officer and crew member.

Once the bunkering process has been explained and roles assigned, a final sounding is taken before the bunkering record is completed. The deck scuppers and save-all trays are then plugged. An overflow tank is provided in the engine room, which is connected to the bunker tank and bunker line. The overflow tank must be kept empty to allow any transfer of excess fuel from the bunker tanks. It is important that adequate lighting at the bunker and sounding position is provided. A no-smoking notice should be positioned near the bunkering station and a no-smoking perimeter established. All onboard communications, signs, and signals must stop to allow the bunkering crew to communicate and understand each other without disruption. The red flag/light must be present/illuminated on the masthead. The opposite side bunker manifold valves are closed and appropriately blanked. The vessel draught and trim is recorded before bunkering begins. The equipment in the SOPEP (Shipboard Oil Pollution Emergency Plan) locker is checked and kept near the bunkering station. When bunker ship or barge is secured alongside, the OIC on the barge is advised of the bunkering plan. The bunker supplier's paperwork is checked against the ship's required oil grade and density. The pumping rate of the bunker fuel is agreed with the bunker barge/bunker truck. The hose is then connected to the manifold. The condition of the hose must be checked properly by the bunkering crew. If the condition of the hose is not satisfactory, the chief engineer must be notified immediately. Most bunker suppliers provide their own crew members to attach the bunker oil pipeline from bunker ship/barge to the receiving ship. The bunkering crew should check the flange to ensure a full connection.

Once the connection is made, the chief engineer will ensure the line valves which lead the bunker fuel to the selected bunker tanks are open, whilst keeping the main manifold valve shut. Most bunkering facilities (ship/barge/terminal/truck) provide some form of emergency stop switch which controls the bunkering supply pump. This should be checked and tested before the supply starts. Once all checks are complete, and the chief engineer is satisfied it is safe to continue, the manifold valve is opened for bunkering. At the start of the bunker, the pumping rate is kept low; this is done to check that the oil is going into the tank to which the valve is open. The bunkering crew must track the sounding of the selected bunkering tank and other tanks not involved in the operation to ensure the oil is fed to the correct tank. After confirming the correct tank is being filled, the pumping rate is increased accordingly. In most situations, it is preferable to fill only one tank, as gauging multiple tanks at one time increases the chance of overflow. The maximum allowable volume to which the tank may be filled is 90%. When the tank reaches close the maximum limit, the barge must be instructed to slow the pump rate. During bunkering, soundings are taken regularly, and accordingly increased when the tank is near to full. Many vessels have tank gauges which show the tank level in the engine control room, though this gauge should never be totally relied on. The temperature of the bunker oil should also be checked; generally, the barge or supplier will provide the bunker temperature. Temperature is a critical parameter, especially for bunker fuel such as heavy fuel oil, and any deviation in the provided temperature value may cause a shortfall in bunker supply. A continuous sample is taken during bunkering by way of the sampling cock located on the manifold. The bunkering crew need to switch (open and close the valves) the internal storage tanks to accommodate the quantity of bunker oil being supplied. Utmost caution needs to be taken when opening the other storage tank valve and closing the valve to the tank which is reaching the maximum fill limit.

Once the bunker is finished, it is a general practice to air blow the bunkering supply line to discharge any oil trapped in the pipeline. At this stage, it is important to ensure all sounding pipe caps are closed and to keep a watch on the storage tank vents which are at their maximum limit. Always avoid opening the bunkering supply line connecting the bunker ship and the receiving manifold. In the event of any discrepancy, the supplier may agree to compensate the shortfall and may resume the bunkering operation. During and after bunkering, the ships draught and trim must be checked and recorded. The bunker tanks should be sounded to confirm the absolute level of bunker supplied. The volume bunkered should be corrected for trim, heel, and temperature. In general, for each degree of increase in temperature the bunker density should be reduced by 0.64 kg/m^3. Four samples are taken during bunkering. One is kept on board, one is retained by the bunker ship or barge, one is sent off for analysis, and one is despatched to the Port State Authority. The chief engineer will sign the bunker delivery note (BDN) and confirm the amount of bunker received. If there is any shortfall of bunker received, the chief engineer can issue a note of protest against the barge/supplier (in case the deficit is disputed by the bunker supplier). The lab sample is sent off to the laboratory for analysis. Only after everything has settled may the hose connection be removed. On completion of the operation, the chief engineer will make the appropriate entry into the ORB together with the BDN. Importantly, the new bunker should not be used until the report is received from the laboratory.

BOILER BLOWDOWN PROCEDURE

The boiler is one of the most important machinery systems on the ship. An efficient working boiler requires timely maintenance and special care in starting and stopping. Routine cleaning is essential to increasing the boiler's working life. One of the main procedures that marine engineers need to perform regularly is the boiler blowdown. The water which is circulated inside the boiler tubes and drum contains Total Dissolved Solids (TDS) along with other dissolved and undissolved particles. During the steam making process, i.e., when the boiler is in operation, the water is heated and converted into steam. However, these dissolved solids do not evaporate, instead, they tend to settle at the bottom of the boiler shell. This layer of detritus prevents the efficient transfer of heat amid the gases and water, which eventually will lead to the boiler tubes and shell overheating. These impurities also lead to scaling, corrosion, and erosion and will also be carried over with the steam into the steam system, leading to deposits inside the heat exchanger surface where the steam is the primary heating medium. To minimise these problems, a boiler blowdown is done. The aim is to remove two types of impurities – scum and bottom deposits – which means there are two types of boiler blowdown. As well as removing these impurities, boiler blowdowns also provide a number of additional benefits. A blowdown removes precipitates formed as a result of chemical addition to the boiler water; it removes solid particles, dirt, foam, or oil molecules from the boiler water. This is mainly done by the scum valve through a procedure is known as 'scumming'; to reduce the density of water by reducing the water level; and to remove excess water in the event of an emergency.

Inside the boiler, the blowdown arrangement is provided at two levels: at a bottom level, which is called a 'boiler blowdown' and at the water surface level, which is called the 'scum blowdown'. The boiler blowdown can be done in two ways depending on the type, design, level of automation, the capacity, and the characteristics of the boiler feedwater system. The first system is the *intermittent or manual blowdown*. When blowdown is done manually by the boiler operator it is known as manual blowdown. This type of blowdown is useful for removing sludge formations or suspended solids from the boiler, usually after oil ingress into the boiler water due to leakage in the heat exchanger. Using the manual scumming process, the oil on the water surface can be easily removed. The main drawback to manual blowdown is the heat loss from the release of hot water out of the water drum. Even though the release valve is opened only slightly, there is still significant heat and pressure loss. The second system is the *continuous blowdown*. Many modern boilers are fitted with blowdown automation. This allows for the continuous blowdown of the boiler water, which helps in keeping the dissolved and suspended solids under boiler operating limits. This process is known as continuous blowdown. In this system, the automation monitors the blowdown continuously and in turn checks the quality of feedwater and the quality of water inside the boiler shell for dissolved and undissolved impurities. Accordingly, it automatically opens the blowdown valves if the boiler water TDS exceeds the boiler's operating limits. As the blowdown valves are precisely controlled, the water discharged from the blowdown removes the maximum volume of dissolved impurities with minimum heat and water loss, maintaining boiler efficiency. Most boilers with continuous blowdown automation are fitted with heat recovery systems. This means the hot water from the boiler blowdown is first sent to a heat exchanger unit which utilises the heat of the water before it goes overboard. The choice of blowdown system used on board will depend on various factors, and the blowdown valves will be fitted with the appropriate utilities for the system.

Procedure for scumming and bottom blowdown

The procedure for carrying out the boiler blowdown is relatively straightforward and set out below.[1] Start by opening the overboard or ship side valve first. Open the blowdown valve;

174 Ship operations

this valve is a non-return valve. The blowdown valve adjacent to the boiler should be opened fully to prevent cutting of the valve seat; the rate of blowdown is controlled by the valve. After the blowdown, close the valve in reverse order. If the boiler is blown down for inspection, the first step is to stop the firing and allow the boiler to cool off. Open the boiler vent plug. This will allow natural cooling at ambient pressure. Ensure the non-return overboard valve is functioning properly so that no seawater can enter the boiler pipeline. If it does, it will create a vacuum due to the sudden steam cooling leading to pipe burst. Once the boiler blowdown is complete, open the belly plug to remove the remaining content in the engine room bilges. Always perform a scum blowdown before the bottom blowdown otherwise the scum settled on the water surface will agitate contaminating the boiler water.

Requirements and regulations

If there is any oil sheen visible in the boiler gauge glass or hotwell inspection glass, do not perform a scum blowdown, as this will lead to oil pollution. The oil leak inside the boiler water must be stopped and all efforts made to clear the oil from the hotwell by filling freshwater and removing the contaminated oily water. Before performing a boiler blowdown, the operator must be cognisant of the Vessel General Permit areas and comply with chapter 12 of the VGP. This prohibits the discharge of boiler wastewater in restricted areas except where safety is compromised. The vessel must not discharge boiler water in any port waters. This is because the water consists of different chemicals or other additives which are added to reduce impurities or prevent scale formations. The boiler blowdown must be done as far from shore as possible. The master and the OOW must be informed before the start of the blowdown operation. The boiler blowdown operation must be recorded in the Engine Logbook, including the start and stop time. If the boiler blowdown or hotwell water is transferred to the bilges, this must also be recorded in oil record book and engine logbook. A boiler blowdown may only occur in territorial or harbour waters in the following conditions: (a) if the ship is entering dry dock; and (b) for any safety reasons.

DIESEL GENERATOR OPERATION

The ship's generator is its heart. It is completely unlike the conventional generators that used on land. Ship generators require a special step-by-step method of operation. Though not very complex, the process must be followed all the same. Missing even one step can lead to the generator failing to start or stop, which in turn can cause a dreaded blackout.

Generator starting procedures

To initiate the automatic start, sufficient starting air must be supplied to the generator. The air valves and interlocks are operated in the same manner as the turning gear operation. With automatic start, there is nothing for the operator to do, as the generator starts itself depending on the load requirement. That said, in restricted areas and during manoeuvring the operator has to start by going into the computerised *Power Management System* (PMS). Once inside the system, the operator goes to the generator page and clicks start. In the PMS system, the automation follows a sequence of starting, voltage matching, and frequency loading of the incoming generator. In the event of a blackout condition or a dead ship condition, the operator might have to start the generator manually. The manual process is totally different from the automatic start system. In this situation, the following steps need to be followed: (1) check that all the necessary valves and lines are open and no interlock is active on the generator; (2) before starting the generator, the indicator cocks should be opened and a small air kick given with the help of the starting lever; (3) the starting lever is brought back to the zero position, which ensures there is no water leakage into the generator. Leakage may occur from the cylinder head, the liner or from the turbocharger; (4) the controller is moved to the local position, after which the generator may be started locally; (5) in the event that water has leaked into the generator, this must be reported to the chief engineer immediately.

It is worth noting that this manual starting procedure is not followed on UMS ships, but it is a common procedure in manned engine rooms. In engine rooms with water mist firefighting systems installed, this procedure is not followed, as when the engine is given a manual kick with open indicator cocks, a small amount of smoke is emitted from the cylinder heads which can lead to a false fire alarm. After fixing the leak, the indicator cocks are closed, and the generator is started again from the local control panel. The generator is then allowed to run on a zero or no load condition for about five minutes. Once this time has elapsed, the generator control is put into remote mode. If the automation of the ship is working after putting in remote mode, the generator will come on load automatically after checking the voltage and frequency parameters. If this does not happen automatically, then the generator panel in the engine control room must be checked with any faults rectified. Once the parameters are satisfactory, the voltage and frequency will equal out. At this point, the frequency can be increased or decreased by the frequency controller or the governor control on the generator panel. The incoming generator is then checked in synchroscope to determine whether it is running fast (high frequency) or slow (low frequency).

In synchroscope, the needle is manipulated in a clockwise and anti-clockwise direction. A clockwise direction means the generator is running fast and anti-clockwise means it is running slow. The breaker is pressed when the needle moves in a clockwise direction very slowly and when it reaches the 11 o'clock position. This process must be carried out under the supervision of an experienced officer. If not, the generator may overload causing a blackout. Once the starting procedure is complete, the generator load will be shared almost equally by the number of generators running. Once this is confirmed, the parameters of the generator should be checked for any abnormalities.

Generator stopping procedures

In automatic setting, the generator is stopped by going into the PMS system and pressing the stop button. This stops the generator. This procedure should be carried out only if two or more generators are running. If only one generator is running, the inbuilt safety function will prohibit automatic shutdown to prevent a blackout condition. When the stop button is pressed the load is gradually reduced by the PMS. Once the load is fully reduced, the generator is stopped. In manual setting, the generator is placed off-load from the generator panel in the engine control room. The load is reduced slowly by the governor control on the panel. This reduces the load to below 100 kW. When the load is below 100 kW the breaker is pressed and the generator is taken off-load. The generator is then allowed to run for five minutes in idle condition after which the stop button is pressed on the panel. This stops the generator.

TRIPS

Overspeed trip

The first type of trip is the *overspeed trip*. An overspeed trip is a safety feature provided on marine diesel engines to restrict the uncontrolled acceleration of the engine, which can lead to mechanical failure. To prevent the speed of the diesel engine going beyond the pre-set speed range, an overspeed trip is installed. The diesel engine is designed to cope with the mechanical stress associated with the centripetal and centrifugal forces of the moving parts inside it within a specified operational range. Centripetal force is directly proportional to the square of the rotational speed; stress increases rapidly with increase in speed. Mechanical connection strength can be overcome by excessive stresses caused by unregulated increases in operational speed. Due to sudden changes in the load on the diesel engine, the speed of the engine may vary. Though a governor is provided to control the speed of the diesel engine, the speed might go out of control. This can result in the breaking of rotating parts or damage to the machinery itself. Overspeed is thus a serious safety hazard and can lead to fatal situations. For this reason, overspeed trips are used. No matter what type of overspeed trip the engine uses, the main aim of the overspeed trip is to cut the fuel supply to the engine cylinders in the event the engine speed rises above a predetermined level.

Reducing the likelihood of an uncontrolled and catastrophic overspeed is essential and can be done through two methods. First, using an electronic overspeed trip; and second, by using a mechanical overspeed trip. To understand the *electronic overspeed trip*, a normal lay out of the system is described below. The electronic overspeed trip consists of (1) a *magnetic flywheel mounted speed sensor*. Due to the discontinuity of actuator surface (i.e., the gear teeth on the flywheel) the voltage is excited in the pick-off coil of the sensor, which produces an electric analogue wave. This cyclic wave is created by the flywheel and read by the sensor. (2) A *signal condition unit*. This unit acts as a receiver to the speed sensor. The basic function of the signal conditioner is to convert one type of electronic signal, which may be difficult to read, into another type which is more easily interpreted. This can be achieved by amplification, excitation, and linearisation of the electrical signal. (3) The *detection and comparison unit*. There is a set value which is normally 10% above the rated speed and acts as base value for this unit. Signal condition unit output is continuously detected and compared against the set value. (4) The *trip signal unit*. If the difference between the set value and the detected value is above the limit, then the unit sends a trip signal which in turn shuts down the generator.

Air circuit breaker

The generators on board ships are the power suppliers for the entire vessel. This means they are primary source of power to all running machinery systems including the propulsion plant. For this reason, the safe and efficient operation of the generator is critical. One of the safety devices used on the generator is *Air Circuit Breaker* (ACB). The ACB is designed to overcome defects and safeguard the generator before it breaks down. The main function of ACB is to either manually or automatically open and close a three-phase circuit and to open the circuit automatically when a fault occurs.[2] The main feature of the ACB is that it dampens or quenches the arcing during overloading. The ACB consists of two sets of contacts – i.e., main and auxiliary contacts. Each set of contacts has a fixed contact and a moving contact. The main contact normally carries most of the load current. All the contacts are made of cadmium-silver alloy which provides very good resistance to damage by arcing. When the ACB is closed, the powerful spring is energised and the ACB is then latched shut against the spring pressure. The auxiliary contact makes first and breaks last – i.e., when the ACB is closed, the auxiliary contact closes first followed by the main contact. The main contact closing pressure is kept high so that the rise in temperature of both contacts when carrying current remains within prescribed limits. A closing coil operating on DC voltage from a rectifier is provided to close the circuit breaker by operating a push button. The quenching of the arc is achieved by using arcing contacts made of resistance alloy and silver tips for the main contacts. The arcing contacts close earlier and open later than the main contacts.

Engine room operations 177

When opening, the contacts travelled at high speed to stretch the resultant arc, which is then transferred to the arcing contact. The cooling and splitting of the arc is achieved by arc chutes, which draw the arc through splitters by magnetic action and quickly cool and split the arc until it snaps. The circuit breaker then opens when the arc is quenched.

Preferential trips

A preferential trip is a type of electrical arrangement on ships which is designed to disconnect non-essential circuits, for example, the non-essential load from the main bus bar in the event of partial failure or overload of the main supply. The non-essential circuits or loads on board are air conditioning, exhaust, and ventilation fans, and galley equipment. These can be disconnected momentarily and reconnected after fault finding. The main advantage of preferential trips is that they help prevent the operation of the main circuit breaker trips causing loss of power to essential services, which in turn prevents blackout and generator overload. The preferential trip circuit consists of an electromagnetic coil and a dashpot arrangement. This provides some delay for disconnecting the non-essential circuits. Along with this, there is also an alarm system, which functions as soon as an overload is detected, and the trips start operating. There are some mechanical linkages in the circuit which instantaneously operate and completes the circuit for preferential trips. The dashpot arrangement consists of a piston with a small orifice which is placed inside a small cylinder assembly. The piston moves up against the fluid silicon and the time delay is governed by the orifice in the piston. The current passes through the electromagnetic coil. The linkages are kept from contacting using a spring arrangement. As soon as the current value increases over the limit, the electromagnetic coil pulls the linkage up against the spring force and operates the instantaneous circuit and the alarm system. The lower linkage completes the preferential trip circuit. The current passes through the coil in the preferential trip circuit which pulls the piston in the dashpot arrangement. The movement of the piston is governed by the diameter of the orifice. This also determines the time delay. The preferential trip operates at 5, 10, and 15 second intervals with the load removed accordingly. If the overload persists, then an audible and visual alarm is sounded. The preferential trip is one of those important electrical circuit diagrams which helps in removing the excessive load from the main bus bar, thus preventing situations such as blackout.

Other important trips

Reverse Power Trip. When multiple generators are running in parallel, a situation may arise where one generator acts as a motor and draws in the current from the system instead of supplying it. This is known as motoring or reverse generator power. A safety device known as the reverse power relay is used to trip the generator to prevent the reversing of the alternator. *LO Pressure/Temperature/Level Trip.* The generator engine is a high revolution machine which requires a continuous supply of LO at the recommended grade to keep the bearing friction-free and at low temperature. LO is one of the most important supplements for the engine and alternator's moving parts. Therefore, various parameters of the engine LO are monitored. The three important LO parameters which are provided alarms and trips are: (1) the *LO LP alarm and trip.* If the pressure of the LO in the generator inlet after the filter is lower than the recommended value, an alarm will sound to alert the engineer to investigate the cause before the pressure goes too low and activates the trip. (2) *LO HT alarm and trip.* If the LO cooler is not functioning or any of the internal parts of the prime mover are damaged, the LO temperature will rise. After a point the LO will start to lose its characteristics causing damage to the rotating parts and contact points. The temperature of the LO is constantly monitored and any abnormal variation triggers the alarm and trip. (3) *LO low level*. The generator is provided with its own sump from where the priming pump and attached lube oil pump takes suction and supplies back to the engine. To safeguard the engine from starvation of LO, a level alarm and trip is fitted in the prime mover. (4) *Cooling water pressure/temperature trip*. The cooling water for the engine jacket, liner, and other high temperature parts keeps them within controlled parameters which prevent the parts from seizing. The two important cooling parameters installed as alarms and trips are the *cooling water low pressure alarm and trip* and the *cooling water high temperature alarm and trip*. If the pressure of the cooling water in the generator is lower than the recommended value, an alarm will sound to the alert the engineer to investigate before the pressure goes any lower. If it does, this will activate the trip to stop the generator from sustaining major damage. If the cooling water temperature in the engine jacket is high, it will also activate an alarm. Any further increase in temperature will activate the trip to avoid the water from boiling off.

(5) *Oil Mist Detector*. The oil mist detector takes continuous samples from the main engine crankcase. It then checks the samples to confirm whether the concentrations of the mist are below the level at which a crankcase explosion may occur. An overall mist density of the crankcase is also measured by comparing the samples with the fresh air once every rotation of the sampling valve is done. A beam of light from a lamp is reflected through mirrors and the output is measured from a photocell. (6) *Crankcase relief doors*. The crankcase relief doors are fitted to prevent damage to the crankcase and ingress of fresh air inside the crankcase. The crankcase doors are spring loaded valves which lift-up in the event of a rise of pressure within the crankcase. Once the pressure is released, they reseat to prevent the ingress of air. This is especially useful when any ingress of air can lead to secondary explosion followed by a surge and damage to the crankcase. The opening pressure and sizes of the valves are specified by different classification societies, depending on the volume of the crankcase. The number of doors present also depends on the bore of the cylinder.

SLUDGE PRODUCTION AND MANAGEMENT

Sludge is an unfortunate biproduct of many of the onboard systems and processes. On most ships, there are six main sources of sludge: (1) the *fuel oil purifier*. The fuel oil purifiers have a designated discharge interval depending on the quality of the fuel oil. After every set interval the bowl of the purifier discharges the accumulated sludge into the sludge tank or a designated fuel oil purifier sludge tank. This sludge contains oily water and impurities which have been separated from the fuel oil by the purifiers; (2) the *LO purifier*. The *LO purifiers* have a designated discharge interval depending on the quality of LO and the running hours of the main engine and auxiliary generators. After every set interval the bowl of the purifier discharges the accumulated sludge into the sludge tank or designated LO purifier sludge tank. This sludge contains oily water and impurities which have also been separated from LO by the purifiers; (3) the *main engine scavenge drains*. When the main engine is running, oil residue in the scavenge spaces is collected from the cylinder lubrication being scrapped down from the liners. This oil is drained through the scavenge drains of each unit of the main engine and is collected by the sludge tank or designated scavenge drain tank; (4) the *main engine stuffing box*. When the main engine is running, oil residue is collected from the stuffing box scraping oil on the piston rod. This oil comes from the stuffing box drains of each unit of the main engine and is collected by the sludge tank or designated stuffing box drain tank. (5) the *machinery tray drains*. All fuel oil machinery – i.e., the pumps, filters, and purifiers – all have a tray under them to collect any leaking oil. The drain of the tray goes directly into the sludge tanks; (6) *miscellaneous*. These are any other drains that go straight into the sludge tanks; for example, the air bottle drains and the fuel oil settling and service tank drains. Each of these contains oily water which is collected in the sludge tanks.

Sludge tanks

The number of sludge tanks varies from ship to ship. It largely depends which shipyard the vessel was built in and what machinery is installed in the engine room. Some ships have one common sludge tank whereas other ships have individual sludge tanks. In either case, the sludge pump is used to make internal transfers and to transfer sludge from the tank to the onshore reception facility. All sludge tanks must comply with the Flag State ORB, into which all transfers must be recorded. All designated sludge tanks and bilge tanks must be annotated on the International Oil Pollution Prevention (IOPP) certificate. Any transfer from or to the IOPP tank must also be recorded in the ORB by the chief engineer.

Sludge incineration and oily water evaporation

Inevitably some of the sludge generated by the ship will have some content coming from the HFO and LO purifiers, from the HFO settling and service tank drains, and the air bottle drains. This water can be evaporated in the waste oil tank. This is done by transferring the sludge from the various sludge tanks into the waste oil tank for incineration. Before incineration can start, the water must be evaporated so that sludge can be burned off efficiently. The sludge is transferred from the HFO purifier sludge tank, and the LO purifier sludge tank and the oily bilge sludge tank into the waste oil tank. The inlet and return steam valves are kept open for the water to evaporate. When the tank temperature reaches 100°C (212°F) the water begins to evaporate. Once the tank temperature rises above 100°C (212°F) this indicates that the water has evaporated and the oil has started to heat up. This means the sludge is ready for incineration. The volume of water evaporated must be recorded in the ORB. If there is a common sludge tank, then water is allowed to settle for a few days in the bottom of the tank. After the water has settled, suction from the bottom is taken and transferred to the waste oil tank for evaporation. Before transferring any sludge into the waste oil tank, the temperature of the waste oil tank should be less than 90°C (194°F) to prevent boil off in the tank. Boil off will result in an instantaneous rise of pressure in the tank. After the water has been evaporated and sludge is heated up, it is ready for incineration.

The incineration process is done by draining the waste oil tank and confirming there is no water left at the bottom of the tank. If a sludge agitator is available, agitate the sludge. This will help in emulsifying the oil into an even mixture for fine atomisation. Start to warm up the incinerator with diesel oil. The incinerator should be operated by SQEP personnel only. After warming the incinerator, open the waste oil feed valve on the waste oil tank. Ensure steam tracing is proper for the waste oil line and the strainers are not choked. Adjust the damper and temperature in accordance with the operations manual. The waste oil pump will take suction from the waste oil tank. Continue burning the waste oil to maintain the incinerator parameters. Depending on the capacity of the waste oil pump, compare and check how much waste oil is being burned by off the incinerator. The final amount of sludge incinerated must be recorded in the ORB. The total amount of sludge generated on board is proportional to the ship's fuel consumption. In general, average sludge production is approximately 1.5% of total fuel consumption. If sludge generation is more than 1.5%, then this indicates that the sludge production of the ship is too high.

180 Ship operations

BILGE SYSTEM

Atmospheric air contains moisture, and when this air is compressed in the turbocharger and then cooled in the air cooler, the moisture condenses to form water droplets. If these water droplets enter the cylinders with the scavenge air they can remove the oil film from the liner, resulting in excessive cylinder liner and piston ring wear. Additionally, removal of water droplets from the air minimises the risk of sulphuric acid formation in the cylinders and uptakes due to the dissolving of acid products of combustion in the water droplets. To prevent these problems, water is removed from the combustion air by water separators fitted after the scavenge air coolers. The water droplets are directed from the air coolers, via drain traps, to the air cooler drain tank. This tank is pumped overboard by the air cooler drain discharge pump or bilge pump. The water flowing to the overboard discharge line passes through an oil detector, which monitors the oil content of the water being discharged. It is also possible to pump the contents of the air cooler drain tank to the bilge holding tank using the oily water bilge pump. All the bilge transfers and bilge discharge must be recorded in the ORB. Whenever the OWS is operated, the position of the vessel at the time of starting and stopping must be recorded together with the time and volume of bilge discharge. The ppm monitor will not allow the discharge of bilge with more than 15 ppm of oil content.

Engine room bilge water generation

Leaks from the freshwater and seawater pumps and coolers are collected in bilge wells in the engine room. These bilge wells are located at the forward end of the bottom platform at the tank top, both port and starboard. In the aft of the engine room, additional bilge wells include the recess bilge well under the flywheel and the shaft tunnel bilge well if a separate space for the shaft tunnel is present. All leakages from the engine room bottom platform are collected in these bilge wells and can be transferred to the bilge holding tank via the oily bilge pump. The oily bilge pump may also pump these spaces to the sludge tank (via the sludge pump bypass line) and the deck connections for discharge to shore or barge. The oily bilge pump transfers bilges to the bilge holding tank via the bilge primary tank. The bilge primary tank has a smaller capacity to separate oil from the bilges. The bilge primary tank is overflowed to the bilge holding tank. Any oil layers formed on top of the bilge primary tank can then be removed. The bilge tanks in the engine room are: (1) the *bilge holding tank*. Bilges from the bilge well are transferred here and stored to be discharged overboard via the OWS and ppm monitor or discharged ashore; (2) *bilge primary tank*. Bilge is transferred here to separate oil by gravity. Any oil layer formed on the top is then removed; (3) *bilge evaporation tank*. Present on some ships, bilge can be transferred and evaporated by heating; (4) *air cooler drain tank*. All the moisture from the main engine scavenge air coolers and generator scavenge air cooler are drained into this tank. They might contain some oil, as engine room air often contains oil vapour. Hence, the bilge is discharged overboard via the ppm monitor.

Cargo hold bilge water production

The cargo holds on container ships have bilge wells located at the bottom on each side: port and starboard. The hold bilges are normally pumped overboard by bilge eductor from the fire and general service pump, as they contain only water. However, before pumping hold bilge wells, a visual inspection must be carried out of the bilge wells. If any traces of oil are found, then this must be pumped to the hold bilge collecting tank or any other designated engine room tank, from where it is processed by the OWS. Before any bilges are pumped directly overboard, the chief engineer must be confident that no local or international anti-pollution regulations will be contravened. The eductor should only be used when at sea. The hold bilge line additionally takes suction from the bow thruster room bilge wells, pipe duct bilge wells, chain locker bilge well, and forepeak void space. All the bilge well valves can be operated remotely from the bridge or the engine control room. Sludge and bilge management on board is very important, as the MARPOL rules are stringent and must be followed properly to prevent pollution at sea. Any violation of MARPOL can lead to imprisonment and substantial fines.

WASTE OIL INCINERATOR

In accordance with Annex VI of MARPOL 1973/78, the guidelines regarding waste material storage and disposal of waste at sea must be strictly followed. Incineration of various materials such as galley waste, food scraps, accommodation waste, linen, cardboard, oil sludge from LO, fuel oil, the bilges and purifiers, and sewage sludge is one of the most effective ways of saving space and disposing of waste. Moreover, the residue left from the incineration can be easily disposed of, as it mainly consists of ash. For all foreign-going vessels, any incinerator installed on board on or after 1 January 2000 must comply with the requirements of the standard specifications for shipboard incinerators developed under resolutions MEPC.76(40) and MEPC.93(45). As such, the following materials are prohibited from being incinerated: (1) Annex I, II, and III cargo residues of the present Convention and related contaminated packing materials; (2) polychlorinated biphenyls (PCBs); and (3) garbage, as defined in Annex V of the present Convention, containing more than traces of heavy metals; and refined petroleum products containing halogen compounds. Incineration of sewage sludge and sludge oil generated during the normal operation of the ship may also take place in the main or auxiliary power plant or boilers but, in those cases, should not take place inside port limits, harbours, and estuaries. The temperature of the flue gases must be monitored and should not be less than 850°C (1,562°F) for continuous feed and reach 600°C (1,112°F) within five minutes (the time may vary depending on the capacity of the incinerator) for a batch feed.

There are different types of incinerators available for marine use. The *vertical cyclone type* and *horizontal burner type* are the two most common incinerators on board ships. The horizontal burner type is like a horizontal fired boiler with a burner arrangement horizontal to the incinerator combustion chamber axis. The ash and non-combustible materials remaining at the end of the operation are cleared out manually. With the vertical cyclone type, the burner is mounted on the top, and the waste to be incinerated in introduced into the combustion chamber also from the top. A rotating arm device is provided to improve combustion and remove ash and non-combustibles from the surface. The important sections of the incinerator are the combustion chamber with the diesel oil burner, sludge burner, pilot fuel heater, and electric control panel; the flue gas fan, which may be fitted with a flue gas damper or frequency inverter; the sludge service tank with circulating pump and heater; the sludge settling tank with filling pump and optional heater; an optional water injector; and in the vertical cyclone type, the rotating arm used for the removal of ash and non-combustibles.

Incinerator operation

A sludge burner is located in the incinerator to burn and dispose of sewage, sludge, and waste oil. An auxiliary oil burner is also fitted to ignite the garbage. Automatic controls provided for the system secure the igniter when the garbage starts burning without the need of the igniter. Combustion air is supplied with the help of a forced draught fan. A loading door, pneumatically operated, is provided to load the garbage. An interlock is also provided with the burner and forced draught fan, which trips when the loading door is opened. Solid waste is fed into the incinerator from the loading door, and the incineration process starts immediately the door is closed. Liquid waste is fed into the system when the refractory of the incinerator becomes hot. After the completion of the incineration process, the incinerator is allowed to cool down, and any residue like ash and non-combustibles are removed by pulling the ash slide door. The rotating arm in the vertical cyclone type scrapes off the entire solid residue in the ash box which is then disposed of. During incineration, it is important to control the exhaust temperature, which should not be too high or too low. A high temperature could lead to the melting of the metal structure and can cause damage to the machinery, whereas a too low temperature will not be capable of burning and sterilising the residue. Temperature control can be achieved by introducing cold-diluted air into the exhaust stream.

It is critical to keep the incinerator chamber inlet, outlet, and burner parts clean. A daily inspection should be carried out before each incineration. Never throttle the air/steam needle valve more than three-quarters of a turn closed. If the pressure increases above the defined limit, clean the sludge burner nozzle. Do not turn off the main power before the chamber temperature is down to below 170°C (338°F). Keep the fan running to cool down the chamber. Any problems with high temperature in the combustion chamber, flue gas, or control of sludge dosing can be rectified by replacing the dosing pump stator.

Never transfer sludge to the service tank during sludge burning in a single tank system, as this can damage the refractory. It is always recommended to heat the sludge overnight, without starting the circulating pump; drain off the free water and start the sludge programme before performing the incinerator operation. Never load glass, lithium batteries, or large quantities of spray cans into the incinerator, and avoid loading large amounts of oily rags or filter cartridges, as these may damage the flue gas fan. Inspect the cooling jacket every six months by opening the cover plates and clean as required with steam or hot water. Flammable materials such as bottles or aerosol cans containing flammable liquids or gases must never be incinerated. Never incinerate metals such as drinks and food cans, crockery, flatware, cutlery, hardware (nuts and bolts), structural pieces, wire rope, chains, or glass such as bottles, jars, and drinking vessels. Loading glass into the incinerator will result in a hard slag, which is extremely difficult to remove from the refractory lining. In the event of a blackout, if the combustion chamber temperature is above 220°C (428°F) it is important to start the flue gas fan as soon as possible to avoid damaging the incinerator through the accumulation of heat in the refractory lining.

FUEL CHANGEOVER PROCEDURE

Many port authorities regulate the use of gas oil for generators and boilers while ships are within the port confines. This is most common in European ports. Subsequently, to comply with the port's regulations, the ship must change over the fuel used by the generators and boilers to diesel oil with a sulphur content of less than 0.1%. The generators are best changed over from one grade to another while at load, as this helps in flushing out the system. If only one generator is being changed over, then the second generator should be kept running in case of emergency. The procedure for changeover starts by shutting off the steam to the boiler fuel oil heaters. When the temperature drops below 90°C (194°F) the diesel oil service tank valve is opened. The local diesel inlet valve is also opened whilst the heavy oil inlet valve is shut simultaneously and slowly. Maintain a close watch on the fuel pressure.

Change only one generator onto diesel by way of a separate diesel pump. Allow the heavy oil outlet to be kept open. Keep the diesel oil outlet shut until the system is thoroughly flushed. After a few minutes open the diesel oil outlet and shut the heavy oil outlet. If the complete system is to be changed to diesel oil, open the diesel oil inlet valve to the generator supply pump whilst simultaneously closing the heavy oil inlet valve. If the return line is linked to the diesel service tank, open the return line whilst simultaneously closing the heavy oil return once the system is properly flushed. It is important to remember that the marine generator is amongst the most vital parts of machinery in the engine room. To ensure it is operated without incident it is provided with several safety alarm and trip systems. This not only ensures that the engineers are notified about any problems with the generator but also ensures the shutdown of the generator in the event of trouble. Therefore, marine engineers should be fully conversant in the different types of trips present in the generator and how they are activated.

FUEL OIL CHANGE OVER PROCEDURE FOR THE MAIN AND AUXILIARY ENGINES

Emission control areas are those designated regions at sea wherein the SOx and NOx emissions are regulated by the laws laid down under MARPOL Annex VI Prevention of Air Pollution by Ships. Some local laws regarding air pollution are more stringent than those laid down by the IMO. For example, in Europe, when the ship is in port, all running machinery consuming fuel must use fuel which has less than 0.1% sulphur content. As the SOx emissions are purely dependent on the quality and sulphur content of the fuel, when entering ECAs it is necessary to switch over to a lower sulphur content fuel. This means flushing out any fuel from the system with a sulphur content higher than 1.0%. Considering that most of ships today operate on high sulphur fuel oil, changing the fuel over at the right time is very important. Moreover, as low sulphur fuel oil is much more costly than high sulphur fuel oil, there is a direct financial impact on the ship if the fuel is not changed over at the most opportune moment before entering the ECA. Most ships today are equipped with one service tank and one (possibly two) settling tanks, which can result in the mixing of two different grades of oils whilst performing the fuel changeover. Every ship is provided with a changeover Low Sulphur Fuel (LSF) calculator which tells the correct changeover time at which the system should be running on LSF before entering the ECA. To work effectively, some important data is needed including the sulphur content of the high sulphur fuel currently in the system; the sulphur content of the low sulphur fuel; the fuel capacity of the main engine system including the settling tank, service tank, main engine piping, and transfer piping from service tank to main engine; and the capacity of transfer equipment such as the fuel oil transfer pump and fuel oil separators.

Once the changeover time is calculated (accounting for the time needed to intermix the two different sulphur grade oils) the following actions are to be taken at least 48 hours prior to entering the ECA: (1) ensure that no further transfer of high sulphur fuel is carried out to the settling tank; (2) ensure that the low sulphur bunker tank stream is open for transfer; (3) if two separate settling tanks are present, one can be dedicated to the low sulphur oil which will reduce the changeover period; (4) ensure the separator keeps running until the settling tank level reaches minimum; (5) if filling the service tank with HSFO increases the calculated time period of changeover, stop the separator and drain the settling tank; (6) the settling tank can be first drained into the fuel oil overflow tank, after which the drained oil can be transferred to the bunker tanks containing the same grade of oil; (7) once the settling tank is drained of all heavy sulphur oil, fill the settling tank with low sulphur oil via

184 Ship operations

the transfer pump; (8) as the separator is stopped, the service tank oil will be consumed by the main engine system; (9) remember not to lower the level of the service tank below which the fuel pumps cannot take suction; (10) move the separator from the settling tank to the service tank, which will now start filling with low sulphur oil; and (11) fill the LSFO oil into settling and service tank as per the quantity required to cross the ECA as calculated by the chief engineer and in accordance with the passage plan.

FUEL OIL CHANGEOVER FOR THE AUXILIARY ENGINE AND BOILERS

Some port authorities enforce regulations regarding the use of gas oil for generators and boilers when ships are in port (again, typically in Europe). This requires changing over from a high sulphur content to a low sulphur content of less than 0.1%. To changeover the boiler, first start by shutting off the steam to the fuel oil heaters. When the temperature drops below 90°C (194°F), open the diesel oil service tank valve which feeds into the boiler system. Shut the heavy oil valve for the boiler system slowly and observe the pressure of the supply pump. Check the flame and combustion of the boiler.

Leave the heavy oil outlet open but close the diesel oil outlet. This is to ensure no heavy oil is released into the diesel oil system. When the line is flushed with diesel oil, open the diesel outlet valve and shut the heavy oil outlet valve. The process for changing over the generators is slightly different, as they must be changed over from one grade to another while at load. This helps in the flushing of the system. If only one generator is being changed over, keep running the other generator for emergency use only. Shut the steam to the fuel oil heaters. When the temperature drops below 90°C (194°F), open the diesel oil service tank valve going to the generator system. Simultaneously open the local diesel inlet valve and shut the heavy oil inlet valve slowly. Keep an eye on the fuel pressure. Change only one generator into diesel at a time. This can be achieved with the help of a separate diesel pump. Leave the heavy oil outlet open and shut the diesel oil outlet till the system is thoroughly flushed. After a few minutes, open the diesel oil outlet and shut the heavy oil outlet. If the complete system is to be changed over to diesel oil, open the diesel oil inlet valve to the generator supply pump whilst simultaneously closing the heavy oil inlet valve. If the return line is provided to the diesel service tank, open this whilst simultaneously closing the heavy oil return. This should only be done after the system has flushed properly. Once the changeover procedure is complete, remember to change the HMI setting on the cylinder oil lubricator system (alpha lubrication) or changeover the cylinder oil daily tank to be suitable for low sulphur operation.

SHORE POWER LOADING DURING DRY DOCK

Drydock is one of the most crucial periods for a ship, as it is the time when all major repairs and surveys take place. As per SOLAS chapter 1, regulation 10, a commercial vessel has to undergo two inspections of its hull every five years. The time-gap between these inspections should never be more than 36 months. The drydock also provides an opportunity for the ship management team to carry out repairs of the main and auxiliary engines, seawater pipes and system, intermediate and tail shaft, propeller, bow thruster, and any other machinery systems whose repairs cannot be performed when the ship is in water. During drydock, the ship must take shore power to ensure that the work inside the ship can be performed uninterrupted. When the ship sits on the keel blocks in the drydock and the water is removed from the dock to inspect the hull, the auxiliary engine-generators, which

Engine room operations   185

produce the electrical power, can no longer work due to non-supply of cooling water to the engine. To avoid the overheating of moving parts in the engine, the auxiliary engine has to be switched off before the water is pumped out of the drydock. If the auxiliary engine and its alternator are to be included as part of a major maintenance package during drydock, these must be switched off to allow personnel to work on the machinery. The only alternative to shore power is to keep the auxiliary engines running. That can only be done if the shore team provide a separate portable cooling water piping system which can be attached to the inlet and outlet of the ship's auxiliary engine cooling system. This set up is complex and requires extensive preplanning. The water provided to the vessel will typically be charged by the quantity (metric tonne) supplied to the ship's system. Hence, shore power supply is much preferred over this method.

When preparing for drydocking, the chief engineer needs to ensure certain checks and preparations are carried out before receiving shore power. These include ensuring the ship's power-receiving terminal is prepared well in advance of the drydock so that shore power can be connected without incurring delay. Normally, the ship's electrical engineer will prepare the ship's power-receiving terminal box. This requires: (1) ensuring the receiving box is not obstructed with any objects, pipes, or spares. It is usually located on deck near the accommodation entrance or in the emergency generator room. If the box is not used or maintained for long periods, the box will need to be cleaned and inspected before use; (2) ensuring the receiving terminals inside the box are checked and confirmed present and in good working condition; (3) ensuring the earthing cable is provided to earth the ship's hull to the shore earth; (4) ensuring the measuring instruments such as voltmeter, phase sequence indicator, and tester are present and in working order; (5) ensuring the shore power indicator is present and in working condition; (6) ensuring a safety device (circuit breaker or fuse) is provided in the terminal to protect the main switchboard; (7) ensuring details of the shore power requirement is posted near the shore-receiving terminal box. This should include details of the required voltage, frequency, and method of connecting the shore supply; and (8) ensuring the ship's batteries are fully charged and tested.

When setting up a shore-to-ship power supply, it is critical the correct procedures are followed, as unprotected connections may lead to the wrong shore supply. This will likely cause damage to the ship's electrical systems and potentially cause machinery-space fires. The following points should be checked before connecting the shore supply to the ship in drydock: (1) check the cable drawn to the ship for providing the shore supply is in good condition; (2) check the insulation resistance of the cable provided for the shore supply; (3) check the insulation resistance of the shore supply box; (4) check the polarity of the shore supply using a voltmeter; (5) check and ensure the frequency and voltage of the shore supply match the specifications required by the ship; (6) check the phase sequence of the shore supply using a phase sequence tester; (7) check the tightness of the shore cable connector clamp to ensure good connection; (8) ensure a warning notice is posted near to the ship's receiving terminal box advising high power cables are in use; (9) check and ensure the ship's generators are disconnected from the ship's main switchboard; (10) one of the engineering officers must check and record the energy meter reading provided on the shoreside meter; and (11) ensure the ship's hull is fully earthed to shore before supplying shore power to the ship.

Taking the shore supply on board

Once all checks are performed by the ship's engineers and the ship is ready to take on shore power, the following procedures must be followed. When the shore power supply is made available to the vessel, the light indicator in the terminal box will illuminate. When this happens, close the breaker to start the supply of the shore power to the ship.

186 Ship operations

To check the phase sequence, a bulb type phase sequence indicator may be used. This involves two lamps which are connected to an unbalanced load across the three-phase circuit via the capacitor and resistors. The phase sequence will be considered satisfactory when the right-side lamp is illuminated and the left-side lamp is unlit. Another instrument used to measure PSI is a small portable three-phase induction motor-driven meter with a rotary pointer. Once the phase sequence has been confirmed, check the frequency of the supply from the provided frequency meter or on the ship's main switchboard. Make sure to keep the emergency generator in manual mode in case the shore power goes off abruptly and uninterrupted power supply is needed.

Common problems

Some of the common problems faced by the ship's staff when bringing shore power on board include when the shore supply is switched on, but the ship is not receiving any shore power. In this situation, check the three fuses that are connected between the ship's terminal and main switchboard. If these are satisfactory, check the circuit breaker located in the shore supply switchboard. If this is satisfactory, check the circuit breaker interlocks which are arranged in the system to avoid paralleling of shore and generator power. The second most common problem is caused by shore power trips during the shore-to-ship supply. The third is caused by faulty shore cables. Before connecting the shore cable to the ship, first check the cables are of the correct size and as per the maximum protective current value for the ship. The fourth problem is an overload in the system. To prevent this from happening, it is important to correctly calculate the electrical load of the ship during the drydock by using an electric power balance table. Fifth are generator circuit breaker trips. It is possible for the safety breaker for the generator to trip the shore supply during inspection or maintenance of generator's interlock. And sixth is the wrong shore supply. Most countries have local regulations regarding the generation of electrical supply. If the voltage and frequency of the shore power do not match the ship's rating, the machinery will operate at lower efficiency and potentially cause overheating. To avoid this from happening, the ship's manager must ensure the ship is drydocked at a facility which can provide adequate shore supply as per the ship's requirements.

NOTES

1. Modern boilers should never be blown down while the boiler is steaming at high rates. While performing the blowdown, the shipside valve should always be opened first, followed by the blowdown valve. This will allow the operator to control the boiler in case of pipe bursts.
2. Faults can be of various types including under- or over-voltage, under- or over-frequency, short circuits, reverse power, earth fault, and so on.

Chapter 13

Bridge operations

Ships are massive vessels spanning hundreds of metres in length and weighing tens if not hundreds of thousands of tonnes. Being able to control and safely manoeuvre such a large vessel is critically important. This is where the bridge comes in. The bridge is the main control centre of the vessel. It is generally located in a position with an unrestricted view and immediate access to the essential areas of the ship. Historically, the bridge was a structure connected to the paddle house that housed the steering equipment. As the structure closely resembled a bridge, the name stuck. As we have said previously, the officer in command of the bridge is always the captain, who retains control and responsibility of the vessel whilst they are on board. During the round-the-clock watch, the highest-ranking officer of the watch is generally placed in charge of the bridge. Only authorised personnel are permitted onto the bridge as it is a restricted area. The bridge houses the main steering equipment, navigation charts, communication systems, engine control as well as various other miscellaneous systems and controls. In addition, some bridges also have adjacent bridge wings, that house equipment for the stern and bow thrusters. These wings extend beyond the main bridge and provide a clear, unobstructed view of the surrounding area. The bridge is always manned by an OOW, who has the responsibility of manoeuvring the vessel and coordinating the ship's propulsion with the engine room. In general, an officer and a lookout are required to be present on the bridge at all times. For complicated manoeuvres, the master may be called to the bridge to take over the controls. This is usually the case in high-risk environments such as stormy conditions, congested sea lanes and when the pilot is required. In summary, the bridge is the eyes, ears and brain of the ship.

MASTER'S STANDING AND NIGHT ORDERS

Ship operations are complex and often challenging. The master, being in overall command of everything on board, is responsible for the functioning of the vessel in every respect. Thus, it is natural for the master to promulgate their commands with respect to the safety of navigation and other operations carried out on board. To avoid any misunderstanding or confusion, the master will often issue their commands in writing. These are called the 'Master's Standing and Night Orders'. *Standing Orders* are a set of instructions provided by the master to ensure safe ship navigation and operations whether at sea or in port. These instructions encompass a wide area from navigation to the rules of conduct of officers. Standing Orders must always be followed and are signed by every officer on board, making them liable. *Night Orders* are a supplement to the Standing Orders and come into force as the master proceeds to take rest during the night. The Standing Orders remain in force and the Night Orders add specific points to be followed when the master is unofficially off duty. The master writes the night orders every night, with specific regard to the prevailing state of

DOI: 10.1201/9781003244615-16

188 Ship operations

the weather, sea conditions, and marine traffic. These are generally handwritten and duly signed by each OOW. The Night Orders are an important document as the master will use their extensive experience and expertise to determine safe navigation during the hours of darkness. Although the master is unofficially off duty, they remain officially in command of the ship and are responsible for the safe passage and conduct of the vessel, even in their absence from the bridge.

TAKING OVER THE WATCH

The navigational watch is one of the most significant shipboard operations for deck officers. When the ship is at sea, the bridge is the only location that is always manned. As the navigating officers must keep bridge watches round the clock, the practice of taking over of the watch by a relieving OWW from the present OOW is followed every day. When taking over the watch, the oncoming OOW must be acquainted with the ship's position, speed, and course; traffic density; past, present, and expected weather and sea conditions; the state and condition of the bridge equipment; logbooks, checklists, and daily orders; readiness of the lookout or helmsman; any activities taking place on deck or in the engine room; and any conditions that may require the master on the bridge. The deck officer assigned with the duties of watchkeeping and navigation on the ship's bridge is known as the OOW. Whilst keeping watch on the bridge the OOW is the representative of the ship's master and has total responsibility for the safe and efficient navigation of the ship. The OOW is also in charge of the bridge team, which is there to assist in the navigation process. The OOW is responsible for complying with the COLREGS and with all standing orders issued by the master. Altogether, the OOW has three core duties: navigation, watchkeeping, and GMDSS monitoring.

We have already covered most of the duties of the watchkeeping in earlier chapters, and we discuss navigation and passage planning in the next chapter, so there is no need to dwell on these here.

THE SHIP'S LOGBOOK

Being a deck officer involves myriad responsibilities that are spread across the many different aspects of the vessel's operation. It is a challenging job where there is much at stake. Not only is safe navigation a prime responsibility but so is the keeping of accurate records and documentation. The term originally referred to a book for recording readings from the chip log that was used to estimate a ship's speed through the water. Today, the logbook has grown to contain many other types of information and is a record of the ship's condition at any moment in time. The information recorded in the logbook includes weather conditions, times of routine events and significant incidents, crew complement or what ports were docked at and when. Most Flag State authorities and specify that logbooks are kept to provide a record of events, and to help crews navigate should radio, radar or GPS systems fail. Examination of the detail in the ship's log is often an important part of the investigative process for official maritime inquiries, in much the same way as a *black box* is used on aeroplanes. The logbook is a legal document and sometimes the entries are of great importance in legal cases involving maritime and commercial disputes. Merchant ships often keep a *rough log*, which is a preliminary draft of the ship's course, speed, location, and other data, which is then transcribed as the *smooth log* or the *official log*. This then becomes the final version of the ship's record. Changes may be made to the rough log, but the smooth log is considered a permanent record and no erasures are permitted. Alterations or corrections to the official logbook may be made, but these must be initialled by the authorised keeper of the logbook and the original data entries which have been cancelled or corrected must remain legible.

During the watch, the OOW must record the following information at regular intervals. The point in time where the log is entered depends largely on the type of information and the specific log keeping procedures for the ship: (1) the position of the ship in latitude and longitude at different intervals; (2) time to be noted when navigation marks are passed; (3) time, details, and reason for any course alterations; (4) meteorological and weather conditions including details of sea and swell together with Beaufort scale (wind) readings; (5) movement of the ship at sea including rolling, pitching, and heaving; (6) details of any abnormal conditions; (7) speed of the propulsion engine and speed of the ship in knots; (8) details of any incidents such as stranding or grounding; (9) any physical contact with floating objects; (10) details of any distress signals received; (11) any kind of assistance rendered to the distress signal sender; (12) complete details of any salvage operations performed; (13) any oil spills or other pollution incident including the position of the ship, time and details of the incident; (14) a record of general watch routines performed including fire watch; (15) time of arrival to and departure from port; (16) if berthing or anchoring is planned, a record of the date, time and position; (17) details of any heading compass errors; (18) drills and training carried out as well as inspections with regard to stowaways and security-related measures; (19) a record of stores, provisions, and freshwater; and (20) any other entries as required by the master, company, and Flag State authority.

Furthermore, as the logbook is a legal document, an original page should never be removed. This is because the logbook serves as an official record of every action and situation that occurs on board the vessel. Only official designations and symbols may be used. If there is insufficient space in the Remarks section, an additional gummed paper strip may be inserted at the appropriate location. At the start and end of each watch, the logbook must be signed by the outgoing and the incoming OOW. Remember that the logbook entry carries the OOW's signature which means that the OOW is responsible for the information recorded by them during their watch.

NAVIGATION AND COMMUNICATION ON THE BRIDGE

Navigation is the core occupation of the OOW. Basic navigation equipment includes a Global Positioning System (GPS), Navtex receiver, Electronic Chart Display and Information System (ECDIS), radar system, and communication channels. Navigation is often controlled using charts that are used to plot routes. To ensure that the vessel stays on course, a combination of GPS and a compass system is used. The charts and equipment are stored in separate locations to ensure the compartmentalisation of the bridge. In addition to this, binoculars are used in the daytime for sighting. However, when the weather is not clear, visibility is low or at night, the radar must be used to accurately place and navigate the ship. When using radar, a range scale must be used based on the speed and traffic around the vessel. Ships weighing more than 10,000 gross tonnes must use two radars for plotting their course and for navigation.

Automatic Radar Plotting Aid (ARPA), Electronic Plotting Aids (EPA), and Automatic Tracking Aids (ATA) are carried on most vessels. Alarms to warn of impending collisions, equipment failure, and so on are also used to indicate errors. When at sea, vessels must maintain strict compliance with the SOLAS and IMO regulations. As the bridge controls the entire ship, it is essential that the bridge and all equipment satisfies the regulations. For

190   Ship operations

navigation purposes, the bridge must be located with a clear view both ahead and abeam. There must also be a minimum vision of 255° for the OOW with at least 112.5° visibility on both the port and starboard beams. For the bridge wings, the side of the vessel must be clearly visible with 180° on the side and 45° on the opposite side. For the officer in charge of steering, 60° on both sides is the minimum clear visibility. Ships weighing more than 10,000 gross tonnes must include a single X band–9 GHz frequency radar. This is in accordance with IMO guidelines for safe navigation and steering. In addition, faults or damage sustained to other parts of the ship are fed back to the bridge.

PRINCIPLES OF PASSAGE PLANNING

Shipping cargo from one port to another involves many coordinated operations both land and at sea. One of the most important roles undertaken by the deck officer is the passage plan. A passage plan is a comprehensive, berth to berth guide, developed and used by a vessel's bridge team to determine the most efficient route and to identify potential problems or hazards along the route, and to adopt Bridge Management Practices that ensure the vessel's safe passage. Passage planning is governed by SOLAS chapter 5, annexes 24 and 25 under the titles *Voyage Planning* and *Guidelines for Voyage Planning* respectively.

We will cover passage planning and navigation in more detail in the next chapter, so again, we need not concern ourselves with it any further at this point.

NAVIGATING WITH RESTRICTED VISIBILITY

One of the most important duties of a ship's OOW is the safe and smooth navigation of the ship. Throughout her voyage, a ship is likely to sail through different weather and tidal conditions. It is the duty of the navigating officer to know and understand the ship's sailing route well in advance and prepare accordingly. One of the most dangerous conditions to navigate in is restricted visibility. This may be caused by fog, heavy rain, snow, hail or dust and sandstorms. When the ship's officer receives information regarding such weather conditions, they must take all necessary precautions to ensure the ship progresses through the restricted visibility area without incurring incident. Some of the main points to be considered when entering a restricted visibility area include: (1) *know the ship inside-out*: An effective navigating officer knows each and every aspect of their ship. From her dimensions to the characteristics of the hull, the officer should know how the ship will respond to different stresses. In restricted visibility situations, it is vital the OOW knows the ship's stopping distance at any specific rpm to control the ship during an emergency stop; (2) *inform the master*: during restricted visibility, it is important that the master is present on the bridge. The OOW must call or inform the master when entering an area of restricted visibility. The officer should also inform the engine room and request the duty engineer to man the engine room in the event it is on *unmanned* mode; (3) *appoint adequate manpower*: it is important that sufficient manpower is present on the bridge to keep a close watch on the ship's course. Additional personnel must be appointed as *lookouts* at different locations on the ship. If there is traffic in the area, the OOW must inform the engine room to have enough manpower available so that the engine is also ready for emergency manoeuvring; (4) *keep the foghorn ready*: ensure the foghorn is working properly. If the horn is air operated, drain the line prior to opening the air line; (5) *reduce speed*: reduce the speed of the ship in accordance with the visibility level. If visibility is drastically reduced, bring the ship down to manoeuvring rpm; (6) *ensure the navigation equipment and lights are working*: ensure that all navigating equipment and navigation lights are operating throughout the area of restricted visibility. The OOW must ensure that the navigation charts are properly checked for correct routeing and that a good radar watch is carried out; (7) *stop all other works*: though it may seem obvious, multitasking during restricted visibility is never advisable. Stop all other deck work and order the crew to attend their respective quarters. This is to prevent injury to personnel from working on the open deck in case a collision or grounding occurs; (8) *open/close the bridge doors*: ensure that the bridge doors are kept open and without any obstruction for easy bridge wing access (assuming the that the bridge wing is not enclosed). During dust or sandstorms, close the bridge doors to prevent the ingress of dust or sand; (9) *shut ventilation*: If the ship is passing through a sandstorm, the ventilation fans and accommodation/engine room ports must be closed to avoid sand particles from entering the bridge, the accommodation, and the engine room; (10) *follow all procedures*: follow all procedures for restricted visibility as laid out in COLREG rule 19. Also, monitor channel 16 and ensure that all important parameters of the ship such as latitude and longitude, time, and speed are noted in the ship's logbook.

RESPONDING TO TROPICAL STORM WARNINGS

Seafarers are, by tradition, a superstitious breed and this is no less evident when it comes to preparing for rough weather. Before joining their ship, many a seafarer is wished 'smooth sailing and calm seas'. Nevertheless, every seafarer has faced rough weather at least once in their career. Some of the most common forms of rough weather are tropical depressions or storms, typhoons, cyclones, and hurricanes. These are often generated by varying atmospheric pressures over different parts of the earth. The Beaufort Scale[1] categories winds and sea states according to their speeds and effects.

The movement of the sun causes pressure belts to build and shift and so the varying temperatures over land masses and water bodies cause pressure differences. Tropical depressions often occur in the middle latitudes and tropical cyclones more often originate in the *Inter Tropical Convergence Zone*. A depression may develop and travel in any direction whereas tropical storms are mostly found to follow a predictable path in both hemispheres. This means tropical storms recurve after following a particular track. It is therefore important for seafarers to predict the location, magnitude and path of the storm. The ship can then either avoid these regions altogether or navigate with caution.

Sailing through rough weather is both unpleasant for the crew and risky for the ship. It is therefore important that precautions are taken when encountering stormy weather. *Always use available information.* Tropical storms and depressions are formed by pressure and temperature variations. The modern seafarer has access to myriad information regarding seasonal areas and frequency of occurrence through MSI notices, Admiralty Sailing Directions, *Ocean Passages of the World*, and various other means. By consulting these sources in advance, it is possible to plan the passage to either avoid likely storm locations altogether or to plan diversions should the need arise. *Study weather reports.* More often that not, weather reports and weather fax warnings are issued well in advance of unsettled weather conditions. A careful review of navigational areas and current weather reports by the navigating officer can be instrumental in obtaining early warning of impending stormy weather. Frequent observations from the various meteorological instruments on board can be used to confirm the veracity of the weather reports. *Keep away from the eye of the storm.* Once the presence of a storm or depression is confirmed, it is vital to establish the distance of the vessel from the eye of the storm, the centre of the depression, and the storm's track and path. Buys Ballot's law states that in the Northern Hemisphere a person who stands

192 Ship operations

Table 13.1 Beaufort Wind Scale

Wind Force	Description	Wind Speed			Description	Probable Wave Height		Sea State
		mph	km/h	kts		Mts	Max	
0	Calm	<1	<1	<1	Smoke rises vertically. Sea like a mirror	–	n	0
1	Light air	1–5	1–3	1–3	Direction shown by smoke drift but not by wind vanes. Sea rippled	0.1	0.1	1
2	Light breeze	6–11	4–7	4–6	Wind felt on face; leaves rustle; wind vane moved by wind. Small wavelets on sea	0.2	0.3	2
3	Gentle breeze	12–19	8–12	7–10	Leaves and small twigs in constant motion; light flags extended. Large wavelets on sea	0.6	1	3
4	Moderate breeze	20–28	13–18	11–16	Raises dust and loose paper; small branches moved. Small waves, fairly frequent, white horses	1	1.5	3–4
5	Fresh breeze	29–38	19–24	17–21	Small trees in leaf begin to sway; crested wavelets form on inland waters. Moderate waves, many white horses	2	2.5	4
6	Strong breeze	38–49	25–31	22–27	Large branches in motion; whistling heard in telegraph wires; umbrellas used with difficulty. Large waves, extensive foam crests	3	4	5
7	Near gale	50–61	32–38	28–33	Whole trees in motion; inconvenience felt when walking against the wind. Foam blown in streaks across the sea	4	5.5	5–6
8	Gale	62–74	39–46	34–40	Twigs break off trees; impedes progress. Wave crests begin to break into spindrift	5.5	7.5	6–7
9	Strong gale	75–88	47–54	41–47	Slight structural damage (chimney pots and slates removed). Wave crests topple over, spray affects visibility	7	10	7
10	Storm	89–102	55–63	48–55	Seldom experienced inland; trees uprooted; considerable structural damage. Sea surface largely white	9	12.5	8
11	Violent storm	103–117	64–72	56–63	Very rarely experienced; accompanied by widespread damage. Medium-sized ships lost to view behind waves. Sea covered in white foam; visibility seriously affected	11.5	16	8
12	Hurricane	118+	73+	64+	Devastation. Air filled with foam and spray, very poor visibility	14+	–	9

facing away from the wind has high pressure on the right and low pressure to the left; in the Southern Hemisphere, the reverse is true. It is advisable to keep a distance of 250 nautical miles[2] away from the eye of the storm however some companies prescribe specific distances in their SMS.

Check the stability of the vessel. A prudent check is required of the stability condition of the vessel and its compliance with intact stability criteria. Damage stability conditions should be carefully evaluated before the beginning of the passage. This means the vessel can take heavy weather ballast before or in the rough weather area. Heavy weather ballast provides additional stability to the vessel by lowering the centre of gravity. This makes the vessel more stable as the GM increases. Heavy weather ballast tanks are designated on board vessels and if those tanks previously carried oil, they must be washed before the heavy weather ballast starts. *Use the ballast tanks to minimise free surface effect.* As part of good seamanship, the ballast tanks which are slack can be pressed up to minimise free surface effect. This will also help to increase the GM. Well planned cargo stowage, ballast or both can minimise the number of slack or partly filled tanks. *Exercise caution when changing speed, angle, and direction.* Often waves associated with storms or depressions causes a reduction in intact stability. This increases the risk of rolling to very large angles or even capsizing. MSC 1228 provides guidance with respect to reductions of speed and changes of angle and direction to adjust the encounter period of waves to avoid parametric or synchronous rolling motions. *Secure loose equipment/cargo on deck.* For vessels with lower freeboards, decks are washed frequently by seas with greater magnitudes. Securing loose deck equipment with additional lashings is strongly advised to prevent them from washing overboard. Safety lifelines can be rigged on vessels carrying cargoes on deck. Additional lashings should be provided to secure anchors, lifeboats, life buoys and life rafts.

Secure weather and watertight openings. The various weathertight and watertight openings like side scuttles, hatch covers, portholes, doors, and manholes must be securely closed to prevent any ingress of water. Leaks, damaged gaskets, or inadequately secured covers can affect the watertight integrity of the vessel. *Secure all doors forward of the collision bulkhead.* Special emphasis is provided to securing the doors and openings forward of the collision bulkhead, for example, forepeak stores and hatches, vents, and forward openings. These spaces often house forward mooring equipment and associated electrical or hydraulic machinery. Spurling pipe covers need to be sealed well in advance. Bilge alarms in such remote compartments should be tried out regularly to provide an early warning of any water ingress or flooding. Openings in subdivisions of watertight compartments, which may cause progressive flooding, must be secured. *Drains and scuppers must be cleared.* All deck drains and scuppers for water drainage must be clear to prevent any accumulation of water on deck. *Secure aerials and antennas.* Antennas, aerials, stay wire clamps, and lashings should be inspected before wind speeds pick up. Winds of gale force and above can easily break and blow away aerials. Storms are associated with lightning and thunder and so all aerials and antennas must be earthed and any low insulation alarms investigated thoroughly. *Keep check on the rpm to avoid load fluctuation on the main engine.* This is something we have touched on previously but due to unsettled movements of the vessel, it is common for load fluctuations to develop on the main engines. By carefully setting and monitoring the rpm, these fluctuations can be managed. *Inform all departments.* All departments (deck, engine, and galley) should be informed well in advance of any storm warning so that deck, engine and galley stores, hospitals, sick bays, and work areas can be lashed and secured. Any major overhaul jobs, working aloft, lifting of heavy machinery on deck and engine room use of overhead or deck cranes must be stopped and postponed. Last but by no means least, *aim to maintain the morale of the crew.* The morale of the crew should be kept high as often heavy rolling and pitching causes giddiness, nausea, and reduced appetite. These can all have detrimental effects on crew members' health and wellbeing.

194 Ship operations

NAVIGATING THROUGH CONGESTED WATERS

Coastal passages are an extremely busy time for the OOW. This sort of high-pressure environment demands skill and perseverance. Being the ship's navigator involves constantly plotting the vessel on the large-scale chart, manoeuvring, and altering course as per the passage plan as well as keeping a sharp lookout at the same time. When the OOW is busy, they must have confidence that the lookout is vigilant. Ironic as it may seem, navigating through congested waters requires the OOW to share their attention between the chart and being on lookout. This requires tremendous skill and ability.

MANNING THE SHIP'S RADAR

The OOW should be familiar with the working of all navigational equipment used on the ship. They should also be aware of the procedures for troubleshooting in case any equipment malfunctions. The radar is one of the most important navigational tools used on board. It should be kept running all the time and must undergo periodic tests to check for any operational errors. However, there are certain points that the OOW should be aware of when operating the radar. These include (1) keeping a close watch on the ship's course as sometimes small vessels, objects, and ice may not be detected; (2) shadow and blind sectors should must be accounted for when navigating by the ship's radar; (3) plotting of targets should be done at longer range and not shorter range; (4) the OOW must use multiple plots to increase accuracy; (5) detection of small targets is better at short range; (6) the OOW should know how to handle video processing techniques; (7) long-range should be used to get advance notice of approaching vessels, ports, and obstacles; (8) when deciding the range scale two things should be kept in mind: marine traffic in the region and the ship's speed; (9) radar operation should be practised in clear and calm weather. This helps the operator to develop a better idea about radar observations and target vectors during restricted visibility; (10) the OOW should consider replotting or rechecking every time there is a change in the ship's speed or course; (11) the OOW should keep a watch on the variable range marker, fixed range lines, and electronic bearing lines. A safe speed for the ship should be decided after using long-range to detect approaching vessels and obstructions; (12) the OOW must know how to use clutter control to avoid unclear objects. Heading markers should be properly aligned with the fore and aft of the ship and also with the compass heading; (13) the parallel index lines should be set correctly; (14) the OOW must check for any gyro errors and accuracy of the heading line arrangement; (15) if a performance monitor is fitted, the quality of the performance should be checked regularly; (16) the OOW must check the identity of any fixed objects; and (17) whilst deciding the closest point of approach (CPA) to avoid collision of the ship, factors such as course, speed, and aspect of the target should be taken into account. Any other important aspects of the ship should also be considered to mark the CPA correctly.

COMMUNICATION SYSTEMS

Communications at sea have undergone wholesale revolution over the past century. Long gone are the days of semaphores and flags (which are still used even today in some situations). The advent of radio telecommunications brought about a drastic change in marine communication ability. In the 1970s, the IMO evaluated a series of studies carried out by the *International Telecommunications Union*. These studies showed that employing radio technology on board ships not only made communications easier but was also far more effective. Subsequently, the IMO implemented automated systems of ship-to-ship and ship-to-shore communication. The days of keeping a 24/7 radio watch were numbered. Today, marine communications systems between ships to shore use highly technical onboard systems that channel messages through satellites to onshore stations. Ship-to-ship communication employs VHF radio and Digital Selective Calling (DSC). Modern DSC controllers are now integrated with the VHF radio as per SOLAS. Satellite services, as opposed to terrestrial communications systems, use geo-stationary satellites for transmitting and receiving signals, where the range of shore stations cannot reach. Marine communication services are provided by two services: a commercial company called *INMARSAT* and a multinational public funded agency, *COSPAS–SARSAT*. Whereas *INMARSAT* provides the full scope of two-way marine radiocommunications, *COSPAS-SARSAT* uses a system that is limited to the reception of signals issued by emergency equipment (such as EPIRBs and SART) and offers no two-way marine communications facilities.

EMERGENCY COMMUNICATIONS SYSTEMS

Under SOLAS, ships must carry a complement of emergency telecommunications equipment. These emergency telecommunications are provided through the *Global Maritime Distress Safety System* or GMDSS. The radio communication systems required by SOLAS to be carried on board depends largely on the vessel's area of operation. GMDSS divides the world into four core areas. These are defined as A1, A2, A3, and A4. A1 operates within a range of approximately 20 to 30 nautical miles under the coverage of at least one coastal VHF station. A1 uses continuous DSC alerting and requires a VHF set, DSC and NAVTEX receiver (a navigational telex for receiving maritime and meteorological information). A2 nominally covers 400 nautical miles but in practice covers 100 nautical miles excluding A1 areas and requires DSC, radio telephone (MF radio range), VHF set, and NAVTEX. A3 excludes all A1 and A2 areas and operates within 70° north and 70° south latitudes. A3 is within the *INMARSAT* geostationary satellite range, where continuous alerting is available. The equipment required includes high-frequency radio and/ or *INMARSAT* set, a system for receiving MSI plus all systems needed for A1 and A2 areas. A4 are all areas outside the scope of A1, A2, and A3. These are effectively the polar regions north and south of 70° of latitude. The equipment needed includes HF radio plus those required for all other areas. All major oceanic areas are covered by HF for which the IMO requires two coastal stations per oceanic region. Today, almost all ships are fitted with a *Ship Security Alert System (SSAS)* for long-range identification and tracking as per SOLAS requirements.

Daily, weekly, and monthly **GMDSS** tests

The development of GMDSS (Global Maritime Distress and Safety System) for the shipping industry has come a long way. The GMDSS system was established with the objective of improving distress and safety radio communications and procedures at sea. The greatest benefit of GMDSS is that it vastly reduces the chances of ships disappearing without trace and enables SAR operations to launch without delay and be directed to the exact site of the incident. But, for GMDSS equipment to function properly and effectively in the event of an emergency, it is critical that the officers and crew understand its purpose and carry out the necessary maintenance to keep the equipment in a working condition.

196 Ship operations

RESPONSIBILITIES OF THE OOW DURING ANCHORAGE

When a ship is due to enter port, but there are no berths available, or the cargo destined for the ship has not yet arrived, it is common for ships to enter anchorage. Anchorage can be an opportunity for the crew to get some well-deserved rest, but it can also be an extremely testing time for the ship's officers. Anchoring in treacherous areas such as the Bay of Calabar (Nigeria) or in busy sea lanes (Singapore) is a major challenge. It is up to the master to decide whether the OOW must stand duty on the bridge or out on deck. There are specific duties and tasks that must be undertaken when preparing to anchor and during the anchoring procedure. We will not go into any more detail here, but we will highlight some of the main issues and challenges the OOW faces during anchorage.

Calculating the swinging circle

When a ship is at anchorage, one or more anchors are used to keep the vessel at a fixed position. As ships are usually fitted with anchors only at the bow, and not the stern, the effect of currents and tides is to rotate the ship around the axis of the anchor. This is called the *swinging circle*. To maintain a safe distance from navigational hazards such as sandbanks, buoys, and other fixtures, the OOW must calculate the swinging circle for the ship. This is done using the following calculation:

$$\text{Swinging Circle}(M) = \text{L.O.A} + \text{Length of Cable} - \text{UKC}$$

Critically, the swinging circle might vary with changes in tidal levels and the weather. Even so, it is important for the OOW to have a fair idea of the radius around which the ship might swing. *Maintaining a Check on own Ship and other Ships in the Vicinity.* At anchoring, the OOW must keep a vigilant watch of their own ship and other ships in the vicinity lest they start dragging after anchoring. Dragging might occur due to changes in tidal levels, changes in the weather or due to the brake giving away to a lot of yawing. *Keep a Constant Check on the Ship's Position.* This point is generally laid down in the Masters' Standing Orders and almost always mentions the intervals at which the position must be plotted on the chart. Using the GPS, the Radar or both will provide an exact position of the ship. *Display Appropriate Lights.* When a ship is at anchorage, she must let other vessels know that the ship is anchored and unable to manoeuvre. This allows other vessels to pass freely without interfering with the ship at anchor. *Keeping a Constant VHF watch.* If slated to receive a pilot on board or for information on vessels in the area, it is important to keep a constant VHF watch. Coastal authorities generally promulgate useful information that might be integral to the safety of the vessel over VHF including wreckages, vessel information, pilots ETA, and berthing information. *Alert Nearby Vessels When Required.* If another vessel is coming in too fast or too close, the OOW must alert the vessel via VHF or by flashing the Aldis Lamp. If this does not gain the other vessel's attention, use any means possible to avert the danger of a collision. Keep an accurate log of the incident and if possible, take photographs and video footage as evidence. Watchkeeping at anchorage might seem easy but the very fact that the vessel has stopped makes it vulnerable to many hazards. It is crucial the OOW is vigilant, and if necessary, requests the support of additional lookouts. In areas prone to piracy, the importance of alertness cannot be stressed enough. The ship being stationary makes it open to attacks and pilferage. Responsibility and diligence on the part of the OOW will keep the vessel safe and away from harm.

PREPARING TO ENTER PORT

'Arrival at port' and 'Departure from port' are two extremely important aspects of a ship's voyage. Both procedures are considered critical because of the complexities involved. Both the engine and deck departments must prepare themselves well in advance to ensure the safety of the ship and her crew. Before arriving at port, the ship's officers will discuss and plan the matters that are required for the safe berthing of the ship and the impending cargo operations. The master will inform the chief officer and chief engineer of the ETA. Once this is done, the OIC will check the conditions of all items mentioned in the 'Checklist for Entering Port'. The outcome of the check must be recorded in the ship's logbook. All officers (including any DOCs) and crew members will be assigned duties during the berthing of the ship. According to the master's orders, all those involved with the berthing procedure are assigned a 'position' to carry out the duties and to guide the ship's operations. The berthing sequence typically follows a 'general plan', which sets out the steps for bringing the ship safely alongside. The general plan will contain stations for both the deck and engine departments. For the deck department, a general plan involving stations for entering port would involve the master taking control of the vessel on the bridge, accompanied by the third officer. The chief officer will position at the ship's bow to command and guide the forward station.

The second officer takes up station at the stern to command the aft station. Deck crew will be tasked by the chief officer or second officer to assist in the berthing procedure. Additional deck crew may be tasked to perform lookout duties. As the senior deck rating, the bosun generally assists the chief officer at the bow. For the engine department, a general plan for entering port would involve the chief engineer taking control of the engine room. The first engineer or second engineer may be tasked to command subordinates for operating the machinery and propulsion systems. The third engineer and fourth engineer station at places in the engine room according to the orders of chief engineer and second engineer. The junior engineers may be tasked with taking rounds of the engine room as per the orders of the second engineer. The motorman or pumpman typically assist the engine room operations under the supervision of second engineer. Other engine room ratings are assigned duties by the chief engineer as required.

PILOT BOARDING AND DISEMBARKATION

When a ship is due to enter a port zone, or navigate a particularly awkward seaway, it is often necessary to arrange for a pilot to come on board. The pilot is an experienced mariner with expert knowledge of the port and its hazards, as well as the rules and regulations for entering and leaving the port's confines. When the ship is coming into the port, the master and pilot work together to bring the ship safely in and alongside. When the ship is ready to leave, the pilot assists the master to depart the port. Prior to the pilot boarding, determine the ETA of the pilot with the VTS on VHF. In busy shipping lanes and ports, pilots are in high demand, so it is important to know when the pilot is due to board and to be prepared for the pilot to board. Close to the ETA rig the pilot ladder. VTS will generally inform which side the pilot will be boarding from and the requirement of height above the water; if advised to do so, it may be necessary to rig the gangway. The pilot ladder should be arranged as per standard procedures with all safety measures on standby (e.g., life jackets, lifebuoy, VHF radios, etc). Check if the required equipment is operational. Synchronise the bridge clocks. Keep both radars ready and operating. Put the echo sounder on to constantly monitor the UKC. Adjust the squelch and volume controls

198 Ship operations

of the VHF to ensure clear communication. Keep the appropriate (large scale) charts ready for plotting. Prepare the master/pilot exchange forms. Inform the ECR of the pilot's ETA. Unless urgent, suspend all work on deck and designate crew to pilotage duties, such as standing by the mooring ropes or on extra lookout. Check and ready the mooring lines and ready the crew for port arrival. Engage the manual steering prior to the pilot's arrival and allow sufficient time for the helmsman to get accustomed to the steering. As the pilot approaches, hoist the pilot flag.

After ushering the pilot on board, the master and pilot will discuss the course of action to be taken by the ship as it closes in on the precautionary zone of the port. At this point, the pilot will take over the verbal command of the vessel and direct the helmsman. Although the pilot is nominally in command of the vessel, the master retains ultimate authority. When the master and pilot are on the bridge, the OOW is expected to take a step back and observe the helmsman and lookout (if posted). The crew might be fatigued in which case the OOW should ensure that there is somebody else on standby to provide relief if required. All the important navigational marks should be annotated in the Ship Manoeuvring Book, as per the chart or ECDIS. The position of the vessel should be plotted on the chart as deemed necessary by the master. If the workload is too much for the OOW to handle by themselves, they may, with the master's authorisation, designate the DOC to plot the position. If the vessel is proceeding to berth, the OOW must follow the master's instructions with respect to manoeuvring, speed, and course. These will likely be relayed by the master from the pilot, which means the OOW must work fast to prevent any incidents from occurring. Once the ship is safely berthed, the pilot is required to sign a bevy of documents. These must also be countersigned by the master *before* the pilot leaves the vessel. As a matter of extending courtesy, the pilot is usually ushered out as they were ushered in. Once the requisite forms are signed, and all other paperwork has been completed, the OOW should ensure the pilot exits safely. It is advisable to inform the crew in advance so they may have the ladder/combination ladder rigged on the required side. Upon boarding the vessel, all safety measures should be adhered to. The process of pilot embarkation and disembarkation is simple but extremely hazardous. Therefore, the OOW should be vigilant that all safe working practices are strictly followed.

MANOEUVRING IN AND OUT OF PORT

Manoeuvring is the operation during which the vessel enters or exits ports, moves through congested channels, passes through canals or navigates separated traffic zones. Most collisions and grounding happen during manoeuvring. For this reason, it is considered one of the most hazardous operations the ship undertakes. It is essential before starting any manoeuvre, to understand the effects of the wind, tide, state of the ship's trim, draught and freeboard, as well as the ship's equipment and manoeuvring aides together with any assistance rendered by tugboats. The master assesses the ship's capabilities and then devises a plan of action. The plan of action needs to be flexible, and the master should also have alternate plans in mind. The pilot contributes towards the safe navigation of the ship in confined waters but the responsibility for the vessel's navigation cannot be transferred to the pilot. The master and OOW always remain responsible for safe navigation. When developing their action plan, the master must take into account the minimum water depth, tide, currents, general condition of the berth, any use of tugboats during mooring, the mooring arrangements (including length of lines, certified bollard strength, etc.), use of anchors, thrusters, and/or tugboats in the event of surge or swell, and any other considerations that may be relevant.

Use of tugboats

Tugboats are used to assist the ship in coming alongside. Larger heavier ships lack the same manoeuvrability as smaller nimbler vessels and need to added power and thrust tugboats can provide. Tugboats can control both the lateral and forward, and the aft movement of the vessel by either pulling and/or pushing as required. If only one tugboat is deployed, then it is usually secured aft. Tugboats deployed forward are usually used for pushing only, are not secured to the berthing ship.

Berthing the ship

As the ship closes in on the berth, the master does not attempt to bring the ship directly alongside the berth, but instead brings the ship parallel to the berth and stops just short of the berthing position, clear of any forward or aft ships (if any). This is normally at one ship's breadth distance between the ship and the berth. Once the vessel has all but stopped off the berth, the master uses the assistance of the tugs and thrusters to get the vessel into position. The master directs the officers in charge of the mooring stations forward and aft to send over the spring lines first. The spring lines keep the vessel from moving forward and aft. The headlines/stern lines are then sent. Once all the lines are made fast, the winches are usually put to 40% auto tension and the springs are kept on brake. If the configuration of the berth is such that long ropes cannot be used, the master may consider changing the configuration of the vessel, i.e., using the spring lines as the headlines and vice versa. When closing a berth, the master monitors the ship's movement and distance to the pier, and of course to the other moored ships. Ships are fitted with various instruments such as the conning display, Voyage Management System and so on which indicate whether the ship is moving ahead or astern. The ship's speed and the amount of set and drift is indicated as the ship makes sideways. These are all excellent aids, but a visual assessment of the relative movements of objects ashore when berthing the ship provide a much quicker and more accurate indication of the direction and speed the ship is making over ground.

BALLASTING AND DE-BALLASTING

Ballasting or de-ballasting is the process where seawater is taken in and out of the ship when the ship is at port or at sea. The seawater carried by the ship is known as ballast water. Ballast or ballast water is seawater that is carried by a vessel in its ballast tanks to ensure its trim, stability, and structural integrity. When no cargo is carried by the ship, the vessel becomes light in weight, which affects its stability. For this reason, ballast water is taken on and stored in dedicated tanks. The tanks are filled with ballast water with the help of high-capacity ballast pumps. This process is known as ballasting. However, when the ship is filled with cargo, the stability of the ship is maintained by the weight of the cargo itself and thus there is no requirement for ballast water. The process of emptying the ballast tanks is known as de-ballasting.

BALLAST WATER MANAGEMENT PLAN

Port State authorities around the world enforce their own specific requirements when it comes to ballasting and de-ballasting. To simplify the requirement for ships to comply with individual Post State ballast control regimes, the IMO implemented a universal *Ballast*

Water Management Plan (BMP). The BMP includes the following information: (1) international rules and regulations for different port state controls; (2) location of ports providing shore discharge facilities for sediment and ballast water; (3) the duties of personnel on board for carrying out ballast operations; (4) ballasting operational procedures; (5) locations of different coastal waters for ballast exchange; (6) ballast water sampling points and treatment methods; (7) records of ballast water exchange to include the following information: (a) date of the ballast operation; (b) ship's ballast tanks used in the operation; (c) temperature of the ballast water; (d) salinity of the ballast water in ppm (salt content in parts per million); (e) position of the ship in latitude and longitude; (f) amount of ballast water loaded or discharged. The ballast records must be signed and dated by a responsible officer, usually the chief officer, although the master remains in overall charge of the operation. The master must also sign off the BMP log. In the event of any accidental discharge of ballast exchange, this must be entered into the BMP log and signed by the chief officer and master. A report of the incident must then be sent to the Port State authorities.

BRIDGE RESOURCE MANAGEMENT (BRM)

BRM was adopted in the early 1990s by the maritime industry as a safety and error management tool and has now become an integral part of officer training. BRM makes use of resources including the equipment and information and human resources available on board to achieve safe operations. BRM plays a critical role in any environment where human error can have devastating effects. It has proven to be an important tool for improving safety in the maritime industry and where important lessons have been learnt, prevented the recurrence of incidents. BRM helps to support a safer and more efficient operation by blending technology with human skills. In short, BRM is the effective management and utilisation of all resources – human and technical – which are available to the bridge team, to ensure the safe completion of the vessel's voyage. BRM includes critical elements without which it cannot achieve its objectives. These include (a) *communication.* The first cluster of BRM skills includes those related to effective communication. Good communication between crew members is key to successful BRM. The transfer of information is a complex process. It requires information to be conveyed when needed, understood, and acknowledged by the receiver and clarified if needed. It is often the case that information that is needed is available, but not communicated well if at all. Poor communication is a common cause of major incidents where inaccurate, incomplete, or ambiguous messages are passed from one crew member to another. It is important when giving and receiving information to acknowledge and repeat to ensure that the information is understood; (b) *Teamwork.* BRM focuses on team building and teamwork. Working in a team helps to solve problems faster. A team approach ensures that all crew members are involved in problem-solving and are not just spectators. As Henry Ford once said, 'coming together is a beginning, keeping together is progress and working together is success'. Team discussions are essential for learning and refining BRM. A good team should anticipate dangerous situations and recognise the development of a chain of error. On the bridge, the OOW and lookout should work together to ensure safe navigation. Safe and effective navigation is not the job of one person. This means it is important that the bridge team share a common view of the intended passage. If in doubt the lookout should speak up. Every individual can contribute something of value, and no one should be ignored based on their rank or position on board; (c) *decision making.* This is a key skill in effective BRM. Decision making often appears to be an individual matter. We all agree that master is the ultimate authority on board.

However, it is equally important for decision-makers to invite input from other officers and the crew. Before making any decision, it is vital to gather relevant information. An ill-informed or poorly made decision can lead to many unintended situations. Conducting regular meetings, interacting with officers and crew members, and taking opinions can help to formulate a final decision from several available options. It must be clearly stated though that the decisionmaker is ultimately responsible for the outcome of their decisions, irrespective of the decision-making process; (d) *situational awareness*. Every officer should think and plan well ahead of time. Officers and crew members should be aware of the external and internal conditions that can affect ship safety. This means keeping eyes and ears open and active and being prepared for the unexpected. Overlooking critical details or being indifferent to what is going on can lower situational awareness. Officers often tend to sit in front of the radar or stand stationary in one position rather than strolling from one side of the bridge to the other. This means they are not aware of what is happening outside their immediate range of view. Situational awareness is always important as it enables better anticipation and faster reaction; and (e) *fatigue*. Fatigue is a major issue among seafarers. Although many operations are now automated, this has led to reduced manning levels on ships. Despite this being recognised as the cause of many an accident, most of which were avoidable, fatigue remains one of the main problems of life at sea.

MANAGING SHIP SAFETY AND SECURITY

Last, but in no way least, the OOW is the person responsible for the safety and security of the ship during their watch. In every shipboard operation, there are three prime factors that should be focused on by the OOW: the safety of the crew, the safety of the ship and cargo, and the protection of marine environment.

NOTES

1. Named after the Irish hydrographer and Royal Navy officer, Rear Admiral Sir Francis Beaufort (1774–1857)
2. 287 miles or 463 kilometres.

Chapter 14

Passage planning and navigation

Shipping cargo from one port to another is a complex task and requires good planning, coordination, and execution. To ensure the voyage goes smoothly, the navigation officer is required to prepare a 'Passage Plan'. This is a comprehensive, berth to berth guide to determine the most favourable route for the vessel, and to identify potential problems or hazards along the route. It also ensures the bridge team can employ the best Bridge Management Practices.

PRINCIPLES OF PASSAGE PLANNING

Passage planning is an official duty and as such is contained within the SOLAS regulations. SOLAS chapter 5, Annexes 24 and 25, entitled 'Voyage Planning' and 'Guidelines for Voyage Planning' respectively, provide navigation officers with specific regulatory information regarding the planning and progress of the ship. When drafting the passage plan, the navigation officer must keep in mind that the ship must reach her destination safely and by complying with both local and international rules and regulations. Drafting the ship's passage plan involves four stages, which are: (1) appraisal, (2) planning, (3) execution, and (4) monitoring. Each stage of writing the passage plan has its own importance and should be followed without exception. To start, a rough estimate is made of the whole voyage. Once the rough plan is ready, it is further modified or refined taking into consideration details obtained from charts, the pilot book, weather forecasts, anticipated sea states and so forth. This process is carried out throughout the appraisal and planning stages. Over the next two stages – execution and monitoring – the plan is used as a guideline, and the passage is executed taking into consideration contemporaneous factors such as weather and sea conditions.

- *Appraisal.* This is the first stage of the passage planning progress and starts with the master discussing the voyage with the chief navigating officer (usually the second officer). The master will set out how they intend to make their way to the destination port. In some cases, it may be necessary for the master themselves to plan the passage. At this stage, the navigation officer will gather the information relevant to the proposed voyage. This involves extracting information from publications as well as those from the chart(s). A typical list of publications that may be consulted during the initial passage planning phase include Admiralty Charts, Admiralty Distance Tables, Admiralty List of Lights and Fog Signals, Admiralty List of Radio Signals, Admiralty Sailing Directions, Chart Catalogue, Draught of Ship Log, Load Line Chart, Mariner's Handbook, Navigational Warnings, Notices to Mariners, Ocean Passages of the World, Routeing Charts, Ships Routeing Manual, Tidal Stream Atlas, and Tide

202

DOI: 10.1201/9781003244615-17

Tables. The officer may also draw on their own personal experience and knowledge. Once the navigation officer has prepared a bare draft-taking into consideration the master's guidelines, company's guidelines, ship's cargo, the marine environment, and all other factors that may affect the ship – the navigating officer is ready to prepare the 'general track', which is the path the ship will follow. For ease of planning, the draft plan is first laid out on a small-scale chart, which is later transferred to larger scale charts, with minor modifications made as and when deemed necessary.

- *Planning.* Once a full appraisal using all information at hand has been completed, the navigation officer, acting under the authority of the master, will prepare a detailed plan for the passage. At this stage, the intended course of the ship is laid out on charts of suitable scale and all additional information is marked. The plan is laid out berth to berth, including pilotage waters. It is good practice to mark dangerous areas such as nearby wrecks, shallow water, reefs, small islands, emergency anchorage positions, and any other information that might aid safe navigation. Some of the reporting areas that should be accounted for in the passage plan are no-go areas, margins of safety, charted tracks, course alterations and wheel over points, parallel indexing, aborts, and contingencies, clearing line and bearings, leading lines, tides, and currents, change in engine status, minimum under keel clearance (UKC), use of the Echo Sounder, head marks, and natural transits. When approaching constrained waters, the vessel might find itself in a position beyond which there is no possible action but to proceed. This might happen when the vessel enters an area so narrow that there is no room to turn. For this reason, a position is drawn on the chart showing the last point where the passage can be aborted. The bridge team must always be aware that events might not go as planned and that emergency action may be required. Contingency plans account for such situations. The chart should clearly show the OOW how they can take swift action. Contingency planning may include alternative routes, safe anchorages, waiting areas, and emergency berths.
- *Execution.* At this stage, the navigating officers will execute the plan as it has been prepared. After departure, the speed is adjusted based on the ETA and the expected weather and sea conditions. The speed should be adjusted so that the ship is neither too early nor late at its port of destination. The master will also continuously calculate how long the voyage is taking, and account for supplies, stores, and fuel.
- *Monitoring.* Monitoring involves continuously checking and confirming the position of the vessel. *Parallel Indexing* can be used to maintain a safe distance alongside any hazards to navigation. A safe and successful voyage can only be achieved by close and continuous monitoring of the ship's progress along the pre-planned tracks. That is not to say that situations may arise where the navigating officer might feel it prudent to deviate from the passage plan. In such cases, the officer must inform the master and carry out any actions that may be deemed necessary for the safety of the ship.

ELECTRONIC CHART DISPLAY AND INFORMATION SYSTEM

The ECDIS is a relatively recent development in the navigational chart system used on board naval vessels and merchant ships. With the use of the electronic chart system, it has become easier for the ship's bridge team to navigate and plot positions with greater confidence and accuracy. ECDIS complies with IMO regulation V/19 and V/27 of the SOLAS Convention as amended, by displaying selected information using a *System Electronic Navigational Chart (SENC)*. ECDIS equipment that complies with SOLAS requirements can be used as an alternative to paper charts. Besides enhancing navigational safety, ECDIS greatly eases the navigator's workload with its automatic capabilities such as route planning, route monitoring, automatic ETA computation, and ENC updating. Furthermore, ECDIS provides many other sophisticated navigation and safety features, including continuous data recording which can be used for later analysis as well as Gyro, RADAR, ARPA, Echo Sounder, and so on. The system can keep an accurate position as it uses GPS satellites which continuously feeds data to the onboard ECDIS system. Further enhancing its usefulness, ECDIS incorporates and displays information contained in many other nautical publications such as Tide Tables and Sailing Directions and integrates additional maritime information such as radar information, weather, ice conditions, and automatic vessel identification. There are two main types of ECDIS charts currently available: the Raster Chart (RNC) and the Vector Chart (ENC). The RNC is a direct copy or scan of the paper chart. It looks identical to a paper chart and presents information exactly as it appears on the paper chart. The chart can be zoomed in or out or rotated. The ENC on the other hand is a computer-generated chart. The details on an ENC can be turned on and off depending on the requirement of the user. Objects on the ENC can be clicked for more detail. Depths can also be monitored to obtain grounding warnings. When zooming in, the features expand but the text remains unaltered.

The ECDIS system conforms to SOLAS requirements as well as several additional regulatory requirements including SOLAS chapter 5, Port State Control Requirements, IMO Performance Standards for ECDIS, S 52 Standard (Display Standard), S 57 Standard (Compilation Standard), and S 63 Standard (IHO Data Protection/Encryption Standard). ECDIS with adequate backup arrangements may be accepted as complying with the up-to-date charts required by Regulation V/20 of the 1974 SOLAS Convention. In addition to the general requirements for shipborne radio equipment forming part of the GMDSS and for electronics navigational aids contained in IMO Resolution A.694 (17), ECDIS should meet the requirements of this performance standard. ECDIS should be capable of displaying all chart information necessary for safe and efficient navigation originated by, and distributed on the authority of, authorised hydrographic offices. ECDIS should facilitate simple and reliable updating of the electronic navigational chart. It should also reduce the navigational workload compared to using the paper chart. It should enable the OOW to execute in a convenient and timely manner all route planning, monitoring, and positioning currently performed on paper charts. It should be capable of continuously plotting the ship's position. ECDIS should have at least the same reliability and availability of presentation as the paper chart published by government hydrographic offices. Finally, ECDIS should provide appropriate alarms or indications with respect to the information displayed or any malfunction of the equipment. Updates to the ECDIS charts may reach the ship in various ways, depending on the capabilities of the service provider and the onboard communication facilities.

- On data distribution media (DVD)
- As an email attachment (SATCOM)
- As a broadcast message via SATCOM plus additional communication hardware
- As an internet download

Key features

Passage recording

- Minute by minute recording for the past 12 hours of the voyage
- Record of four- hourly intervals of voyage track for a period of six months
- Dual Fuel: Dual Fuel is the use of RNCs when ENCs are not available with approved paper chart backup

Alarms

- Exceeding cross track limits
- Crossing selected safety contour
- Deviation from the route
- Critical Point Approach
- Different datum from the positioning system

Alarms or indication

- Largest scale for alarm (present chart too small a scale)
- Area with special conditions
- Malfunction of ECDIS

Indication

- Chart over scale (zoomed too close)
- Larger scale ENC available
- Different reference units
- Route crosses safety contour
- Route crosses specific area activated for alarms
- System test failure

For ease of understanding, indications may be visual or audible whereas alarms must be audible and may be visual as well.

WATCHKEEPING

The deck officer assigned with watchkeeping and navigation duties on the ship's bridge is called the OOW, sometimes referred to as the Officer of the Watch. Whilst keeping watch on the bridge, the OOW is also the master's representative and has total responsibility for the safe and smooth navigation of the ship. This means they are responsible for ensuring the ship complies with SOLAS, the COLREGs, and the Masters' Standing Orders. The OOW has three primary duties: navigation, watchkeeping, and GMDSS radio watchkeeping. Each of these three duties consists of discreet tasks, some of which we explore below:

- *Compare the compasses:* This is done to ensure there is a precise estimate window within which compass errors can affect the course to be steered and thereafter, made good. In case a gyro fails, the OOW must be aware of the extent to which the error of the magnetic might affect the course being followed/to be followed. Also, a comparison of the repeaters is essential to know if the repeaters are aligned with the master gyro and showing the correct reading which is needed when reading from the bridge or when calculating the compass error using the Azimuth
- *Check soundings by the echo sounder:* The UKC and the depth of water at any point are imperative to the safe navigation of the ship. While a record is made of the depth if need be and if instructed by the Master to do so, it is also necessary for the OOW to account for the errors of the echo sounder to ensure that the correct reading is obtained (basically, avoiding under or over-reading of the depth). This is especially

206   Ship operations

crucial when in shallow waters as failure to understand the actual depth can have devastating effects such as grounding of the vessel.

- *Ensure that the lookout is alert:* Not just the lookout but also the helmsman should be always alert. Rule 5 of COLREGs puts special emphasis on lookout and states that

Every vessel shall at all times maintain a proper lookout by sight and hearing as well as by all available means appropriate in the prevailing circumstances and conditions so as to make a full appraisal of the situation and of the risk of collision.

Again, the importance of this can be best explained when considering the vessel in restricted visibility (rule 19 of COLREGs) wherein the role of the lookout man is paramount.

- *Check the position:* The OOW must check the position plotted by the outgoing OOW and not depend entirely on the displayed information on the chart. While this is not to question the outgoing OOW, it is necessary to do so for personal convincing and rechecking it to ensure that there have been no errors. The precious positions affect the future position and therefore, to maintain maximum accuracy of the plot, this must be done.
- *Discussing the watch with the outgoing OOW:* Navigation of the vessel is extremely dynamic and therefore all conditions at any given time affect the ship in a certain way and helps us to ascertain the trend regarding the movement of the ship and the surroundings. The current OOW must discuss with the outgoing OOW if there has been any unusual activity, any changes in the CTS, any points where the master needs to be called or informed, any weather warnings or messages, any VHF communication with other ships etc. Also, the current OOW must ask the outgoing OOW if the master or chief officer has left any verbal instructions to be complied with or any night orders that there might be confusion with.
- *Read log entries:* The OOW must read any log entries made by the outgoing OOW before he leaves the bridge. If there is any confusion, he must ask the outgoing OOW for its explanation. Remember that the current bridge watch is under the responsibility of the current OOW so to reduce the margin of error as much as possible, this checking and rechecking must be done.
- *Check the draught:* The ship's draft must be displayed on bridge, updated when there are any changes, for ready reference by the OOW. This is to be always aware of the UKC
- *Check the gyro and its error:* Most of the equipment on the bridge might have some errors associated with it. While they are all important to be factored in, the gyro is something that is used at every second of the bridge watch to plan, execute and monitor the courses and any changes associated with it. Different makes of the gyro call for different inputs and some might require input to be fed to it which means that the OOW must take precautions to ensure that it done accordingly after accounting for all errors.
- *Check the GMDSS:* The GMDSS watch is crucial to safety and must be maintained on the stipulated frequencies as per regulations. Additionally, all MSI promulgated via the NAVTEX or the SAT C EGC or the VHF must be always checked. Whether or not such information affects the ship immediately is not the primary task at hand but to obtain, read and understand such a message to determine if it affects the ship is what the OOW must do.
- *Carry out general rounds of the ship:* Soon after handing over the watch, the OOW relieved may take a round of the ship to ascertain that fire safety is maintained, there

Passage planning and navigation 207

are no signs of breach, nothing unusual, no unsecured articles in the accommodation; having completed this, the outgoing OOW must inform the current OOW that such an inspection has been carried out satisfactorily and that nothing is amiss or if anything is amiss.

SHIP'S LOOKOUT

In accordance with the COLREGs, a lookout is required to always provide their uninterrupted attention to the ship's navigation to inform the OOW about other ships, shipwrecks, debris, flotsam, and so forth. Though the task might sound simple, the duty of a lookout is a responsible one and should be taken with the utmost regard. The lookout should inform the OOW should they observe any of the following: (a) any kind of floating object; (b) navigation marks or lights; (c) any type of distress signal from other ships or ports; (d) land; (e) ice, irrespective of size or form; (f) any type of ship irrespective of its size; (g) sandbanks or prominent navigational hazard; (h) any problem with any of the ship's navigation systems, including navigational lights; and (i) any kind of hazards or derelicts that may present a hazard to the ship's navigation. The job of lookout is mostly carried out by an experienced AB or OS. When on lookout duties, the AB (or OS) must be either free from their other onboard duties or be officially relieved from their other duties. In pirate affected areas, the job of the lookout is more important than at any other time.

OPERATING THE MARINE RADAR

Marine radar is by far the most used equipment on the bridge. The term 'Radar' is an acronym for *Radio Detection and Ranging*. The radar works on the basic principle of electromagnetic waves. The radar antenna sends out a high-speed electromagnetic wave. If another object is within range of the radar, the wave will bounce off and return to antenna. This is then shown on the radar screen. The wave can establish the position, speed, and direction of the object. On most ships, the wave travels more than 300,000 kilometres per second or roughly the same as the speed of light. This makes radar an essential 'aid to navigation'. Marine radars are categorised according to whether they operate on the x-band (10 GHz) or S-band (3 GHz) frequencies. The x-band, being higher frequency, is used for generating sharper images through better resolution whereas the S-band is used primarily in rain or fog conditions for identification and tracking purposes. Ship tracking devices are compulsory as per the COLREGs. Indeed, SOLAS chapter 5, regulation 19 states that

> all ships of 3,000 GT and upwards shall, in addition to meeting the requirements of paragraph 2.5, have a 3 GHz radar or where considered appropriate by the Administration, a second 9 GHz radar, or other means to determine and display the range and bearing of other surface craft, obstructions, buoys, shorelines and navigational marks to assist in navigation and in collision avoidance, which are functionally independent of those referred to in this paragraph.

There are two main components to marine radar. The first is the screen (referred to as the Plan Position Indicator (PPI)). The PPI displays all the targets that are present within the radar's range. The second is the parabolic radar antenna, which transmits and receives the electromagnetic waves. The radar antenna continuously rotates on top of the ship sending and receiving signals. As the radar rotates 360°, it sends out pulses which gives the OOW full visibility around their vessel. When the pulses are received back, the computer screen logs the position. The subject of marine radar is of course much more complex than has been laid out here. That said, as an OOW, it is important to be thorough with the radar and to study its operation and features extensively and to appreciate the limitations of radar.

Chapter 15

Stowaways, piracy, and drug trafficking

Political and social unrest, civil wars, famine, and poor economic opportunities are all stimulants for people seeking to better their lives. Unfortunately, this often means resorting to illegal activities. In this chapter we will briefly look at three of the most problematic for the shipping industry: stowaways, piracy, and drug trafficking.

STOWAWAYS

In accordance with maritime law, no ship or any member of its crew is permitted to enter a coastal state's territorial waters without valid documentation. A stowaway is any person who illegally and secretly boards and hides on a ship without the consent of the master. The intent is to travel into international waters to reach another country without any monetary payment or legal documentation. Stowaways employ many ingenious methods to secret themselves on board. As port facilities are a restricted area controlled by the ISPS Code, stowaways often require the support of dock workers to gain access to the quayside. This support is usually given in return for money. Once the stowaway has gained access to the restricted area of the port facility, they often break their way into containers. Once inside the container, stowaways are known to construct false walls using any means possible that will help them hide from casual inspections.

More desperate stowaways may employ methods that are far more dangerous, for example, and climbing up the stern ropes or jumping into the water and clambering up the rudder stock. Once on board, the stowaway is free to hide anywhere inside the ship including the engine room, paint locker, and steering flat. Stowaways have always been a problem for the maritime industry. To try and deal with the problem, the IMO has passed guidelines that apply to all ships and ports in every country across the world. These guidelines were implemented partly in response to the rise in stowaway incidents but also in part to the way crews react when discovering stowaways on board their ships. In the most extreme cases, stowaways have been found inside oil drums and crates with meagre food and water and left afloat on the open seas. Whilst illegal, the consequences for the crew if stowaways are found on board are severe.

Whenever a stowaway is found on board, it becomes the responsibility of the master to deliver the stowaway to the nearest coastal authority. Despite maritime law being clear on this, many countries refuse to accept stowaways and so refuse the ship access to their ports. Once a stowaway has landed ashore, they become the responsibility of the coastal state. This means the stowaway must be fed and accommodated, their identity ascertained, and eventual repatriation to their country of origin. This is fraught with legal issues and the costs of dealing with stowaways can very quickly escalate. To minimise the risk of stowaways boarding ships in port, the IMO has issued guidelines for ships, shipping companies and

DOI: 10.1201/9781003244615-18

209

IMO signatory countries. These guidelines are split into general duties, the master's responsibilities, the responsibilities of shipping companies, ship-owners and ship managers, Flag State responsibilities, and the responsibilities of the country of first port of call, country of original port of embarkation, and countries of transit during repatriation. We will briefly summarise these responsibilities below. The IMO has established a stowaway checklist that must be followed prior to departure. The checklist involves carrying out inspections of all areas of the ship and mandates that a proper gangway ISPS Watch is to be implemented whilst the ship is alongside.

RESPONSIBILITIES

Master, shipowner, and Flag State

When a stowaway is detected, it is the responsibility of the master to inform the ship's Flag State, the next port of call, and the port authorities of the original port of embarkation. The master must also endeavour to establish the identity and nationality of the stowaway. Whilst the stowaway is in the master's custody, the ship's crew are to ensure the general health, welfare, and safety of the stowaway until deportation can be arranged. The shipowner or vessel manager must ensure the master carries out their responsibilities regarding the notification of the relevant authorities. They must also comply with the instructions pertaining to and support of the removal of the stowaway from the ship. The Flag State of the ship should assist the master and the relevant port authorities in issuing the required documentation pertaining to the arrest and custody of the stowaway. This includes making representation to the relevant authorities to assist in the deportation of the stowaway at the next port of call and to assist the master, shipowner, and port authorities in making arrangements for the removal and repatriation of the stowaway to their country of origin.

Country of first port of call following detection of the stowaway and the country of original port of boarding

The country of first port of call following the detection of the stowaway is obliged under maritime law to accept the stowaway for investigation according to local laws and to allow the disembarkation and repatriation of the stowaway at the expense of ship-owner and agent. If the stowaway is a national of the country of original boarding, that country is required to repatriate the stowaway. If the stowaway is found on board whilst the ship is still alongside in the same port where the stowaway boarded the ship, the stowaway must be detained immediately with no charges imposed on the ship-owner or agent. When a stowaway is repatriated to their country of origin, and must transit through third-party countries, it is expected the third-party country will issue the relevant visas and exemptions to allow the stowaway to be escorted and transit unhindered.

STOWAWAY CATEGORIES

Stowaways are categorised according to their legal status: (a) refugees; (b) asylum seekers; (c) economic migrants; (d) illegal immigrants; and (e) criminals. A refugee is defined as any person forced to escape their country of domicile, or attempting to escape, for reasons of war, civil unrest, or religious persecution. The word 'forced' is used because in this situation as the person is in genuine fear for their life. An asylum seeker is an individual who seeks protection in another country without the fear of repatriation. Most asylum seekers are trying to avoid persecution in their home country because of political, social, or sexual discrimination. Asylum seekers may or may not be refugees. Economic migrants are people who wish to leave their country of domicile for the sole purpose of having a higher quality of life in another country. Illegal immigrants can be any one or more of the above categories. Stowaways are generally treated as illegal immigrants at the port of disembarkation though this depends on the laws of the countries involved. That said, a stowaway who claims refuge or asylum should be treated in accordance with the relevant UN conventions regarding the recognition and treatment of refugees and asylum seekers. The most concerning type of stowaway are hijackers whose intention is to take command of the ship and hold the ship and its crew for ransom.

STOWAWAY PREVENTION CHECKLISTS AND INTERROGATION QUESTIONNAIRES

Ships carry a stowaway prevention checklist which provides guidance to the master to ensure the best preventative measures are enacted to avoid stowaways. When a stowaway is found on board, an interrogation questionnaire is used to ascertain the particulars of the stowaway including their identity, their nationality, and port of boarding. The questionnaire, developed by ARM International, is available in several languages and once completed is sent to the appropriate authorities.

ONBOARD MEASURES FOR MANAGING STOWAWAYS

Security. First and foremost, any crew member that has found stowaways on board their ship must ensure their own safety above all else. Stowaways are, by definition, desperate and tend to react violently when found. If it is known or suspected that a stowaway is on board, the entire ship must be searched thoroughly. The safety of the crew is of paramount concern and full security precautions must be followed including locking all cabin and office doors. If the stowaway is found, they must be immediately arrested and placed into the master's custody. They should be searched for any weapons or sharp objects that could be used to injure themselves or members of the ship's crew. The body search should be carried out whilst respecting the stowaway's dignity. The stowaway must be kept confined in a secure location such as a cabin or storeroom where the opportunity to escape is minimal. Of the stowaway acts or threatens to behave violently, it may be necessary for the master to authorise the use of shackles. Care must be taken not to assault or cause injury to the stowaway. *Health and Welfare.* The mental and physical health of the stowaway must be taken into consideration. This includes monitoring for the symptomatic indications of infectious or communicable diseases. Confining the stowaway to their quarters and keeping minimum contact between them and the crew is critical. Provide the stowaway with separate eating utensils and crockery, bed linen and personal hygiene products. Once the stowaway has been removed from the ship, these should be disposed of. *Work.* Whilst it is not illegal to make the stowaway work during their confinement on board, it is strongly advised not to put stowaways to work. There are various reasons for this. First the master is personally responsible for the stowaway's health and welfare; any injuries or accidents involving the stowaway are the master's responsibility. Ironically, forcing stowaways to work on board a ship they have illegally boarded may give rise to a claim of employment, payment of wages, and employee rights. These are complications any master would want to avoid.

P&I CLUB COVER FOR STOWAWAYS

Insurance cover for ship-owners and operators is provided by Protection and Indemnity (P&I) Clubs. This insurance covers a vast array of incidents, including liabilities related to stowaways. In most cases, the costs of dealing with stowaways are covered by the Club in accordance with their policy terms and conditions. Most P&I policies include clauses that reduce or nullify cover if it is deemed by the Club that inadequate steps were taken to protect the ship against the risk of stowaways. This is important as in most cases it is the ship-owner, operator, and sometimes even the master and their crew who are held liable for the costs of repatriating stowaways. These costs can be substantial and include actual and punitive fines, food and accommodation, security, clothing, linen, and bedding, embassy fees, detention expenses, flights and other repatriation costs, and expenses incurred by agents associated with managing the repatriation process. Diversion expenses are another cost incurred by ship-owners but are usually recoverable from the P&I Club. Diversion happens when the ship is either ordered to divert to the first friendly coastal state or where the master deems it necessary to divert to the nearest coastal state. In either situation, the appropriate authorities must be contacted beforehand to confirm whether the diversion is authorised as the contract of carriage of cargo may be violated by the diversion. There may also be legal issues around the issuance of consent to enter territorial waters. These costs are generally recoverable under additional Ship-owners Liability (SOL) insurance which covers necessary breaches of contract.

PIRACY

Maritime piracy is a global issue that presents significant risks to the maritime sector with estimated worldwide losses of US $16 billion per year. The worst affected areas include the waters between the Red Sea and the Indian Ocean, the Somali coast, and the Strait of Malacca. These waterways are essential to the global economy with over 50,000 merchant ships every year passing through each year. In the Gulf of Guinea, piracy has led to pressure on offshore oil and gas production, with security for offshore installations and supply ships often paid for by individual oil companies. In the late 2000s, the emergence of piracy off the coast of Somalia spurred the US to form a multinational task force to patrol the waters off the Horn of Africa. Some of the world's major shipping routes take commercial shipping through narrow straits – often referred to as 'choke points' – including the Gulf of Aden and the Strait of Malacca. The volume of marine traffic in these sea routes means ships must often slow cruise. This makes them vulnerable to attack by small motorboats. Other active areas include the South China Sea and the Niger Delta. It is not just the open ocean where piracy is a problem. In response to the murder of the New Zealand world champion yachtsman, Sir Peter Blake in 2001, the Brazilian government formed an anti-piracy unit on the Amazon River. River piracy also happens in Europe, with ships reporting pirate attacks in the Serbian and Romanian sectors of the Danube River. Modern pirates tend to use small fast boats that can easily outmanoeuvre lumbering merchant ships, often taking advantage of the small number of crew on board.

Professional pirates operate from larger *mother ships* that supply the smaller attack/boarding craft. This enables the pirate gangs to operate further out at sea and for longer periods of time, which aids their ability to evade detection and capture. Pirates predominantly operate in regions with developing economies. These countries often have very small or non-existent navies and large trade routes. The end of the Cold War in 1991 has seen national navies decrease in size, with fewer expeditionary patrols, while global seaborne trade has continued to grow. This has made maritime piracy not only easier but also increasingly profitable. The International Maritime Bureau (IMB) maintains statistics regarding pirate attacks dating back to 1995. Their records indicate hostage-taking overwhelmingly dominates the type of violence perpetrated against seafarers. IMB records show in 2006, there were 239 attacks, of which 188 were taken hostage, 77 were kidnapped and 15 seafarers were murdered. In 2007 pirate attacks rose by 10% to 263. The IMB reported a 35% increase in attacks involving firearms. In 2009, the number of pirate attacks involving firearms was 176, compared to 76 the previous year.

Most maritime pirates prefer to target the crew, their personal belongings, and the contents of the ship's safe rather than capture the ship and its cargo. Ships often carry large amounts of cash to pay for payroll and port fees, which make for rich pickings. Less commonly, professional pirates and syndicated crime gangs have been known to capture vessels, repaint and rename them using false papers, and use the vessel for shipping narcotics and contraband products subject to embargo. In perhaps one of the worst cases of modern-day piracy, pirates attacked UN chartered ships bringing much-needed charity supplies to Somalia during the 2009 (to present) civil war. During the same conflict, sophisticated pirates armed with machine guns and a rocket-propelled grenade (RPG) managed to highjack the cruise ship *Seabourn Spirit* some 100 miles (160 km) off the coast of Somalia. Somali pirates have, on average, netted in excess of US $120 million every year since 2008, reportedly costing the global shipping industry between US $900 million and US $3.3 billion each year.

Ship defences against piracy

Most coastal states forbid commercial ships to enter their territorial waters with arms on board, even if the purpose is to protect against maritime piracy. Subsequently shipping companies have turned to novel ways for protecting their ships, crew, and cargo against the threat of piracy. Shipping companies have increasingly contracted private armed security guards who board ships at a waypoint, provide a visible deterrent against pirate attacks, then disembark at a further waypoint. Though a questionable practice, armed security guards do provide protection against modern-day pirates. Whilst armed guards are a potent defence mechanism, non-lethal defences are the preferred method of responding to piracy. In April 2009, the Israeli flagged cargo ship *MV Africa Star* was attacked by nine pirates. The ship's crew used coils of barbed wire to prevent the pirates from boarding the ship. This has since become a common technique to protect ships passing through piracy affected areas. Anti-piracy technology has greatly improved over the past two decades. A variety of powerful non-lethal weapons have been introduced onto ships to prevent pirate attacks. Merchant ships plying high piracy affected areas such as the Gulf of Aden (GOA) frequently carry a Long-Range Acoustic Device (LRAD), which is a non-lethal device that produces pain-inducing sound beams. The BAE Systems LSD 100 Anti-Piracy Laser Device uses a non-lethal laser beam to visually warn pirates not to come close. The laser can be operated during both daylight and night-time hours. Less sophisticated defences include water cannon and high-pressure hoses. There are many other technologies and defence systems available on the market that can be deployed against attacking pirate crafts.

The 'citadel'

The citadel is a compartment on the ship where the crew can seek refuge and hide in the event of pirates boarding the ship. The use of citadels to protect crews against piracy has increased since they were first introduced in the mid-2000s. To be effective, the citadel needs

214 Ship operations

to be installed in accordance with the regulations set out by the International Maritime Security Centre (IMSC). The IMSC recommends the citadel is kitted out with dry food and water supplies, effective communication equipment, ventilation, a first aid kit, CCTV cameras, and remote controls for switching off the main and auxiliary engines.

DRUG TRAFFICKING

Since the 1970s trafficking in narcotics such as cocaine, heroin and marijuana has been a major bane for law enforcement and customs officials the world over. Drug trafficking is not limited to the infamous cartels of Central and South America. The production and marketing of narcotics are often used by terrorist groups as a way of financing their nefarious activities. Drug trafficking is a problem that affects everyone, everywhere. Illegal drugs are trafficked by sea partly because ships move freely around a global trade network that often takes them to obscure ports where enforcement is either non-existent or open to corruption. This makes merchant ships an unwitting target for traffickers and gangs. If drugs are found on board by port or customs authorities, it is not unusual for charges to be levied against the master and crew, and the seizure and confiscation of the ship and her cargo.

In some parts of the world, particularly in Southeast Asia, the consequences of being caught in possession of narcotics are severe with long prison sentences and even the risk of the death penalty. When preparing to enter port, officers should account for the threat posed and implement measures to minimise risk. Even simple measures such as placing additional lighting across all exposed deck areas to eradicate possible shadow spaces can be effective, though this must never hinder safe navigation. Physical barriers may be installed so far as is possible in areas below the waterline such as the rudder trunking, overboard openings, and exposed thruster and propeller regions as these may be used as conduits for storing narcotics. Crew education and holding regular team meetings to reinforce awareness of the risks of being involved in drug trafficking are also effective ways of combatting drug trafficking. When shore leave is approved, the master should take time to brief the crew on the potential for drug traffickers to accost and entice accomplices to bring narcotics on board. Training sessions regarding personal safety, ISPS Code, Security Plans, security duties, port operations, and overall general awareness supported by warning signs and posters are all effective ways of reinforcing awareness. When alongside, especially in ports susceptible to drug smuggling, it may be advisable to hire additional guards from approved shore suppliers.

The ship may double up watches and post extra lookouts, especially when at anchorage. Unusual and erratic behaving craft and bubbles in the water around the hull make indicate divers. On completion of cargo operations and before the ship departs, the crew should perform a thorough search of the ship – to include the cargo holds, engine and machinery spaces – for the presence of suspicious objects. This should be carried out separately from the regular rounds performed by the crew whilst in port. All events and searches must be recorded in the ship's logbook as well as in the security log maintained by the SSO. In locations vulnerable to drug smuggling, port authorities along with customs officials are more likely to inspect the ship prior to departure. Sniffer dogs, amphibious remotely operated vehicles (ROVs), and divers may be used to search the vessel. If narcotics are found on board, the master and SSO must be informed immediately. The master should inform the local authorities, customs, police, the ship's agent, P&I Club, the ship's managers or owners, and the Flag State authority. Evidence should be collected including photographs if safe and permitted to do so. Always avoid moving or touching the item, and certainly not with bare hands. Under no circumstances should the item be taste-tested. This might work well as a Hollywood film trope but in real life, this is extremely dangerous and unnecessary. Only remove the package if it is small and if instructed to do so by the police, and always under the supervision of a senior officer. Secure the package in a locked compartment until it can be collected by the relevant authorities. If ordered not to remove the package, cordon off the immediate area, and prevent any unauthorised access. Continue searching the ship for other suspicious packages. Maintaining accurate records of the incident is critical. Aim to record as much detail as possible including the approximate quantity of substance found, the date and time, the exact location of where it was found on board, the names and ranks of each crew member in the search party and any witnesses. Record an accurate log of all communications taking place during and after searches. The records must be countersigned by the crew member and officers, any witnesses, the SSO, and the master.

Part IV

Cargo operations

Chapter 16

Hague–Visby Rules and bills of lading

The Hague–Visby Rules is a set of international rules for the international carriage of goods by sea. They are a slightly updated version of the original Hague Rules which were drafted in Brussels in 1924. The premise of the Hague–Visby Rules (and of the earlier English common law from which the Rules are drawn) was that a carrier typically has far greater bargaining power than the shipper, and that to protect the interests of the shipper/cargo-owner, the law should impose some minimum *affreightment obligations* upon the carrier. The Hague and Hague–Visby Rules are not a charter of new protections for cargo-owners; in fact, the English common law prior to 1924 provided more protection for cargo-owners and imposed more liabilities upon 'common carriers'. The official title of the Hague Rules is the rather awkward '*International Convention for the Unification of Certain Rules of Law relating to Bills of Lading*'. After being amended by the Brussels Amendments (which are equally as awkward but officially known as the 'Protocol to Amend the International Convention for the Unification of Certain Rules of Law Relating to Bills of Lading') in 1968, the Rules became known colloquially as the Hague–Visby Rules. A final amendment was made in the SDR Protocol in 1979. Many countries declined to adopt the Hague–Visby Rules and stayed with the 1924 Hague Rules. Some other countries which upgraded to Hague–Visby subsequently failed to adopt the 1979 SDR protocol. The Hague–Visby Rules were incorporated into English law by the Carriage of Goods by Sea Act 1971.

Although the rules were meant to clarify the relationship between carriers and shippers, it is important to note that some discrepancies exist in the text of the protocols. For example, Article I(c) of the Rules exempts live animals and deck cargo, yet section 1(7) restores these items into the category of 'goods'. Further, Article III (4) declares a bill of lading to be a mere 'prima facie evidence of the receipt by the carrier of the goods', whereas the Carriage of Goods by Sea Act 1992 section 4 promotes the bill of lading to 'conclusive evidence of receipt'. Under Article X, the Rules apply if '(a) the bill of lading is issued in a contracting State, or (b) the carriage is from a port in a contracting State, or (c) the contract (of carriage) provides that [the] Rules … are to govern the contract'. If the Rules apply, the entire text of Rules is incorporated into the contract of carriage, and any attempt to exclude the Rules is voided under Article III (8).

CARRIER'S DUTIES

Under the Rules, the carrier's main duties are to 'properly and carefully load, handle, stow, carry, keep, care for, and discharge the goods carried' and to 'exercise due diligence to … make the ship seaworthy' and to 'properly man, equip and supply the ship'. It is implicit (from the common law) that the carrier must not deviate from the agreed route nor from the usual route; though Article IV (4) provides that 'any deviation in saving or attempting

DOI: 10.1201/9781003244615-20

220 Cargo operations

to save life or property at sea or any reasonable deviation shall not be deemed to be an infringement or breach of these Rules'. The carrier's duties are not 'strict', but require only a reasonable standard of professionalism and care; Article IV provides the carrier with a wide range of exemptions from liability on a cargo claim. These exemptions include destruction or damage to the cargo if caused by fire, perils of the sea, act of God, and act of war. A controversial provision exempts the carrier from liability for 'neglect or default of the master ... in the navigation or in the management of the ship'. This provision is considered unfair to the shipper; and both the later Hamburg Rules (which require contracting states to denounce the Hague–Visby Rules) and Rotterdam Rules (which are not yet in force) refuse exemption for negligent navigation and management. Also, whereas the Hague–Visby Rules require a ship to be seaworthy only 'before and at the beginning' of the voyage, under the Rotterdam Rules the carrier will have to keep the ship seaworthy throughout the voyage (although this new duty will be to a reasonable standard that is subject to the circumstances of being at sea).

SHIPPER'S DUTIES

By contrast, the shipper has fewer obligations (mostly implicit), namely: (1) to pay freight; (2) to pack the goods sufficiently for the journey; (3) to describe the goods honestly and accurately; (4) not to ship dangerous cargoes (unless agreed by both parties); and (5) to have the goods ready for shipment as agreed; (q.v. 'notice of readiness to load'). None of these shippers' obligations are enforceable under the Rules; instead, they would give rise to a normal action in contract.

CRITICISM

With only ten articles, the rules have the virtue of brevity, but they have several faults. When, after 44 years of experience, the 1924 rules were updated with a single minor amendment, they still covered only carriage wholly by sea (thereby ignoring multi-modal transport), and they barely acknowledged the container revolution of the 1950s. Also, UNCTAD felt that they had diluted the protection to shippers once provided by English common law, and proposed instead the more modern Hamburg Rules of 1978, which were embraced by many developing countries, but largely ignored by ship-operating nations. The modern Rotterdam Rules, with some 96 articles, have far more scope and cover multi-modal transport but remain far from general implementation.

DOCUMENTS REQUIRED FOR SHIPPING

There are many documents that need to be prepared by the various parties involved in shipping a container from one location to another. Many of these documents concern the ship, and so it is worth spending a few moments going over the basics of the documentation involved in a sea freight shipment. For an average container shipment, there are no less than nine different bodies involved and each has a specific role. The first step in the process is occupied by the *exporter*, who prepares the commercial invoice, packing list, certificate of origin or similar certificates and shipping instructions for the *Bill of Lading* (B/L). We will discuss the B/L later. Next, is the *freight forwarder* (FF). The FF prepares the delivery notes, FF's cargo receipt, and shipping instructions for the B/L;

and arranges marine insurance, the cargo inspection certificates, and hazardous packing declarations. Third are the *clearing agents* (CA). The CA prepare the customs documentation, port documentation, and duty and VAT exemptions where applicable. The fourth step is where we step in – the shipping line (or their) agent (SLA). The SLA prepares the booking confirmation and container release form. They also generate the B/L, cargo manifest, manifest correctors, Telex Release, freight invoices, stowage plans, loading lists, dangerous goods manifest, and OOG manifest. Once the cargo has arrived at the port of discharge, the SLA prepares the arrival notification, delivery orders, discharge lists, and freight invoices. Once the cargo has been unloaded, it becomes the responsibility of the contracted *haulier*, who prepares the TREM card (if the cargo is hazardous), road permits, over-border permits and port entry documents. Supporting the haulier are *intermodal operators* (IOs). The IO prepares the documentation for inland haulage or rail movement to the destination, at which point, the cargo is finally delivered to the customer. In addition to those who are involved in the actual shipment of the cargo, various other bodies must also be included in the process. *Surveyors* prepare the cargo inspection and survey reports based on what they have been asked to survey. The shippers or receivers bank may need to prepare letters of credit, bills of exchange, sureties, and guarantees. And of course, the shipment needs to be insured with marine insurance, cargo insurance, and other general insurances as may be required. This is by no means an exhaustive list of the documentation involved in the shipping process. Depending on the cargo, exporter, importer, bank, destination, shipping line, government, and so on there may be many more documents required. These typically include the port and terminal authorities, customs and excise, the police, public health authorities and veterinary authorities. As you can see, one single shipment is a complex process made up of many moving parts which depend on the cooperation of various entities to make it happen.

WAYBILL

The 'waybill' is a document issued by a shipping company that provides the details and instructions relating to the shipment of a consignment of goods. Typically, it shows the names of the consignor and consignee, the point of origin of the consignment, its destination, and route. Most freight forwarders and trucking companies use an in-house waybill called a 'house bill'. These typically contain 'conditions of contract of carriage' terms on the back of the form that cover limits to liability and other terms and conditions. The waybill is akin to a courier's receipt, which contains the details of the consignor and the consignee, the point of origin, and the destination. The UK Carriage of Goods by Sea Act, 1992 s.1(1) applies to bills of lading s.1(2), sea waybills s.1(3), and ships' delivery orders s.1(4). Under s.1(3) of the Act, a sea waybill is defined as

> any document which is not a bill of lading but is such a receipt for goods as contains a contract for the carriage of goods by sea; and identifies the person to whom delivery of the goods is to be made by the carrier in accordance with that contract.

S.2 continues

> a person who becomes the person who (without being an original party to the contract of carriage) is the person to whom delivery of the goods to which a sea waybill relates is to be made by the carrier in accordance with that contract ... shall (by virtue of

222 Cargo operations

becoming the person to whom delivery is to be made) have transferred to and vested in him all rights of suit under the contract of carriage as if he had been a party to the contract of carriage.

BILL OF LADING

The B/L is one of the most important documents in the whole shipping and freight chain. The B/L serves three basic roles: it acts as evidence of Contract of Carriage; it acts as a Receipt of the Goods; and it provides a Document of Title to the goods. These have very specific legal implications – which we will discuss shortly – but before we go on, bear in mind that every shipping company will have their own format of the B/L. Therefore, this is 'generic' information and does not refer to any specific shipping line. As such, the main parts of the B/L are as follows:

- *Shipper.* This is the name and address details of the person or company who is shipping the cargo. They may or may not be the actual owner or manufacturer of the cargo but may be a trader or FF depending on the type of B/L that is issued. This could also be different from the exporter of the cargo. In simple terms, the shipper is the person or company who is shown on the shipping documentation (B/L, commercial invoice, packing list, etc). The exporter is a person or company that is authorised by customs and excise to export the cargo to another country
- *Consignee.* This is a key entity in the shipping chain and this field reflects the name and address details of the person or company that is to legally receive the cargo listed in the B/L. This may or may not be the actual owner or recipient of the cargo as they may be a bank, trader or forwarder depending on the type of B/L issued. Being named as the consignee on the B/L also comes with the risk and responsibility of being held accountable for many issues such as non-clearance of cargoes, late clearance and claims arising from the shipment of the cargo
- *Notification Party or Notify.* This is the name and address details of the person who should be notified upon the arrival of the cargo. Depending on the B/L that is issued this could be the actual buyer or receiver of the goods, a clearing and forwarding agent or the trader
- *Bill of Lading Number.* This is the unique number provided to the shipment covered under a specific B/L. This is allocated by the shipping line and must be quoted by the client for any queries, sailing information, arrival information, claims and so forth
- *Reference Numbers.* This space can be used to update any reference numbers specific to the client or the freight forwarder which they will use to trace the shipment during transit
- *Carriers Agents.* In this space, the details of the agents at the port of discharge are usually recorded by the shipping line so that the destination agent of the client/forwarder can contact the shipping line's agents to query the status of the shipment or approve for release

So far, we have covered the details pertaining to the shipper (consigner), the receiver (consignee), and their agents. The B/L also has important information relating to the carrier.

- *Pre-Carriage by.* Imagine there is an inland point which is connected to the mainland port by means of a feeder (connecting) vessel. The name of that feeder vessel is shown here. For example, Felixstowe to Aberdeen by feeder vessel *MV Antarctica*.

Hague–Visby Rules and bills of lading 223

- *Place of Receipt*. This is the place where the cargo is handed over by the shipper or their agent to the carrier (shipping line) or their agent. This is very important in terms of the contract of carriage between the shipper and the shipping line. If this area is completed, it is assumed that the carrier has done the movement from point of collection to the Port of Loading and if there any incidents, damages, etc. to the container or cargo between the Place of Receipt and Port of Loading, the liability will lie with the carrier.
- *Port of Loading*. This is the place from which the container or cargo is loaded by the carrier onto the nominated Ocean Vessel.
- *Ocean Vessel/Voyage*. This is the name of the vessel and the voyage number that carries the container from the (mainland) Port of Loading (e.g., New York) to the Port of Discharge (e.g., Durban). Remember that the combination of vessel and voyage number will be unique and never repeated.
- *Port of Discharge*. This is the place at which the container or cargo is discharged by the carrier from the nominated Ocean Vessel.
- *Place of Delivery*. This is the destination of the container for delivery from the perspective of the carrier. If this area is completed, for example by showing Cooper Pedy, it means the carrier has undertaken to move the container from the Port of Discharge (e.g., Adelaide) to the final Place of Delivery (Cooper Pedy). Again, as in the case with the Place of Receipt, the shipping line must be careful when annotating this field as they will become liable for the delivery of the container to the point of delivery, rather than the port of discharge. If there is a Place of Delivery shown on the B/L, generally carriers will not allow the consigner to take delivery of the container at the Port of Discharge and move it to the Place of Delivery. The simple reason being that if anything should happen to the container enroute to the Place of Delivery, the carrier may still be held liable.

EVIDENCE OF CONTRACT OF CARRIAGE

Here, the emphasis is firmly on the word 'evidence'. The B/L is often misunderstood by people to mean a contract between the seller and buyer and a Contract of Carriage between the Carrier and Shipper. Both are wrong. The contract between the buyer and seller is established when the buyer places the order with the seller and they both discuss and agree (verbally or in writing) the 'what', 'where', 'when', 'how', and 'how much' of the transaction in detail. The contract between the shipper and the carrier established when the shipper or their agent makes the booking with the carrier (the shipping line) to carry the cargo from location A to B. Therefore, the B/L is the *evidence* of the contract of carriage between the 'Carrier' and the 'Shipper' or the 'Cargo Owner'. The second emphasis is on the word 'receipt'. The B/L is issued by the carrier or their agent to the shipper or their agent in exchange for the receipt of the cargo. The issuance of the B/L is proof that the carrier has received the goods from the shipper or their agent in apparent good order and condition, as handed over by the shipper. The third emphasis is on the term 'title'. This means the goods may be transferrable to the holder of the B/L which then gives the holder of the B/L the right to claim the goods or transfer the goods to another party. Based on these three roles, there are several variations of the B/L. The most important are discussed below.

When a B/L is issued in original(s) form to a 'named' consignee it is referred to as a 'Straight B/L'. The straight B/L is a non-negotiable and non-transferrable document. Release of cargo at the destination of delivery may be issued only to the named consignee and only upon surrender of at least one of the original bills issued. This type of B/L satisfies roles one

224 Cargo operations

and two above but does not satisfy role three (Document of Title) as the document is non-negotiable and non-transferable. When a B/L is issued to a 'named' consignee but without any originals, it is considered a 'Sea Waybill'. This type of B/L is also non-negotiable and non-transferable. A Sea Waybill is usually issued for inter-company shipments, for example, from the *ACME Corporation*, Los Angeles, to the *ACME Corporation*, London, or where the shipment takes place between two different companies but there are no negotiations required between the two either directly or via bank for release of the cargo; and where the shipper does not need to submit an original B/L to secure their payment. As no originals are issued with a Sea Waybill no surrender is required. The release of the goods is immediate. Where a Sea Waybill is issued, this must be clearly annotated on the body of the B/L and the shipping manifest. Again, this type of B/L only satisfies roles one and two above but does not satisfy role three (Document of Title) as the document is neither negotiable nor transferable. When a B/L is issued in original(s) form and consigned 'TO ORDER' or 'TO ORDER OF SHIPPER' or even 'TO ORDER OF XYZ BANK' it is termed as a 'Negotiable B/L' or 'Order Bill'. One of the most important aspects of a B/L is that it can be used as a negotiable instrument for payments between the buyer and seller using Letters of Credit. A negotiable B/L must be treated like cash and with due care as there are several cumbersome procedures to be followed should an original B/L become lost or damaged. Another notable feature of this type of B/L is that it contains the Terms and Conditions of the Carrier on the first page of the B/L. The first page is what is commonly referred to as the 'back of the B/L'. Sea Waybills issued by some carriers do not have these Terms and Conditions on the back (also known as a 'blank back short form B/L'). The destination port agent may authorise the release of the cargo only after at least one of the issued originals are surrendered and after checking the endorsements on the back of the B/L. This is because it is possible for this type of B/L to be endorsed or transferred to another company. Unlike the first two types, the third B/L satisfies the three roles.

There are also various ways in which the B/L may be called or titled; the purpose of which is to identify the carrier's responsibility in terms of the carriage. These include *Port to Port B/L*. When a B/L is issued as a Port-to-Port B/L (also known as an *Ocean B/L*), the carrier's responsibility begins at the port of loading and ends at the port of discharge. Subsequently, the Place of Origin / Receipt or Place of Destination / Delivery should not be annotated in the B/L. *Combined Transport B/L*. When a B/L is issued as a Combined Transport B/L, it involves multiple modes of transport from the Place of Receipt to the Place of Delivery and all these movements are carried out as a single contract by multiple service providers under the umbrella of the carrier. Carrier takes responsibility for any loss or damage for the entire transport including the sea and other modes of transport. When a B/L is released as a Combined transport B/L, boxes like 'Pre-Carriage by', 'Place of Receipt by Pre-Carrier', 'Place of Delivery by On-Carrier', and 'On-Carriage By' will be completed. Some agents may refer to the *Multimodal Transport B/L*. This is the same as a Combined Transport B/L. Lastly, the *Through B/L* is like the Combined Transport B/L except that in the case of the Through B/L, the carrier is directly responsible only for the sea part of the goods transit and for the inland movement the carrier acts only as an agent in arranging the inland movement. The terms on the Through B/L as issued by the carrier will be specifically listed. When a B/L is released as a Through B/L, the boxes 'Pre-Carriage By', 'Place of Receipt by Pre-Carrier', 'Place of Delivery by On-Carrier', 'On-Carriage By' etc., will be completed. A common misconception that some people have is to refer to the B/L as a *Telex Release B/L*.

In fact, there is no such document as a Telex Release B/L. By *Telex Release*, we are simply referring to a message that is sent by the shipping line or agent at the load port to their office or agent at the port of discharge advising that the shipper or exporter has surrendered one or all the original bills of lading that have been issued to them, and that the cargo can be released to the consignee shown on the B/L without presentation of an original B/L. This is usually requested only if the consignee is a direct consignee (i.e., not a bank or To Order).

SHIPPER'S LOAD, STOW, AND COUNT

Shipper's Load, Stow, and Count or Shipper's Load and Count (SLAC) is a term that is used extensively when drafting a B/L. In all break-bulk and bulk vessels, there is a document called *Mate's Receipt*. This document is akin to a delivery note and has all the information pertaining to the shipment such as cargo description, number of bundles, weight, measurements, and so on. This note is handed over to the ship at the time of loading. If any discrepancies are found between the actual cargo delivered and the Mate's Receipt, the chief officer (after whom the receipt is named) aka the first mate, will check the cargo and note any discrepancies to confirm that the cargo was received in that condition. This absolves the ship/owner/charterer of any claims relating to missing or damaged cargo that might be charged upon them by the shipper at a later stage. This was mostly possible in the era of pre-containerisation as the carrier, or their agents, could easily and physically check and verify the cargo. Since the introduction of containerised cargo and especially full container loads (FCL), the carrier/agent is not privy to the packing of the containers and the nature of the cargo. The carrier relies on the information provided by the shipper in terms of the cargo, the number of packages, the weight, and its measurements. Henceforth, the clauses 'SHIPPERS LOAD STOW AND COUNT (SLAC)' and 'SAID TO CONTAIN (STC)' is entered onto the B/L to protect the carrier from any claims that the shipper might charge them at a later stage. For example, let us say the B/L states 1×20 ft container STC 55 boxes of laptop computers. When the container reaches its destination and is opened, the container only has 45 boxes of laptop containers. The carrier is protected against any liability for the missing boxes as the B/L has not been opened since it was collected from the shipper, and the B/L states STC. So long as the seal has not been altered or tampered with, the consignee or shipper cannot question or hold the carrier liable for the shortage because the carrier was not present at the time of the packing of the container and carrier does not know what the Shipper Loaded, Stowed or Counted. In these situations, the B/L clearly shows the details of the shipment as provided by the shipper. The consignee must contact the shipper to take up the dispute. If the seal has been broken, or the seal number tampered with, that becomes an entirely different proposition for the carrier altogether.

HOUSE BILL OF LADING AND MASTER BILL OF LADING

Without being drawn into the intricacies of maritime and commercial law, it is important to recognise the differences between a House Bill of Lading (HBL) and a Master Bill of Lading. An HBL is issued by a Non-Vessel Operating Common Carrier or NVOCC operator or an FF. An MBL is issued directly by the shipping line (the carrier) to the NVOCC operator or FF. When issued for a FCL shipment (non-groupage), an HBL should always be issued on a back-to-back basis with an MBL which means that the HBL should be an *exact* replica of the MBL issued by the actual shipping line in respect of all details except the shipper, consignee, and notification parties. With the HBL the shipper will usually be the actual shipper/exporter of the cargo (or as dictated by the letter of credit (L/C); the consignee will usually be the actual receiver/importer of the cargo (or as dictated by the L/C); the notification party may be the same as the consignee (or any other party as dictated by the L/C). With the MBL, the shipper will usually be the NVOCC operator, or their agent or the FF. The consignee will usually be the destination agent or counterpart or office of the NVOCC operator, or the FF; and the notification party may be the same as consignee or any other party. In the interests of the NVOCC operator and their insurance coverage/exposure, it is recommended that the details on the HBL and MBL – such as the vessel/voyage information, cargo description, number of containers, seal numbers, weight, measurements – remain the unchanged. The only difference should be in the shipper, consignee, and notification party details. Unless disallowed by L/C, the HBL is also used/treated as a negotiable document and can fulfil the roles of the B/L. Due care must be taken when using HBLs as a negotiable document as it is possible to create two sets of B/L each issued by two different entities for the same cargo!

Chapter 17

Dangerous cargoes

All IMO member states are required to implement national legislation to address the transport of dangerous goods, through their legal obligations under the SOLAS and MARPOL Conventions. However, to assist them, the IMO has produced a detailed set of requirements covering the transport of packaged dangerous goods by sea in a separate Code; the IMDG Code. The requirements of the IMDG Code are based on the Model Regulations known as the 'Orange Book', which is published by the United Nations Committee of Experts on the Transport of Dangerous Goods in Geneva, Switzerland, together with recommendations for good practice. The requirements of the IMDG Code are published in two volumes with an additional Supplement volume, which contains several additional IMO related publications. Most parts of the IMDG Code became mandatory on 1 January 2004, under the mandatory requirements of the SOLAS Convention. Whilst most signatories have incorporated the requirements of the IMDG Code without further amendment into their national legislation, others have applied some different (usually more stringent) national requirements in addition to those of the IMDG Code. Therefore, when shipping dangerous goods, it is important to be mindful of any further restrictions or requirements, which may apply in a particular country, in addition to the IMDG Code. The IMDG Code is updated on a two-yearly basis with each amendment valid for up to three years. Amendments overlap each other so that there is always a transition period for the maritime industry to make the necessary adjustments to the latest amendment. The IMDG Code adopts a standard reference format, which is harmonised with the United Nations Model Regulations ('Orange Book') and forms the basis of all international modal regulations covering the transport of dangerous goods (i.e., road, rail, inland waterway, air, and sea).

DANGEROUS GOODS LIST

The Dangerous Goods List (DGL) is central to the IMDG Code. This contains a list of all dangerous goods assigned under the United Nations System in Numerical (UN Number) Order, together with their specific transport requirements in a codified system. The Code is presented in two parts: Volume 1, and Volume 2, with a third Supplement volume containing related IMO publications and IMO resolutions. It is necessary to use the first two volumes to obtain the required information when shipping dangerous goods by sea. Volume 1 contains Parts 1, 2, 4, 5, 6, and 7 and Volume 2 comprises mainly Part 3 which contains the DGL, a list of all the dangerous goods in UN Number order, together with their transport requirements presented in 18 columns. Columns 7 and 16 are divided into two parts (a and b). The transport requirements contained in the DGL include:

- Special provisions applicable to certain substances and articles in the DGL
- Limited quantity and excepted quantity provisions

DOI: 10.1201/9781003244615-21

228 Cargo operations

- Stowage and segregation requirements
- Packaging and tank requirements
- Volume 2 contains two appendices and an alphabetical list of the substances, materials, and articles listed in the DGL. The Supplement volume comprises separate IMO publications that relate to the IMDG Code including:
- Emergency Procedures (EMP) for use on ships in the event of an accident (e.g., spillage or fire)
- Medical First Aid Guide (MFAG) for use on ships in accidents involving dangerous goods
- Reporting procedures, for use by ships to report incidents involving dangerous goods, harmful substances, and/or marine pollutants
- Recommendations on the Safe Use of Pesticides in Ships (e.g., fumigation)
- Irradiated Nuclear Fuel (INF) Code
- Various relevant IMO Resolutions, Circulars, and so forth

The primary purpose of the IMDG Code's classification system is to identify goods that are considered dangerous for transport; identify the dangers which are presented by dangerous goods in transport; and to ensure the correct measures are taken to enable these goods to be transported safely and without risk to persons or the environment (both within port and on board).

UN CLASSIFICATION NUMBERS

UN Classification Numbers are unique four-figure, Arabic numeral numbers allocated by the *UN Committee of Experts on the Transport of Dangerous Goods* to specific or generic Proper Shipping Names (PSNs) to overcome language barriers. For example, the English name for *Nitrous Oxide* is *Hemioxide D'Azote* in French and *Distick Stuffoxide* in German. It also helps to avoid confusion caused by similar names (e.g. *Sulphuryl Chloride, UN 1834*, and *Sulphuryl Flouride UN 2191*); and to avoid mispronouncing and misspelling complicated chemical names (e.g., *isocyanatobenzotrifluorides UN 2285*). UN Numbers starting with '0' are allocated to UN Class 1: Explosives whereas UN Numbers starting with '1', '2' or '3' are used to identify goods of any other class. The UN Number for a substance or article must be quoted whenever there is a need for identification such as during an incident and must appear on containment systems and on documentation. Each UN Number is allocated a Proper Shipping Name (PSN). The PSN is the accepted name that must be used for transport purposes on documentation, packaging, and so on. The PSN is the portion of the entry in the DGL which is shown in uppercase characters (plus any numbers, Greek letters, 'sec', 'tert', and the letters 'm', 'n', 'o', 'p' which form an integral part of the name).

CLASSES

In accordance with the principles of the UN Recommendations, the IMDG Code divides dangerous goods into nine classes, some of which are subdivided further. Some dangerous goods may present hazards associated with more than one class. For example, some flammable liquids (Class 3) may also be toxic (Class 6.1) and corrosive (Class 8). When classifying dangerous goods, the main hazard presented is considered the primary hazard and any other hazards (up to a maximum of two) are considered subsidiary hazards. Dangerous goods must be labelled to show the primary and subsidiary hazards they present during transport.

Pure chemicals and dangerous goods transported in sufficient quantities are allocated individual UN Numbers. However, as many of the chemicals available today are mixtures, solutions and formulations containing many different hazardous constituents, they are shipped under a general 'Not Otherwise Specified' (NOS) entry, which describes the dangerous goods by their main hazards. For example, any flammable liquid which does not have its own individual UN Number is shipped under UN 1993 Flammable Liquid, NOS. Similarly, any corrosive solid, which is also toxic, is shipped under UN 2923 Corrosive Solid, Toxic, NOS. Generic entries for products based on their chemical properties may also be used (e.g., UN 3271 ETHERS NOS or UN 1987 ALCOHOLS NOS). Most classes contain multiple NOS or generic entries which may be used. Appendix A of Volume 2 lists the possible entries by class.

Organic peroxides and self-reactive substances

Organic Peroxides in Class 5.2 and Self-Reactive Substances in Class 4.1 are classified into seven types according to the degree of hazard they present. The types range from type A, which is not accepted for carriage in the packaging in which it is tested, to type G, which is not subject to the provisions of the IMDG Code. The classification of types B to F is directly related to the maximum quantity allowed in one package. They are further subdivided according to whether they are solid or liquid and whether they require temperature control during transport. This results in 20 group UN Numbers being available to ship both Organic Peroxides and Self-Reactive Substances (e.g., UN 3101 for Organic Peroxide Type B, Liquid and UN 3235 for Self-reactive liquid, Type D, Temperature-Controlled).

Marine pollutants

Since MARPOL 73/78 Annex III came into force on 1 January 1991, items that are harmful to the marine environment but not to people or the ship (hitherto the only basis for inclusion in the Code) have been included in Class 9. All marine pollutants, whether in Class 9 (because they do not fall under the criteria of Classes 1–8) or one of the other classes, must carry the marine pollutant mark. The term marine pollutant is referred to in other modal regulations as *Environmentally Hazardous Substances* (EHS).

Degree of hazard

Dangerous goods in most classes are subdivided into three packing groups (PG) reflecting the degree of hazard they present during transport.

- Packing Group (PG) I: representing great danger
- Packing Group (PG) II: representing medium danger
- Packing Group (PG) III: representing low danger

When selecting packaging to contain dangerous goods, the PG of the dangerous goods determines the type of packaging and the standards to which it is manufactured and tested. Packaging used to transport PG I dangerous goods must be manufactured and tested to a higher standard than packaging used to transport PG III dangerous goods.

MARKING, LABELLING, AND PLACARDING

To ensure correct identification of dangerous goods in the transport chain they must be correctly marked, labelled and 'placarded' to ensure that the hazards are easily communicated.

230 Cargo operations

Table 17.1 Classification of dangerous goods

Class 1: Explosives	1.1:	Substances and articles which have a mass explosion hazard
	1.2:	Substances and articles which have a projection hazard but not a mass explosion hazard
	1.3:	Substances and articles which have a fire hazard and either a minor blast hazard or a minor projection hazard or both
	1.4:	Substances and articles which present no significant hazard; only a small hazard in the event of ignition during transport with any effects largely confined to the package
	1.5:	Very insensitive substances which have a mass explosion hazard
	1.6:	Extremely insensitive articles which do not have a mass explosion hazard
Class 2: Gases	2.1:	Flammable gases
	2.2:	Non-flammable, non-toxic gases
	2.3:	Toxic gases
Class 3: Flammable Liquids		A flammable liquid is defined as a liquid, a mixture of liquids, or liquids containing solids that require a much lower temperature than others to ignite. These temperatures are so low that there is a high risk of the liquids igniting during transportation. This makes flammable liquids very dangerous to handle and transport, as they are very volatile and combustible. Flammable liquids are usually used as fuels in internal combustion engines for motor vehicles and aircraft. This means they make up the largest tonnage of dangerous goods moved by surface transport. Many household products also contain flammable liquids, including perfumery products and acetone (which is used in nail polish remover)
Class 4: Flammable Solids	4.1:	*Flammable solids:* These will burn easily than normal combustible materials. The burning of flammable solids is also fierce and rapid; they are also incredibly dangerous because they can decompose explosively, burn vigorously, or produce toxic gases
	4.2:	*Spontaneously combustible:* These can be either solids or liquids. They ignite spontaneously when in contact with oxygen
	4.3:	*Dangerous when wet:* These goods react with water to generate flammable gas that can be ignited by the heat of the reaction
Class 5: Oxidising Agents and Organic Peroxides	5.1:	*Oxidising Agents:* Also known as oxidisers, these substances that can cause or contribute to combustion as a product of chemical reactions. Oxidisers are not necessarily combustible on their own, but the oxygen they produce can cause combustion with other materials
	5.2:	*Organic peroxides:* The molecular structure of these materials makes them extremely liable to ignition. This means they are liable to combust individually. They are designed to be reactive for industrial purposes, so they are unstable and can be explosive
Class 6: Toxins and Infectious Substances	6.1:	*Toxins:* Toxic substances are liable to cause death because they are, as the name suggests, toxic. They can cause serious injury or harm to human health if they enter the body through swallowing, breathing in, or absorption through the skin. Some toxics will kill in minutes; however, some might only injure if the dose is not excessive
	6.2:	*Infectious substances:* These are goods that contain micro-organisms that cause infectious diseases in humans or animals, otherwise known as pathogens
Class 7: Radioactive Material		Radioactive materials contain unstable atoms that change their structure spontaneously in a random fashion. They contain 'radionuclides', which are atoms with an unstable nucleus. It is this unstable nucleus that releases radioactive energy. When an atom changes, they emit ionising radiation, which could cause chemical or biological change. This type of radiation can be dangerous to the human body. Examples include smoke detectors and yellowcake
Class 8: Corrosives		Corrosives are highly reactive materials that produce positive chemical effects. Due to their reactivity, corrosive substances cause chemical reactions that degrade other materials when they encounter each other. If these encountered materials happen to be living tissue, they can cause severe injury. Examples include batteries, chlorides, and flux
Class 9: Miscellaneous Dangerous Goods		This category covers substances that present a danger not covered in the other classes. Examples include dry ice, GMO's, motor engines, seat belt pretensioner, marine pollutants, asbestos, airbag modules and magnetised material

Packaging should normally be marked with the UN Number and PSN. There are also additional marks that may be required including:

- Marine Pollutant mark
- Limited quantity mark
- Excepted quantity mark
- Lithium battery mark
- Orientation arrows

Each class is assigned a specific diamond-shaped label or labels indicating the main hazard pictorially and showing the class number in the bottom corner. Each package containing dangerous goods must bear the appropriate label(s) to warn of all the hazards (both primary and subsidiary) presented by the dangerous goods. Containers containing such packages must bear enlarged labels, known as placards. However, in addition to the class placard, there are also additional marks and signs that must be shown on the exterior of cargo transport units in certain circumstances. These include the *Fumigation Warning Mark* to be displayed on units carrying dangerous goods under fumigation; the *Elevated Temperature Mark* to be displayed on tanks carrying dangerous goods which are carried hot; the *Limited Quantity Mark* for goods declared as Limited Quantities; and the *Marine Pollutant (Environmentally Hazardous Substance) Mark*.

DANGEROUS GOODS CONTAINMENT

Product containment is dealt with in six distinct categories.

Conventional containment

Conventional containment (e.g., drums, bags, fibreboard boxes) must:

- Have a maximum capacity of 450 litres/400 kg
- Meet certain manufacturing standards
- Pass specified performance tests
- Bear UN packaging codes as evidence of meeting the required standards

The IMDG Code indicates a range of possible packages for every substance, however these are subject to the prime requirement that the packaging materials must be compatible with the proposed contents and be suitable for use. Conventional packaging permitted for use for dangerous goods are coded according to packing instructions ('P Codes') which are given in column 8 of the DGL. Any special packing provisions which apply are called 'PP codes' are listed in column 9 of the DGL. Details of these packing instructions and special packing provisions are found in chapter 4.1, paragraph 4.1.4.1 of Volume I of the IMDG Code. Details of testing and examples of UN packaging codes are given in chapter 6.1 of Volume 1.

Intermediate bulk containers (IBCs)

Intermediate Bulk Containers are large rigid or flexible packaging with a capacity of up to 3,000 litres and are designed for mechanical handling. Six types of IBC are specified, together with performance tests and details of which substances are allowed in which type of IBC. If IBCs are permitted for shipping dangerous goods, they are coded according to the IBC packing

232 Cargo operations

instructions (IBC codes) which are given in column 10 of the DGL. Any special IBC packing provisions which apply are coded (B codes) in column 11. Full details of the packaging instructions and special packing provisions are found in chapter 4.1.4.2 of Volume I. Details of testing and examples of IBC packaging codes are given in chapter 6.5 of Volume 1.

Large containments

Large packaging is defined as an outer packaging having a capacity exceeding 400 kg or 450 litres capacity with a maximum volume of 3 m³ and contains either inner packaging or articles. Large packaging is designed to be handled by mechanical means. If large packaging is permitted to be used for dangerous goods, they are coded into large packing instructions (LP codes) which are given in column 8 of the DGL. Any special packing provisions for large packaging which apply are coded (LP codes) in column 9. Full details of the Large Packaging instructions and Special Packing provisions are found in chapter 4.1.4.3 of Volume I. Details of testing and examples of Large Packaging codes are given in chapter 6.6 of Volume I.

Bulk containers

Certain solid dangerous goods may be transported in bulk when indicated in the DGL by a 'BK' code in column 13 of the DGL.

- BK1: transport in sheeted bulk containers is permitted
- BK2: transport in closed bulk containers is permitted
- BK3: transport in flexible bulk containers is permitted

Closed bulk containers include freight containers, skips, offshore bulk containers, bulk bins, swap bodies, trough-shaped containers, roller containers, and the load compartment of vehicles. BK1 sheeted bulk containers may only be used for sea transport for UN 3077 not considered to be Marine Pollutants and BK3 are not permitted in cargo transport units but may only be transported in the ship's holds.

Portable tanks

Portable tanks range in size from 450 litres upwards and come in different types depending on the requirement of the cargo. Different requirements for various liquids and gases are detailed in the Code. Items such as maximum allowable working pressure, relief valves, filling ratios, etc., are all dealt with, together with specific requirements for individual substances (Volume I, chapters 4.2, 6.7, and 6.8). Multiple-Element Gas Containers (MEGC) are built to similar standards as portable tanks and are used for the transport of non-refrigerated gases (see chapter 4.2 and 6.7).

DANGEROUS GOODS DOCUMENTATION

The IMDG Code requires that anyone who submits dangerous goods for transport must provide a dangerous goods transport document to communicate details of the dangerous goods being shipped. This document must include the Dangerous Goods Description consisting of the UN Number, Proper Shipping Name (PSN), Class / Division (including compatibility group letter for class 1), Subsidiary Hazard and Packing Group. The sequence in which this information appears is vitally important and is laid down in the IMDG Code.

Information required in addition to the dangerous goods description includes the number and kind of packages (there is no requirement to mention inner packages) and the total quantity of dangerous goods. In addition, further information may be required including the technical name for goods allocated SP 274 or 318 in column 6 of the DGL. Additional notations such as 'waste', 'salvage packaging', or 'hot' may be required as well as the flash point; marine pollutant; limited quantity; and excepted quantity. There may also be specific additional information required for certain classes of dangerous goods. The provisions of chapter 5.4 of the IMDG Code should always be consulted when preparing the transport document. The dangerous goods declaration must be signed by or on behalf of the shipper certifying that the Code requirements have been complied with together with the container packing certificate declaration certifying that permitted dangerous goods have been properly packed and secured in a suitable container. This is not required for portable tanks. These are important considerations when both loading dangerous goods into CTUs and loading CTUs containing dangerous goods on board vessels.

STOWAGE AND SEGREGATION

Stowage refers to where (on deck or under deck) and on what type of ship (cargo or passenger) different dangerous goods may be stowed. For Classes 2 to 9 there are five stowage categories (A to E) and the stowage category indicating the applicable requirements for each UN Number appear in column 16a of the DGL and are defined in chapter 7.1, paragraph 7.1.3.2. For Class 1 there are also five stowage categories (1 to 5) defined in paragraph 7.1.3.1. In addition, for individual substances there are also 30 'SW' (stowage) codes and 4 'H' (handling) codes which add further requirements. These codes are defined in paragraphs 7.1.5 and 7.1.6 of the IMDG Code, respectively. For Limited quantities and Excepted quantities, the stowage category is always A and any 'SW' or 'H' codes do not apply. Dangerous goods, which may interact dangerously with each other, must be segregated from each other. In the IMDG Code general segregation provisions are covered in chapter 7.2 with the following chapters covering segregation provisions within CTUs and segregation requirements between CTUs on board different vessel types. General requirements to segregate various classes of dangerous goods are provided in table 7.2.4, whereas substance-specific segregation requirements are identified via 'SG' codes in 16b of the DGL and further explained in chapter 7.2, paragraph 7.2.8. The segregation provisions provided by these codes take precedence over the general requirements in table 7.2.4. To further aid segregation there are also 'SGG' codes provided in column 16b. These group together dangerous goods with similar chemical properties. There are 18 segregation groups e.g., SGG1 – Acids, SGG2 – Ammonium compounds, SGG13 – Perchlorates, SGG17 – Azides. They are all listed in 3.1.4.4 and 7.2.5.2. For limited quantities and excepted quantities, there are exemptions from these segregation requirements provided they do not react dangerously with each other.

Segregation requirements on board

The IMDG Code also has ship specific stowage and segregation provisions included in part 7. These further requirements are dealt with in separate chapters, accordingly:

- Chapter 7.4: Container Ships
- Chapter 7.5: RORO Ships
- Chapter 7.6: General Cargo Ships
- Chapter 7.7: Shipborne barges on barge carrying ships

234 Cargo operations

Oily Water Separator (OWS) *operation.* Today, the Oily Water Separator function (OWS) is an important ship machinery check carried out by Port State Control on every vessel visit. It is important for marine engineers to inform the bridge and take position on the ship when starting and stopping the OWS. In addition, OOWs are required to record the operation in the Bridge Logbook. An overside check is also required to be carried out by the bridge for any evidence of oil sheen in the water once the OWS operation has commenced. Oil pollution from ships is a serious offence which is punishable by substantial fines and, in the worst cases, even imprisonment. OWS operation therefore requires clear and sound communication between the officers from both departments.

Manning and unmanning of the engine room. The EOW of a UMS ship must inform the bridge before turning on the Unmanned mode and leaving the engine room unattended. The EOW should inform the bridge and Chief Engineer about every visit and manned/unmanned situation including when initiating the dead man's alarm. This informs the bridge of the engineer's presence in the machinery space.

Pilot and or Port State Control on board. It is the duty of the OOW to inform the engine room about the pilot boarding time or whenever any outside authority is about to visit the ship. This provides the engine department time to prepare for any checks or inspections. Running a ship safely and efficiently is a team effort, which requires clear communication between the bridge and engine room. The abovementioned situations are just a limited example of some of the most important situations that require close coordination between the bridge, deck, and engine departments.

Chapter 18

Container specifications

Container units are the keystone to the entire container sector. Without them, the container industry simply could not function. These containers are the metal box structures that store all kinds of products that need to be shipped from one part of the world to another using different types of container ships. Using containers protects the contents on the long passage from the port of loading to the port of discharge. This passage could be as little as a couple of days to several weeks. As such, depending on the type of product to be shipped or the provision of service needed from them, container units vary in dimension, structure, materials, and construction. In this chapter, we will briefly examine the most common types of shipping containers in use today. The ISO or 'intermodal' refers to the utilisation of multiple modes of transport necessary to ship cargoes from one location to another. In the maritime sector, cargo transportation operations have benefited tremendously from the development of the intermodal shipping container, which allows for easy cargo movement between road, rail, and water transportation networks. The intermodal container provides fast-paced cargo shipping with decreased operational costs as the unnecessary repackaging and offloading of cargo is avoided. As we discussed in the previous chapter, the intermodal container was the brainchild of the American entrepreneur, Malcolm Mclean, but it was not until the ISO and IMO, and several other leading marine authorities, established strict guidelines with respect to the design and dimensions of intermodal container that they realised their full potential. These guidelines were also aimed at setting a common intermodal container measure. In terms of its size, a cargo container can either measure eight feet breadth-wise x eight feet height-wise with lengths of either 20 feet or 40 feet. Alternatively, certain cargo containers may also be built to different specifications with a breadth of nine feet x height of 10 feet with lengths ranging to a maximum of 53 feet. The load-carrying capacity of intermodal containers is measured in terms of TEU. A TEU refers to the volume of cargo that one standard 20 foot container with a breadth of eight feet can hold. To ensure compliance with these standards, all containers must bear an ISO certification, together with details of the company that owns the container.

This has led to intermodal containers sometimes being referred to as ISO containers. Various goods and commodities can be shipped in intermodal containers. Since they are constructed of materials such as steel or aluminium, even commodities requiring refrigeration systems can be safely transported using refrigerated containers or reefers. The design and structure of a cargo container is quite simple in nature and features only a cargo hatch. Simple holding mechanisms help to position the container as required on railway wagons or flatbed trailers. Though there are protocols established for the container sizing, at times problems emerge where terminals lack the necessary facilities to process and store containerised freight. This translates into huge losses for the shipping company while also resulting in the spoiling of perishable cargoes. Other issues have evolved as intermodal containerisation has increasingly replaced other transportation methods, namely the lack of optimum utilisation of all available intermodal containers,

DOI: 10.1201/9781003244615-22

235

236 Cargo operations

which results in loss; the adoption and utilisation of container shipping for unlawful activities such as drug and people trafficking; and loss of cargo arising from theft and pilfering from containers. Despite these problems, cargo containers are still very highly rated in the maritime sector. Industry statistics show that nearly 90% of all global trade is carried in intermodal containers. This equates roughly to a container fleet of at least one-quarter of a billion TEUs in operation at any one time.

One of the most significant transformations in the history of shipping and the maritime sector was the introduction of the intermodal container. Today, there are over 16 different categories of shipping container and by one estimate, over a quarter of a billion containers are in transit or in situ for use at any one time. These shipping containers are ISO certified, which means that they are brought into use only when they are manufactured and tested as per the specifications provided by ISO. This helps to ensure that the goods carried are suitable for multiple transportation modes, that is by ship, truck, or rail. In this chapter, we will discuss the core specifications of the shipping container, including container dimensions and the markings found on them. Almost all containers are manufactured from corrugated steel, though aluminium is becoming increasingly popular. Steel and aluminium are excellent materials for shipping dry and packaged cargo.

Though steel is by far the most common material used, the advantage of aluminium dry containers over a steel container is that the former has a slightly larger payload, whereas the dry steel containers have a slightly larger internal cube. This is because aluminium is much lighter than steel but is not as strong as steel. Most shipping containers are manufactured to a standard length. These are usually 20 ft and 40 ft long though width and height dimensions may differ from one manufacturer to another. In addition to the standard 20 ft, 40 ft, and 45 ft containers, there are other dimensions available on the market, which are used mostly for road and rail transportation. These come in a range of 8 ft, 10 ft, 53 ft, and 60 ft lengths. The specifications given below are a representation of the commonly used containers. Specific container dimensions and capacity the ISO containers may vary depending on the manufacturer, the age of the container, and the container owner.

20 FT (TEU) CONTAINER DIMENSIONS

The standard ISO container with a length of 20 ft is the most popular of all and is carried on ships of all sizes. The dimensions are shown in Table 18.1.

40 FT (FEU) CONTAINER DIMENSIONS

The 40 ft container offers double the volume of a standard 20 ft container, and costs approximately 15–25% more to purchase. This makes the 40 ft container the most cost-efficient container to ship goods by sea (see Table 18.2).

Table 18.1 20 ft ISO container dimensions

Specifications		Dimensions
Length		6.06 m / 19.88 ft
Width		2.44 m / 8.00 ft
Height		2.59 m / 8.49 ft
Gross capacity	General purpose	30,480 kg / 67,200 lbs
	Flat rack	45,000 kg / 99,207 lbs
	Reefer	27,000 kg / 59,524 lbs

Container specifications   237

Table 18.2 40 ft ISO container dimensions

Specifications		Dimensions
Length		12.19 m/39.99 ft
Width		2.44 m/8.00 ft
Height		2.59 m/8.49 ft
Gross capacity	General purpose	30,480 kg/67,200 lbs
	Flat rack	60,000 kg/123,276 lbs
	Reefer	35,000 kg/77,161 lbs

45 FT CONTAINER DIMENSIONS

The 45 ft container provides slightly better cubic feet capacity than a 40 ft container, giving valuable extra space to the shipper. This means improved cargo carrying efficiency and potentially lower transportation costs though it should be noted the payload capacity of the 45 ft container is almost identical to the 40 ft container (see Table 18.3).

REEFER CONTAINERS

Insulated containers

The trillion-dollar shipping industry transports a wide variety of goods all over the world. Regardless of whether the goods are meant to be kept hot or cold, dry, or wet, packaged, or fresh, the shipping industry has got it covered. But transporting so many different commodities is not as simple as filling containers with goods, and then loading them onto container ships. For example, what do you do if you must maintain fresh produce at sub-zero temperatures? Obviously, they cannot be transported in the same container as items meant to be stored at room temperature. The solution is to transport similar goods in the same container. This is where insulated shipping containers come into play. Without them, it would be near impossible to ship fresh produce around the world without the cargo spoiling. To understand why a considerable amount of logistic expenditure goes on maintaining an insulated and temperature-controlled state for certain goods, we should first look at the main products that use this facility. Pharmaceutical products, fresh produce, beverages, frozen goods, and chemicals often need to be maintained at specific temperatures. They also need to be protected from contamination, by ensuring that air entering and leaving the container is filtered.

This is where insulation plays an important role. It completely seals the shipping container from the outside atmosphere and helps maintain a fixed condition for the transported goods.

Table 18.3 45 ft ISO container dimensions

Specifications		Dimensions
Length		13.71 m/44.98ft
Width		2.44 m/8.00 ft
Standard height		2.59 m/8.49 ft
High cube height		2.89 m/9.48 ft
Gross capacity	General purpose	30,480 kg/67,200 lbs
	Flat rack	60,000 kg/123,276 lbs
	Reefer	35,000 kg/77,161 lbs

An important point to be considered when discussing insulated shipping containers is the cold chain. This term refers to the supply chain methodology that keeps certain goods in a permanent cold state throughout its journey from the supplier to the customer. By retaining a constant cold condition, there are no abrupt changes in temperature that might cause a variety of problems. For instance, frequent thawing and cooling cycles of food and other produce might cause spoilage. For pharmaceutical drugs, their composition and reactions might change if the pills or medication are not kept below a certain temperature.

The main idea behind the cold chain is that low temperatures lock in freshness for produce, prevent the growth of bacteria, maintain the required composition of drugs and medicines, help to transport fresh foods, and improve the overall shelf life of foodstuffs. To illustrate the importance of the cold chain for perishable food produce, we can use the example of tomatoes. Tomatoes are extremely sensitive and incredibly easy to spoil. To transport a shipment of fresh tomatoes from Morocco to the United Kingdom, the produce must be cooled and kept at a constant temperature as the ship passes from a hot climate to a temperature climate. Given the average sailing time varies from a few days to a week, by the time the tomatoes are unloaded, in a normal ISO container they would be bruised and inedible. By keeping them refrigerated, the shipper can ensure their freshness is maintained and the produce arrives on the supermarket shelves in top condition. Since unloading an entire container onto other smaller modes of transport can break the cold chain, most companies prefer to hire a full container, fill it with their goods, and then haul it to their warehouse facilities using flatbed trailers.

Cooling the temperature of the container

There are several options available to cool the internal temperature of the container. The easiest and cheapest option is to use ice or coolant gels. When the container is first loaded, a coolant such as ice or chemical gel is used to bring the temperature down to the desired level. These work by absorbing the heat present within the container; the turns into a slightly dense vapour when exposed to hot conditions. The next option to seal in the cold is to use gas-filled chambers, either around the entire container or around individual pallets that fill up the unit. The most commonly used gases include inert gases that do not conduct heat and provide a cushion between the surroundings and the interior. Bubble wraps that are used to protect fragile goods can be filled with these gases so that they serve the dual function of preserving the cool temperature and providing protection. The important point to keep in mind when choosing an insulation method is that each type of consignment has a different requirement. For example, reefers are built to function with either liners or vacuum panels. However, produce stored on pallets can use thermal blankets or inert bubble wrap. Depending on the type of goods to be transported, it is always best to consult with an expert to determine the best option for preserving the cargo.

Other cooling methods

In addition to the main methods described above, there are other options available depending on the type of goods being transported. These options range from conventional units like large refrigerators to chemical agents that change phase to induce lower temperatures depending on the external ambient climate. To induce a cool condition, the easiest method is installing blocks of ice or artificial slurry ice within the container. These blocks lower the temperature, after which insulation materials keep the temperature constant. Slurry ice is a form of micro-crystal suspended in water that has a decreased freezing point when compared to normal ice. It is easier to use since it has an efficiency of nearly 70% as opposed to 45% for conventional ice. In addition, it can be densely packed which allows for more cooling within the same space constraints. Other methods of lowering the temperature within a container include using dry ice and chemical Phase Changing Material (PCM). Dry ice is simply solidified carbon dioxide. It is commonly used as it does not leave a residue unlike other types of coolants. It is easily identifiable by the thick white smoke that rises as it changes phase. Dry ice is toxic in large concentrations and should only be used under the right conditions. PCMs are substances that absorb heat to lower the temperature and use this heat to change their phase or state. Common PCMs generally come packed as a solid, although some varieties may be liquid. As they gradually lower the temperature, they convert into a gaseous state.

Along with coolants, several additional features are optionally provided by shipping companies in their containers. These are useful for certain types of fresh products. For instance, fresh produce can become stale if the same air is circulated within the container for the duration of the passage. Air filters are placed in such containers so that there is some form of air circulation. In addition, some types of produce also require a small amount of nitrogen to be pumped into the container. The nitrogen helps to prevent spoilage. Nitrogen reacts with the oxygen present in the air and prevents it from causing foodstuff to rot. This nitrogen is introduced into the container through filtration systems. In addition to filters, a necessity on insulated containers such as reefers is a generator set or gen-set that provides a backup for power during transit. During transit, power is provided by the ship to keep all refrigeration units functioning. However, since the container must continue the cold chain long after discharge gen-sets are provided to power the cooling units. Most containers use a temperature sensor to constantly monitor heat fluctuations. These sensor readings should be regularly checked to ensure that there is no spoilage. If registered with shipping companies, there are often provisions made to monitor the temperature and provide constant feedback to the company that has hired the container.

As with every good idea, insulated shipping containers also have their own share of issues. First and foremost is properly maintaining the cold chain. No matter what effort is taken during shipment, if the chain is broken during transit, whether by road or rail, the goods will inevitably spoil and become unsellable. This presents a significant challenge to the logistics industry, as it is sometimes difficult to keep tabs on each container in circulation. To illustrate this problem, during the transportation of vaccines and medications to sub-Saharan countries during the polio epidemic in 2018–2019, a cold chain was maintained until the container was unloaded at the port. From there onwards, it became difficult to power the refrigeration unit, as sufficient supplies of diesel to run the gen-set were not available, and because a constant supply of electricity was not provided during the journey by road. Thus, by the time the vaccines reached patients, they had turned either ineffective at best or toxic or worst. This created quite the opposite effect of what was intended. Thus, a small break in the cold chain had far-reaching consequences. Even though the medications were within insulated chambers, they were very much at the mercy of the national infrastructure available in the country of unloading. In areas with a shortage of resources, it may be difficult to carry on a cold chain for days on end. To circumvent this problem, several large facilities have been established in and around major cities throughout Africa that allow insulated chambers to function.

Also, companies have begun exploring the possibility of using other types of refrigerants in place of reefers. The next major problem that affects the insulated container industry is the proper disposal of waste materials, by-products, packaging material, and left-over coolants. Present technology does not allow for the recycling of packaging material such as gel packs and bubble wraps. Therefore, they are often simply discarded after their lifetime use, and end up in landfills and incineration sites. These products are almost always made from plastics which are extremely harmful to the environment. Thus, with no other greener alternative, companies are often forced to continue using disposable packaging material. Another major problem is the disposal of coolants. These substances are toxic chemicals that can cause substantial damage to the natural and marine environment, as they pollute the air as well as water bodies. They often include toxic substances such as oxides of poisonous elements and other various contaminants. Trials and experiments into different materials are ongoing to reuse or to at least improve the recyclability of packing materials that would otherwise go to waste. Coolants must always be handled properly after their use and disposed of in certified containers. Some coolants can be released back into the air or integrated into water bodies without harming the natural ecological system. However, the vast majority need to be destroyed and or incinerated. For this, dedicated facilities that carry out incineration in a safe and environmentally managed fashion are required.

In summary, the shipping industry is a modern marvel that allows almost every type of commodity to be shipped thousands of miles around the globe. This would not be possible without insulated containers, that keep items fresh and safe. From fresh produce, meats and medicines to pharmaceutical drugs, a variety of conditions must be met to allow for long-distance transportation. For logistics and supply chain specialists, it is important to recognise that different goods require different techniques to remain fresh and usable. Identifying the correct method, and inspecting insulated containers are the first steps in ensuring quality control. Some of the factors to consider include the temperature sensitivity of the goods, the changes they undergo when exposed to low temperatures for prolonged periods, and the size of each individual pallet or crate that is used. Many shipping companies offer multiple types of insulated containers. When choosing the right solution, shippers must look for important qualities such as in-built refrigeration systems, warranty and quality checks, filter systems, the quality of insulation seals around the edges of the container, standardisation certificates and forth. If properly assessed, these insulated shipping containers can be a huge asset for companies and will allow them to ship a wider variety of goods almost anywhere in the world, at any time of the year.

REEFER CONTAINERS

The reefer system is the backbone of ships that carry refrigerated cargo. Any malfunction in any of the components of the system can lead to the degradation and waste of perishable and cold storage cargo, including the provisions and stores for the ship. It is therefore important to maintain and run the refrigeration plant properly to avoid any potential breakdowns. To understand how to maintain and operate the reefer systems safely, we must first understand how the reefer and refrigeration system works. The refrigeration plants on merchant ships play a vital part in carrying refrigerated cargo and maintaining provisions for the crew. On reefer ships, the temperature of perishable or temperature-sensitive cargoes such as food, chemicals, or liquefied gas, is controlled by the ship's refrigeration plant. The same plant or a smaller unit may also be used for maintaining the temperature of storerooms. It goes without saying that the primary purpose of the ship's refrigeration plant is to avoid any damage to the cargo or to perishable materials so that they are transported and delivered in good condition. This is because refrigeration prevents the growth of micro-organisms, oxidation, fermentation, and dehydration. All refrigeration plants and units work with the same components albeit in different ways depending on the design and construction of the plant.

The main components typically found on board reefer refrigeration ships are:

- *Compressor.* Reciprocating single or two-stage compressors are commonly used for compressing and supplying the refrigerant to the system
- *Condenser.* Shell and tube type condensers are used to cool down the refrigerant in the system

- *Receiver.* The cooled refrigerant is supplied to the receiver, which is also used to drain out the refrigerant from the system when undergoing periodic maintenance
- *Drier.* The drier consists of a silica gel that removes any moisture from the refrigerant
- *Solenoids.* Different solenoid valves are used to control the flow of refrigerant into the hold or room. A master solenoid is provided in the main line and other solenoids are present in all individual cargo holds or compartments
- *Expansion Valve.* The expansion valve regulates the flow of the refrigerant to maintain the correct hold or room temperature
- *Evaporator Unit.* The evaporator unit acts as a heat exchanger to cool down the hold or compartment by transferring heat to the refrigerant
- *Control Unit.* The control unit consists of various safety and operating circuits for the safe operation of the refrigeration plant
- *Low Pressure (LP) Cut Off.* This is a compressor safety function that cuts off the compressor in the event of a pressure drop in the suction line. The pressure of the suction line is continuously monitored by the control unit. When the pressure falls below the value set, the LP cut out will auto trip the compressor. When the pressure rises, indicating there is a flow of refrigerant in the line due to an increase in room temperature, the LP switch restarts the compressor
- *High pressure (HP) Cut Out.* As the name suggests, the HP cut out activates and trips the compressor when the discharge side pressure increases above the limit value. The HP cut out is not auto reset and must be done manually. The reason behind this is to manually attend the fault which is leading to a rise in pressure. A failure to rectify high pressure faults in the refrigeration system can lead to an overloading of the compressor parts resulting in extensive damage
- *Oil Differential Cut Out.* This safety mechanism is designed for the compressor as it is the only machinery in the circuit that has rotational parts, which require continuous lubrication. In the event of low supply or no supply of lube oil to the bearing, the differential pressure will increase activating a trip signal to safeguard the bearing and crankshaft
- *Relief Valves.* The relief valves are fitted to the discharge side of the compressor and lift and safeguard the compressor in the event of an accumulation of overpressure. One relief valve is also fitted in the condenser refrigerant line to avoid causing damage to the condenser in the event of high-pressure accumulation in the discharge line
- *Solenoid Valves.* The master solenoid valve is fitted in the common or main line after the condenser discharge. It closes when the compressor stops or trips to avoid an overflow of refrigerant into the evaporator. All refrigerated cargo holds are fitted with an individual solenoid valve which controls the flow of refrigerant
- *Oil Heater.* The oil heater is provided for the compressor crank case oil and prevents the compressor from getting too cold, which would inhibit the lubrication of the rotational components

HOW THE SHIP'S REFRIGERATION PLANT WORKS

Now that we have briefly explored the various components that make up the ship's refrigeration system, we can begin to look at how all these parts and components come together to form a fully functional reefer system. The compressor acts as a circulation pump for the refrigerant and has two safety cut outs: a low pressure (LP) and high pressure (HP) cut out. When the pressure on the suction side drops below the set valve, the control unit stops the compressor. When the pressure on the discharge side rises, the compressor trips. The LP

242 Cargo operations

cut out is controlled automatically so that when the suction pressure drops, the compressor stops, and when the suction pressure rises again, the compressor restarts. The HP cut out is provided as a manual reset. The hot compressed refrigerant is passed to a receiver through a condenser to cool down. The receiver can be used to collect the refrigerant when any major repair work needs to be performed. The master solenoid is fitted after the receiver and is managed by the control unit. In case the compressor sudden stops, the master solenoid also closes, avoiding the flooding of the evaporator with refrigerant. The hold or compartment solenoid and thermostatic valve regulate the flow of the refrigerant into the hold or compartment, thus maintaining the temperature of the room. For this, the expansion valve is controlled by a diaphragm movement, which operates according to pressure variation and is triggered by a bulb sensor that is filled with expandable fluid fitted at the evaporator outlet. The thermostatic expansion valve supplies the correct volume of refrigerants to the evaporator where the refrigerant absorbs the heat from the room, which then boils off into vapours resulting in the atmospheric drop in temperature.

OTHER TYPES OF CONTAINERS

Double Door Containers. These are a kind of storage unit that are provided with double doors, which provide a wider room for loading and unloading. *Drums.* As the name suggests, these are circular shipping containers made from a choice of materials including steel or other lightweight metals, fibre, and hard plastic. They are mostly suited to bulk transportation of liquids. Although smaller in size, drums generally require extra space because of their shape. *Flat Rack Containers.* With collapsible sides, flat rack containers are like simple storage shipping containers where the sides can be folded to make a flat rack for shipping awkward shaped or oversized cargoes such as excavators and yachts. *Half Height Containers.* Another kind of shipping container is the half-height container. Made predominantly from steel, these containers are half the height of a standard full-sized ISO container. Half-height containers are used especially for loose bulk cargoes such as coal and gravel as these require easy loading and unloading. *Insulated and Thermal Containers.* These are the shipping storage containers that come with a regulated temperature control allowing them to maintain a higher temperature. *Intermediate Bulk Shift Containers.* These are specialised shipping containers made solely for the purpose of intermediate shipping of goods. They are designed to handle large amounts of materials and are made for the purpose of shipping materials to a destination where they can be further packed and sent off for further manufacturing or processing. *Open Top Containers.* Open top containers are fitted with a convertible roof that can be completely removed to make way for an open-top so that materials of any height can be shipped easily.

Openside Storage Containers. These storage units are provided with doors that can change into completely open sides providing a much wider room for loading of materials. *Refrigerated Containers.* These are temperature regulated shipping containers that always have a carefully controlled low temperature. They are exclusively used for shipment of perishable substances like fruits and vegetables over long distances. *Special Purpose Containers.* As the name suggests, these are not ordinary containers, as they are custom designed for specialised purposes. Special purpose containers are mainly used for sensitive cargoes or materials that require extra protection such as weapons or radioactive waste. As such, their construction and material composition depend entirely on the special purpose they need to cater for. *Storage Roll Containers.* A foldable container, this is one of the specialised container units manufactured especially for transporting sets or stacks of materials. They are made of thick and strong wire mesh together with rollers that allow easy movement. *Swap*

Container specifications   243

Bodies. These are a special kind of container used mostly in Europe. Not made according to ISO standards, swap bodies are not standardised shipping container units, but they are extremely useful all the same. They are provided with a strong bottom and a convertible top making them suitable for shipping a vast array of products and goods. *Tanks.* Container storage units used mostly for transportation of liquid materials, they are used by a huge proportion of the entire shipping industry. They are mostly made of strong steel or other anti-corrosive materials providing them with long life and protection to the materials. *Tunnel Containers.* These are container storage units provided with doors on both ends of the container. They are extremely useful for quick loading and unloading. *Vehicle Carriers.* Vehicle carriers are specially designed container storage units made specifically for the shipment of cars and other smaller mobile vehicles. They come with collapsible sides that help the vehicle fit snugly inside the container without running the risk of damaging the vehicle.

CONTAINER MARKINGS

The standard for the coding, identification, and marking of containers is DIN EN ISO 6346, which came into force in January 1996. The different markings provided on ISO containers are the container identification number, the owner or vendor's logo or name, the ISO code, the relevant weights and payload information, approved classification society label, cubic volume and any warning or operational signs and labels: (1) *Container Identification Number.* The container identification number is the primary identification marking on the door of the ISO container. It consists of seven numbers and four letters, which are allotted by the ISO to identify every container to its owner. The number is unique and is registered in a database maintained by the Bureau International des Containers (BIC) in Paris, France. A typical container identification number would look something like ABCD 123456. In this example, the first three letters, i.e., 'ABC', denotes the code for the owner of the container. The fourth letter 'D' provides the container category. The first six digits, i.e., '123456' is the serial number of the container and the last digit, '7' is the check digit which is used to validate if the owner or product group code and the registration number have been accurately transmitted; (2) *ISO Code.* The ISO container code is stencilled below the container identification number and provides the details of the type of container, for example GP for general purpose, DV for a dry van and so on. The ISO code also denotes the size of the container so if the ISO code below the container identification number is 45 G0, the first number '4' denotes the code length (40ft) and the second number '5' is the width code. The last two alpha-numeric character shows the type and subtype of the ISO container; (3) *Weights and Payload.* The details of the container weight and cargo weight are painted directly onto the door, usually in the upper righthand corner. There are three weights annotated: (a) *Tare weight* of the shipping container. This is the net weight of an empty container as provided by the manufacturer post manufacturing; (b) *Payload.* This is the maximum cargo weight the approved ISO container can safely carry; (c) *Gross weight.* This is the total weight of the container and the cargo when fully loaded to the maximum safe weight limit; (4) *Cube or Volume.* The cubic capacity or the volume of the container is marked on the door; (5) *Owner's Logo.* The shipping line or container vendor's logo or name is usually provided on one or both door panels and on the lengthwise sides of the container; (6) *Approved Classification Society Label.* Before the container can be used by a shipping company it is tested for seaworthiness and compliance with the ISO standards by an approved classification society. The label of the class is also provided on the door of the container; (7) *Warning and Operational Signs.* The container may carry various warning labels and signs depending on its type and the cargo it is carrying. For example, a heightened container will

244 Cargo operations

contain height or warning stripes at the highest most point of the container. Similarly, a container carrying hazardous cargo will carry a warning sign advising the type of cargo or the hazards associated with it; (8) *Certifications*. Containers typically carry a certificate that demonstrates the container is subject to an ongoing inspection regime, and that inspections have been performed in accordance with that regime. There are two main types of container certification: the CSC plate and ACEP. The Container Safety Convention (CSC) plate shows the ISO container has been inspected and tested by an appropriate approved authority. It also contains the details of the owner and other technical specifications. The Approved Continuous Examination Programme (ACEP) may also be provided on the container. This is a safety regime for shipping containers, where the container undergoes an extensive inspection in a container depot once every 30 months of service. The container owner renews the ACEP certificate every ten years.

CONTAINER SEALS

Just as you would lock the door to your house to safeguard your personal belongings, shipping containers also need to be secured and locked to prevent pilferage and tampering of the goods inside during transit. Container seals are 'one-time door locks' that are used to secure containers. As the name suggests, each seal-lock can be used only once. Heavy-duty container seals are designed to withstand the natural elements and to last the entire voyage of the container from the point of collection to the point of delivery at the customer. This voyage may last anything from a couple of days to several months! Unfortunately, delays can and do frequently happen due to wrong documentation, port and labour union strikes, the ship breaking down, and an almost limitless number of other reasons. In any case, before removing the container seal, the customer must ensure that it is intact and has not been tampered with. Container seals come in a variety of types. They come in different shapes, sizes, and price range. Each seal has a unique alphanumeric identification number that is used to confirm that it has not been changed during the container's voyage. Very infrequently, seal numbers may be duplicated but this really is an exception rather than the rule. The Bill of lading always includes the container seal number for verification by port authorities, port customs and the customer receiving the cargo.

Container seals are used to secure the container doors once the loading of cargo is complete. In certain cases, empty containers are locked and sealed before being sent for stuffing. This is done to prevent tampering and to maintain container cleanliness or a set temperature, as is most often the case for containers destined for loading of high-value products, highly perishable food items, and medicines. It is a requirement by port authorities, government regulators, and importers/exporters that all Full Container Loads (FCL) and Less than Container Loads (LCL) are sealed during transport. With the manifold increase in global trade, container movement between points of trade has increased significantly in recent times. An equally large number of empty containers are often required to be shunt from port to port to meet demands. Depending on the type of consignment, the consignor or consignee or the person sending and receiving the goods may decide to use a specific mode of transport and in a specific type of container. These containers change hands at several points from the moment it leaves its storage location. For example, the stuffed cargo is taken to the port from where it is due to set sail. It then passes hands to the shipping vessel on which the container and its cargo transit from one port to the next. The ship may stop at one or more transhipment ports. At its destination, the container is unloaded and transported to the consignee's address or warehouse. It is therefore important that the cargo remains safe during its journey until it reaches its final point of offloading. Even though security and features such as CCTV surveillance in warehouses, container yards, and even on board ships, help to deter criminal activities such as pilferage and theft, the dangers posed by smugglers, counterfeiters, human traffickers, drug traffickers, and exploitation by terrorist groups remains large. To help counteract this risk, while shipping empty containers, some shipping lines stack them back-to-back. In this method of stacking, the door end of any two containers is placed facing each other so that they cannot be opened during transit.

Container seals come in a vast array of types and styles including lead wire and a seal, plastic seals, metal strip seals, bolt seals, e-seals, and sometimes even number padlocks. Of these, the safest and the most used is the bolt seal. This consists of a metal pin that is driven into a plastic-coated steel barrel, forming a one-time lock and tamper-proof seal. Bolt seals are made of heavy-duty steel, coated in tough weather-resistant, anti-corrosive plastic. A unique seal number is shown on both the pin as well as the barrel of the seal. E-seals that are read-write capable usually contain basic data about the container and can be read using Radio Frequency Identification (RFID) readers. RFID technology is used to collect data from the computer chip that is embedded in the seal. The power to read data from these seals is taken from the radio frequency transmitted by the RFID reader. Those with their own power source and transmitter are also available. These seals can accommodate more data but are also more expensive. The major drawback to the RFID e-seals is that data can only be read at points where there are RFID readers. Almost all sea containers are now constructed from Corten Steel, which is a kind of weather-resistant, heavy-duty steel. The container is fitted with two hinge-swing open doors, each having two lock-rods. These lock-rods run vertically, from the top to the bottom of the container. Their job is to lock the doors in place. Separate handles attached to these lock-rods have small catches that have holes through which the seal is fixed to anchors on the container doors.

The door on the left-hand side is closed first followed by the door on the right. When opening the container, the door on the right-hand side must be opened first followed by the door on the left. This is because the vertical edge of the right-side door presses against the vertical edge of the door on the left, keeping it closed. Thus, the seal can be put on any one of the lock-rods of the right-hand side door. There are three openings on each of the lock-rods through which bolt seals can be fixed. They can also be fixed onto the lock-rods of both doors for extra security. A bolt seal comes as a single unit with its unique number embossed or laser-engraved on both the pin as well as the barrel. It is considered good practice to check that the numbers match between the two, before fixing the seal. The barrel is first separated from the pin by snapping the plastic connector between the two. It can then be easily fixed by pressing the open end of the pin firmly through the appropriate openings in the lock-rod, into the sealed barrel. If fitted correctly, there should be a soft click as it locks itself into place. Experienced warehouse hands and container handlers ensure that the seal is firmly in place by trying it with their hands. Once locked, the only way to open the container seal is to cut the pin with a seal or bolt cutter. Some consignors send pictures of the locked seal to the consignee, with the date and time stamp clearly visible on the photograph. These pictures are particularly useful in the event of loss or damage to cargo as they help surveyors and insurance companies to decide on the veracity of a claim.

Container seals and cargo theft

Container seals are designed to deter tampering and theft. However, containers can be broken into, and the cargo stolen. Essentially, there is nothing stopping thieves from just breaking open the container seal and gaining access to the cargo within the container. With that in mind, a tampered, broken, or replaced container seal (except as in the case of Port Customs inspection) simply provides evidence that the container has been opened on its way

246   Cargo operations

to its destination. This means the consignee is entitled to take appropriate action for claiming insurance or compensation. Generally, port and customs authorities around the world insist on at least having a single seal on each container, so long as it is fixed in the appropriate hole of the lock-rod on the door to the right. However, it is left to the discretion of the shipper on the number of seals that are used to seal the container. The maximum number possible is six, as container door lock-rods have at a maximum, only six openings through which container seals can be placed. Since the 1980s drug smugglers have resorted to narcotics through normal supply chains as normal sea consignments. With strong financial backing, international criminal organisations can often find newer and increasingly novel ways of smuggling drugs in shipping containers. Latin American countries such as Columbia, Peru, and Bolivia are notorious centres for illegal drug production. From these countries, the drugs find their way to the US, Europe, and Asia. Similarly, drugs from Asian countries also find their way on the streets of the US and Europe. Smugglers have become adept at disguising their illicit cargoes under the guise of legitimate cargo. One of the ways to counteract this illegal trade in narcotics is for Port and Customs officials to carry out random checks on shipping containers. To gain access to the container and to carry out their inspection, the officials must cut open the container seal. In these situations, a new Customs seal will be fixed. Random checks on containers are usually done by Port and Customs officials to ensure that the goods carried within are as per the bill of lading and customs declaration.

It is usual practice to check the container seal for signs of tampering before the customer receives the container. When the metal bolt of the seal shows signs of having been cut, or if the barrel is out-of-shape or has crimp marks signifying that a heavy tool has been used to remove it, the customer must immediately notify the cargo handler as well as their insurance company. The container will then be opened only in the presence of each party's representatives. The seal number should match the seal number on the Bill of Lading, the Shipping Manifest, and the seal on the container. The number should also match between the seal pin and its barrel. To prevent erasing or removal of the seal number from the container seal, it is marked using different techniques such as thermal printing or laser engraving. Any mismatch among the numbers should be immediately brought to the notice of the shipping line. In such instances, the cargo handler's representative, the insurance surveyor, and the consignee's representative will conduct a joint survey to ascertain the cause and establish that the contents of the container have not been tampered with. Container seals are removed using a heavy-duty metal seal or bolt cutters. The only way a container seal can be removed is by cutting it. This ensures that there is no scope for opening the container and refitting the same seal. The seal should be cut along its length, which is the pin of the seal. Some consignees retain the seals that have been cut and removed until the cargo is confirmed as mentioned in the manifest and that there is no longer a need to lodge any claim with the shipper.

Standards for container seals

The prescribed standard for container seals that is recognised worldwide is ISO 17712:2013. This classifies and lays down the standards for all mechanical seals are used to seal freight containers. Certain countries, such as the US, require all inbound containers to be sealed with 'High-Security' ISO certified seals. Similarly, other countries may have container seal requirements to satisfy their own security standards. Any seal that conforms to ISO 17712:2013 may be used for transit on any mode of transportation.

Chapter 19

Container planning, handling, stowing, and lashing

When a container ship is approaching port, there are preparations and procedures that need to be made to ensure the loading operation is carried out safely and efficiently. Container ships have special cell guides and lashing equipment that are used to stow containers in the below deck holds. These help to secure the containers during passage. Correct lashing and stowing of containers on deck are extremely important to prevent any kind of imbalance and loss of ship stability. This requires careful prior planning and execution both before and during the container loading operation. This chapter sets out the main procedures for preparing a container ship and making it ready in all respects to receive or discharge cargo in port. The main responsibilities for deck officers are the safe navigation of the ship and safe cargo handling and stowage. As the rank and responsibility of the deck officer rises, so must the officer's knowledge of cargo handling and stowage. On container ships, a stowage plan is prepared for each container to be discharged and for each container to be loaded at each port along with the ballast conditions and other critical stability considerations. This planning is done to ensure the stability of the ship is maintained. This responsibility falls to the chief officer as the most experienced deck officer after the master. When drafting the stowage plan, the chief officer must take into consideration various factors, which include safeguarding the stability and physical integrity of the ship; safeguarding the cargo; obtaining the maximum use of available capacity; facilitating the rapid and systematic loading and discharging of cargoes; and ensuring the safety of the crew and quayside workers. As might be expected, developing the stowage plan is often a complex undertaking with contradictory factors undermining one another. Over stowage must always be avoided, therefore cargo planning should be done as per the latest loading. For example, cargo destined for a later port should not be placed over those destined for earlier ports. Loading conditions must be calculated for intact stability, shearing force, bending moment, torsion moment, trim, and draft. The torsion moment, bending moment and shear force values must never be allowed to exceed 100% at any time. The IMO visibility line should be taken protected when planning the stowage of containers on deck. This ensures clear and unobstructed visibility from the bridge to the most forward part of the vessel. The stowage of IMDG containers must be planned as per the ship's Document of Compliance with the special consideration given for dangerous goods.

When loading, adjusting, and discharging containers, the GM value will inevitably be affected, most often by placing lighter containers over heavier containers and vice-versa. If we recall from earlier, the GM is also known as the metacentric height, which is the distance between the centre of gravity of the ship and its metacentre. The GM is responsible for deciding the stability factor of the ship. In a low GM situation, it is always preferable for lighter containers to be stowed higher up and heavier containers to be stowed lower down. That said, it is common for the GM values of a ship to be high. This means stowing light containers over heavy containers will only increase the GM leading to a 'stiff' ship with

DOI: 10.1201/9781003244615-23

247

248 Cargo operations

short rolling periods. This increases stresses on the lashing. In these situations, conversely, it is preferable for heavy containers to be loaded on top but with due regard to lashing stresses and staking weight. Out of Gauge or OOG containers refers to containers where standard lashing equipment and procedures cannot be used. OOG should not be stored in outboard rows to prevent OOG cargo from falling overboard should the lashings break. Stowing OOG on deck in the foremost bay must never be permitted; also, if possible, avoid stowing OOG in the second most forward bay.

CONTAINER PLANNING AND STOWAGE

In simple terms, stowage planning is the process of allocating space on board for containers that must be loaded from one port to be discharged at another port, without having to rehandle those containers at ports along the way. This is one of the most important of all ship operations and can be quite intensive in terms of tasking and function. To begin drafting the stowage plan, various tools and information is needed first. These include the scheduled list of ports that the ship will call at, in the order of rotation; a summary of the containers to be loaded such as the quantity, type, size, and weight; a summary of the number of hazardous, reefer and OOG containers per port that are planned to be loaded; and a list and summary of the containers already on board. To understand the stowage plan, we must first grasp the abbreviations and terminology frequently used in the planning process: (a) *profile*. This is the cross-sectional view of the entire ship covering both the deck and the holds. The profile gives the total view of the stow positions of which containers are to be discharged at which port. This enables the port operations team and stevedores to readily identify the sequence of loading and which bays must be discharged and or loaded; (b) *bayplan*. This is the complete cross-sectional view covering both the deck and holds of the entire ship but displayed or printed for each bay; (c) *bay*. Container ships are split into compartments which are called 'bays' where Bay 01 is the forwardmost bay and Bay 88 (for example) is the furthermost bay. Odd-numbered bays (e.g., 1, 3, 5, etc.) hold 20 ft containers and even-numbered bays (2, 4, 6, etc.) hold 40 ft containers; (d) *row*. This is the position where the container is placed across the width of the ship. It starts with 1 in the centre and progresses outwards with odd numbers on the starboard side and even numbers on the port side; (e) *tier*. The tier denotes at which level the container is stowed – in other words, how high the container is stacked on board; (f) *hatch covers*. The hatch covers are shown in the stowage plan as thick black lines separating each deck and compartment. The area above the line is called the deck (the area that is visible when we look at the ship) and the area below the line is called under-deck (the area that is not visible to us from outside the ship).

CONTAINER POSITIONING

Although most modern ships use computerised stowage programmes to manage the positioning of containers, deck officers need to understand the underlying principles. These are first that the list of containers to be loaded on board is segregated by destination; and secondly, that space is allocated to each of the containers first in the order of destination with the furthest destination at the bottom and the next port of call right on top and second in order of weight with the heaviest boxes at the bottom and the lightest at the top. For reasons of lashing and securing, a 40 ft container may sit on top of two 20 fts, but two 20 fts cannot sit on top of one 40 ft (unless it is under deck and surrounded by other containers or within cell guides). We will discuss more about 20 ft and 40 ft containers in the next chapter.

Container planning, handling and stowage   249

To simplify the stowage process, abbreviations are used to denote important information. For example, when inputting information into the system, it is customary to abbreviate port names, for instance: (F) Felixstowe, (A) Antwerp, (Ae) Antwerp Empty, (H) Hamburg, (L) Le Havre, (R) Rotterdam, and (X) which indicates 40 ft containers. To illustrate how containers are positioned on board, we can use a fictional example. Let us say our ship is sailing from Shanghai to Southampton, Antwerp, Le Havre, Hamburg, and Rotterdam. As our ship is due to call at Southampton first, the containers destined for Southampton will be stacked on top of the other containers, with containers destined for Antwerp placed directly underneath, followed by Le Havre, then Hamburg and finally Rotterdam. In this fashion, the entire ship is filled with the containers that are to be loaded at each load port while also considering the containers that are already on board. Sometimes it is necessary to move or remove containers from the ship. This is called a 'restow' and is done a container is offloaded from the ship and then reloaded either at the same stow position or a different stow position. This may be necessary due to incorrect stowage of a container – for example, a container stowed for Le Havre instead of Southampton, or when a change of destination is requested at a later stage to now discharge this container in Southampton. To reach this container, the 12 containers meant for Antwerp (A and Ae) must be 'restowed' because Antwerp is the next port after Felixstowe. Then the hatch cover (the dark line between the deck and under deck) must be opened to reach under deck. Then the 1 container to Le Havre must be 'restowed' as well and only then can the container be discharged in Southampton. It is easy to imagine this involves a considerable waste of time and money. Potentially moving twelve 40ft and one 20ft container just to discharge one container!

To avoid this waste of time and money, it is imperative containers are stowed in the right position according to their destination, weight, and cargo (if hazardous). Each of the bays has deck stress or tier weights which is the maximum permissible weight that each of the tiers/rows can carry as per the design of the ship. For example, if there are four containers in a tier each weighing 26 tonnes, it may not be possible to accommodate all four containers in one tier as this might affect the ship's stability due to the heavy nature of the cargo. However, if there are five tiers of empty containers, it might be possible to load all of these into one tier. These calculations will be automatically performed by the computer. Deck officers can usually identify where a container has been stowed on board their ship just by reading the stow position (also known as the cell position) and whether it is a 20 ft or a 40 ft container. This skill is mainly based on experience in handling stowage plans, but there is a formula behind it. Let us take 090482R as an example of a stow position. We know the stow position is divided into three parts: 09/04/82, where 09 is the bay, 04 is the row and 82 is the tier. In simple terms this means 09 bay – each container vessel is split into compartments which are called bays and depending on the size of the ship will proceed from 01 to 40 (for example) where Bay 01 is the bay towards the bow and bay 40 is the stern. We know that odd-numbered bays refer to 20 ft stows and even-numbered bays refer to 40 ft stows. Returning to our stow position, we can see the reference ends with a letter 'R'. Using our previous example, we can assume this container is destined for Rotterdam. We can now interpret the stowage position: it is a 20 ft container in bay 09, row 04, and tier 82. If tier 82 is shown above the thick black line on the stowage plan, we know the container is on deck.

Estimates put the annual cost of cargo crime worldwide at between US $30 and 50 billion. Shipping lines, terminal operators and vessel operators must constantly watch out for theft, pilferage and crime at ports, terminals, and transport depots. If a container is correctly packed and the doors secured properly, access is possible only by cutting open the container's body, by breaking the seal of the container or removing the entire door. The presence of a seal (with the same number) on a container proves that its cargo has remained secure from the time it was packed until the time it was discharged. It is not an anti-theft

250 Cargo operations

device, and it is easy for any criminal to break open the seal or section of a container to gain access. This information might seem innocuous, but when we consider that containers are loaded from the stack onto the trucks in the port and moved to the ship for loading, they are loaded with the doors facing outwards as the details of the container including the seal number and the condition of the seal are recorded by most ports. Depending on the loading plan of the ship and where that container is stowed, the door of the container may end up facing inwards or outwards. But, as the trucks will be travelling in a circular direction around the stack area, the containers will all arrive under hook with the doors facing outwards. This means the cranes will load it in the same direction, therefore the containers will be loaded on board the ship in the same direction. If we look at any photograph of a loaded container ship, it is almost impossible to see any one container facing the opposite way. Incidentally, reefer containers are generally stowed with the machinery facing outwards so that it can be monitored on board.

CONTAINER LOADING

The main responsibilities of the deck officer are the safe navigation of the ship and the safe and efficient handling and stowage of cargo. As the rank and responsibility of the deck officer rises, so must the knowledge the officer has of cargo handling and stowage. On container ships, a stowage plan is prepared for each container to be discharged and loaded in a particular port along with the tank condition, i.e., the mass carried by the ship other than cargo. This is done to maintain the stability of the ship. The chief officer is responsible for the safe and secure stowage of the cargo on ships and is supported in that duty by the deck officers. The primary objective when loading and stowing cargo on a ship is to first and foremost protect the integrity of the ship, followed by the cargo; to utilise the maximum available capacity of the ship; to facilitate the rapid and systematic discharging and loading of cargo; and finally, to provide for the safety of the crew and shore workers. When carrying out cargo loading and discharging, it is important that the officers in charge of the operation are cognisant that over stowage must be avoided with cargo planning done as per the ship's logical passage plan – i.e., cargoes to be loaded in the immediate present should be prioritised over cargoes to be loaded at later ports. Loading conditions must be calculated for intact stability, shearing force, bending movement, torsion movement, trim, and draft. Torsion movement, bending movement and shear force values must never exceed 100% of the rated allowance at any time. The IMO visibility line should be accounted for when planning for the stowage of containers on deck. The stowage of IMDG containers must be completed as per the ship's *Document of Compliance with the Special Requirements for Ships Carrying Dangerous Goods.*

The GM value of the ship can be manipulated (increased/decreased) by stowing lightweight containers on top of heavyweight containers and vice-versa. GM is also known as the Metacentric height, which is the distance between the centre of gravity of the ship and its metacentre. The GM is responsible for deciding the stability factor of the ship. In a low GM situation, it is preferable to stow lightweight containers higher up. However, usually the GM values for ships are high and stowing lightweight containers on top of heavyweight containers will only increase the GM leading to a 'stiff' ship with short rolling periods. This in turn increases the stress on the lashings. In this situation, it is preferable for heavy containers to be loaded on top with due regard given to the lashing stresses and stacking weights. Although we covered out of gauge (OOG) containers earlier, it is worth mentioning them again here as they present unique challenges for the stowage plan. OOG containers require special lashing as standard lashing equipment cannot be used. Subsequently,

Container planning, handling and stowage 251

outsized cargoes should never be stored in outboard rows to prevent the OOG cargo from falling overboard should the lashing break. Furthermore, the stowage of OOG cargo on deck in the foremost bay is strictly prohibited and every effort should be taken to avoid stowing OOG cargo on deck in the second most forward bay as well. After the stowage is complete, always double-check and inspect the lashings applied to OOG cargoes to prevent their shifting and breaking free. As we have discussed previously, port stays can be extremely testing for the crew and deck officers, especially as the industry moves towards greater efficiencies and less time spent alongside. These factors combined with smaller ships crews and greater automation makes it easier to forget or overlook even simple textbook tasks. Indeed, cargo operations on container ships are an extensive activity that demands deck officers to simultaneously handle different tasks and to keep track on various other things happening in their mind's eye. Draught of course is the most important thing to be checked and confirmed after cargo completion. A proper visual check of the draught should be made by the OOW. The draught reading obtained should be compared with the expected departure draught with any discrepancies investigation and modifications actioned. If the actual draught deviates too much from the expected departure draught, the chief officer should be advised immediately. Unless required otherwise, the ship should always be on even keel.

Lashings need to be thoroughly checked including the lashing bar and turnbuckle unit, the twist locks, hatch cover pins and cleats and the lashing of OOG cargoes. Any missing lashing units or twist locks should be notified to the lashing foreman and should be fixed before the termination of cargo operations. It is always good practice to check the lashings as soon as the cargo operations are complete of each bay. This helps to avoid an unnecessary rush to complete the lashing checks at the time of cargo completion. As lashing gears are handled by shore stevedores, there is a fair chance of finding misplaced twist locks and lashing rods on deck, lashing bridges and catwalks. Good housekeeping is required to prevent accidents such as slips, trips, and falls. The securing of cargo gears and lifting gear equipment such as derricks and cranes should also be completed during final rounds. It is the responsibility of the OOW to ensure that the loading and discharging of containers are done in strict accordance with the loading and or discharge plans. Any containers that are moved and restowed should be cross-checked against the original stowage plan. Special attention should be given to IMDG containers and reefers. Any loading or discharge of containers that do not comply with the stowage plan should be recorded and brought to the attention of the chief officer and planner. As we discussed previously, IMDG containers should be checked and documented with great care: (a) ensure that IMO Class and HAZMAT labels are present on all visible sides of the container; (b) ensure that the containers are positioned as per the loading plan; (c) IMDG spotting plans, manifests and other documentation should be done prior to departure; (d) Fire plans should be updated with the final IMDG spotting plans during the port stay.

Reefers contain very sensitive cargoes, which demand similar care and attention as IMDG cargoes: (a) all reefers loaded on board should be checked with a proper crosscheck with reference to the reefer manifest; (b) the set points of the reefers, electrical connections, terminals, and water hose connections should be carefully checked; (c) reefers loaded on board should be plugged in and connected as soon as possible; (d) the electrician is the delegated person responsible for the maintenance of reefers; OOWs should make use of and defer to his guidance when handling reefers; and (e) any issues or complications involving reefers should be immediately notified to the cargo planner with any faulty reefers rejected from being loaded on board.

The ship's logbook must be updated with the latest status of the cargo operations from time to time and upon the completion phase if the cargo operation with reference made to the time of cargo completion, the time when lashings are completed and the time when stevedores are

252 Cargo operations

offboarded. It is also usual to record the ship's final draught reading along with any other important or pertinent data. There are also various checklists to be examined and completed after the termination of cargo operations. Such checklists include vital factors that need to be confirmed and then documented. This again is the responsibility of the OOW. Visibility from the conning position of the wheelhouse must always conform to the IMO regulations. Chapter V, regulation 22 of SOLAS clearly defines the visibility requirements of the ship from the bridge. Although visibility criteria are accounted for when planning cargo stowage, it is the responsibility of the deck officer to ensure visibility is unimpeded upon cargo completion. Most modern stowage and loading software programmes have an integrated feature that includes the IMO visibility criteria with users notified should the software detect visibility is impeded. The ship is required to conduct ISPS security checks for stowaways, as well as any suspicious packages, or contraband items as soon as the cargo operations are complete, and the shore stevedores are offboarded. Although the ship may comply with the security measures as per the ISPS Code during its port stay, it is very important to carry out a ship search prior departure. The intensity of the search will often depend upon the ship's and the port facility's security level. The OOW must have good knowledge of the ISPS security levels, and the measures required for each level. As the cargo operations are completed and the ship is readying for departure, the pilot and company agent are expected to board the ship. It is a good practice to anticipate the cargo completion time and contact the pilot and agent well in advance. This will avoid unnecessary and expensive delays.

When contacting the pilot, the expected time of pilot boarding should be confirmed with the ship and crew readied for the pilot's boarding. The company agent is required to come on board after cargo completion to exchange any necessary documents with the master or chief officer, and to sign off any other actions in preparation of the ship's departure. If the ship is required to establish communication with port control prior to departure, it should be done soon after the completion of cargo operations; doing so will prevent any unnecessary delays. Gearboxes are open-topped bins that are kept with the flat racks. They contain the lashing gear units including twist locks, mid locks, and stackers. Gearboxes are loaded back on board from the quayside normally after all container units have been loaded, making it one of the last actions of the port visit. The cargo superintendent and or cargo foreman should be advised of the position of the gearboxes to be loaded well in advance of the cargo completion time. When choosing such positions, it is important to keep in mind that the best preferable position will be the centre pontoon of the hatches as loading on the extreme ship side pontoons are not suitable. If practical, the gearboxes should be loaded together in one bay. Once loaded, the OOW must visually examine and confirm the position of the gearboxes; the position to be recorded accordingly.

On modern container ships, most of the cargo is carried within standardised containers, which are placed one over the other and secured using a lashing device. While at sea, the ship is subjected to heavy rolling and pitching, which can not only disturb the cargo but also upset the stability of the ship. Parametric rolling – a unique phenomenon experienced by container ships – must be carefully considered to ensure the safety of cargo containers at sea. Keeping a watch on the loaded containers when the container ship is sailing is as equally important as preparing a container ship for loading. Furthermore, officers are required to know the important equipment and tools which are used to handle cargo on container ships. The following points are vital for taking care of cargo containers whilst the ship is at sea. It cannot be stressed enough that proper container lashing is one of the most important aspects of securing cargo safely on board. Every officer in charge of cargo loading and unloading must know and understand the important points for safe container lashing. Moreover, when the ship is sailing, lashing must be checked at least once a day and tightened whenever necessary. If the ship is about to encounter rough seas or a period of heavy weather, the lashings should be frequently checked and additional lashings provided if required. Containers carrying dangerous goods must be checked at regular intervals, and especially so in bad weather. Dangerous goods containers must be frequently checked for leaks or damage while the ship is sailing. Reefer containers must also be checked and monitored at least twice daily for proper functioning. Frequent monitoring is required in case of special reefer cargoes or containers that are suspected of malfunctioning. Adverse weather conditions may result in damage of cargo caused by leaks from water and oil systems. This is referred to as 'wet damage'. Remember that rainwater may also accumulated inside cargo holds causing damage to cargoes in lower tier holds.

Regular soundings of cargo hold bilges is of utmost importance for the early detection of problems related to water or oil ingress in the cargo holds. Bilges must be checked at least once a day in normal weather conditions and at regular intervals in rough weather. When the ship is at port, cargo hold bilges must be drained into the holding tanks. Regular rounds of the cargo deck compartment must be made to check the condition of container lashings. Sometimes, it might so occur that despite taking all the necessary precautions, damage to the cargo or the ship's hull may occur. In such cases, the master must take the necessary precautions to minimise the damage. This should be recorded in the ship's log. A master's report on the damages sustained must also be made along with a sea protest to be produced at the next port of call.

CONTAINER LASHING

The estimated value of the world's sea-borne trade for container shipping industry is about 52%, which is the highest economic value among all types of maritime trade. The container or liner trade is one of the fastest and easiest modes of transporting vast volumes cargo in a relatively simple and cost-effective way. As of 2021, the largest container ship in operation – the *HMM Algeciras* – can carry a maximum of 23,964 TEUs at any one time. With a length of 399.9 m and a beam 61.0 m wide, this ship truly is a leviathan of the seas. However, container lashing, the process of securing containers together on board ship, remains one of the greatest areas of risk in the marine cargo handling sector. When a container is loaded over a ship, it is secured to the ship's structure and to the container placed below it by means of lashing rods, turn buckles, and twist-locks. Combined these prevent the containers from moving about their position or from falling overboard into the sea during heavy seas. Normally, stevedores are responsible for the lashing and de-lashing of containers in port. However, due to the decreasing amount of time ships spend in port, it is becoming increasingly necessary for the deck crew to assume responsibility for this critical task. Before arrival in port, the ship's crew will normally de-lash the containers so that the containers can be discharged immediately after berthing with substantial time saved in port. Whilst this creates more work for the officers and crew, it does have the benefit of providing ample opportunity to check the container lashings are properly fixed to avoid any type of accidents occurring due to improper lashing.

EXAMPLE: EVER SMART

On 30 October 2017, the UK registered container ship *Ever Smart* suffered a container stow collapse while on passage between Taipei, Taiwan, and Los Angeles, USA. The master had changed the ship's passage plan to avoid severe weather caused by a developing depression east of Japan.

254 Cargo operations

The ship continued in heavy seas, with constant rolling and heavy pitching with frequent bow flare slamming. Once the weather had abated, the crew discovered that the container stacks on the aft-most bay had collapsed and toppled to port. Of the 151 containers in the stow, 42 were lost overboard, and 34 were damaged. Superficial damage was caused to the ship.

SAFETY ISSUES

The loss of the containers most likely occurred during a period of heavy pitching and hull vibration in the early morning of 30 October 2017. A combination of factors resulted in a loss of integrity for the whole deck cargo bay; in particular, the containers were not stowed or secured in accordance with the cargo securing manual. The container lashings might not have been secured correctly.

SAFETY RECOMMENDATIONS

Recommendations (2020/125, 2020/126 and 2020/127) have been made to Evergreen Marine Corp. (Taiwan) Ltd to improve standards of stowage plans produced ashore, knowledge of the dangers of bow flare slamming and lashing gear maintenance management.

As lashing and de-lashing is such a dangerous task, there are several safety critical points that must be always observed. These include wearing appropriate personal protective equipment such as reflective vests, steel toe capped shoes, hard hat or helmet, and gloves. Before starting the lashing and de-lashing job, be mindful that it is physically demanding work, and so it is strongly advised to limber up in advance by stretching and warming up the leg and arm muscles. If possible, wear a back support belt or brace and always bend the knee and not the back when carrying out manual handling. Be cautious when walking around the ship as the ship structure can be a tripping hazard. Watch out for slip, trip, and fall hazards while boarding or leaving the ship from the gangway whilst carrying loads like rods and clits. Never stand or walk beneath a suspended load such as gantry or hanging container. Maintain a safe distance with clear visibility and line of sight. Any work platforms, railings, steps, and catwalks must be inspected prior to starting cargo operations. All manhole covers or booby hatches must be closed while lashing. Exercise extreme caution while walking over rods and twist locks and always keep the lashing equipment in their designated location or clear of the walking path.

Reefer containers require extra attention and coordination for plugging and unplugging when loading or unloading is carried out. Be aware of trip hazards caused by reefer power cords. Do not touch any electrical equipment or power cord until instructed that it is safe to work on. Remember that all lashing and other equipment must be removed and secured from the top of the hatch cover prior to the removal of the hatch cover. Be careful of any potential drop and fall hazards when lashing the outside container on the hatch cover or pedestal. To help prevent potentially fatal accidents, fall arresters or safety harnesses must be used worn when operating aloft. Try and maintain a safe distance from other crew members and stevedores during the lashing or unlashing of containers as the long rods can be particularly hazardous if not handled properly. Be conscious of any hazards around the immediate work area and maintain constant vigilance; avoid shouting and startling others as they drop the lashing rod causing damage to the deck, other containers or worse. It is normal practice to not lash or unlash within a three-container radius of another crew member or stevedore.

Wherever possible, always work in pairs when handling rods and turnbuckles. Walk the bars up, slide them down and control the rods. Do not leave or throw the rod or any other equipment unless it is safe to do so, and then only if necessary. Do not loosen any turnbuckles and leave rods hanging. When securing a rod, the turnbuckle must be tightened immediately. Several container lashing incidents have happened in the past where crew members have lost their lives because the correct procedures were not followed. Handling containers is not an easy job, and it requires a committed attitude towards safety to carry it out without incident. To that effect, by following the safety points listed below, the opportunity for sustaining potentially life-threatening or life-changing injury will be reduced to as low as reasonably possible (ALARP) although no risk or hazard can be completely eradicated.

- *Wear personal protective equipment.* Wearing the right kind of personal protective equipment is of paramount importance while moving cargo from one place to another. Equipment such as safety harnesses, hard hats and helmets, safety shoes and various other bits of PPE must be worn when handling cargo. Working without such equipment puts lives at grave risk. Understanding how to use PPE is equally as important as wearing it. Make sure it is appropriate, fits properly and meets the correct safety standards. Always check PPE before using it for signs of damage and maintain PPE in accordance with the manufacturer's instructions
- *Do not interfere with safety devices.* Before handling cargo, the ship's crew should be told of the various on-site safety devices that will protect them in case of emergency. The crew should in no way interfere with the working of these devices nor should they alter their functioning in any way
- *Identify shelter positions.* If working on the open deck while handling cargo, it is important to be aware of the shelter options that will offer some protection from falling objects. Shelter positions also exist to provide guidance where it is safe to wait until hoisted cargo has been placed on the deck or amidships
- *Securing the Cargo.* It is of paramount importance that all cargo is secured when it arrives on deck and is not 'piggybacked' against other cargo. A secure cargo is safe cargo, and it needs to be secured as soon as it is placed in the storage area. Loose items of cargo are extremely dangerous and can affect the safety and stability of the ship. Any cargo that is not containerised must be properly secured
- *Use the right type of lifting equipment.* Cargo handling on ships requires the use of lifting equipment such as wire ropes, wire rope slings, hooks, forklifts, cranes and so on. This equipment must be regularly inspected and maintained in accordance with the appropriate maintenance schedule. Only ever work this equipment if fully trained and competent to do so. Incorrect use of lifting equipment can put the lives of people working in and around the equipment at risk
- *Never stand beneath suspended cargo.* In an environment where cargo is being handled, there is always a danger of being hit by a load if standing in its path or under it. There are two facets to this safety aspect. Firstly, the crane operator must ensure a safe path for the hoisting of the cargo and, secondly, the on-deck personnel must make sure they are aware of the loading path and stay clear of the incoming cargo
- *Entering enclosed spaces.* In many cases, the personnel in charge of handling cargo will need to enter an unventilated cargo hold. Not adhering to the proper safety procedures can result in entering an oxygen-deficient confined space or a space that is packed with toxic vapours. As can be imagined this can lead to serious health risks. Therefore, such spaces must be checked for their oxygen content and thoroughly ventilated before entry

256   Cargo operations

- *Importance of proper visibility.* Never handle cargo in poor visibility. If the visibility is affected by changes in weather conditions, for example, take the necessary steps to improve the lighting of the workspace and on deck. It is equally important that the lighting does not dazzle or create shadows
- *Handling bulk cargo.* Close supervision is needed to ensure work safety when handling bulk cargoes. This type of cargo loading requires numerous operatives to position in the cargo holds and around the hatches. Always maintain proper and unimpeded supervision
- *If in doubt, shout!* If, at any point in time, the safety of the workplace is compromised in any way or form, it is important to inform the chief officer and superintendent as soon as practicably possible

CARGO WATCHES

Today, most container ships follow a fixed route from one port to the next, in accordance with a predetermined and often very tight delivery schedule. This is called the 'liner schedule' and is usually one of the major sea trade routes (such as Asia to Europe, South America to Europe, West Africa to Europe, Australia to North America and so on). During the port stay of the ship, the deck officers are responsible for monitoring the loading and discharging of cargo as well as other critical onboard activities. This is called the 'cargo watch'. Given there is so much to do and turnaround times in port are getting progressively shorter, it is perhaps entirely natural that many deck officers find being in port much more stressful than being out at sea. That notwithstanding, with the right knowledge and plan of action, cargo watches can be a lot easier than they first appear. This chapter provides some useful guidance and ideas on how to maintain a relatively straightforward, and – hopefully – less stressful, cargo watch.

First and foremost, plan and monitor the loading and discharging of cargo. The most important factor or the ultimate reason for the port stay is the loading and discharging of containers, therefore the priority must be to carry out this duty as quickly and efficiently as possible. Make sure the loading and discharge plan is prepared and checked before commencing the watch. It is good practice to clearly mark out which bays each gantry crane will be working on and, also, to note the gantry number. This makes tracking gantry movements easier. If practical, aim for an even discharging or loading of cargo as this avoids listing and heeling the ship and avoids continuous running of the auto-heeling system and heeling pumps. Give special attention to under deck cargo operations inside the cargo hold and ensure safekeeping and safe removal of hatch covers without damaging the ship's superstructure. If any cargo loading operation is not compliant with the cargo plan, then it needs to be checked with the cargo superintendent and or the cargo planner. Any damage caused to the ship's structure due to the improper operation of cranes should be immediately brought to the attention of the superintendent with a stevedore damage report completed and submitted to the port authority.

As we might expect, deck officers are required to have knowledge of any IMDG containers to be loaded on board. Cargoes recognised by the IMO as IMDG must be transported in containers that are specially designed to carry IMDG classified cargoes. As the name suggests, IMDG containers should be treated with utmost care and attention. The paperwork and documentation that should accompany IMDG cargo, including the IMDG Spotting Plan, is the responsibility of the deck officers, therefore good familiarisation of the IMDG Code is strongly recommended. The loading plan will almost always dictate that IMDG cargoes loaded as far away as possible from the ship's accommodation block and critical infrastructure such as the engines and steering machinery. However, during the cargo watch OOWs need to constantly check the position of every IMDG container loaded on board is as per the cargo plan. Any changes in positioning should be brought to the immediate attention of the chief officer and loading planner. In accordance with the IMDG Code, container containing IMDG cargo must have a clearly visible and legible HAZMAT and IMO Class label affixed to the exterior of the container. It is recommended, though not mandated, to have HAZMAT and IMO Class labels positioned on all sides of the container for maximum visibility. The discharging of IMDG containers without an IMO Class label is a serious offence with the ship fined and the deck department arrested. To avoid unnecessary legal complications, always confirm the presence of IMO Class labels during the loading. Any missing labels should be brought to the immediate attention of chief officer and the planner. Loading of IMDG containers should cease until the necessary labels are affixed to the chief officer's satisfaction.

Always handle reefer containers with care. Reefers and refrigerated containers have very sensitive equipment and sensors fitted and should be handled with care. Ships whose primary cargo are reefers or refrigerated goods should have a qualified electrical engineer as part of the ship's roster and whose primary responsibilities are the handling and supervision of the refrigeration systems. Though the chief officer is ultimately responsible for the loading and discharging of reefers, the operation is best performed when supported by the electrical engineer or electrician. Avoid disconnecting the reefers from the power supply too early prior to discharge. It is recommended to coordinate the loading operation with the superintendent so that the reefers which are due to be transported are unplugged just in time before they are loaded onto the ship. Reefers and refrigerated cargoes should never be unplugged and left without electrical power for any amount of time as this will spoil the cargo. This is especially important in warmer climates or where the cargo is particularly sensitive to heat and humidity. The electrician is the responsible and qualified person for connecting and disconnecting the reefers, though in practice often officers, cadets and deck crew will assist the electrician. Whilst doing makes the loading and discharging operation must faster, it should only be done by personnel who are fully trained and competent.

When loading containers, it is critical to check the lashings thoroughly. It is the OOW's responsibility to ensure every lashing is found satisfactory and able to withstand all sea conditions. A good understanding of the ship's lashing plans and lashing gears is necessary to ensure cargoes are safely secured. The 'Cargo Securing Manual' should be read and followed without exception. Lashings are considered good if they are moderately tight. There should be no slack on the lashing bar-turnbuckle unit and such slack should be tightened with spanners. Excessive force should be avoided as this will make the unit too tight and stiff. Any lashings found unsatisfactory or any missing lashings on containers should be brought to the immediate attention of the superintendent, with the lashings re-tighten to the required tension. Lashing checks are not limited to the lashing bar-turnbuckle units but also the twist locks used in between individual containers. The type of twist lock – whether semi-automatic or fully automatic – depends on the ship's lashing plan, but a missing twist lock between any two containers does not form any part of the plan. Therefore, any missing twist locks should be communicated to the superintendent and fitted immediately. The hatch cover cleats/pins must also be locked and checked. It is a good practice to check the lashings as soon as they are fitted as this generally saves time and energy at the end of the cargo operation. Always check the lashings for OOG cargo. The lashings used for OOG cargo are different from normal container lashings. In most cases, the stevedores working on lashing the OOG cargo are skilled and know what they are doing, but it is always strongly recommended to supervise and inspect the lashings before the stevedores move onto the next load; ensure the lashings are good enough to withstand all rough seagoing conditions. If safe and practical, take photographs of the cargo once it is lashed and secured. If any defects or poor lashings are found, these should be resolved immediately.

It is of critical importance to visually inspect and manage the ship's draught as the cargo loading and discharge operation changes the buoyancy characteristics of the ship. Though it is standard procedure for the arrival and departure draught to be measured and recorded, it is equally important to observe and manage the draught of the ship when it is alongside. In ports where the available water depth is less, the deck officers must maintain a careful watch over the ship draught and the under-keel clearance as cargoes are lifted and shifted around the holds and deck. This means coordinating the intake and discharge of ballast accordingly. There should be a visual examination of the draught at least once during every watch as the draught gauges may give inaccurate readings. Ordinarily, it is the chief officer who is responsible for managing the ballast and stability of the ship though all OOWs are required to have comprehensive knowledge about ballast operations as OOWs may be required to watch over the inclinometer to monitor the ship's list. Whenever ballast water is pumped into the same side as where the cargo is being loaded, the ship will tend to list. Keep in mind that any more than 1° of list on any side must be corrected immediately. In addition, and in so far as is practical, it is best to minimise the intake of ballast water when in port and to use the internal transfer of ballast. This is simply because the water in port tends to be laden with all sorts of detritus, which can block the intake pumps. In any case, all ballast operations should be recorded in accordance with the ship's Ballast Water Management Plan. When discharging ballast water, be mindful of any local restrictions where de-ballasting is prohibited.

Performing efficient watch changes in port are just as important as at sea. The relieving officer should be officially handed over with all the necessary information relating to progress on deck, the stage of the cargo operation, and any ballast operations carried out during the preceding watch period. It is a good practice to carry out deck rounds just before the end of watch so that the correct status of the cargo operation can be shared. The cargo plans should be updated as well. Any bays completed should be checked before handing the watch over to the relieving officer. Any out of the ordinary information should be exchanged and recorded in the ship's log. Overseeing the safety and security of the ship when in port is one of the main responsibilities of the deck officer. A significant duty when in port is compliance with the ISPS Code. Security rounds and gangway watches must be kept at all times when the ship is alongside. The ISPS Code contains different security levels, each with respective security measures to be followed. A detailed knowledge of the ISPS Code and the responsibilities and duties required to comply with the ISPS Code is strongly recommended for all deck officers and crew. When the ship is alongside and cargo operations are underway, the risk of accidents on deck is higher than when ships are at sea. The safety of the ship's crew and shore stevedores is of paramount importance and any unsafe working practices should be stopped and brought to the attention of the chief officer and the cargo superintendent.

Lastly, always aim to carry out cargo loading and discharging operations without error or incident. This might seem obvious, but port stays in general, and cargo operations, can be extremely hectic and stressful. During last rounds, count how many more containers are left to be loaded to each bay and total it to find how many moves altogether are remaining. Shortly before the anticipated departure window, the master is likely to ask how many moves are left. Be ready with that information as this will aid the ship in making a timely departure. When the time comes to finally depart visually examine and record the draught. Inspect all lashings and confirm the lashing certificate has been signed. Ensure the lashing gearboxes are landed back on board and record the location. Ensure that good housekeeping was maintained by the stevedores and deck crew; if not already done so, square away any equipment or tools left out and dispose of rubbish. Inform the engine room and deck

Container planning, handling and stowage **259**

department and advise of the impending departure. Advise the officer in charge to prepare the bridge accordingly. Confirm the presence of the agent and planner on board and complete and sign any final documentation and paperwork. Confirm the pilot has been booked in advance and is ready to attend the ship at the required time. If during the final stages of the cargo operation it is felt there is too much left to complete, arrange for extra hand on deck to assist in the checking of lashings and any non-critical tasks that need doing. The above points should be kept in mind as cargo watches can be busy with lots of different things happening on board and ashore. But with the right balance of knowledge, skills, experience and support, nothing should be too complex or difficult to achieve in good time.

CARGO VENTILATION

One of the important considerations when transporting cargo by seas is to prevent any kind of damage from happening to the cargo. It is important to take proper care of the cargo on board ships to avoid loss of property and to prevent claims arising from manhandling and mismanagement. Damage to cargo can occur for many different reasons and it falls on the ship's officers and crew to ensure every possible care is taken to safeguard the integrity of the cargo from the time it is loaded to when it is unloaded. Of all the causes for cargo damage, moisture is by far the most common and the primary source of significant claims. To prevent cargo damage because of moisture, ships are fitted with a range of natural and mechanical ventilation systems. These systems help to avoid a phenomenon often found on ships 'sweat'. Sweat generally forms in one of two ways: (1) cargo sweat, and (2) ship sweat. Cargo sweat refers to the condensation that often occurs on the exposed surface of the cargo because of the warm, moist air that is introduced into holds containing substantially colder cargo. This type of sweat occurs when the ship is travelling from colder to a warmer location and where the exterior air has a dew point that is above the ambient temperature of the cargo. Ship sweat refers to the condensation that occurs on the surface of the ship when the air inside the hold is made moist and warm by the cargo, and later meets the ship surface as the ship moves from a hot to a cold region. Ship sweat leads to the formation of overhead drips inside the hold and or the accumulation of condensed water at the bottom of the hold. This can lead to substantial cargo damage. In addition to reducing cargo and ship sweat, ventilation systems also help to (a) supply fresh air to the cargo; (b) prevent the build-up of poisonous gases and vapours; (c) remove the odours of previous cargoes; and (d) absorb the heat and moisture given out by some types of cargo.

Furthermore, cargo ventilation is important for managing both hygroscopic and non-hygroscopic cargoes. Hygroscopic cargoes have natural water moisture content and consist mainly of natural plant-based products such as timber, which absorb, retain, and release water within the hold. This water leads to the significant heating and spreading of moisture and can result in the caking or spoiling of the cargo. Non-hygroscopic cargoes have no water content; however, they can be spoilt in moist environments. The dew point of the air, both inside and outside the cargo hold plays an important role in determining the quality of the cargo. Here, the 'Dewpoint Rule' is taken into consideration to provide the level of ventilation required and to maintain the hold temperature within a favourable range. The Dewpoint Rule refers to the dewpoint of the air inside the hold compared to the dewpoint of the air outside the hold. This means the dewpoint of the air within the hold must always be higher than the air outside the hold. Ventilation should not be provided if the dewpoint of the air inside the hold is lower than the dewpoint of the air outside the hold. Sometimes it is impracticable to measure the dewpoint temperature of the cargo hold. In such circumstances, ventilation is provided by comparing the average cargo temperature at the time of

260 Cargo operations

loading with the outside air temperature. In summary, cargo ventilation is important for both hygroscopic and non-hygroscopic cargoes, however, the former requires more careful monitoring and checks together with appropriate ventilation.

LOSS AND DAMAGE OF CARGO

Cargo is loaded onto a ship when she is floating steadily in the water, upright, or with a practical trim astern. When the ship sails out to sea, it encounters external forces which result in six different forms of motion acting on the ship. These motions are a threat especially for those ships which require cargo lashing and securing on the open deck. If the storage of cargo is not secure enough then there is no way for the tensions and stress that builds up in the ship structure to escape. This in turn takes a toll on the loaded cargo, which can cause damage to other cargo in the vicinity or to the ship's structure and fittings. In the worst scenarios, cargo may even end up overboard. Improper cargo lashing and failure to adhere to the procedures required for cargo stowage on ships is extremely dangerous to property, life, and the marine environment. To avoid getting into situations like these the deck officers should be competent enough to plan and uphold the principles of safe carriage. This is done through the proper planning and implementation of container lashing and securing.

It obviously goes without saying that it is the responsibility of the ship's officers and crew to deliver their cargo as quickly, as safely and as economically as possible. However sometimes cargoes are lost at sea completely or delivered in a damaged condition. Some of the key reasons for this happening are discussed as follows: (1) *severe and adverse weather conditions and lack of appreciation of the various forces of* nature. The open sea can be a very unforgiving place with extreme conditions starting and dissipating almost at a moment's notice. Sometimes officers overseeing the loading and carriage of cargo can fail to appreciate the ship's characteristics and how she responds to adverse bad weather conditions and sea states; (2) *lack of knowledge and training of the relevant rules and guidelines.* Failure to follow the regulations and guidelines for cargo stowage, securing, and lashing can be catastrophic for the cargo and the ship; (3) *cost control pressures.* The maritime sector is a highly competitive industry with razor-thin margins. Time spent alongside is extremely costly. Berthing fees, stevedore fees, crew costs, fuel, ship maintenance and so on; the list is almost endless. This can lead to cost-cutting, which in turn results in lower quality cargo security; (4) *inadequate time and personnel to complete the securing of cargo before departure.* Due to excessive paperwork and short port turn-around times, the basics of cargo lashing, and handling can easily be overseen or neglected; (5) *basic seamanship techniques not applied adequately.* Dunnage that is not utilised in an effective manner or for that matter taking lashing materials around sharp edges which then causes them to part, or insufficient force, steadiness and/or number of lashings can all result in cargo breaking in extreme weather; (6) *improper usage of cargo securing gear.* Cargo securing equipment such as wire loops and eyes can easily be applied incorrectly. A lack of knowledge or training in the use of bulldog grips, bottleneck screws, wire slings and strops can all lead to cargo slippage; (7) *lack of continuity in strength between the various securing components.* These problems are largely determined by the ship's design and construction, the quality of the materials used in the construction of the ship, its age and state of repair; (8) *unbalanced stowage and inadequate weight distribution.* Unbalanced stowage and inadequate weight distribution can all adversely affect the ship's stability in heavy seas.

To counterbalance these issues, it is important to remember when securing cargo that: (a) tight stowage of cargo containers on ships may avoid the need to totally secure it, provided the cargo is adequately packaged and there are no heavy components; (b) bulky and heavy units may still require to be secured even if the space around them is filled with other cargo. Particular attention should be paid to the chances of such units sliding or tripping; (c) several units can be secured or lashed together into one block; (d) permanent securing points on the cargo should be used, but it must be remembered that these securing points are intended for inland transport and may not necessarily be suitable for securing other items on board ships; (e) independent lashings must only be secured properly to suitable strong points of the ship's fittings and structure, preferably onto the designated lashing points; (f) cargo lashings must be taut, and as short as possible for a better hold; (g) If possible multiple lashings to one item of cargo should be kept under equal tension. The integration of different material components having different strengths and elasticity should be completely avoided; (h) cargo lashings must be able to be checked and tightened when underway; and (i) lashings should be enough to prevent the load from moving when the ship rolls through 30° with 13-second duration.

In the next part, we will turn our attention to maritime emergencies and incidents. We will look at the main types of emergencies and incidents that can occur on board and what equipment and facilities are available to respond to emergencies at sea.

Part V

Maritime emergencies

Chapter 20

Maritime incidents and emergencies

Incidents and emergencies at sea happen with alarming regularity, and often with catastrophic consequences for the ship, crew, marine environment. Most incidents tend to fall into one or more of the following areas: offshore installation-related incidents, cruise ship accidents, accidents involving commercial fishing vessels, incidents involving tugboats, accidents on oil tankers and cargo ships, ships running aground, incidents involving alcohol and drugs, accidents involving cranes and derricks, accidents in shipyards and drydocks, accidents involving diving support ships and divers, accidents on barges, and finally cargo handling related incidents. Sadly, container ships are both some of the safest – and deadliest – ships in operation. In this chapter, we will briefly examine some of the common incidents that have occurred on container ships over the past couple of decades. Fortunately for us, we can cross out half of the categories above, though that still leaves us with substantial risk. The first category we want to look at is *ships running aground*. This type of incident occurs when the bottom of the hull touches the seabed. This may be caused by many different reasons, but the most common cause is overloading the ship, miscalculating the draught, or miscalculating the volume of ballast needed to keep an even trim. Grounding may also occur when tides are miscalculated or during rough weather when the ship is forced off course running aground on sandbanks or rocks.

The second type of incident that concerns us involves the *consumption of alcohol and drugs*. Alcohol consumption at sea has always been a major issue for the industry. Fortunately, attitudes towards alcohol consumption are changing with fewer incidents involving officers and crew being drunk on duty. Recreational drug use, however, has increased over the past 20 years or so and is showing signs of becoming a problem. Inebriation from alcohol or drugs is dangerous under any circumstances, and even more so on board. Being caught drunk or high whilst on watch or during work hours is a criminal offence punishable by loss of licence, fines, and imprisonment. Where the ship is involved in an incident, and the root cause is either alcohol or drugs, the consequences will be much graver. Incidents involving *cranes* and *derricks* are often caused by poor maintenance, poor training and supervision, or negligence. It has been known for strong winds and heavy seas to dislodge cranes from their cradles, but these are very rare. *Drydocks* are dangerous places and extreme care should always be exercised. Slips, trips, and falls, dropped objects, loose fittings, hot work such as welding and slippery surfaces are some of the many hazards crew members are likely to encounter whilst the ship is in drydock. Last of all, *cargo handling incidents* are unfortunately common and often lethal. Cargo handling is a dangerous operation, especially in ports where infrastructure is old and poorly maintained.

Any emergency on board must be handled calmly. Rash decisions made on the spur of the moment can have unintended and detrimental effects. Though it is impossible to prepare for every type of incident and emergency on board, an effective response is

DOI: 10.1201/9781003244615-25

265

266 Maritime emergencies

best achieved through clear planning, continuous training, and practical drills. Specific actions will be contained in the ship's *Fire Training Manual* (FTM) and *Training Manual on Life Saving Appliances* (TM-LSA). All members of the crew from the master to the wiper are strongly advised to read the FTM and TM-LSA on joining the ship for the first time, and at regular intervals thereafter.

ALARMS AND SIGNALS

Ship signals and alarms are designed to alert the crew to the presence of an incident or emergency on board. Ships have a range of signals and alarms that mean different things. It is incumbent upon every crew member to be aware of the signals and alarms and what they signify. Some alarms are audible only; audible and visual; or visual only. Dual audible and visual alarms ensure crew members can be alerted to an incident even when they are wearing ear defenders or when visibility is obscured. The most common types of alarms used on board are the general alarm, fire alarm, MOB alarm, navigation alarm, engine room alarm, machinery, and cargo space CO_2 alarm, ship security and intruder alarm. Ships are also fitted with an abandon ship alarm. *General Alarm*. The general alarm is sounded to alert the crew that an incident has occurred. This might include fire, collision, grounding, or any scenario that may lead to the abandonment of the ship. The general alarm is recognised by seven short rings of the ships' bell followed by one long ring. Alternatively, the general alarm may be sounded on the ship's horn: seven short bursts followed by one long blast. The activation point for the general alarm is located on the bridge. Once the general alarm has sounded, every member of the ship's crew must follow the procedures of the muster list and make way to the muster point. It is likely the master, OOW and EOW will issue secondary commands to be carried out.

Fire alarm. Whenever fire is detected on board, the fire alarm must be raised immediately. This is done by pressing the nearest fire alarm point or by shouting 'FIRE; FIRE; FIRE'. The fire alarm signal is the continuous ringing of the ship's electrical bell or the sounding of the ship's horn for at least ten seconds. The signal to indicate the fire has been extinguished is three blasts on the ship's general alarm followed by three short bursts on the ship's whistle. *MOB Alarm*. MOB is one of the most serious incidents that can happen. When a crew member is known – or is thought to have – fallen overboard, the MOB alarm must be activated. The MOB alarm comprises of three long blasts of the ship's general alarm to notify the crew, and three long blasts on the ship's whistle to alert other ships in the vicinity. *Navigational Alarm*. Most navigation equipment and navigational lights are fitted with failure alarms. Should any malfunction, an alarm on the bridge will activate together with a visual display of the location, the equipment affected and an error message relating to the type of malfunction.

Engine room alarm. The engine room is jammed packed with machinery that is continuously monitored using various control and monitoring systems. If any of this machinery malfunctions a common engine room alarm will activate. The location and cause of the alarm will be displayed on the ECR panel. Machinery space alarms are designed to be audible throughout the engine room with all machinery running. *Machinery Space and Cargo Hold CO_2 Alarm*. Machinery spaces and cargo holds are often fitted with CO_2 fixed fire extinguishing systems. When activated, these systems are highly toxic, and anyone caught in the compartment will likely suffer an excruciating death. To prevent this from happening, an alarm will sound several seconds before the gas starts to flow. This provides precious time for anyone in the compartment to make a sharp exit. The audible and visual alarm is separate to the machinery space alarm and any other alarms used on board. The alarm is designed to be heard and seen with all machinery working. The alarm is activated when the release cabinet doors that accommodate the CO_2 bottle tanks are opened. For safety, specific instructions must be followed when activating the CO_2 fire extinguishing system.

Ship security and intruder alarm. In accordance with SOLAS chapter XI, regulation XI-2/5 all ships must be fitted with a Ship Security and Intruder Alarm System (SSAS). The SSAS is a silent alarm that is activated in the event of a pirate attack. When activated, the system sends an emergency alert to the nearest coastal authorities. The signal is sent via a global satellite system which advises the authorities of the current position of the ship. As the alarm is silent, no signal can be heard throughout the ship to alert the crew of the proximity of pirates; nor does not alert other ships within the vicinity. This prevents the attackers from knowing the alarm has been activated. *Abandon Ship Alarm.* When an emergency on board exceeds the capability of the crew and equipment to control it, the ship becomes no longer safe to remain on board. At this point the master will issue the command to abandon ship. This command is given verbally to the OOW first, followed by the crew via the PAS.

Once the command to abandon ship has been given verbally, the abandon ship alarm must be activated. This consists of six short bursts and one prolonged blast on the ship's whistle or the same on the ship's general alarm.

TYPES OF MARITIME INCIDENTS AND EMERGENCIES

MOB is an extremely dangerous situation for any crew member. In 2019 alone three seafarers on UK-registered ships lost their lives after falling overboard. When a MOB occurs, it is critical for the ship's crew to respond immediately and to execute the recovery procedures without hesitation. To minimise the risk of MOB incidents, minimum safety measures should be followed such as donning lifejackets on deck, wearing a safety harness and appropriate safety footwear when working near to or over the sideboard, or when working aloft. Furthermore, extra precautions should be taken when working in heavy weather or when the decks are wet or icy. As a matter of safety, the bridge must always be informed of work activities in advance; and when the work activity starts and when it ends. When someone falls into open water it is almost always unexpected and often during difficult sea conditions. This means quick rescue is imperative for the long-term survival of the casualty. In most cases, the greatest risk to survival is hypothermia. Hypothermia is a condition that affects the human body when exposed to extremely cold temperatures. When a crew member falls into water or is otherwise exposed to extreme conditions, they stand the risk of developing hypothermia unless immediate action is taken. Hypothermia will occur when the core body temperature falls below 35°C. The mortality rate of hypothermia ranges from 20% to 90% depending on factors including the temperature of the water, the time spent in the water, and the weight and build of the casualty.

There are two types of hypothermia that affect seafarers. The most common is *accidental hypothermia* and is usually the result of falling overboard. The second type is *secondary hypothermia* which is caused when the patient is already ill, and the core body temperature naturally falls to below 35°C. Whichever the type or cause, hypothermia is measured in three levels: mild, moderate, and profound. *Mild hypothermia* occurs when the body's core temperature drops to between 35 and 32°C, with effects ranging from suppression of the central nervous system, impaired decision making, slow and sluggish body movements, and shivering. *Moderate hypothermia* occurs when the core body temperature drops to between 32 and 28°C. The effects include an alarming suppression of the central nervous system resulting in unconsciousness and coma; slowing of the heartbeat, which reduces oxygen supply to the brain and main organs; difficulty breathing leading to reduced oxygen intake;

268 Maritime emergencies

slowing down of the main organs including the heart and lungs; improper function of the digestive system leading to intestinal obstruction; and rigidity of the muscles. *Profound hypothermia* is a condition which almost always results in death. The body's core temperature must fall to below 28°C, leading to coma and heart and respiratory failure resulting in the blood pressure dropping to dangerously low levels. If the body temperature continues to fall below 22°C, the casualty will be entirely incapacitated and unable to breathe. If the core temperature reaches 20°C or below, the casualty will suffer profound cardiac arrest and expire. If a crew member is showing signs of hypothermia, immediate action is required. Provide the casualty with a thermal protective aid (TPA). If the respiratory function is affected, provide cardiopulmonary resuscitation by blowing air five times directly into the mouth whilst pinching the casualty's nose. Whilst two times is generally accepted practice, in the case of respiratory failure due to drowning, five times is more suitable as this stands a better chance of clearing obstructions from the airway). If the casualty's heart has stopped, perform a heart massage at a rate of 100–120 times per minute. If available, use an AED to stimulate the electric pulses in the heart. If cardiopulmonary recovery has been achieved, it is important to warm the casualty using a blanket and TPA. Avoid giving the casualty food and fluids as they may be drowsy and could choke. At the earliest possible opportunity, remove the casualty to a shore-based hospital for further medical treatment.

Early realisation that a crew member has fallen overboard is key to increasing the chances of their survival. The actions to be taken are time-critical. If the crew member was seen falling overboard, shout '*MAN-OVERBOARD STARBOARD/PORTSIDE*'. Inform the OOW immediately. The OOW will change from autopilot to manual steering and pull the wheel hard over to the starboard or port side. When in proximity to the last known location of the MOB, release the MOB marker from the bridge wing – the marker is buoyant and comes with a self-illuminating light and self-activating smoke signal. Press the MOB button on the bridge-mounted GPS to mark the position. Sound 'O' on the ship's whistle (three prolonged blasts) – this will inform the master and the crew of the incident. Raise the 'O' flag. Post extra lookouts at vantage points along the ship. Sound the general alarm and announce '*MAN-OVERBOARD*' on the PAS. Inform the engine room of the incident and warn that MOB manoeuvring will be required. Execute any of the accepted MOB manoeuvres. These may include the Williamson Turn, Scharnow Turn or Anderson Turn. Maintain a visual fix on the radar and ARPA and put the VHF on Channel 16. It is important to maintain an accurate record of all events and actions in the ship's logbook.

Blackouts are one of those situations that most seafarers have experienced at least once in their careers. It is a bane of life at sea. Blackouts affect everyone on board from the bridge to the engine room. Blackouts occur when the main propulsion plant and associated machinery including the boiler, purifier and other auxiliary systems stop working due to a loss of power to the ship's generator and alternator. On modern ships, power system redundancies are installed which help avoid blackout incidents. These work by operating the generator in parallel so that if one fails the other will continue to function albeit on reduced capacity. A near miss can be defined as 'a sequence of events that have the potential to lead to an accident, but where there is a break in the sequence of events that stops the accident from occurring'. If a near miss occurs on board, it must be reported to the OOW and the master, who in turn will report the near miss to the appropriate authorities. An initial investigation should be carried out to ascertain the cause of the near miss. The purpose of the investigation is not to portion blame but to establish how and why the near miss incident occurred, and to establish ways of avoiding similar incidents in the future. The investigation should conclude with a list of actions that should be taken to stop the near miss from happening again.

Though collisions at sea are often the result of a sequence of events, the root cause is usually one of three things: negligence, incompetence, and miscommunication. The consequences of collisions can be catastrophic. One of the worst maritime collisions occurred on 20 December 1987. The Philippine registered ferry *MV Donna Paz* collided with the oil tanker *MT Vector*. The ferry sank with the deaths of 4,386 passengers and 11 crew. When it becomes apparent that the ship is on course for collision, the OOW must summon the master to the bridge immediately. The master will order evasive manoeuvres. If the ship has lost control of its steering, the OOW must issue the NOT UNDER COMMAND (NUC) distress signal via VHF, MF, HF, SAT-C, and any other means available. Channel 16 must be left open with ship to ship and ship to shore communications carried out using any other VHF channel. If the ship is unlikely to survive the collision, the master may decide the only option is to abandon ship. This must always be the last resort. If, after the collision, the ship remains stable and seaworthy, it may be possible to seek a place of refuge. The concept of refuge for ships has existed for centuries, though it was only in 1980 that the concept was first formally mooted. It was suggested that coastal states had an obligation to offer safe refuge to any distressed ship seeking safety. Though not legally recognised, the concept of safe refuge is broadly recognised worldwide though there are examples of where distressed ships have been refused safe refuge. In 2000 the oil tanker *MV Erika*, which was carrying heavy fuel oil, sustained damage off the coast of France. The French maritime authorities refused to offer or provide safe refuge to the *Erika*, resulting in the contamination of a substantial stretch of the French coastline. In a separate incident, a second ship – the *MV Castor* – developed structural problems and sought refuge in Spain. The ship tried unsuccessfully to seek refuge for more than 30 days resulting in the mass contamination of the Spanish and French coastlines. The ship was fully laden with unleaded petroleum.

In response to these two incidents, the IMO felt it necessary to issue standard guidelines for the provision of refuge for distressed ships. In November 2003, the IMO adopted two resolutions: resolution A.949 (23), and resolution A.950 (23). In summary, the two resolutions defined a place of refuge as any location into which a ship in distress can safely navigate to, therein preventing further damage or deterioration of the ship. The IMO guidelines set out two situations where a distressed ship should seek refuge. The first situation when the structural integrity of the ship is beyond repair, but the safety of the crew is not diminished; and secondly, when the safety of the crew is diminished or in immediate danger. The guidelines do not stipulate that the place of refuge must be a port, but rather any location where the ship can be moved without causing further damage to the ship or damaging the marine environment.

EXAMPLE: MSC CHITRA AND MV KHALIJA

In August 2010, two vessels collided off the coast of India. The incident resulted in the loss of containers and an oil spill along the Indian coastline around Mumbai. One of the vessels, the *MSC Chitra*, was carrying 1,219 containers, 2,662 tonnes of fuel, 283 tonnes of diesel, and 8,804 litres of lube oil. As a result of the collision the *MSC Chitra* took on excessive water and eventually sank causing extensive ecological damage. An investigation into the incident found there were various factors that had led to the collision occurring, the majority of which were entirely avoidable. The investigation report concluded that:

1. One or both vessels failed to comply with the Rules of the Road (ROR). The ROR or the Rules of Navigation state as per rule 9d that 'a vessel should not cross a narrow channel or fairway if such a crossing impedes the safe passing of the vessel in that they can safely navigate

within the narrow channel or fairway'. In this incident, the *MV Khalijia should have waited until the MSC Chitra* was fully out of the channel. The *MSC Chitra* should have sounded the wake-up call of five short rapid blasts on the ship's horn to indicate their presence.

2. As per rule 9a, 'a vessel using a narrow channel or fairway shall pass near to the outer limit of the channel or fairway that lies to her starboard side is as safe as practicable'. The *MV Khalija*, for some inexplicable reason, altered course towards port. The reasons for this bizarre behaviour could have been steering failure, wrong application of the rules, misjudgement of the manoeuvring characteristics of the vessel, confusion due to proximity of the vessels, or lack of experience of the navigation officers. The prevailing situation also demanded both vessels to apply rule 2b of the ROR. This states that 'no vessel should rely on the rules alone to keep them out of danger'. This means that vessels must always obey the ROR unless where there is a clear and present danger to one or both vessels, in which case appropriate actions must be taken to avoid or reduce the impact of collision. In this incident, the *MSC Chitra* should have taken evasive action after seeing the *MV Khalija* change heading towards port. The fact the *MSC* Chitra did not react accordingly demonstrates extremely poor sea-manship. Moreover, the deck officers failed to use the sound signalling apparatus on board to alert the crew of the *MV Khalijia*. Both vessels failed to follow rule 5 by not posting sufficient lookouts, and rule 6, by not observing the safe speed rule. As both vessels were entering or exiting the channel they should have proceeded at a safe speed.

3. One or both vessels failed to comply with the Merchant Shipping Act (MSA) 1958, section 285. Under section 285, the Indian Government has the appropriate authority to implement and enforce rules and regulations that apply to Indian-flagged and foreign-flagged vessels operating in Indian territorial waters. The investigation found both vessels did not follow the regulations set out in section 285.

4. One or both vessels failed to comply with SOLAS chapter 5. Regulation 34 mandates that the master of the ship must ensure the passage plan is followed using appropriate charts and publications. Both vessels involved in this incident did not follow the passage plan, subsequently deviating off course. This was found to be a major contributing factor to the collision. Furthermore, as per regulation 11 of SOLAS, the master must maintain close contact with Vessel Traffic Services via the Vessel Traffic Information Management System (VTIMS). On this occasion, neither master's contacted VTS and failed to heed the calls of VTS. As per regulation 34-1, the master retains ultimate authority over their vessel. In this instance, the master of the *MV Khalija* should have requested tugboat assistance from the port authorities as well as a pilot to board the vessel whilst at anchorage; this was especially important as the vessel had previously run aground on 18 July 2010.

Whilst the real reasons for the incident will probably never be known, it is evident a catalogue of errors contributed to a needless maritime incident that could have been easily avoided had the crew on both vessels applied the regulations designed for avoiding incidents such as these.

Capsizing occurs when a ship lists to one side to such an extent that it is no longer able to maintain an upright position. This causes the ship to tip over into the water. There are several reasons why a ship might lose its stability and roll over on its side. These include free surface effect, shifting cargoes, cargo absorption of moisture, ship grounding, flooding, heavy weather and wave damage, fire damage and synchronous rolling. Most of these problems affect container ships, all of them affect ROROs. Although we have touched on some of these already, it is perhaps useful to remind ourselves of what these phenomena mean. Free surface effect is more prominent on tankers and gas carriers than on container ships, though the latter may experience free surface effect if appropriate precautions are not in place. A large free surface, usually resulting from slack tanks and improper tank subdivisions (i.e., lack of longitudinal divisions) can result in a reduction in metacentric height which increases the risk of capsizing. On container ships and ROROs, the risk of off-side metacentric (GM) is higher due to the profile of on-deck containers and free-standing cargoes. The hazard is increased further when the ship is heavily laden and making way through heavy seas where large amounts of seawater wash on deck. If inadequate drainage is provided, the risk of capsize increases dramatically. Shifting cargo such as vehicles or oversized plant and machinery can result in heavy listing. This increases progressive rolling and the potential for full capsize. It is imperative therefore to ensure static cargoes are sufficiently lashed and constantly checked. Some types of bulk cargoes are susceptible to absorbing moisture. This called having a *hydroscopic nature*.

When the moisture content rises above a certain limit, the dry cargo starts to behave like a liquid causing free surface effect. This in turn contributes to progressive rolling and the risk of capsize. When a ship runs aground, specifically at a spot off the centre line, and the water depth drops, there is a virtual rise in the centre of gravity. This makes the metacentric height negative resulting in the ship capsizing. Any type of flooding on board a ship will cause a loss of buoyancy. If this loss is greater than the reserve buoyancy, the ship will capsize. Heavy sea damage that leads to progressive flooding will cause a loss of buoyancy. If this loss of buoyancy is greater than the reserve buoyancy, the ship will capsize. To prevent this from happening, the navigation officer and OOW should make every effort to avoid heavy seas and to plot their passage plan to take account of seasonal weather conditions. Firefighting with pumps, especially at higher decks, can result in a substantial addition of deadweight weight which raises the 'G' centre of gravity and reduces the GM leading to possible capsize. For this reason, it is important to consider the effect of using pumps when firefighting. Every ship has a natural rolling period which is inversely proportional to the square root of the metacentric height and directly proportional to the beam of the ship. If the ship encounters a series of swells in such a manner that the wave period matches the roll of the ship, the ship will have no time to correct itself before the next wave strikes. This situation is called synchronous rolling and if not corrected, can result in capsizing.

EXAMPLE: MV TRICOLOR

One of the most famous examples of ship capsize is the Norwegian flagged vehicle carrier, *MV Tricolor*. The *MV Tricolor* was a £25.1million ($39.9m) 50,000-tonne vehicle carrier that has the unfortunate reputation of being involved in not one but three collisions within a fortnight, all in the English Channel. The first collision resulted in the *MV Tricolor's* capsize resulting in massive damage, marine pollution and probably the biggest loss in the automotive export industry. The second and third collisions occurred when two passing vessels refused to heed the instructions of the French Police and Royal Navy to avoid the vessel, resulting in their colliding with the partly submerged *MV Tricolor*. By the time, the *MV Tricolor* was salvaged, some 2,862 BMWs, Volvos and Saabs and 77 units of rolling stock were damaged beyond repair and an estimated £25million of damage was caused. Over 1,000 seabirds were found dead, having washed onshore covered in diesel oil.

The drydock is an inherently hazardous location. The most common and by far most dangerous incident during dry docking is fire. Fire can lead to damage to the ship and the drydock facility. Dry dock fires are most frequently caused by hot work, such as welding and gas cutting near oily rags, oil spills, and other types of flammable materials and chemicals. Slips, trips, and falls and falling objects are also major causes of accidents in drydock.

Chapter 21

Ship fires, firefighting systems, and firefighter equipment

Ship fires can break out literally anywhere, but the worst fires tend to occur in the cargo holds, the engine room and machinery spaces. In the ship's generator room, the biggest danger of fire is from leaking high-pressure fuel pipes. Oil leaking from these pipes can fall on high-temperature exhaust manifolds or indicator cocks, both of which are sensitive points for fires. On modern marine engines, there are typically push-type covers that conceal the indicator cocks; however, in older engines there is no such provision which makes it quite difficult to lag the indicator cocks. Newer engines have sheathed fuel high-pressure pipes. This sheath enables leaks to drip down into a small tank at the bottom of the engine known as the fuel leak off tank. To function properly, it is imperative to keep this system in good working order by regularly testing the tank alarm and the fuel leak off tank high-level alarm. Engine leaks are mainly caused by pipes breaking due to vibrations, clamps rubbing against pipes to create holes, ageing pipe connections behind pressure gauges, and leaks emanating from the fitting at the boiler furnace and incinerator frontages. These leaks are the most common causes for engine and machinery space fires. Engine and machinery space fires can be largely prevented by providing effective lagging to hot surfaces such as the generator turbocharger bellows, the main engine exhaust uptakes after the turbocharger, the steam pipes and pipes carrying hot oil. Lagging can be easily done by the ship engineers. Whenever lagging is removed, it is important to put it back after the work is complete.

CARGO HOLD FIRES

When responding to a cargo hold fire, the following actions should be taken – assuming the cargo is of a dry and general nature and not an IMDG cargo: shout *FIRE* loudly to alert anyone in the immediate vicinity. Sound the fire alarm from the closest call point. This will alert everybody on board to proceed to the fire stations and for the authorities to be informed of the incident. Use the PAS to announce the location of the fire and, if known, the cause or type of fire. Maintain constant contact with the master and chief engineer by handheld VHF radio. Immediately cease all operations in the hold and evacuate any persons that might be inside or in the periphery of the hold. If loading, send all stevedores ashore and cease operations in all other holds. Inform the fire brigade. Follow the master's orders. In the master's absence (for example, if on shore leave), try and contact the master by all reasonable means. In the interim, the chief officer will assume authority. If the chief officer is also on shore leave, the second officer will assume authority although it is highly unlikely that both the master and the chief officer will be ashore considering that most companies require one of the senior officers to be present on board at all times. Inform the ship's agent as soon as possible. Switch off the blowers in the hold. If safe and practical to do so, attempt to fight fire, but take care to avoid unnecessarily damaging the cargo. The Port State Control might

DOI: 10.1201/9781003244615-26

273

274 Maritime emergencies

request the ship to move out to anchorage to not jeopardise surrounding ships, in which case stations need to be called and the engine put on standby. If the above actions do not extinguish the fire, then ensure there is nobody left inside the hold and shut the hatch. Shut off the fire dampers in the ventilator coamings of the hold. Start infusing CO_2 into the hold. Carry out boundary cooling. Do not open the hatch until advised to do so by the master or fire brigade (if in attendance) as the hold will be full of CO_2. The OOW must ensure that the crew execute their duties as assigned. This is essential to avoid confusion and panic. In the event the fire brigade attends the ship, be ready to render all information and aid as required. They are far better trained and equipped to fight fires and they will expect and need your support but remember – the master is the ultimate authority on board the ship.

As soon as the fire brigade arrives, the incident commander or senior attending officer must be introduced to the master to coordinate the operation. The fire brigade will need to know the location of the fire, the nature of the fire, any special or specific dangers that firefighters might be exposed to such as hazardous or toxic chemicals and explosive cargoes, firefighting actions carried out so far, any structural problems that might result in the ship losing stability.

EXAMPLE: CARGO HOLD FIRE

A very large, recently constructed container ship was loaded and underway in darkness when a smoke alarm sounded in the nos.3 cargo hold. With the master on the bridge, the chief officer went to the muster/fire control station. He oversaw the Emergency Team; besides mustering the crew and carrying out a headcount, he would oversee the firefighting and boundary cooling operation. The master noted the apparent wind about four points on the starboard bow and adjusted the ship's heading to starboard to minimise the effect of smoke on the accommodation, whilst still maintaining speed. On the starboard side main deck, the crew closed all 16 natural ventilation flaps for nos.3 but were unable to complete this task on the port side due to heavy smoke and heat. Several members of the crew reported a strong chlorine-like smell while closing the ventilation flaps on the cross deck, suffering breathlessness and itchy burning-like sensations about the eyes and mouth. After 30 minutes from the first alarm sounding, the master took the decision to release the CO_2 into the hold. His reasoning was the safety of the ship and its crew, although the ventilation flaps on the port side could still not be closed. Boundary cooling activities continued deck but with copious amounts of smoke coming from nos.3. Another 30 minutes following the first release of CO_2. The master ordered all non-essential crew to the bridge and ordered a second release of CO_2. About seven minutes after the second release of CO_2, the water mist system in the engine room auto activated, indicating that temperatures in the engine room were possibly elevating. Soon afterwards, the master ordered a distress call. The remaining crew were ordered to the bridge.

About 15 minutes later, the master ordered the release of all remaining CO_2 into nos.3, with little to no effect. Ten minutes after, with most of the crew now on the bridge, acrid smoke entered the space and created a panic reaction. The crew evacuated the bridge and broke up haphazardly into four groups. Almost an hour after the evacuation of the wheelhouse, a group of seven crew and the master boarded the starboard lifeboat and successfully abandoned the ship. Once in the water, they brought on board another 14 crew members who already abandoned in a life raft and one crew member who had jumped overboard. Of the 27 crew, 23 survived. The crew member who was rescued from the water was later pronounced deceased. The official investigation found, among other things, that nos.3 cargo hold contained a block stowage of 55 containers of sodium dichloroisocyanurate dihydrate (SDID). It is possible that the cargo in one or more of these containers underwent self-decomposition. The block stowage exacerbated the rate of reaction and the heat produced, which resulted in the uncontrollable spread of the fire.

LESSONS LEARNED

The complexities and interconnected risks of large modern container ships, including the carriage of certain dangerous cargoes below deck, may have outstripped the current accepted best practices and firefighting arrangements, not to mention the firefighting training of crew members. One problem highlighted by this incident was the inability of the crew to safely close all the ventilation flaps manually when there is so much heat and smoke present. Although the arrangement on board conformed to class rules, it was proven that the arrangement – in this situation – was not suitable. It is important to close the ventilator flaps/dampers in the accommodation and machinery spaces for the protection of the crew, even for an underdeck cargo fire. For at least 90 minutes after the fire was discovered, the master maintained a high speed of at least 15 knots. Best practice would have the ship brought quickly to bare steerage to reduce apparent wind while keeping the management of smoke in mind. Although the master was intending to reduce the effect of the smoke on the crew engaged in firefighting, this could have been done at a very slow speed with helm adjustments and thrusters. There are many more lessons learned from this report than it is possible to list here and interested readers should visit the full report on the Singapore Ministry of Transport website.

OPENING THE SHIP'S HATCH

Extreme caution must be taken when opening the ship's hatch as there will be a sudden gush of CO_2 exiting the hold. Clear out all unnecessary crew members or other persons from the vicinity of the hold. All remaining personnel must don breathing apparatus. Keep everybody well clear and open the hatch slowly. The use of an exhaust blower may be made at this point to rid the hold of smoke and residual fire gases. When authorised, 'masked' personnel may then enter the hold to check if the fire has been fully extinguished. The time spent inside inspecting and or extinguishing any residual pockets of fire must be kept to the absolute minimum. The hatch must be left open after the personnel have left the hold to ensure maximum ventilation. All events and actions must be accurately logged for reference. Although these methods hardly make sense when there is absolute chaos on board, following a certain procedure streamlines the actions that need to be taken. Above all else, however, it must always be remembered that preservation of life is of utmost importance and that should always be given the highest priority over all other considerations.

CO_2 FIRE EXTINGUISHING SYSTEMS

The most frequently used system for fighting fire in the cargo holds of a general cargo ship is the CO_2 flooding system. The CO_2 system consists of a fire detection system (smoke detectors) and an alarm system, along with several CO_2 cylinders. When a fire is detected in the cargo hold, the contents of the CO_2 bottles are released depending upon the cargo permeability (how much space is empty over the cargo for CO_2). The firefighting system for cargo hold consists of a 20mm diameter sampling pipe in the cargo hold compartments of the ship. This is controlled from a cabinet placed on the bridge or in the ship's control centre. Air is continuously drawn through these pipes to the cabinet with the help of suction fans, which delivers air from the diverting valve up to the bridge.

When there is a fire in any of the cargo hold compartments, the smoke is sucked into the sampling pipes and is passed through diverting valves into the bridge, warning the bridge about the fire. Simultaneously, the sample from the pipes is passed over a smoke detector which senses the smoke and activates the audio-visual alarm, indicating the outbreak of fire. The advantage of the audio-visual alarm is that even if the bridge is unattended – for example, in port – there is still an alarm that sounds signalling the outbreak of fire. In the cabinet, the sample is passed over small propellers made of nylon, through a transparent 13 mm tube, which indicates the airflow. If the propellers are not running it indicates that the pipe is choked and must be cleared immediately. When there is a fire, the sampling pipe turns dark which can be seen in the transparent pipe of the cargo hold. The same sampling pipe is connected to the bank of CO_2 bottles with the help of a changeover valve. The CO_2 is released by opening the appropriate valve for the hold. The important point to consider before releasing the CO_2 is to calculate the amount of CO_2 to release. This means calculating the free volume of the affected cargo hold. We do this by calculating the total hold volume–volume of the cargo. A minimum of 30% of the volume calculated is to be flooded with CO_2. For one bottle of CO_2, the volume is calculated as 45.2kg.

EXAMPLE: CHARCOAL FIRE BREAKS OUT IN CONTAINERS

On two container vessels, fires broke out in containers loaded with bulk charcoal despite the charcoal passing the UN N.4 test. The cargo was rated as self-combusting. In both cases, the charcoal cargo originated from the island of Borneo, Indonesia, and were destined for the same consignee. Due to the similarities of both fires, both incidents were investigated by the German Federal Bureau of Maritime Casualty Investigation (BSU) with the findings issued in one investigation report. It was found that on both vessels, the fires were controlled and extinguished with minimal damage to the surrounding containers. The report's findings concluded that it was not possible to fully determine the hazardous material properties of charcoal-based on the UN N.4 test alone, especially where the charcoal passes the preliminary test and is then transported in large packages or in bulk in containers. The report further found that the UN N.4 test did not sufficiently address the dependency on the volume of the goods being transported. In other words, on multiple instances, the cargo manifests that were examined in connection with the incident could not be definitively linked to the cargo being transported. Following the incident, various 'lessons learnt' were promulgated in relation to the carriage of cargoes in general and charcoal where the cargo is not classified as dangerous goods, including:

1. Checking that the laboratory certificate is applicable to the customer
2. Checking that the laboratory is accredited by a competent authority
3. Checking that the manufacturer's name is shown on the laboratory certificate
4. Ensuring the laboratory certificate accompanies the shipment.

Ensuring after the containers have been filled, the container numbers are added to the certificate and carried on board till the time of discharge.

Ship fires and firefighting systems   277

EXAMPLE: APL AUSTRIA CARGO FIRE

On 12 February 2017, a fire broke out in one of the cargo holds on board the 71,867 tonne Liberian-flagged container vessel, *APL Austria*. The vessel was sailing 30 nautical miles southwest of Cape St Francis, South Africa, when she had to be diverted towards the port of Ngqurha for emergency firefighting and rescue. In an operation overseen by the SAMSA Maritime Rescue Coordinating Centre in Cape Town, responding units battled the blaze throughout the Sunday and Monday before eventually extinguishing the fire early on the Tuesday morning. In a press release, Master Nigel Campbell – executive head of the SAMSA MRCC, reported it appears that the fire in the hold has been extinguished but the space has not been deemed safe to enter yet. There are still smouldering containers on deck which are being fought by the fire brigade, a harbour tug is providing boundary cooling. Containers with hazardous cargo are being removed from the area around the fire.

EXAMPLE: CONTAINER FIRE ON BOARD THE YANTIAN EXPRESS

In the early hours of 3 January 2019, a fire broke out in a container stowed on deck above hold 2 of the German-flagged *Yantian Express*, a 7,510 TEU container vessel en route from Colombo, Sri Lanka, to Halifax, Canada. The fire occurred approximately 800 miles east of Halifax in the North Atlantic. Weather conditions were particularly foreboding with Force 8–9 winds, freezing temperatures and rain. By the evening of the 3 January, the onboard supply of SCBA air had been exhausted and the crew were forced to cease firefighting efforts. The decision was made to try and contain the spread of the fire by setting up fire hoses to cool the perimeter and slow the spread. On request of the shipowner, the offshore tug *Smit Nicobar* was dispatched to the location of the vessel to aid and firefighting support. By the late evening of 4 January, the *Smit Nicobar* was able to direct her firefighting monitors towards the scene of the fire. Despite this, the fire still managed to spread to other containers. In response, on 5 January 11 crew members were evacuated to the *Smit Nicobar* with the remainder evacuated in the afternoon of 6 January. A small team returned to the *Yantian Express* on 7 January to set up an emergency towing connection to the large offshore tug *Maersk Mobiliser*, which had also been diverted to the scene. On 15 January 15, a team of professional firefighters and salvors arrived on board the *Boskalis AHTS Sovereign*. The deck fire was fully extinguished by 21 January however the effort to put out the last burning containers belowdecks in Hold 1 continued till 26 January. The *Maersk Mobiliser* towed the *Yantian Express* to Freeport in the Bahamas, where the damaged containers were offloaded, and inspectors boarded the ship. When investigators from the German Federal Bureau of Maritime Casualty Investigation (BSU) entered the containers that were stowed near the location where the fire broke out, they found that one box with a declared cargo of coconut pellets (compressed fibre used for feed or fertiliser) was a cargo of coconut charcoal, also known as pyrochar.

Laboratory testing of some of the surviving charcoal cubes from the container showed that they had potential for autoignition below a temperature of about 50°C (122°F). As there were no other obvious indications for ignition sources in the area where the fire broke out, the BSU concluded that this cargo was the likely cause of the fire. The intense heat generated by the burning pyrochar within the container likely ignited an adjacent boxload of polypropylene bags, which allowed the fire to spread. Flammable goods with the potential for self-ignition typically require testing and certification for shipping. In this instance, the BSU investigators could not rule out the possibility that the shipper had mis-declared the cargo to avoid compliance requirements. The BSU also noted several difficulties that the crew encountered during firefighting. First, the CO^2 flooding system for Hold 1 did not fully discharge due to a malfunction of its time-delay system. This did not affect the course of the fire, but under different circumstances it could have created additional complications. Second, the crew reported that firefighting and cooling underneath containers on deck were difficult due to the transverse bars welded between the container pads, which made it hard to spray water below containers in the middle of the stack; this was recorded as a structural design feature, but it created challenges for fire-fighting purposes. Third, accumulated water from firefighting efforts disabled the electrical bilge well valve controls in Hold 2, making it impossible to dewater the compartment until adequate portable bilge pump capacity was deployed. Bilge pumping for Hold 1 failed as well, potentially due to debris and clogging. By 11 January, the water in Hold 2 was 40 feet deep with the *Yantian Express* trimmed by the head by about four feet.

BACTERIA FIRES

Despite the stringent safety measures and various techniques available today, it is impossible to completely eradicate the possibility of fire. We know that is the result of a tetrahedron: heat, fuel, and air and sustaining chain reaction. There are many potential causes for fire on board ship but one of the most obscure are bacteria fires. This used to be called the 'fire triangle'.

EXAMPLE: ENGINE ROOM BACTERIA FIRE

To put this into context, it was a fine calm morning on a cargo ship and the engineers were busy with their routines. The chief engineer was also on his regular rounds after the evening meal. On the cylinder head platform, as he was checking the parameters and engine components, he observed some hazy white patches of smoke emerging out of a partially covered waste bin. The chief engineer attempted to open the cover to check what was going on inside the bin. As he opened the bin, the in rush of air caused the fire to spike out from the bottom of the bin. The chief engineer immediately raised the fire alarm and, taking a nearby dry powder extinguisher, managed to safely extinguish the fire. After the commotion settled down, an investigation was made to analyse the cause of the fire. The chief engineer suspected that other engineers or engine crew might have dropped a lit cigarette butt into the bin. When interviewed, it transpired none of the engine crew were smokers! The chief engineer immediately informed the master about the incident and despite the initial investigation, no obvious cause was identified.

ROOT CAUSE ANALYSIS

The chief engineer asked the oiler, who oversaw that platform for clearing out the garbage from the bin daily. The oiler explained that he followed standard procedure. The oiler dumped milk packs, oily rags, some waste bread, and other organic materials such as cotton waste into the bin. At the end of the day, the bin was emptied, and the contents incinerated the next day. The master informed the ship manager about the incident, who decided to send samples ashore for further laboratory investigation. After a month, the laboratory established what they considered was the most likely cause for the fire. The entire sample was divided into 25 to 30 equally sized smaller samples, with each sample kept at a certain temperature to observe their behaviour. The samples which were kept at a temperature of 20 to 30°C did not show any considerable change in its behaviour. However, the samples which were kept at 40°C and above showed unusual behaviour. Even after the heating element for the sample was turned off, their temperature continued to rise inexplicably to more than 9°C. Later upon testing, it was found that the steep increase in temperature was due to a peculiar kind of bacteria called 'thermophilic bacteria'. Thermophilic bacteria grow in warm and moist environments. Ship engine rooms are an ideal breeding ground for Thermophilic bacteria. When they multiply, the bacteria give off intense heat, which in the scenario above, was sufficient to ignite the oily rags disposed of in the bin. Further investigation found the auto ignition temperature of oily cotton rags is 120°C with oily cotton rags having a greater affinity for self-heating and spontaneous combustion. The outcome of the investigation was to demonstrate the importance of having a well thought out garbage management plan on board and to follow it. This incident led to the now mandatory practice of segregating garbage. For example, oily rags must be disposed of in a separate bin with food waste, metal scraps, ash and batteries assigned to different colour coded bins. Though not mandatory, it is good practice to clear out the bins before unmanning the engine room.

BATTERY ROOM FIRES

The battery room of a ship is always at risk of explosion as batteries release hydrogen during charging. Hydrogen is a highly explosive gas, and it is therefore important to take the following necessary steps while working inside the battery room during maintenance: (a) provide proper ventilation inside the compartment; and (b) prevent any source of ignition inside the compartment. Ventilation is provided with the help of ventilation fans. The ventilation arrangement should be such that there is no accumulation of hydrogen in the space. Hydrogen is lighter than air and thus tends to accumulate at the top of the compartment. The fans should be of a non-sparking type and should not produce any static charge. The ventilation ducts should be below battery level, which helps forcing the gases out. The motor used should be of a standardised approved type so that there is no spark from the motor. The tools used for maintenance should be coated in a rubberised layer to prevent any chance of short circuiting by mistake. The coating will also prevent any kind of spark occurring should the tool falls on the floor. The paint used in the battery room and the materials for ducting should be corrosion resistant. Metal jugs should not be used for filling distilled water inside the batteries. Additional precautions include preventing the usage of naked lamps and prohibiting smoking in the battery room. The battery must never be placed in the emergency switchboard room as there is a high chance of sparking due to circuit breakers arcing.

MAINTENANCE OF THE BATTERY

The batteries should be maintained in a fully charged condition. This is done by the charging circuit. The state of charge can be seen with the help of a hydrometer. A sample is taken using the hydrometer which checks the condition of specific gravity. For a fully charged lead acid battery, the specific gravity is 1.280 at 15°C. There is no change in specific gravity in alkaline batteries during charging and discharging therefore the hydrometer test is used only for lead acid batteries. Top the batteries up with distilled water to compensate for the loss of water during charging. Always keep the battery terminals clean. This can be achieved by smearing the terminals with petroleum jelly.

CRANKCASE EXPLOSIONS

A crankcase explosion is caused by the crankcase overheating. In the crankcase of the main engine, oil particles are churned into small particles approximately 200 micrometres in diameter. These particles cannot ignite easily, even with a naked flame. If, however, a hot spot develops and touches these small particles, the particles further reduce in size, resulting in the formation of a flammable mist. This mist can be very easily ignited when in contact with the hotspot. With crankcases, there is a mixture of lubricating oil, air, and abundant heat; all of which are needed to start what would be a very serious fire indeed.

HOTSPOTS

A hotspot is caused by two metal surfaces rubbing together, such as the friction between two metal parts (e.g., the piston rod and gland, cross head guides or chain and gear drive). Hotspots are generally caused by poor maintenance and insufficient clearance within the crankcase. When oil leaks, it is drawn towards the hot spot. On contact, the oil vapourises into smaller oil particles, which are then drawn towards the cooler areas of the crankcase. At this point, the vapours turn into a fine white mist. Over time the mist increases in volume. As the mist expands, it again touches the hotspot resulting in a crankcase explosion. The extent of the explosion will depend on the volume of the mist produced inside the crankcase. The force of the primary explosion may be sufficient to lift the crankcase relief valves, which in turn can lead to a more severe and dangerous secondary explosion.

SECONDARY EXPLOSION

The primary explosion produces a shock wave which propagates inside the crankcase with increasing force. This shock wave has the effect of further reducing the size of the oil particles, which produces yet more fuel for ignition. As the pressure front moves forward through the crankcase space, it is followed by a low-pressure area directly behind it. This low-pressure area sucks in yet more air from the outside. As the pressure inside the crankcase rises, the air is forced out into the scavenge space through the piston glands and relief valves. If the mixture of enriched air and oil mist that was produced during the primary explosion touches another hotspot, the result is a secondary explosion. This tends to be much worse than the initial primary explosion as by now the air inside the crankcase is fully enriched with fuel and lubricating oil vapours. The force of the secondary explosion is often sufficient to seriously damage the crankcase beyond repair, as well as causing extensive damage to the surrounding machinery. It is therefore imperative that all engine room crew are aware that crankcase explosions can almost always be avoided through proper scheduled maintenance and performing regular engine checks.

STARTER AIRLINE FIRES

One of the most common causes of engine room fires is the starting airline explosion. In the air starting system of the main engine, fuel is often present in the form of lube oil which is carried over from the air compressor. This is joined by an abundant supply of oxygen. The heat source is usually caused by a leaking starting air valve fitted on the cylinder head. The combination of fuel, oxygen and heat in the appropriate ratios may lead to an airline explosion. For preventing explosions in the starting airline, a variety of safety devices and arrangements are often used: (a) *the relief valve*. This is fitted on the common air manifold which supplies air to the cylinder head. The relief valve is normally located at the end of the manifold and lifts the valve in the event of excess pressure inside the manifold. The advantage of the relief valve is it will sit back after removing the excess pressure and thus continuous air is available to the engine in case of manoeuvring; (b) *bursting disc*. This is in the starting air pipe and consists of a perforated disc protected by a sheet of material which will burst in case of excessive pressure caused by an airline explosion. It also consists of a protective cap constructed that if the engine is required to run even after the disc has been ruptured, the cap will cover the holes when it is turned. This ensures that when manoeuvring air is always available for the engine; (c) *non-return valve*. This is positioned between the air manifold and the air receiver. The non-return valve prevents the explosive mixture of heated oxygen to reach the air bottle; (d) *flame Arrestor*. This is a small unit consisting of several tubes which arrests or stops any flame coming out of the cylinder through a leaking start air valve. It is fitted on every cylinder before the starter air valve.

Preventing starter airline fires is relatively simple provided good maintenance of the system is carried out regularly. This means ensuring that all safety devices fitted to the starter airline system are working correctly. It also means draining the air bottle during each watch; checking the auto drain for proper function; ensuring the air compressor is well maintained to avoid oil carry over; ensuring the oil separator at the discharge point of the compressor is working efficiently; ensuring the starter air manifold pipe is cleaned and checked for paint deformation, as this indicates overheating pipes; overhauling the starting air valve regularly to avoid leakage; and ensuring the starter air valve seat is regularly inspected and lapped.

PURIFIER ROOM FIRES

The purifier room is one of the most likely places in the engine room to catch fire. There is an abundant supply of fuel oil (lubricating oil in the lube oil separator and fuel or diesel oil in the fuel oil separator), air for combustion, and many potential heat sources such as hot oil and electrical short circuits. When all these factors combine within the flammable range, a fire can spontaneously break out. For example, if a leaking pipe sprays oil over a hot surface or over an electrical point, this can lead to a purifier room fire. Preventing and avoiding purifier room fires is quite simple provided basic standards of maintenance are carried out regularly. All pipes leading to the separator should be double sheathed. The reason being that if the inner pipe leaks, then it will not spray hot oil over the engine compartment and machinery but instead will leak into the outer pipe. Drip trays should be provided below the purifier and separator. All flanged pipes and connections should be covered with anti-spill tapes that can prevent flange leaks. Fire detection and alarm systems must be provided and firefighting systems such as water mist and CO^2 should be installed and tested regularly. Quick closing valves and systems that allow the remote stopping of pumps and purifiers should be installed and again tested on a regular basis.

SCAVENGE FIRES

The most lethal type of engine room fires is the scavenge fire. There are many reasons why scavenge fires may break out, but the most common causes are: (1) excessive wear of the liner; (2) piston rings may be worn out or have loose ring grooves; (3) broken piston rings or rings seized in the grooves; (4) dirty scavenge space; (5) poor combustion due to leaking fuel valves or improper timing; and (6) insufficient or excess cylinder lubrication. There are a few indications that a scavenge fire is in the process of developing and it is extremely important that marine engineers and engine room crew can recognise these signs, which typically include: (a) increasing temperature of the scavenger; (b) turbocharger surge; (c) abnormally high exhaust temperatures; (d) loss of engine power and reduction in rpm, caused by back pressure under the piston space; (e) smoke rising from the scavenge drains; and (f) development of paint blisters on the scavenge doors.

In the event of a scavenge fire breaking out, the actions to be taken depends largely on the stage of the fire, i.e., whether it is incipient or involved. Involved fires usually easier to identify as there will be peeling or blistering paint, large fluctuations and reductions in engine power and turbocharger surge. Incipient fires are much harder to identify though it is critical to tackle an incipient scavenge fire before it becomes involved. The best actions to take when an incipient fire has been identified is to reduce the engine rpm to slow or dead slow. Increase the cylinder lubrication of the affected unit, paying special attention so as not to feed the fire. Where the fire is growing, avoid lubricating the cylinder entirely. If it is obvious the fire was caused by leaky fuel valves, lift-up the pump of the affected unit keeping the scavenge drain closed. Keep monitoring the scavenge and exhaust temperatures and allow the fire to starve and burn itself out. Once the fire has been extinguished, start increasing the rpm slowly. Continue to monitor the scavenge temperature for any signs of reignition. For larger involved fires, stop the engine immediately and engage the turning gear and keep the engine rotating. Extinguish the fire using the fixed firefighting systems for scavenge fires. This may be the CO^2 system, or a steam connection designed for smothering. In the event the fixed system is not available, apply external cooling to prevent heat induced metal distortion. After confirming the fire is extinguished, allow the scavenge space to cool down fully before opening for inspection and remedial work.

FIRE DETECTION EQUIPMENT

Modern ships are fitted out with a wide range of fire detection systems and firefighting equipment. In this section, we will briefly look at the main types of systems found on board container vessels. Other types of ships, and particularly oil tankers, product tankers and gas carriers will have fire detection and firefighting systems specific to the types of hazards unique to these ships. *Flame Detectors*. The light produced by a flame has a characteristic flicker frequency of about 25 Hz. The light spectrum in the infrared or ultraviolet range can be monitored to trigger fire alarms. As oil fires do not emit much in the way of fire gases (i.e., smoke), these types of sensors are used mainly near fuel handling equipment and boilers. *Heat Detectors*. Heat detectors are of various types though the most common is the rate of temperature rise type. This consists of a bimetallic detecting element which is a thin metal strip and a thick metal strip. The thin strip is more sensitive to temperature rises than the thick strip. If there is a sudden rise in temperature, the thin strip bends faster than the thick strip, bringing both strips into direct contact. During normal temperature rises both strips deflect heat by about the same distance, exhibiting no reaction. This means if the rate of temperature rise is less than 10°C in any given 30 minute period, the detector will not trigger the alarm. If, however, the temperature rises to 75°C or above at any time, the two strips will come into direct contact, setting off the alarm. *Smoke and Heat Detectors.* There are two types of smoke detectors commonly used on board container ships: (1) light obscuration; and (2) ionisation. The first type works by monitoring the amount of light that passes through a sensor. As fire gases contain a mixture of vapours and soot, creating 'smoke', this obscures the sensor which triggers the alarm. The second type works by monitoring the composition of air. If the sensor in the alarm detects any of the common particles found in smoke, this triggers the alarm. It is important to remember that liquid or gas fires may not emit much smoke in the initial stages of development. Therefore, smoke detectors are not considered an effective precaution for such fires. Smoke detectors are mostly used in the crew accommodation areas where fires are more likely to generate smoke.

FIRE PREVENTION

In the engine and machinery spaces, waste bins are often used for storing oily rags. These must be fitted with lids. It is never acceptable to leave oily rags lying around. Waste baskets and bins with covers should be provided on each deck and on both sides of the machinery. High pressure fuel oil pipes should not be tightened to control leaks whilst the engine is running. Furthermore, oil should never be allowed to flow into the turbochargers when in operation. Short sounding pipes should be kept shut with plugs and never left in the open position as hot oil is easier to spill from short sounding pipes. The pet cocks and small cocks on common rail pipes should be inspected and checked for signs of wear. Lastly, exhaust and steam leaks should be promptly investigated and wherever possible, resolved immediately. Although the engine and machinery spaces are the most likely areas on board to catch fire, the ship's crew should be equally prepared for galley and accommodation fires. The galley is at risk of electrical fires if galley equipment is not maintained and kept in good working order. Fires may break out during the loading and storing of provisions as this is really the only time when the galley is left unattended for long periods. Smoking remains a constant threat and fires caused by unattended cigarettes are still a common cause of ship fires. Care should be taken to dispose of cigarettes using self-closing ashtrays and avoid smoking in bed.

Most cargoes are safe when packaged properly and stowed appropriately. Even so, cargo fires can spontaneously erupt given the right conditions. Checking the cargo manifest, following all precautions and guidelines, and abiding by the shipper's instructions will go a long way in avoiding cargo fires. The FCP is a mandatory requirement of the SOLAS Convention, and is described in chapter II, regulation 15. The FCP provides information about the fire station on each deck of the ship, on various bulkheads, and in spaces enclosed by 'A' class divisions and 'B' class divisions. It also explains the type of fire detection system and firefighting systems available on the ship such as fire alarms, firefighting appliances, escape routes, fire switches and so on.

The FCP advises on the different fire alarm systems; sprinkler installations; extinguishing appliances; means of escape to different compartments and decks; ventilation systems; the position of various dampers, their markings, and which fan is for which compartment or deck. With the permission of the ship's Classification Society, the details of the FCP may be provided to the ship's officers as a booklet. The graphical symbols used in the FCP should be as per the fighting equipment symbols set out in IMO Assembly Resolution A.654(16). It

284   Maritime emergencies

is the responsibility of every crew member to know the meaning of these symbols. The FCP must be available in the working language of the ship and in English. At least one copy of the FCP must be available onshore at the offices of the Company. A copy of Fire Control Plan should be permanently stored in prominently marked weathertight enclosures outside the deckhouse for the assistance of shoreside firefighting teams in case the ship is in port or drydock. The General Arrangement Plan (GAP) should be conspicuously exhibited for the guidance of the crew and posted locations such as the bridge, engine room and throughout the accommodation block. The FCP should be kept current and if any alterations are made, these must be formally recorded. It falls the master, the shipowner and the ship's onshore manager to ensure the FCP is regularly reviewed and updated as required. The FCP must be reviewed, and new versions circulated in any of the following circumstances: (1) following a change in firefighting systems, alarm systems, escape route designs or anything related to the current FCP; the new system or design must be approved by Class; (2) following any modification in the ship's structure or ship's particulars which affect the current FCP; the new system or design must be approved by Class; (3) in the event of revisions of statutes related to FCP under SOLAS, the IMO or similar authority; (4) when a change of Flag happens, Class must review and approve the FCP; (5) following a change in Class, the FCP must be reviewed and approved.

SURVEY REQUIREMENT

The Class surveyor must ensure that there are no discrepancies between the content of the FCP and the record of approved cargo ship safety equipment carried on board. In addition, the various entries in the record should correspond to the particulars of the equipment carried and with the associated service and maintenance reports. As part of the ongoing FCP management process, ships are required to submit for Class inspection the following surveys: (a) *initial survey*. This is the survey to be done for issuing the approved FCP to the newly built ship; (b) *annual survey*. The FCP survey comes under the continuous ship safety equipment survey (CSSE), which is performed annually; and (c) *renewal survey*. If the CSSE certificate is under a renewal period requiring a survey, the FCP will require this survey. The attending surveyor is required to make a specific and explicit statement in the report of the relevant survey as to whether they have examined and verified the content of the fire control plan as legible, current, and approved (or examined for compliance) and in accordance with the requirements of the regulations set out in SOLAS.

FIRE SAFETY SYSTEM CODE

Fire is one of the most dangerous emergencies that can happen on board any ship. Fire has the potential to cause disastrous damage including loss of property and life. As the resources available on board to fight fire are limited, fire prevention measures are more effective than firefighting measures. For this reason, an international fire safety system (FSS) was developed and promulgated in chapter II-2 of SOLAS; otherwise known as the Fire Safety System (FSS) Code. The FSS Code came into force in July 2002 following its adoption by the Marine Safety Committee (MSC) in session 73 and was made mandatory by resolution MSC 99(73). The main purpose of the FSS Code is to provide specific standards of engineering specification for FSS on board. The FSS Code consists of a total of 15 chapters with each chapter relating to a specific fire prevention or firefighting system.

EXAMPLE: MAERSK KENSINGTON

On 19 March 2018, the *Maersk Kensington* (2007), a vessel owned and operated by the US subsidiary Maersk Line Limited (MLL), reported a container on fire in a cargo hold while making way from Salalah, Oman, towards the Suez. All 26 crew members were safe and accounted for and the fire was reported to be contained. Safety measures in accordance with the FCP were taken immediately. The crew reacted swiftly and as per procedure, releasing CO_2 into the cargo hold to contain the fire. The *Maersk Kensington* was able to make way to the port of Salalah, where it was placed at anchor. At the time of the fire, the vessel was carrying 3,518 containers (the equivalent of 5,616 TEU) with a maximum capacity of 6,188 TEUs.

FIRE RESPONSE EQUIPMENT AND SYSTEMS

The sprinkler system is an automatic fire detecting, alarm, and extinguishing system, which is designed to respond quickly and effectively to an outbreak of fire. Sprinklers are most often found in the accommodation block and other crew spaces such as the paint room. The system consists of a pressurised water tank with water pipes that lead to various locations within the compartment. These water pipes terminate in a sprinkler head, which automatically activates when fire is detected. The pressurised water tank is half filled with fresh water through the freshwater supply connection. Compressed air is delivered from the electrically operated compressor or from air bottles, which raises the pressure of the tank to a predetermined level. The pressure in the tank is set to be able to deliver pressure at the highest sprinkler head in the system at not less than 4.8bar. The sprinkler heads are grouped into different sections with not more than 200 sprinkler heads in each section. Each section has its own alarm system which sounds the fire alarm. The sprinkler head consists of a quartzoid bulb which bursts when the temperature increases beyond the limit set. This starts the water flowing from the sprinkler head. The quartzoid bulbs are colour coded according to their heat resistance rating. Red bulbs have a heat resistance rating of 68°C; yellow is 80°C; and green is 93°C. Each sprinkler head covers a deck area of approximately 16m². The flow of water in each head corresponds, as per SOLAS, to a standard discharge rate of five litres per minute. When the sprinkler head bursts, the non-return valve in the line opens and the water starts to flow. When the water flows, the pressure in the line drops activating the alarm. This system is also commonly connected to a seawater pump that can supply water to the system in case the water in the pressure tank is exhausted.

The CO_2 fixed firefighting system works by suppressing the oxygen in the fire-affected compartment. Before using the CO_2 system, it is important to ensure the compartment is completely sealed. If not, the CO_2 will leak out of the compartment. Before sealing the compartment, check that no crew members are present as once the CO_2 is released, the system cannot be stopped until the bottles are fully discharged. Any crew members left in the compartment will quickly succumb to CO_2 poisoning and suffocation. The requirement for CO_2 fire extinguishing is to discharge 85% of the CO_2 gas into the affected space within two minutes in the engine room and 10 minutes in the cargo holds. After the CO_2 has been fully discharged, the compartment must be ventilated before being accessed. Entry should only be authorised using full SCBA. Given the hazardous nature of the CO_2 system, it is critical that the crew are familiar with the system and competent in its operation. The CO_2 room comprises segregated CO_2 bottle banks for the engine room and cargo holds. The CO_2 gas is carried to the ship's compartments via small pipelines. These pipelines must be checked for signs of corrosion and damage. Any detection of leaks must be rectified immediately. Checking the level measurements is an important procedure to be performed at regular intervals using a CO_2 bottle level measuring instrument. As the ship passes through varying temperature zones, it is common for the pipes accumulate condensed water. This can lead to line blockages and corrosion therefore it is important to clear the lines by blowing pressurised air through the system regularly.

The FM-200 Waterless Fire Extinguishing System is stored in cylinders as a quick release pressurised liquid. Due to its low boiling point, this liquid discharges as a gas which extinguishes the fire through a combination of chemical and physical heat removal. Unlike other fire extinguishing products, the FM-200 does not muffle flames by removing oxygen from the environment but instead absorbs the heat energy from the fire. It does this by absorbing heat from the flame zone and disrupting the combustion chemical chain reaction. This helps to put out the fire quickly, minimising the risk of explosion and collateral damage. The FM-200 is specially designed for marine firefighting and is distributed uniformly throughout the protected areas of the ship including the engine enclosures, electrical controls, machinery compartments, and other critical operational areas. Whereas water or water mist may not penetrate inside cabinets or reach fires beneath machinery fixtures, the FM-200 can penetrate obscure and hard to reach areas.

The types of fire extinguishers that may be used to put out a fire depends on the cause and type of fire. Fires are classified according to their fuel source and so fire extinguishers are classified accordingly. There are three main types of fire extinguishers approved by SOLAS and carried on board. These are the portable fire extinguisher, the semi-portable fire extinguisher, and fixed type equipment. There are five categories or classes of fire recognised by SOLAS. These are shown in the table below. By classing fires according to their fuel source, it is easier for the crew to respond immediately by choosing the correct type of fire extinguisher for the class of fire.

Semi-portable fire extinguishers hold a higher capacity than portable extinguishers but are substantially heavier. They are generally considered the second line of defence where portable fire extinguishers have failed to extinguish the fire. As it is much heavier to lift, they are fitted with a wheel-trolley arrangement which can be dragged to the fire location. Semi-portable fire extinguishers use either foam or DCP as the extinguishing media. Semi-portable extinguishers are ordinarily stored in locations where there is a substantial risk of fire, for instance, in the engine room near the boiler and incinerator and in the galley.

Table 21.1 Classes of fires, fuel, and extinguishing media

Class	Fuel	Extinguishing media
Class A	Wood, glass fibre, upholstery, and furnishings	Water Dry Chemical Powder (DCP) Foam
Class B	Oil fires involving lubricating oils, fuels, paints, and cooking oils	CO_2 DCP
Class C	Electrical fires involving energised electrical equipment such as motors, switches, and wiring	CO_2 DCP
Class D	Metal fires involving magnesium and aluminium	DCP
Class E	High voltage fires involving magnesium and aluminium	DCP

FIXED FIREFIGHTING SYSTEMS AND EQUIPMENT

In addition to the fixed firefighting systems discussed earlier, ships are also fitted out with various other fixed systems such as hydrants, manual fire pumps, remote shut and stop systems and international shore connection systems. Different classes of fire-retardant bulkheads – i.e., Class-A, Class-B and Class-C – are used in the construction of different areas such as the accommodation, machinery space, and pump room. The purpose of these special bulkheads is to contain and restrict the spread of fire. Fire doors are fitted within fire-retardant bulkheads to provide access to and from the compartment. These are self-closing type doors with no hold back arrangement. Fire dampers are provided in the ventilation system of cargo holds, the engine room, and the accommodation block and work by inhibiting the oxygen supply to the fire. As per SOLAS regulations, ships must carry main fire pumps and an emergency power pump of approved type and capacity. The location of the emergency fire pump must be outside the space where the main fire pump is located. The Fire Main piping which is connected to the main and emergency fire pump must be of an approved type and capacity. Isolation and relief valves must be provided to avoid a build-up of over-pressure in the line. Fire hoses with A length of at least 10m must be carried on board. The quantity and diameter of the hoses are determined by Class. Most ships carry nozzles with an output diameter of 12m, 16m and 19m. These may emit either a spray or a jet. Fire hoses are connected to fire hydrants from which the water supply is controlled. They are made from heat retardant material and are designed to withstand sub-zero temperatures. The remote station shutdown is provided to all fuel lines from the fuel oil and diesel oil tanks in the machinery space. This is done via the quick closing valves. Remote stop systems are also provided to stop the fuel pumps, purifier, ventilation fans and boiler in the event of fire or before discharging the fixed firefighting system. Last of all, most modern ships are fitted with an International Shore Connection (ISC). The ISC is used to connect shore water supplies directly to the ship when fighting onboard fires. The size, dimensions and couplings of the ICS are universal and designed to be used anywhere in the world where standard firefighting facilities exist.

FIREFIGHTER PPE

Chapter II-2, regulation 10.10.2 of the SOLAS regulations sets out the requirements and quantity for ships to carry onboard firefighter PPE (Ff PPE). In summary, all ships regardless of size of type must carry at least two firefighter sets on board. Additional firefighter sets are needed for passenger ships depending on the design of the ship – i.e., length of passenger spaces, number of decks, vertical zones, and passenger-carrying capacity. For tankers, an additional two firefighter sets must be carried. Firefighter sets must be stored in the fire control room and in places that are easily accessible during emergencies. Firefighting sets will likely differ from ship to ship but the minimum requirement includes heat resistant outer clothing, boots, and gloves; heat resistant helmet and face visor; SCBA; fireproof line; electric intrinsically safe hand lamp with minimum three hours battery power; fire axe; and heat resistant belt for carrying ancillary equipment.

The protective hood is designed to cover all parts of the face. It has an eye-cover (visor) that enables the wearer to see and allows oxygen to pass continuously from the air cylinders to the mouth and nose. The Portable Transporting Bag is an important piece of equipment as it can be filled with air cylinders, protective hoods and any other protective equipment that may be necessary for the rescue operation. The bag is made from a special fire-resistant material. The Portable Hauling Bag is like the Portable Transporting Bag, with the main difference being that extra weight can be carried. It is used for carrying SCBA and other rescue equipment from the locker to the incident zone. In addition to the personal protective equipment that firefighters must wear when attending to a fire, they must also don SCBA. As the name suggests, SCBA uses an oxygen tank to provide breathable air for the wearer. The set is designed to be completely self-contained with no openings to allow the ingress of smoke and other toxic fire gases. The capacity of the air cylinder must provide at least 1,200 litres of oxygen and should be capable of providing a minimum of 30minutes of air under normal working conditions. The set is fitted with a bypass valve and a pressure gauge with an anti-bursting assembly which is connected to the high-pressure air supply system. The maximum weight of the cylinder and its associated equipment should not exceed 19kg including lifelines, safety belt, and harness. An adjustable safety belt or harness made from heat resistant fabric is provided to which a fireproof personal line with a snap hook can be attached. The personal line must have a minimum length of three metres and be able to reach the furthest point within any given compartment. Furthermore, the line should have a minimum tensile strength of 500kg. To protect the face and provide breathable air, a sealed face mask is worn. This is connected to the air cylinder via a hose. For safety, the cylinder sounds an audible alarm when 20% of the air is left in the bottle with a maximum operating pressure of between 180 and 200bar. Spare cylinders should be available with a full 2,400-litre capacity. For ships carrying five sets or more, the total spare capacity should be 9,600 litres or if a charging facility is available on board, a prefilled capacity of 4,800 litres. The cylinders should be hydraulically pressure tested at intervals not exceeding five years with the hydrostatic test date permanently marked on each cylinder.

There are two types of SCBA available: the Closed-Circuit SCBA (CC-SCBA) and the Open Circuit SCBA (OC-SCBA). The CC-SCBA is designed to be worn when operations are expected to take considerably longer. The air is continuously re-processed or recycled so that the wearer gets a continuous supply of air. With OC-SCBA, the oxygen is compressed into air cylinders which are carried on the wearers back. Once the cylinder is empty, the oxygen is exhausted, and wearer must replace the empty cylinder for a full cylinder. Shore-based firefighters tend to use OC-SCBA as the time spent in the incident zone is generally much shorter than on ship. Subsequently, the SCBA used on board is predominantly the CC-SCBA type. The air cylinders contain about 1,240 litres of compressed air at 200 bar of atmospheric pressure. This gives the wearer around 31 minutes of air supply at full use or about 21 minutes during heavy use. The 'reducing valve' lowers the pressure by about 4bar which is further reduced by the demand valve attached to the mask. The demand valve is the one that supplies the air to the wearer when they inhale. The exhalation valve releases the air from the facemask. When the air left inside the apparatus is at about ten minutes (40–45bar), a warning alarm or whistle sounds continuously until the cylinder is fully emptied. The sounding of the alarm is an indication for the wearer to begin moving out of the incident zone. The face mask is formed from soft moulded natural rubber and is fitted with a speech diaphragm and nose guard. It has a foam filled or air cushion seal and shatterproof full vision visor. The mask has five adjustable head straps and a nylon lanyard or neck strap. To correctly position the mask over the face and head, the straps should be tightened in a sequence where the first two upper straps are tightened, followed by the middle pair and finally the lower strap. Care should be taken not to overtighten the straps as this will cause the wearer discomfort. A gauge is provided which is either clipped or attached to the harness that carries the cylinder. This gauge monitors the pressure within the cylinder and is positioned to be visible to the wearer.

Ship fires and firefighting systems 289

Table 21.2 Approximate air consumption limits for SCBA

Degree of exertion	Air consumption (litres / minute)	Duration/cylinder (1,200 litre capacity)	Duration/cylinder (1,800 litre capacity)
Resting	12–8	150–100	225–150
Light work	20–12	100–60	150–90
Moderate work	40–20	60–30	90–45
Heavy work	60–40	30–20	45–30

CALCULATING THE AIR CAPACITY AND REMAINING DURATION

To approximate the amount of air remaining in a cylinder, the wearer can use the following calculation:

$$\text{Nominal Working Duration} = \frac{\left(\text{Fully Charged Cylinder Capacity}\right)}{40} - 10$$

We subtract '10' as 10 minutes is when the alarm activates, and it is a safe period which must be considered. Hence, a 1,200litre cylinder will last for 1,200/40 = 30 minutes minus the 10 = 20 minutes. Remember though that nervousness and excitement can cause heavy breathing, which in turn reduces the amount of oxygen available.

To don the SCBA, the wearer opens the cylinder cradle by squeezing the two sides of the cradle lever then the cylinder strap. Line up the cylinder valve with the reducer valve handwheel. Turn the handwheel counterclockwise till tight. Hook the cylinder strap over the cylinder. Pull down the operating lever onto the tension spring to clip into place. Attach the demand valve assembly to the facemask. Line up the assembly with the red bypass valve knob in an upward position with the centreline of the facemask. Turn the assembly clockwise through 90° until it clicks into place. Hang the facemask from the neck by the neck strap. Lift the cylinder with the cylinder valve on top and the backplate facing the wearer and raise over the head. Straighten the hands to slide the shoulder straps over and onto the shoulders. Fasten the waist belt and tighten the shoulder straps. Slide the arms through the shoulder straps and place the back plate on the back with the cylinder valve facing downwards. Tighten the shoulder straps and fasten the waistbelt till tight. Open the cylinder valve by turning the handwheel slowly in a counter-clockwise direction. Check the pressure on the gauge. Open the facemask straps fully. Holding the breath, place the chin into the facemask. Pull the head harness and straps over the head. Ensure the mask is correctly placed on the face with the nose guard over the nose. Tighten the upper straps first then tighten the lower straps. Both side straps should be tightened together for a snug fit. Slowly exhale and start to breathe deeply – this will activate the positive pressure sensor. Once activated, breathe normally.

Once the SCBA has been donned, it is important to carry out the following pre-use checks. First, close the cylinder valve. Breathe normally to vent the system. During the venting observe the gauge. The whistle alarm should sound at the pre-set pressure of 55bar +/– 5bar. When the gauge indicates zero, hold breath. The facepiece should hold onto the face indicating a positive seal. Open the cylinder valve slowly but fully to pressurise the system. Inhale and hold. There should be no audible leak from the mask or the hoses. Exhale slowly and continue to breathe normally. The expired air should easily flow out of the exhalation valve. Press the centre of the rubber cover on the demand valve to check the supplementary air supply. Prior to entering the incident zone, the cylinder pressure should never be less than

80% when full. When in the incident zone, keep checking the gauge reading. If the whistle sounds, make way out of the incident zone and to a safe area. Never wait till the cylinder is completely empty and never remove the set until outside the incident zone and in a free air space. After leaving the incident zone, it is important to carry out some post-use actions. Start by pressing the reset lever and switch to OFF. Press and hold down the OFF button and remove the demand valve. Insert a finger behind the neck strap and press the buckles forward. Pull the mask forward and then up and back over the head. Close the cylinder valve and remove the facepiece. Unbuckle the waist belt. Loosen the shoulder straps and remove the backplate. Never drop the cylinder or facemask on the deck as this may cause internal damage. Wipe down the facemask with a mild disinfectant and rinse under cool running water. Always wipe dry.

For safe use and operation, the SCBA must be maintained and checked routinely. This includes checking the backplate and the shoulder/waist straps for any signs of damage. Check the facemask straps and any other rubber parts for signs of deterioration. To perform an alarm test, open the cylinder valve. The line will be pressurised at 200bar pressure. The pressure gauge will indicate that the pressure is at 200bar. Close the cylinder valve. Observe the pressure gauge and check that the pressure does not drop 10bar within one minute. Open the demand valve to let the pressure reduce from the high-pressure line. When the pressure reaches 50–60 bar, the alarm will sound. This indicates there is approximately only 10 minutes of oxygen left in the cylinder.

Chapter 22

Emergency distress equipment and signals

Seafarers have long used all manner of methods to signal distress; the earliest method being the flag. Ships in distress would hoist their flag upside down to alert passing ships that they were in trouble. This later evolved into the flag and ball system. Around 1850 an English widow, Martha Colston, developed a colour-coded flare system that could be fired and seen over the horizon. This marked the beginning of the marine flare. Following the invention of the radio, Morse Code became the dominant form of ship to ship and ship to land communication. Though the exact circumstances have long been forgotten, it is believed the first radio signal for help was sent sometime in the 1890s. Within a few years the system of Morse Code was developed, with 'SOS' being adopted in 1909. There is an ongoing disagreement over what 'SOS' means. Some maritime historians claim it an abbreviation of 'Save Our Ship'; others argue it stands for 'Save Our Souls'. The likeliest reason is the three letters 'S-O-S' are easy to spell out using Morse Code and are easy to decipher. Today, Morse Code has been replaced by more technologically advanced distress signals.

Throughout the late 18th and early 19th centuries, ships in distress depended on Morse Code to communicate their position to other passing ships. Though advanced for its time, Morse Code was far from perfect. Signals were often ignored, misinterpreted, or lost in the ether. Following the sinking of the *RMS Titanic* in 1912, the international maritime community realised a new method was needed for ships to communicate their distress. This led to the development of the GMDSS. GMDSS was fully adopted by the IMO under SOLAS chapter IV on 1 February 1999. GMDSS sets a universal standard for communication protocols, procedures, and equipment that ships must use to communicate in times of distress. Under the GMDSS regulations, all cargo ships and passenger ships above 300 gross tonnes, and sailing in international waters, must carry GMDSS equipment on board. When the ship is in distress, the GMDSS transmitter on the ship sends a signal via satellite or radio wave which is then picked up by other GMDSS receivers. GMDSS is also used for sending and receiving maritime safety information (MSI). As the earth has a circular shape, the GMDSS signals are transmitted using different frequency bands depending on the location or 'area' of the vessel. This means for a signal to be sent and received, the GMDSS transmitter must be set to the correct area.

TYPES OF GMDSS COMMUNICATIONS EQUIPMENT

As per the GMDSS regulations, ships over a certain tonnage must carry specific types of GMDSS equipment on board. These include VHF radio, Inmarsat, NAVTEX, and DSC. VHF is a set of radio frequencies that ships can use to communicate distress and send and receive MSI. The VHF range for distress signals is between 156 MHz and 174 MHz Channel 16, which is set at 156.800 MHz is specifically set aside for Distress, Urgency, and

DOI: 10.1201/9781003244615-27

291

292 Maritime emergencies

Table 22.1 GMDSS areas, ranges, and bands

Area	Range	Frequency
A1	50–20 miles	VHF + DSC
A2	400–50 miles	VHF + MF
A3	70° N–70° S	VHF + MF + One Inmarsat
A4	Above 70° N–70° S	HF + MF + VHF

Safety Communications. Channel 70, set at 156.525 MHz, is used for routine VHF DSC communications. GUARD channels are set above and below Channel 16 to avoid cross channel interference. The GUARD channel frequencies are between 156.775 MHz and 156.825 MHz. The VHF set runs off a 24-volt DC power supply with J3E type transmission for radiotelephony and G2B type for the transmission of VHF DSC comms. Inmarsat or the *International Maritime Satellite* is a system that connects ships to earth to station terminals through INMARSAT B, C and F77. The system provides telex, telephone, and data transfer services between ship-to-ship, ship-to-shore, and shore-to-ship as well as priority telex and SAR telephony. NAVTEX is an internationally adopted automated system which is used to distribute MSI as well as weather forecasts and weather warnings, navigational warnings, SAR notices and other relevant safety information. DSC is a calling service that connects ships-to-ships, ships-to-shore, or shore-to-ships. The service transmits safety and distress information usually on a high or medium frequency or VHF maritime radio.

Ships are legally required to have on board certain documents relating to GMDSS. These include the ship's radio licence, the radio operator's licence, the safety radio certificate, GMDSS radio logbook, ITU List of Cell Signs and Numerical Identities of Stations used by Maritime Satellite Services, ITU List of Coastal Stations, ITU List of Ship Stations, ITU List of Radio Determination and Special Service Stations, an antenna rigging plan, and a valid shore-based maintenance certificate. The operation of GMDSS equipment requires specialised training as well as licensing from an approved maritime authority. For deck officer's to be authorised to operate GMDSS, they must hold a *General Operator's Certificate (GOC)*. To obtain the GOC, the officer must attend a compulsory GMDSS Operator course. This is generally aimed at deck officer cadets and consists of written and oral examinations. On passing both the paper and oral assessment, deck officer cadet is awarded the GOC and is authorised to use GMDSS equipment. The *GMDSS Endorsement Certificate* is a legal document that permits the certificate holder to work on foreign-flagged ships. Obtaining a GMDSS endorsement certificate qualifies the holder to operate specialised emergency radio equipment including DSC, NAVTEX and SART, take command of emergency situations on board in place of the master or other senior officer, and to work on board foreign-flagged ships. The GMDSS Endorsement Certificate must be revalidated every five years. The revalidation process involves the re-evaluation and renewal of the original GMDSS certificate. This is necessary to maintain the authenticity of the original GMDSS certificate. Though different maritime authorities set their own criteria, the universally accepted conditions for GMDSS Endorsement Certificate

Table 22.2 GMDSS frequencies

Frequency	Frequency range
MF	300 KHz
HF	3 MHz to 30 MHz
VHF	30 MHz to 300 MHz

revalidation include performance of radio operations on board a seagoing ship that is fully fitted with GMDSS equipment for a period of at least 12 months within a preceding five-year period or at least three months within the preceding six-month period; successful completion of an approved training or GMDSS revalidation course provided by a recognised training provider within 12 months of sending the application revalidation; and completion of revalidation training every five years.

The criteria for transmitting GMDSS distress signals are set out in SOLAS and includes the following mandatory provisions:

- *Ship to Shore*. Every seagoing ship must have at least two separate transmission and receiver methods for sending ship-to-shore distress communications using either EPIRB, DSC, or Inmarsat C
- *Shore to Ship*. Every seagoing ship must be capable of receiving shore-to-ship warnings and distress alerts by DSC and NAVTEX
- *Ship to Ship*. Every seagoing ship must be capable of transmitting and receiving distress signals ship to ship by VHF Channel 13 and DSC
- *Search and Rescue Coordination Communications*. Every seagoing ship must be capable of transmitting and receiving SAR Coordination Communications by NAVTEX, HF, MF, VHF, and Inmarsat
- *On Scene Communications*. Every seagoing ship must meet the required standard to coordinate SAR and other distress communications between ships at the scene of the incident through either HF, MF, or VHF
- *Location Transmissions*. Every seagoing ship must be equipped with approved facilities for responding to maritime distress operations such as radar in accordance with SOLAS chapter V
- *Transmitting and Receiving MSI*. Every seagoing ship must be capable of receiving MSI such as navigation warnings, chart corrections, weather forecasts, and distress alerts through NAVTEX and DSC
- *Shore-Based Networks*. Every seagoing ship must be fitted with general communications equipment for official, business, and personal and private crew communications. This is usually provided through DSC and Inmarsat
- *Bridge to Bridge*. Every seagoing ship must be capable of transmitting and receiving bridge to bridge communications. This is usually required in port or during pilotage using VHF for normal ranges and HF, MF, and Inmarsat for other ranges

SAR SIGNALLING EQUIPMENT

Modern SAR signalling equipment also uses radio waves and satellite signals to help rescuers locate distressed ships, or in the worst cases to locate lifeboats and life rafts and MOBs. There is a veritable selection of SAR signalling equipment available on the market and most ships will carry a variety of some, if not all. The most used SAR signalling equipment includes the EPIRB, SART, and the Portable Marine Radio (PMR). The EPIRB is a type of emergency locator beacon that when activated transmits a continuous radio signal that can be picked up and triangulated by SAR teams. There are three types of EPIRB currently in operation:

- *COSPAS-SARSAT*. EPIRBs that function as part of the COSPAS-SARSAT system work on the 406.025 MHz and 121.5 MHz frequencies and are applicable for all sea areas

294 Maritime emergencies

- *Inmarsat E.* INMARSAT E devices work off the 1.6GHz band and may be deployed in sea areas A1, A2 and A3
- *VHF CH 70.* This works on the 156.525 MHz band and is deployable only in sea area A1

The EPIRB device contains two radio transmitters: one 5-watt and one 0.25 watt. Each operates at 406 MHz, which is the standard international frequency for distress signalling. The 5-watt radio transmitter is synchronised with a GOES weather satellite, which orbits the Earth in a geosynchronous pattern. When deployed, the EPIRB transmits a signal to the satellite. The signal consists of a digitally encrypted identification number that holds information such as the ship registration number or identifier, the date of the incident, the nature of the distress and the EPIRB's position. A unique identifier number (UIN), or Hex ID, is programmed into each beacon during the manufacturing process. The UIN consists of 15 digits comprising numbers and letters and provides the unique identity of each beacon. UINs can be found on the external casing of each beacon–usually on a white label. The Local User Terminal (LUT) is a land-based satellite receiving unit or ground station that calculates the position of the beacon using *Doppler Shift*. Doppler Shift is the change in frequency or wavelength of a radio wave relative to the receiver and the transmitter. The LUT sends the beacon data to the closest regional Mission Rescue Coordination Centre (MRCC). From here the MRCC coordinates the rescue operation. In the event the EPIRB is not compatible with GPS signal receiving equipment, the geosynchronous satellite orbiting the Earth will only pick up the signals emitted by the radio. This means the location of the transmitter, or the identity of the owner, will not be transmitted and received. This is because the satellite will only pick up trace elements of the radio signal reducing the amount of information the receiver can interpret. As a result, the LUT will receive only a rough location of the distressed ship rather than an exact fix.

In practical terms this means SAR crews can use the vague signal to plot an approximate location of the beacon, and gradually close in as the signal increases in strength, usually at around three miles. If an emitter transmits signals at 121.5 MHz SAR crews can pick up relatively precise locations at up to 15 miles. Accuracy can be improved if the beacon is fitted with a GPS receiver. To function, the EPIRB must be activated to emit signals. This is done by pushing a button on the unit; alternatively, some devices activate automatically when in contact with water. Water-activated EPIRBs are referred to as hydrostatic EPIRBs and are generally considered the best type as they do not require manual activation. That said, both hydrostatic and manually activated EPIRBs will only work when dislodged from their permanent brackets. This is achieved physically by a member of the crew or when immersed in water. All EPIRBs are battery powered which is essential as power is most commonly the first utility to be affected during an emergency. The batteries are 12v and provide up to 48 hours of transmitting capacity. Battery expiry date checks should be carried out as part of the regular safety inspections. Most EPIRBs have an operational lifespan of between two and five years.

It is possible for EPIRBs to activate accidentally. When an accidental activation has occurred, it is imperative that the false transmission is cancelled immediately by contacting the nearest coastal station or MRCC otherwise an unnecessary SAR operation will be initiated. EPIRBs should be tested once a month to ensure they are fully operational. The procedure is simple: (1) press and release the test button on the EPIRB; (2) wait for the red lamp to flash once; (3) within 30 seconds the red light and strobe should flash several times; and (4) after 60 seconds the device should automatically switch off. EPIRB maintenance is necessary and straightforward and should be completed as part of the scheduled health and safety maintenance programme. The EPIRB must be inspected for visual signs of damage or impairment such as cracks and chips. Once inspected, the device should be wiped clean with a dry cloth to remove any residues such as salt. When wiping the device clean, carefully inspect the buttons and switches. The lanyard must be neatly packed into the container with no loose threads. The battery expiry date should also be checked regularly. Once an EPIRB has been activated, it must never be reactivated. Always return the device to an approved servicing agent for safe disposal.

The second type of SAR signalling equipment carried on board all ships is the Search and Rescue Transponder or SART. This is a self-contained, waterproof transponder designed specifically for maritime emergencies. There are two types of SART: radar-SART and GPS-based AIS-SART (automatic identification system SART). The radar-SART is used to locate survival craft or distressed vessels by creating a series of dots on the rescuing ship's radar display. The SART will only respond to a 9 GHz X-band (3cm wavelength) radar and will not be seen on S-band (10cm) or any other radar. The radar-SART may be triggered by any X-band radar within a range of approximately eight nautical miles (15km). Each radar pulse received causes the SART to transmit a response that is swept repetitively across the complete radar frequency band. When interrogated, it sweeps rapidly (at 0.4 microseconds) through the band before beginning a relatively slow sweep (at 7.5 microseconds) through the band back to the starting frequency. This process is repeated for a total of twelve complete cycles. At some point in each sweep, the radar-SART frequency will match the interrogating radar, being within the pass band of the radar receiver. If the radar-SART is within range, the frequency match during each of the 12 slow sweeps will produce a response on the radar display. This line of 12 dots is equally spaced by about 0.64 nm (1,185 km). When the range to the radar-SART is reduced to about one nautical mile (1,852 km), the radar display may also show the 12 responses generated during the fast sweeps. These additional dot responses, which are also equally spaced by 0.64nm (1.2 km), will be interspersed with the original line of 12 dots. These appear stronger and larger the closer the interrogating radar gets, slowly becoming arcs at first until the SART is within one nautical mile, at which point the arcs will become full circles indicating the active SART is in the general area.

The general self-test procedure for the SART is simple: (1) switch the setting to TEST mode; (2) hold the SART in view of the radar antenna; (3) check that the visual indicator light is operational; (4) check the audible beeper is operational; (5) observe the radar display and identify the presence of concentric circles on the PPI; (6) check the battery expiry date. Should the SART accidentally activate in live mode, switch the device off immediately and transmit a DSC alert cancellation message on VHF Channel 70; and VHF channel 16 to all coastal stations indicating the identification and position of the vessel. AIS-SART is a self-contained radio device used to locate survival craft or distressed ships. It works by sending automatic updated positions using an Automatic Identification System Class-A position report. The position and time synchronisation of the AIS-SART is derived from an inbuilt GNSS receiver (e.g., GPS). The Portable Marine Radio (PMR) is a critical component of GMDSS and is located on the bridge. Being lightweight and durable, it consists of a portable handheld radio that can be used to communicate from the rescue craft. The IMO has mandated that PMRs must: be easily operated by unskilled personnel, must transmit and receive at 156.8 MHz (Channel 16) and 156.3 MHz (Channel 6); be able to withstand a drop of one metre onto a hard surface; be watertight to a depth of one metre for a minimum period of five minutes; and have a minimum power rating of 0.25 watts complete with a power reduction switch. Furthermore, the antenna must be omnidirectional and vertically polarised, and the battery must have a power capacity of eight hours. Personal Location Beacons or PLBs are essentially EPIRBs but for individuals. PLBs are used to indicate distress when out of range of the emergency services. PLBs work in the same manner as EPRIBs and transmit on the COSPAS-SARSAT satellite system in the 406.025 MHz band range. PLBs are much smaller than EPIRBs and are designed to be carried on the person, whether at sea or on land. Once activated, PLBs transmit for approximately 24 hours.

296 Maritime emergencies

Pyrotechnic distress signals are a special type of distress signal that uses a self-contained and self-sustained exothermic chemical reaction for producing heat, light, gas, smoke, and sound. Ships use pyrotechnic distress signals to alert other ships of their distress. The use of pyrotechnic distress signals is covered at Annex 4 of the COLREGs and in SOLAS. The location of pyrotechnic distress signals and the minimum quantities to be carried on board are set out in both the COLREGs and SOLAS. Accordingly on the bridge there must be a minimum of 12 rocket parachute flares, six handheld flares, four buoyant smoke signals with two on the port and two on the starboard sides and one line throwing appliance. In each lifeboat, there must be a minimum of six handheld flares, four rocket parachute flares and two buoyant smoke signals. Each type of pyrotechnic distress signal has attributes that must be taken into consideration when deploying them in an emergency. *Handheld flares* are small cylindrical stick that, when activated, produce an intense red smoke or light without an explosion. The flare should be held out leeward when activated. Handheld flares can be used during both daylight and night-time hours. *Rocket parachute flares* are designed to fire a single red star to a height of approximately 300 m. When launched, the flare self-activates to produce an intense red smoke. At the peak of ascent, a parachute opens which reduces the rate of descent. This increases the time that the flare can be seen. *Buoyant smoke signals* are stored in compact floating containers. Used mainly during daylight, the buoyant smoke signal cloaks the position of distress with a bright orange smoke. This can also be used to aid rescue helicopters by indicating prevailing wind directions. Though not strictly a pyrotechnic distress signal, the *line throwing appliance* is counteracting device that can be used in emergency situations. When fired, it creates a connection or bridge between the distressed ship and the rescuing ship, upon which towing lines can be attached.

The SOLAS regulations set out the maintenance and disposal criteria for pyrotechnic distress signals. The general provisions for pyrotechnical distress signals are:

Pyrotechnics must be kept in a lockable watertight storage container

These containers should be kept in a dry but accessible location

Flares must be kept away from fuel and other combustible materials

Weekly maintenance routines must be carried out in accordance with the manufacturer's instructions, LSA maintenance schedules and company ISM procedures

When pyrotechnic distress signals expire, they must be removed from service and quarantined pending later disposal

Pyrotechnics must be disposed of in port and never discarded overboard

The provision and use of handheld flares are contained in SOLAS chapter III regulation 25, accordingly handheld flares must:

Be contained in a watertight casing

Have a self-ignition system

Not cause discomfort to the person using the flare

Not cause damage to the vessel or survival craft

Illuminate with a bright red colour

Contain a simple and easily understood instruction diagram on the outside casing

The provision and use of rocket parachute flares are contained in SOLAS chapter III regulation 26; accordingly, rocket parachute flares must comply with the same provisions set out in SOLAS chapter III, regulation 25; and in addition, must:

Have a minimum vertical height, when fired, of 300 m
  Contain a parachute that automatically deploys when the flare reaches the top of its ascent
  Burn for a period of not less than 40 seconds with a minimum luminous intensity of 30,000
  candelas
  Have a minimum rate of descent of five metres per second
Have such an arrangement that the flare will not damage or burn the parachute once activated

The provision and use of buoyant smoke signals are contained in SOLAS chapter III regulation 37; and accordingly, must:

Be contained in a water-resistant buoyant container with a clear diagram for operation
  Not ignite or explode if used in accordance with the correct operational procedures
  Emit a high visibility smoke with a uniform rate over a minimum period of three minutes
  Only emit smoke and not a flame when floating in calm water
Emit smoke for a period not less than 10 seconds if immersed in water

The provision and use of pyrotechnic line throwing devices are contained in SOLAS chapter III regulation 49; and accordingly, must:

Have good accuracy
  Be contained in a water-resistant container with a clear diagram for operation
  Contain a minimum of four projectiles, each with a line length of 230 m in calm water
Contain four lines with a SWL of not less than two kilos Newton.

NON PYROTECHNIC DISTRESS SIGNALS

Non-pyrotechnic distress signals are the opposite of pyrotechnic signals in the sense that they do not involve an exothermic chemical reaction to operate. The most common forms of non-pyrotechnic distress signal equipment carried on board ships include EPIRBs, emergency radios, flying the NC flags in accordance with the ICS, operating the ship's horn, marker dyes, 'MAYDAY' or 'SOS', mirrors, orange signal flags, and slowly and repeatedly raising and lowering the arms. Other than the emergency distress telecommunications methods already discussed above, ships in distress can utilise other non-pyrotechnic means of getting the attention of passing ships and aircraft. The floating man, overboard pole or Dan buoy is a compact, self-contained device specially designed for maritime rescue and recovery. The Dan buoy is usually used during MOB incidents and is thrown overboard towards the casualty. The buoy is fitted with a yellow and red flag (ICS 'O') and either a flashing lamp or strobe light. Prior to the adoption of modern distress technology, hoisting the national flag upside down could be used to indicate a ship in distress. This method is generally avoided today as it is easily misinterpreted as error and in some cases, some national flags are the same irrespective of whether they are hoisted the right way up and upside down. As per the ICS regulations, the flag combination 'NC' indicates distress. Listed under Annex IV of the COLREGs, the Maritime Distress Signal Flag may be flown which consists of a square orange cloth flag adorned with a black ball. Orange is used as it is the internationally recognised colour for distress.

If a Maritime Distress Signal Flag is unavailable, hoisting a length of orange cloth with a black square and a circle will also indicate a vessel is in distress. Also listed under Annex IV of the COLREGs are marker dyes, which have an approximate range of 50m. Rarely used today, marine mirrors, better known as Heliographs, may be used to attract the attention of other ships, or passing aircraft. The mirror works by reflecting sunlight in the direction of the approaching vessel. Mirrors not only reflect sunlight to pinpoint the position of the distressed ship or survival craft but are non-corrosive and never expire. They can be used for as long as their sunlight. The ship's foghorn may be continuously sounded to alert other vessels and shore authorities of the ship's distress. If all other methods have failed, slowly and repeatedly raising, and lowering the arms, outstretched by the sides, can attract the attention of passing aircraft and small boats.

Chapter 23

Lifesaving appliances

Safety is of paramount importance on board any vessel. The ship is both the home and workplace for the crew. Unfortunately, incidents do happen and whilst the majority can be resolved relatively easily, there is always the risk that they may escalate out of control. On these occasions, it is necessary to use LSA. By law, ships must LSA, which includes everything from handheld radios to lifeboats. These are a legal requirement under SOLAS, and every crew member must be trained in their use. It is incumbent upon the ship's officers – usually the second officer – to inspect the LSA regularly. On most ships, these inspections form part of the PMS. Inspections typically involve the lifeboats, davits, inflatable life rafts, radios, smoke signals and buoys, lifejackets, FCP and firefighting equipment, pilot ladders, and indeed any other critical lifesaving equipment. Lifeboat drills should be carried out regularly to ensure crew members are fully conversant in the preparation, operation, and deployment of the lifeboat under emergency pressure. The exterior of the lifeboat should be renewed in accordance with OEM instructions, and the information written on the outside of the lifeboat kept legible. During drills, the lifeboat should be lowered with checks carried out on its forward and astern movements. Lifeboat davits must be de-rusted, repainted and greased together with the winches and blocks. It is important to test these during drills to ensure their smooth operation.

Inflatable life rafts should be checked regularly to comply with servicing and renewal requirements. Information stickers and labels can lose their legibility over time and these need to be inspected, and replaced, as necessary. Portable handheld radios are essential for lifesaving communication between the rescue craft and rescuers. This means they should be checked and tested to ensure they are in optimal working condition. The ship's crew should be fully trained in the use and operation of portable handheld radios including charging and battery replacement. Pyrotechnic smoke signals and lifebuoys should be inspected and overhauled as required. Any equipment that has expired, is damaged, or no longer usable should be removed from service and quarantined in an area of the ship where it will not be mistaken as active. Any quarantined LSA must be disposed of shoreside using an approved disposal service. They must never be disposed of overboard. As part of the regular safety check regime, lifejackets should be inspected and rigorously checked for signs of defect or damage. Expired lights and faulty lifejackets must be replaced. Regular drills should be held to practice the donning and doffing of lifejackets in the quickest time possible. As crew members are replaced, new drills should be carried out to maintain currency. It is a legal requirement under maritime law that ships must carry sufficient lifejackets in accordance with the number of crew and passengers on board.

Lifejackets are designed to keep the wearer afloat when immersed in water. It consists of a sleeveless vest made from a buoyant or inflatable material and wrapped in bright orange fabric. The standards of construction and function of lifejackets are provided in SOLAS chapter II under the LSA Code, which was amended in July 2010. There are two main types

DOI: 10.1201/9781003244615-28

299

of lifejackets currently available: non-inflatable lifejackets, which are fitted with a buoyant foam; and auto and semi-inflatable lifejackets, both of which use a gas canister inside the jacket compartment which inflates when immersed in water. Automatic and semi-inflatable lifejackets provide the same level of buoyancy; the only difference being that the semi-inflatable lifejacket must be triggered by the wearer.

The least buoyant form of lifejacket is the nylon-lined foam buoyancy aid, which is used predominantly in water sports such as kayaking, canoeing, and dinghy sailing. These types of buoyancy aid are designed to allow freedom of movement whilst providing the wearer with sufficient buoyancy to keep them afloat. They are designed for minimal maintenance and are the cheapest to manufacture. Some buoyancy aids are designed specifically for children and adolescents. These lifejackets may include one or two under-straps to be worn between the legs of the wearer and a headrest flap. The under-straps are designed to keep the vest from riding up when immersed in water. They also help prevent the wearer from slipping out of the lifejacket. The straps are fully adjustable. The headrest flap is designed to help support the head and keep it out of the water. A grab handle is attached to the headrest to be used if needed to rescue or lift the wearer out of the water. Buoyancy aids are rated by the amount of buoyancy they provide measured in Newtons with the minimum rating considered suitable for an adult at 150 newtons (34 lbf).

Lifejackets carried on merchant ships and commercial aircraft typically consist of either a single air chamber or a pair of (twin or double) sealed air chambers constructed of coated nylon (sometimes with a protective outer encasing of heavier, tougher material such as vinyl), joined together, with a side release buckle. The twin air chambers provide for redundancy in case one of the air chambers leaks or fails to inflate. When the wearer jumps into the water – usually from a height – the automatic inflating lifejacket will inflate slowing bringing the wearer back to the water's surface. Semi-inflatable lifejackets require the wearer to manually trigger the release mechanism which then inflates the lifejacket. Most lifejackets are fitted with a plastic whistle for attracting attention and a light that is activated when in contact with water. Quality lifejackets always provide more positive buoyancy than that provided by buoyancy aids alone. The design and location of the buoyancy on the wearer's torso ensure the wearer always faces upwards with their mouth, nose, and eyes clear of the water. This offers a distinct advantage over buoyancy aids as unconscious casualties may be face down in the water putting them at risk of drowning. Drifting in open seas involves prolonged survival in water. Subsequently, lifejackets are often attached to a vest with pockets and attachment points for distress signalling and survival aids. Depending on the available time and the urgency of the situation, it is always advisable to try and load as much survival equipment into the lifejacket as possible without being overbearing. A recommended selection of LSA to carry in the lifejacket includes a radio, emergency beacon (406 MHz frequency), signal mirror, sea marker dye, smoke or light signal flares, strobe light, first aid supplies, concentrated nutritional foods, water purification supplies, shark repellent, knife, and pistol. Additional accessories such as leg straps may be utilised to keep the inflated chambers in position for floating in a stable attitude. Some lifejackets are fitted with a face shield of transparent vinyl which covers the head and face to prevent waves from inundating the face and entering the airway through the nose and mouth.

The SOLAS regulations set out the minimum quantity of lifejackets that must be carried on board each type of ship. Accordingly, for passenger ships, the following must be carried: (a) a minimum of one lifejacket for every crew member and adult passenger onboard; (b) a minimum of one lifejacket for every child passenger or 10% of the total capacity of passengers, whichever is higher.

Ordinarily, ships will carry more lifejackets than the total crew or passenger capacity to compensate for any lifejackets are lost or damaged. The SOLAS regulations also set the minimum quantity of lifejackets that must be carried on board cargo ships; accordingly: (a) a minimum of one lifejacket for every crew member (and their family members if) onboard; (b) a minimum of one lifejacket for every child family member. In addition to the quantity of lifejackets to be carried, the SOLAS regulations (amended 2010) also stipulate that each lifejacket must be fitted with a whistle secured by a lanyard. Lifejacket lights and whistles must function in a way that their simultaneous use is not hindered by each other. Each lifejacket must be fitted with a releasable buoyant line or some other means of securing it to another lifejacket when worn by another person in the water. Each lifejacket must be constructed with the means for a rescuer to lift the wearer out of the water and into a survival craft or rescue boat. Lifejackets must be able to withstand burning or melting when exposed to fire for a minimum period of two seconds. Lifejackets must be capable of being worn in only one way, or as far as is practicably possible, cannot be donned incorrectly. When jumping from a height of at least 4.5 m into water, the wearer must not sustain any injury caused by wearing the lifejacket, nor should jumping from height cause the lifejacket to dislodge. Lifejackets should have a sustainable buoyancy that is reduced by no more than 5% following submersion in freshwater for 24 hours.

An immersion suit is a type of whole-body covering that is worn specifically for remaining afloat in open water. Immersion suits are sometimes referred to as survival suits or rescue suits. It is the responsibility of the second officer to ensure regular checks are carried out on emergency lifesaving equipment including the quantity, location and function of immersion suits and thermal aids. Immersion suits are generally made from neoprene, a type of rubberised fabric that is waterproof and able to withstand extreme hot and cold temperatures. The immersion suit fits the wearer's body in such a way that no part is exposed. It also comes with a protective hood to cover the head and face and protective gloves. Immersion suits generally come in two colours – orange and red. Both colours are fluorescent so that they can be easily spotted by rescue crews. There are three types of immersion suits, each one serving a particular purpose. The first type is worn by trawlermen who operate in extreme temperatures and must keep their immersion always suits on. This ensures they are safe should they fall overboard whilst working on deck. The second type of immersion suit is mandatory under SOLAS for all ships, boats, and offshore platforms such as oil and gas rigs. The third type of immersion suit is inflatable but unlike the first two, does not fully cover the body. The inflatable parts are worn only on the hands and legs, which provides buoyancy and is much easier to carry and don in emergency situations. Some premium immersion suits are fitted with an inbuilt torch, whistle and tagline that can be connected from the suit to another person. The tagline is often called a 'Buddy Line' and is provided to ensure no one floats away and is lost from the group.

The SOLAS regulations set very strict criteria for the design and function of immersion suits. To know what type of immersion suit is available, onboarding personnel should refer to the FCP as part of their initial health and safety induction. The main provisions that SOLAS provides relating to immersion suits are every individual onboard must have their own immersion suit with extra immersion suits provided for watchkeepers on the bridge. There is no requirement for immersion suits to be insulated or wearable with a lifejacket however they must provide sufficient buoyancy. They must be made from a waterproof material and must be either international RED or ORANGE in colour. The suit should be unpacked and donned within two minutes without any extra help or assistance. The wearer must be able to jump from a minimum height of 4.5 metres (14.7 feet) into open water without sustaining any injury from or causing damage to the immersion suit. The immersion suit must be capable of covering the entire body except the face. The hands should be covered unless gloves or mitts are permanently attached. The suit must be fitted with retro-reflective tape strips. The suit must be able to withstand total envelopment in fire for a minimum period of two seconds without melting. The wearer must be able to carry out their normal duties whilst dressed in the suit and the wearer must be able to climb up and down a vertical ladder of at least five metres without being encumbered by the suit. The wearer must be able to swim a short distance in the suit. The wearer must be able to don the suit in freezing conditions, resulting in a drop of body temperature of not more than 2°C when immersed in water (between 0°C and 2°C) for a period of six hours. The wearer must be able to turn from a face-down position to a face-up position in water, with or without the aid of a lifejacket, in five seconds or less. Finally, where a lifejacket is worn with the immersion suit, the lifejacket must be worn over the suit.

Anti-exposure suits are like immersion suits though there are some distinct differences. The main features of the anti-exposure suit are they must be manufactured from non-flammable and waterproof materials. They must be made from high visibility international ORANGE. The suit should be unpacked and donned within two minutes without any extra help or assistance. The wearer must be able to jump from a minimum height of 4.5 metres (14.7 feet) into open water without sustaining any injury from or causing damage to the suit. The suit must be capable of covering the entire body except for the face and hands, unless separate separate gloves or mitts are permanent attached. The suit should be fitted with a pocket that can hold a handheld VHF radio transceiver. The suit should provide a lateral field of vision of at least 120 degrees. The suit must be able to withstand total envelopment in fire for a minimum of two seconds without melting. The wearer must be able to carry out their normal duties whilst wearing the suit. The wearer must be able to swim a minimum distance of 25 metres (82 feet) in the suit unincumbered. The suit must not allow the body temperature to drop by more than 1.5°C per hour for the first 30 minutes when the water temperature is at 5°C. The wearer must be able to turn over from a face-down position to a face-up position in water, with or without the aid of a lifejacket, in five seconds or less. Finally, where a lifejacket is worn, the lifejacket must be worn over the suit.

In addition to immersion and anti-exposure suits, some ships may carry thermal protective aids or TPAs. The main features of TPA are they must be manufactured from non-flammable and waterproof materials. They must be coloured in highly visible international ORANGE. They should have a thermal conductance of not more than 7,800 W/m 2.K. They should reduce convective and evaporative heat loss from the wearer's body. They should function in air temperatures between -30°C and +20°C. The wearer should be able to doff the TPA in water within two minutes if it impairs their ability to swim short distances. They should cover the entire body except the face, and they should be easily unpacked and donned without assistance in a survival craft or rescue boat.

The Emergency Escape Breathing Device (EEBD) is a lifesaving appliance that provides a limited supply of oxygen to the wearer that allows them to escape compartments with irrespirable atmospheres. Accommodation compartments are required to have a minimum of two EEBDs whereas engine rooms and machinery spaces depend on the size of the compartment and the number of crew members. EEBDs are strictly emergency escape devices and must never be used for firefighting or evacuating casualties. EEBDs must comply with the standards set out in the FSS Code. This includes providing a minimum of 10 minutes of oxygen, which is considered sufficient for an average-sized, able-bodied male to exit an affected compartment under medium hazard conditions. Most EEBDs are of a standard design, which includes (a) a *cylinder* consisting of approximately 600 litres of compressed air, which equates roughly to 15 minutes of breathing time. The cylinder is charged with a breathing air compressor; (b) *hood and face mask*. This component covers the wearers head and face and prevents the ingress of smoke and toxic vapours; (c) *transparent visor*. The face mask is fitted with a transparent visor that enables the wearer to see out through the mask.

The visor is usually manufactured from a heat resistant material that prevents facial burns; and (d) *pressure indicator* to inform the wearer of how much air is left in the cylinder.

Maintenance requirements for EEBDs are minimal. Regularly check the indicator needle is in the green zone. This shows whether there is any air leaking from the cylinder. Ensure the device case is clean and free from grease, oil, and other contaminants. Regularly check and record expiry dates. Most EEBD have a shelf life of 15 years. The SOLAS regulations set the standards for EEBDs. Cargo ships are required to carry a minimum of two EEBDs in accommodation areas whereas passenger ships must carry a minimum of two EEBDs in the main vertical zones. For ships with a passenger-carrying capacity of 36 or more, two additional EEBDs must be carried in each main vertical zone. An additional EEBD must be carried onboard solely for training purposes. EEBDs must be stored in clearly marked and accessible locations, together with simple diagrams or pictorial instructions.

Most ships carry a selection of emergency equipment on board in case the worst happens. One of these is the *Neil Robertson Stretcher (NRS)*. This is designed for the removal of injured persons from spaces where access, doors and hatches are too small to allow regular stretchers to be used. This includes spaces such as the engine room, cargo holds, pump rooms, boiler rooms and ballast tanks. The NRS is manufactured from semi-rigid canvas and is easily stowed when not in use or when handed down through confined spaces. The stretcher is fitted with strong straps which, when firmly wrapped around the casualty's body, provide support to hold the casualty in place. This is particularly important when handling casualties with suspected neck and spinal injuries. The straps are designed to confine the casualty in a mummy-like fashion, which prevents them from moving around or falling off the stretcher when positioned vertically.

Chapter 24

Abandoning ship

Sea survival pushes the human body to its absolute limits. In the anticipation rescue, survivors often experience near-fatal challenges such as seasickness, saltwater sores, hypothermia, constipation, dehydration, and sunburn; most of which can become fatal if left untreated. In addition to the physiological challenges, survivors often succumb to depression as the hope of rescue gradually fades. For these reasons, abandoning ship must always be the very last resort as the best lifeboat is the ship itself. Abandoning ship has as many legal implications as it does practical. For this reason, only the master can issue the command to abandon ship. If the master is incapacitated for whatever reason, the authority passes to his appointed deputy. This is important as abandoning the ship without the correct legal authority amounts to dereliction of duty and is a criminal offence. If, following an incident, the vessel is no longer able to stay afloat or becomes too dangerous to remain on board, the master will issue the order abandon ship. This order must be given verbally; first to the OOW and then as a general call to muster over the ship's PAS. On receiving the command, the OOW will issue a distress call, collect all relevant documents from the bridge, activate the EPIRB and carry the SART to the lifeboat. The master will arrange for the collection and safekeeping of all personal documentation relating to the ship's crew including passports, identity cards, Certificate of Competency's and STCW certificates. The master will also collect any funds or other valuables from the ship's safe.

It cannot be stressed enough that abandoning ship must be the very last resort after all other options have been tried and failed. Abandoning the ship and taking to the high seas in a lifeboat or life raft is a dangerous and unpleasant experience and should be avoided at reasonable costs. As mentioned above, crew members are likely to experience physical and mental conditions that make survival in a small and cramped space uncomfortable, including seasickness, hypothermia, sunburn, saltwater burns, infections, constipation, and dehydration. The most consequence of being adrift in a lifeboat or life raft is seasickness. This is caused by the relentless rocking and unsteadiness of the craft. Treating crew members suffering from seasickness can be especially hard on the person providing the treatment. It becomes progressively easier to succumb to the influence of the patient. To counteract this, it is advisable to place the patient in a horizontal position. Remove any vomit or other bodily fluids from the craft as quickly as possible and if safe, allow fresh air to circulate. Restrict food and reduce water intake to a minimum. Ensure the patient is given seasick tablets. If possible, allow the patient to focus on the horizon. This should help alleviate some of the motion disparity that causes seasickness. Wind chill is a hazard faced by survivors everywhere, but particularly so in colder regions. When cold wind contacts exposed skin, a wind-chill effect is created. By combining the wind speed and air temperature, the wind-chill factor can be calculated. Cold temperatures weaken the senses and reduce the body's ability to think and adapt quickly. When the body temperature drops dangerously low, it quickly begins to shut down by reducing the blood flow to the extremities. Eventually the

304   DOI: 10.1201/9781003244615-29

heart stops leading to unconsciousness, and death. Hypothermia can be avoided by keeping dry and warm, and avoiding water immersion.

Direct sunlight can cause sunburn, which is a painful condition that can lead to long term illnesses such as skin cancer. Sunburn is not caused by the heat of the sun, but rather by the sun's rays. This means exposed skin in the polar regions and along the equator are both just as likely to suffer the effects of sunburn. To avoid sunburn always try and keep out of direct sunlight. Stay within the shaded or covered areas of the survival craft and cover up any bare skin such as the face, top of the head and crown, back of the neck, feet, and hands. Try to avoid sea glare and regularly apply sun creams or balms from the first aid kit. Saltwater burns are caused when broken skin is exposed to saltwater. This causes painful sores to develop. It is important to leave these alone. Clean the sore with fresh water (if available) and apply regularly antiseptic cream. Try to avoid picking and scratching the sore as this may lead to infections. It is very easy to contract eye infections in lifeboats and life rafts. Dust, smoke, and other particles can get trapped between the eyelid and the eyeball. If foreign objects do get caught around the eye, apply an eye ointment, and bandage the affected eye. Avoid looking at the water and sun. It is advisable, if possible, to wear sunglasses to avoid glare. Dehydration and constipation are among the most common problems associated with sea survival. Treating constipation usually means ingesting more water to loosen the bowels. This aids the passage of stools from the body. Unfortunately, stranding at sea makes fresh potable water a premium resource. This will likely exacerbate dehydration leading to constipation. Even so, it is important never to drink seawater. Many good survival guides suggest ways of distilling potable water from condensation and rain.

The lifeboat is an extremely important component of LSA. It is used only in the most extreme emergencies. Lifeboats are small rigid boats that are secured on deck and lowered using davits. By law, the construction, size, and utility of lifeboats must comply with the SOLAS regulations. This includes the rations, potable water, first aid equipment, compass, and distress signalling equipment such as radios and distress rockets that must be carried on board the lifeboat. The SOLAS regulations mandate that any ship of 20,000 GT or more must be capable of launching a lifeboat when the ship is making way at a speed of five knots. The hoisting time for the boat launching arrangement should not be less than 0.3 m per second with the lifeboat loaded to its full capacity.

There are three types of lifeboats carried on merchant ships: open, closed, and freefall lifeboats (1) *Open Lifeboats*. As the name suggests, the open lifeboat has no roof and is normally manually propelled using handheld ores. A compression ignition engine may be installed. It is unusual to find open lifeboats on modern ships though many older ships still carry them. Open lifeboats provide no protection against the elements or high waves which makes them susceptible to swamping; (2) *Closed Lifeboats*. Closed lifeboats are more commonly found on passenger ships. Closed lifeboats are fully enclosed which provides protection against rain, strong winds, and rough weather. Watertight integrity is vastly improved, and the lifeboat can upright itself should it capsize in high waves; and (3) *Freefall Lifeboats*. Freefall lifeboats are virtually the same as closed lifeboats; the only difference being in the manner of launch. Whereas closed lifeboats are lowered by the sideboard of the vessel, freefall lifeboats sit atop a frame arrangement overlooking the far stern. When the launch is initiated, the lifeboat freefalls directly into the water below.

Open and closed type lifeboats are stowed in metal cradle arrangement and kept in place by ropes called *gripes*. The lifeboat is lowered and raised from its cradle using wires called falls. The descent of the lifeboat is regulated by centrifugal brakes. To maintain the stability of the lifeboat even when the ship is tilted at an angle of 15°, a series of gravity davits are used which slide down with the lifeboat. Lifeboats must be painted in international orange with the ship's call sign clearly legible on the sideboard. The lifeboat station must be easily accessible for all crew members. Safety awareness posters and launching procedures are usually posted around the lifeboat station. Different manufacturers use different launching arrangements for their lifeboats. Whilst the specific details may differ from one arrangement to the next, all lifeboats must follow a broadly universal launching sequence. There are three such launch sequences: offload, onload and freefall. Onload and offload systems are like each other in that the mechanisms release the boat from the davit, which is attached to a wire or fall by means of a hook. By releasing the hook, the lifeboat can be set free to propel away from the ship. The offload mechanism releases the lifeboat after the load of the boat is fully waterborne. The release is made via a hydrostatic piston unit at the bottom of the craft. The piston is connected to the operating lever via a link. As the craft touches the water, the water pressure pushes the hydrostatic piston up. The piston continues upwards, pushing the lever and operating the hook arrangement which releases the fall wire. A safety pin arrangement is provided near the clutch, which disables the offload release (in case of rough weather or hydrostatic piston malfunction). This allows the helmsman to perform an onload release. The onload mechanism can release the lifeboat from the wire, with the boat above the water level and with all the crew members inside the craft. The load is still in the fall as the boat has not yet touched water. Normally the onload release is operated when the boat is about to touch water so that the fall is smooth without damaging the boat and injuring the crew. A lever is provided inside the craft to operate this mechanism. As the lever is operated from inside the craft, it is safe to free the boat without being positioned outside the craft. This is particularly useful when the ship is on fire. With a freefall lifeboat, the launching mechanism is like the onload release. The only difference is that the freefall lifeboat is not lowered till one metre above water level, where it is then launched from the stowed position by operating a lever located inside the craft. This lever releases the boat from the davit. The boat slides down the tilted ramp and direct into the water.

The size, quantity, and capacity of lifeboats carried on merchant ships are dictated by the type of ship and number of ship's crew. Ordinarily, lifeboats should not be less than 7.3 m in length and at least lifeboat should be carried on both sides of the ship (i.e., port and starboard). Ships must carry one rescue boat for MOB rescue operations. Where the ship has more than one lifeboat onboard, one lifeboat may be designated as the rescue boat. A few basic checks carried out during routine inspections can identify potential defects and avoid added stress and confusion during a ship abandonment. Listen to the sound the engine makes when it is turned on. Check to see if it is making familiar running noises. If irregular noises or sounds are coming from the engine, a simple diagnostic test can be carried out using a standard long-handled screwdriver. Place one end of the screwdriver to the ear and the other end where the abnormal sound is coming from. This will help pinpoint the general location of the sound. Carry out visual checks for rust, oil leaks, and kinks in the fuel lines, chaffed hoses, paint discolouration in heat areas, distorted electrical cables, or damaged cable junctions and housing.

It is an unfortunate reality that even the best-maintained lifeboat engines can fail at the most inopportune moments. Engine failures can be caused by any number of reasons from the smallest to most catastrophic including empty fuel tank, incorrectly attached fuel hose, damaged fuel supply hose, defective fuel pump, contaminated fuel, improper starting procedures, faulty, spoiled, or incorrect positioning of spark plugs, deactivated emergency shut off valve, undercharged starter battery, loose electrical connections, bad ignition coil, and defective starter motor.

Life rafts are easier to launch compared to lifeboats and in case of emergency situations, evacuation from the ship can be done without manually launching them as the life raft is designed with an auto-inflatable system. SOLAS chapter III provides details for the quantity of life rafts to be carried as per the size and type of ship. Life rafts are normally located at the muster station on the port and starboard sides, often close to the lifeboat station, and always forward and aft of the ship. The location generally depends on the size of the ship. Life rafts are stowed on deck in fibreglass containers. Inside the container is a high-pressure gas canister that inflates the life raft when deployed. A Hydrostatic Release Unit (HRU) connects the life raft to the ship. The HRU automatically releases the raft when immersed in water. The container has important markings which include the manufacturer's name and trademark, the unit's serial number, the name of the inspection authority, the number of persons the life raft can carry, the date of last service, the length of the painter line, maximum stowage height and launching instructions. A SOLAS emergency pack is also enclosed.

All life rafts onboard ships are stowed with its painter line permanently attached to the ship. Each life raft or group of life rafts should be stowed in a float-free arrangement that enables each raft to float free of the vessel. If it is an inflatable raft, it should inflate automatically when immersed in water. Davit-launched life rafts are stowed within reach of the lifting hooks. The process for launching davit operated life rafts is as follows:

Remove the ship's handrail
  Remove the lashings from the canister
  Lower the davit and lock it with the lifting shackle
  Secure the canister lines outboard
  Secure the bowsing line
  Pull the painter out approximately 5–6 m
  Secure the painter line
  Pull the painter line to its full length
  Lift the canister
  Pull the painter line sharply and let the raft inflate
  After inflation, secure the life raft
  One person climb-in and check the condition and integrity of the life raft
  Enter the life raft and position equally to maintain balance
  Release the bowsing line and pass to the raft
  Check the launching area is clear
  Lower the raft using the brake release
  Operate the hook release one metre above the water line or allow the raft to ride a wave
crest
  Put the load on the water and allow to release automatically
Cut the painter and clear away

Life rafts intended to be thrown overboard are stowed to be readily transferable for launching on either side of the ship. The procedures for launching the free-throw life raft are as follows:

Remove the painter line
  Fasten it to the ship side at a strong point
  Remove the railing and check overboard for any obstructions
  Unfasten the hook from the cradle
  Lift the life raft over the sideboard and into the water

308 Maritime emergencies

> Give the painter line a short sharp tug to inflate the life raft
> If the life raft inflates upside down, the raft has a strap that can be used to right it
> Using the painter line, pull the life raft towards the ships' side
> Lower the embarkation ladder or jump directly onto the life raft if safe to do so
> Cut the painter line using a sharp implement clear away

If the ship is sinking and there is insufficient time to operate the davit or throw the life raft overboard as described above, the third option is to wait for the vessel to sink to a depth of four metres. This automatically triggers the HRU. A pressure-sensitive sharp point will cut the straps around the canister releasing them into the open water. As the ship sinks further, the painter line will stretch, inflating the life raft. Due to the increase in buoyant pressure, the painter line will break at around 2.2 kN +/−0.4 leaving the raft to float back to the surface. As per SOLAS regulations, life rafts are kitted out with lifesaving equipment, emergency first aid kits and sea survival items. These typically include rescue quoits with a minimum 30 m attached line; non-folding knife with a buoyant handle; bailer; sponges; buoyant paddles; tin openers; sea anchors; scissors; waterproof first-aid kit; whistle; waterproof torch for communicating Morse Code with spare bulbs and batteries; signalling mirror or heliograph; radar reflector; waterproof lifesaving signals card; fishing tackle; anti-seasickness medicine sufficient for at least 48 hours and one sickbag for each person; instructions on how to survive (Survival Booklet); instructions on immediate actions to be taken on abandoning ship; six handheld flares; four rocket parachute flares; and two buoyant smoke signals. In addition, it is recommended that sufficient food is brought on board (10,000 kJ per adult is the recommended amount); and 1.5 litres of potable water per adult.

As per SOLAS regulations, life rafts must have minimum space for at least six adults. Furthermore, life rafts should be capable of withstanding exposure for 30 days afloat in all sea conditions. When dropped into the water from a height of 18 m, the life raft and all the equipment on board should remain fully operational. The life raft should be capable of withstanding repeated jumps onto it from a height of at least 4.5 m above its floor, with and without the canopy erected. The life raft should be able to withstand towage at three knots with its full equipment, complement of persons, and one anchor streaming. The canopy must provide insulation and protection against heat and cold with two layers of material separated by an air gap. The interior of the life raft must not cause unnecessary discomfort to the occupants. The life raft must admit sufficient air for the occupants, even with the entrance is closed. The life raft must be provided with at least one viewing port. The life raft must be provided with a means of collecting rainwater. The life raft must be provided with a means to mount a SART unit at a height of at least one metre above sea level. The life raft should have sufficient headroom for the sitting occupants under all parts of the canopy. The maximum weight of the container, as well as the equipment inside, should not exceed 185kgs. The life raft should be fitted with a sufficiently long painter with a length equal to a minimum of 10m plus the distance from the stowed position to the waterline in the lightest seagoing condition or 15m, whichever is greater. A manually controlled lamp should be fitted on the top of the canopy; this light must be white, and it must operate for at least 12 hours with a luminous intensity of not less than 4.3 candela. If a flashlight is fitted, it should flash at a rate of not less than 50 flashes and not more than 70 flashes per minute for a minimum period of 12 hours. A manually controlled lamp must be fitted inside the life raft, capable of continuous operation for a period of at least 12 hours. When the life raft is loaded with a full complement of occupants and equipment, it should be capable of withstanding a lateral impact against the ship side at a velocity of not less than 3.5 m per second and drop into the water from a height of not less than three metres without sustaining damage. In accordance with SOLAS, all life rafts must be serviced at intervals not exceeding 12 months. If necessary, Class may extend this to 17 months in exceptional circumstances. Davit-launched life raft automatic release hooks should be maintained in accordance with the PMS.

Beaching a lifeboat in good weather is doable, although tricky, but when it is to be done in bad and inclement weather, it is positively a nightmare. A boat can easily topple over on its broad side when approaching dangerous breakers and surfs near the shore if not handled properly. Once a landing point has been chosen, take time to adjust to the situation. Landing onto the leeward side of the mainland or an island, or on a point projecting out into water is more favourable than crashing in from the windward side. Avoid the glare of the sun as far as possible to prevent being baffled when finding the correct landing spot. Choosing a sandy beach for landing is strongly advised. If possible, avoid beaching at night. Watch out for rip currents or tides as they may carry the lifeboat further out or into danger. Look for openings in the surf lines, and head for them. A good lookout is important for corals or rocks protruding out from the shallows. Use the lifeboat's engine to close in, to a position that is comfortable for manoeuvring – this will usually be a point where the swell breaks or a position from where the breakers rise. Turn the boat round to face the sea with the boat's stern towards the shore. Stream the sea anchor along with the tripping line attached to it. This will help to hold the bow into the sea and swell. Secure the rudder to any side and use the boat oars to steer ashore. The moment breakers hit the bow of the boat, the person handling the sea anchor should trip the line whilst at the same time, the boat should be oared astern. The person at the bow should watch for the next wave and release the tripping line to have the lifeboat stemming the sea. Take the oars out of the water. This will take the boat astern slowly and safely while keeping the bow offshore. Once the boat hits shallow ground, alight the lifeboat and pull it all the way in. Where there are breakers flowing rapidly, it will not be possible to outrun them, therefore it will be necessary to lifeboat aground simply by using the engines. Heaving onto the sea when heading inshore might lead the boat to lose its steerage way causing the boat to broadside the sea or swell and keel over. If the lifeboat capsizes, take care to swim clear of the boat as soon as possible to avoid being trapped underneath.

Index

abandonment 26, 266, 306
abandon ship 41–43, 48, 146, 266–267, 269, 247, 304, 308
Able Seaman 12, 20, 98
admiralty 3, 72, 191, 202
advanced firefighting 13
aft perpendicular 136–137
air compressor 23, 40, 108–111, 113, 163, 281, 302
AIS-SART 96, 295
Aker Finnyards 55
Alzheimer 32
Anchor Handling Tug 97
anchoring 22, 156–158, 162, 169, 189, 196
Anchor Winch 158
APL Austria 227
Argentina 3
Articles of War 3
asbestos 40, 230
as low as reasonably possible 36, 255
Associated Steamships Pty. Ltd 50
asylum seeker 19, 210–211
Australia 50, 256
Autocarrier 49, 50
automatic identification system SART 295; *see also* AIS-SART
Automatic Radar Plotting Aids (ARPA) 21, 189, 204, 268
average freight rate assessment (AFRA), Aframax 6

ballast tank 25, 85, 90, 93–95, 100, 146, 147, 149, 193, 199, 200, 303
Bay: Algoa of 43; Calabar of 196; class 52; container 21, 54, 86, 87, 248, 249, 251, 252, 254, 256, 258; sick 97, 98, 193; stowage 52; water 41
benzene 40
Bernoulli's Equation 84, 100
bilge/bilges 25, 35, 82, 114, 130, 135, 146, 174, 179, 181, 253, 278; alarm 29, 114, 193; drain 117; pump 180, 278; strake 82; suction pumps 95; water 113; wells 181; water tanks 95, 180

Bill of Lading (B/L) 25, 219–222, 225, 244, 246
Birkenhead Drill 43
blackout 33, 45, 46, 93, 120, 124, 131, 174, 175, 177, 182, 268
boiler 23, 39, 40, 45, 46, 107, 120, 121, 124, 126, 128, 129, 149, 168, 173, 174, 181, 182, 184, 186, 268, 273, 282, 286, 287, 303; blowdown 173, 174; suit 30, 39
bosun 8, 22, 23, 42, 43, 86, 197
breathing apparatus 13, 30, 35, 36, 44, 48, 275; Self-Contained Breathing Apparatus 42
bridge 8, 9, 20, 21, 23, 26, 29, 32, 33, 37, 38, 42–44, 60, 66, 86, 88, 92, 93, 96–99, 101, 106, 107, 112, 117, 132, 146, 155, 157, 158, 163, 164, 166, 181, 187–191, 196–198, 200, 201, 205–207, 234, 247, 251, 252, 259, 266–269, 274, 276, 284, 293, 295, 296, 301, 304; communications 293; flying 96; management practices 190, 202; resource management 200; team 87, 200, 202, 203; watchkeeping 7; wings 34, 96, 99, 100, 187, 191
bulbous bow 84, 85, 100, 158
bulk carrier 4, 6, 9, 33, 36, 50, 52, 53, 56, 57, 64, 78, 79, 82, 85, 88, 91
bulkhead 41, 53, 79, 81, 83, 89–92, 95, 113, 135, 283, 287; aft peak 94; Class A 91; Class B 91; Class C 91; collision 94, 193; fire class 91; watertight 29, 33, 92
bunker 65, 94, 123, 147, 168–172, 183; bunkering 23, 58, 94, 168–172; bunkering crew 171, 172; bunkering plan 171; bunkering station 171; bunker training 46; bunkerage 59
buoyancy 22, 86, 134–139, 141–145, 147, 258, 271, 300, 301; aids 30, 300; centre of 137; low coefficient 82; reserve 271
buttress system 54, 55

312 Index

cabotage 16, 17
Cape Horn 6
Cape of Good Hope 6
car carrier 4, 51, 55, 56, 146; Pure 60, 146; Pure Car and Truck 60
cargo: care of 22, 252; securing manual 71, 254, 257; stowage 19, 22, 53, 63, 70, 71, 82, 90, 193, 252, 260
Casualty Investigation Code 63, 69, 70
cell guides 54, 55, 79, 87, 247, 248
centre of floatation 136, 138
centre of gravity (CG) 85, 88, 134–138, 143–148, 193, 247, 250, 271
Certificate of Competency (CoC) 10–16, 20, 22, 23, 304
Certificate of Equivalent Competency (CEC) 12, 16
chemical exposure 39
Chief cook 8, 24, 42
chief engineer 7, 19, 23, 24, 26, 37, 42, 44, 46, 47, 97, 99, 115, 117, 120, 166–168, 170–172, 175, 179, 181, 184, 185, 197, 234, 273, 278
chief officer 7, 8, 11–13, 15, 16, 19–23, 41, 42, 44, 47, 93, 99, 146, 147, 155, 160, 197, 200, 206, 225, 247, 250–252, 256–258, 273, 274
citadel 97, 98, 213, 214
City of Glasgow College 11
classification rules 74, 150
classification society 62, 74, 75, 80, 81, 89, 90, 135, 149, 150, 243, 283
CMA CGA 56, 57, 60
Code of Conduct for the Merchant Navy 8, 63
Code of Safe Practice for Cargo Stowage and Securing 63, 70, 71
Code of Safe Working Practices for Merchant Mariners (COSWP) 28, 29, 63, 156
cofferdam 35, 93–95, 100, 116
confined spaces 35–37, 45, 161, 303; enclosed spaces i, 91, 255
CONRO 55, 60
containerisation 49–51, 54, 225, 235
container seals 244–246
contract of carriage 212, 219, 221–223
control air system 110, 111, 163, 166
control unit (CU) 114, 241, 242
corona laurèa 18
corona navalis 18, 25
corrosives 230
crankcase 35, 105, 115, 117, 166, 178; explosion 46, 178, 280

Daewoo Shipbuilding 56
dangerous goods 21, 22, 39, 62, 72, 227–233, 247, 253, 276; classes of 228, 230; *Document of Compliance with the Special Requirements for Ships Carrying Dangerous Goods* 250;

International Maritime Code for the Storage and Transportation of Dangerous Goods (IMCSTDG) 64; *International Maritime Dangerous Goods Code* (IMDG) 62, 71; list 227; *Supplement to the International Maritime Dangerous Goods Code* 39; *UN Committee of Experts on the Transport of Dangerous Goods* 228
deck department 7, 18–20, 22–24, 26, 157, 162, 197, 257
dementia 32
Dengue Fever 41
Denmark 4, 60
designated person (DP) 27, 28, 68
Det Norske Veritas (DNV) 75, 150
Digital Selective Calling (DSC) 20, 195, 292, 293, 295
discontinuity 81, 84, 85, 109, 176
disease 41; cardio-vascular 38; communicative 211; contagious 40; epidemic 38; infectious 230; sexually transmitted 38
Document of Compliance (DOC) 68, 247, 250
double bottom 80–82, 89, 93, 116; hull 53, 81, 82, 89; tanks 93, 95
double door container 242
drug trafficking 209, 214
drydock 147, 174, 184, 272
dry ice 230, 239

Ebola 41
Edward VIII 4; Prince of Wales 3
Egypt 6
Electronic Chart Display and Information System (ECDIS) 14, 25, 99, 170, 189, 198, 203, 204, 205
electro-technical: department 7; officer 8, 24, 25
Emergency Escape Breathing Device (EEBD) 302, 303
Emergency Position-Indicating Radio Beacon (EPIRB) 20, 42, 195, 293–295, 297, 304
emergency response team 21, 42
engine room 7, 23, 24, 32–34, 39, 43, 45, 53, 81, 94, 95, 98, 99, 101, 105–107, 109, 111, 114, 159, 160, 171, 175, 180, 187, 188, 190, 191, 193, 197, 234, 258, 268, 273, 274, 278, 279, 284–287, 302, 303; alarm 266; Bilges 174; drains 122, 123; fire 40, 45, 111, 113, 281, 282; machinery 8, 24, 121, 167, 183; operations 163, 165; pumps 129–131; Sounding Log 168; team 42, 162, 280, 282; watch 24; unmanned 33, 124; ventilation 29
engineer on watch (EOW) 533
European Highway 56
Evergreen Marine Corp. (Taiwan) Ltd 56, 60, 254
exhaust gas boiler (EGB) 107

Index 313

Exhaust Gas-Piping System 107
explosives 65, 95; classification of 71, 228, 230

Falkland Islands 3
fatigue 31, 32, 35, 89, 102, 160, 198, 201
Fire Control Plan (FCP) 42, 283–285, 299, 301;
prevention and firefighting 13, 21, 163
first aid 21, 24, 29, 42, 97, 300, 305; elementary
13, 15; kit 214, 305, 308; medical
13, 15; Medical First Aid Course 14;
Medical First Aid Guide 228
First Line Management 'Leadership and
Management' (L&M) certificate 12
first officer, 1/O, first mate 7, 19, 225
flag of convenience 4, 57, 73
Flag State 18, 19, 27, 29, 30, 41, 42, 57, 61,
67–70, 73, 74, 135, 179, 210; authority
62, 73–75, 188, 189, 214
Flame Detectors 282
flammable liquids 182, 228, 230
flammable solids 230
flat rack container 236, 237, 242
Fleetwood Maritime Academy 11
flooding; CO_2 flooding system 42, 109, 275,
278; down flooding angle 140, 147;
drill 45; seawater 21, 45, 80, 89, 92,
135, 136, 141, 145, 147, 156, 157, 163,
193, 270, 271
Formal Safety Assessment 27
Forty-foot equivalent unit: 40FT / FEU 5, 54,
60, 236, 243, 249
forward perpendicular 89, 136, 141
foundation degree 11
fourth engineer 8, 23, 24, 197
free surface effect 33, 94, 135, 147, 193, 270, 271

galley 9, 21, 24, 32, 33, 42, 43, 60, 91
geared: ship 51, 53, 56, 60
general alarm 266–268
Global Maritime Distress and Safety System 8,
13, 15, 17, 20, 26, 63, 146, 188, 195,
204–206, 291–293, 295; endorsement
certificate 292; frequencies 292;
General Operator Course 292
Greece 4
Guinea 41, 212

Hague–Visby Rules 219, 220
half height container 242
Hamburg Express Class 7
Hamburg Index 58
Hamburg Shipbrokers' Association 58
Hapag-Lloyd 7, 56, 60
hatch coaming 54, 89
Health and Safety Executive 35
heat detectors 282, 283
heat exhaustion 34
heat stroke 34
heave 136

Human Element and Leadership and
Management (HELM) 12–14
Higher National Certificate 11
Higher National Diploma 10, 11
high prismatic coefficient 82
High sulphur fuel oil (HFSO) 95, 101, 133,
183, 184
HMM Algeciras 56, 57, 253
HMS Birkenhead 43
Höegh Autoliners 56
hotspots 280
hydrostatic load 79
hydrostatic pressure 80, 90, 92
Hydrostatic Release Unit 307
hypothermia 30, 34, 35, 267, 268, 304, 305;
mild 267; moderate 267; profound 268
Hyundai Merchant Marine 56

Ideal X 50
inert gas (IG) 36, 94, 238
infectious substances 230
INMARSAT 20, 195, 291–294
intercostal girders 80–82
Inter-Governmental Maritime Consultative
Organisation (IMCO) 61
Intermediate Bulk Shift Containers 242
intermediate shaft 101, 102
International Air Pollution Prevention (IAPP) 75
International Association of Classification
Societies (IACS) 75
International Code of Signals (ICS) 20
International Convention for the Unification of
Certain Rules of Law relating to Bills
of Lading 219
International Convention on Standards
of Training, Certification and
Watchkeeping for Seafarers 1978
(STCW) 7, 10–16, 24, 28, 31, 47, 63,
74, 75, 304
International Fire Safety System Code (FSSC) 63
International Life Saving Appliances Code 63
International Maritime Organisation (IMO) 61, 62
International Prevention of Pollution from Ships
(MARPOL) 39, 46, 61–64, 69, 74, 113,
114, 125, 126, 128, 129, 181, 183,
227, 229
International Regulations for Preventing
Collisions at Sea (COLREG) 21, 62,
72, 73, 188, 191, 205–207, 296–298
International Safety Management Code (ISM
Code) 27, 62, 64, 67
International Sewage Pollution Prevention
(ISPP) 75
International Ship and Port Facility Security
Code (ISPS) 18, 61, 62, 64–67, 209,
210, 252, 258
International Standardisation Organisation
(ISO) 5
Isherwood system 79

314 Index

James Brindley 49–51
Japan 4, 50, 57, 59, 60, 105, 253
John Moore University 11

keel 5, 9, 20, 35, 53, 55, 79–84, 86, 88, 94, 100,
    135–138, 141, 145, 146, 184, 203, 251,
    258, 309
K Line 55

laurus 18, 25
length: between perpendiculars 136; Length of
    Waterline 136; Length overall (LOA)
    5, 6, 136
lifeboat 24, 26, 41, 43, 91, 147, 274, 296, 299,
    304–307, 309
lifejackets 30, 43, 44, 267, 299–301
lifesaving appliances (LSA) 20, 26, 42, 63, 266,
    296, 299, 300, 305
light tonne displacement (LTD) 57
liner sector 4
liquefied natural gas (LNG) 4, 171
liquefied petroleum gas (LPG) 4, 62
Lloyds of London 4
load line 151, 152, 202; calculations 62, 149,
    150; convention 150; mark 150, 151
Local User Terminal (LUT) 294
longitudinal stiffening 79
lookout 20, 22, 23, 39, 98, 99, 187, 188, 194,
    197, 198, 200, 206, 207, 309
lube oil 29, 32, 95, 102, 103, 113, 115, 116,
    241, 269, 281; filter 104; pump 121,
    178; samples 166; tank 95, 111

Maersk: Line 56, 60, 285; Kensington 285;
    Triple E 51, 88, 105
magister navis 18
malaria 41
Man overboard (MOB) 19, 33, 38, 39, 267, 268,
    297, 306; alarm 266
manually handling 38
Maritime Accident Investigation Branch
    (MAIB) 160
Maritime and Coastguard Agency (MCA) 11,
    12, 14–16, 73, 74
Maritime Labour Convention (MLC) 29,
    31, 107
maritime safety information (MSI) 191, 195,
    206, 291–293
Maritime Security (MARSEC) 18, 61, 64–66,
    68, 214
mass displacement 136
McIlwraith, McEarchen & Co 50
McLean, Malcom 49, 235
McLean Trucking Co 49
Mediterranean Shipping Company 56
medium frequency (MF) 195, 269, 292, 293
Merchant Marine Act of 1920, Jones Act 16
Merchant Navy Training Board (MNTB) 11, 14
Merchant Shipping Act 1995 42

mess 9, 32, 43, 60, 97, 100
metacentre 134–139, 141, 142, 144, 145, 148,
    247, 250
metacentric height 135–139, 142, 144–148, 247,
    250, 271
metacentric radius 136, 138, 139
Mission Rescue Coordination Centre (MRCC)
    294, 277
MOL Triumph 56, 57
moment to change trim 136, 140
monkey island 96
mooring 26, 143, 145, 155–157, 162, 169,
    193, 198; area 155; lines 20, 22,
    33, 155, 156, 198; station 156, 199;
    winch 157
mosquitoes 41
motorman 24, 197
MSC Chitra 269, 270
MS Color Magic 55
MS Estonia 148
musculoskeletal disorder 38
muster: card 41, 42; list 33, 41–43, 266
MV: *CSCL Pusan* 54; *Kanimbia* 50; *Khalija*
    269, 270; *Kooringa* 50; *Manoora* 50;
    Torrey Canyon 62; *Tricolor* 271

NAEST: management 13, 14; operational 13, 14
Navigational Alarm 266
NAVTEX 20, 99, 195, 291–293
New ConTex Index 58
Night Orders 26, 187, 188, 206
Norway 4

Ocean Network Express 56
officer cadet (OC) 8, 10–12, 15, 21, 292
Officer of the Watch (OOW) 11–16, 20–22, 28,
    33, 44, 47, 51, 86, 96, 98–100, 106,
    120, 174, 187–191, 194, 196, 198,
    200–208, 234, 251, 252, 257, 258,
    266–269, 271, 274, 304
Oil Content Monitor (OCM) 113
oiler 24, 278
oil spill 39, 46, 171, 269
oil tanker 5, 9, 10, 62, 82, 269
oily water separator (OWS) 46, 113–115,
    180, 234
openside storage containers 242
open top containers 242
Ordinary Seaman 23, 24
Organic Peroxides 229, 230
orlop deck 96
outer bottom longitudinals 82
Overseas Collaborative Programme 12
oxidising agent 230
oxygen 35, 36, 45, 94, 108, 113, 160, 161,
    165, 230, 239, 267, 281, 285–290,
    302; content 94, 128, 255; cylinder
    161; deficiency 36, 255; depletion 36;
    poisoning 36

Index 315

Pan American Steamship Company 50
Panama 6, 25, 57, 58
Panama Canal 6, 51; Panama Canal
    Authority 51
Panamax 6, 51, 52; Post-Panamax 52
parametric rolling 86, 87, 252
passage planning 64, 188, 190, 202
permit to work (PTW) 36, 37, 39, 161
personal protective equipment (PPE) 28, 29, 36,
    48, 254, 255, 288
Personal Safety and Social Responsibilities
    13, 15
Personal Survival Techniques 13, 15
Phase Changing Material 239
Pierre Bouguer 134, 152
pilot 98, 187, 196–198, 234, 252, 259, 270;
    pilotage 75, 93, 198, 203, 293; pilot
    book 202; pilot flag 198; pilot ladder
    14, 197, 299
piracy 25, 65, 98, 196, 209, 212, 213
pitch 85, 86, 132, 133, 135, 136, 148, 158
Plymouth University 11
Polar Code 63, 64
poop deck 96, 97
Port Facility Security Officer (PFSO) 67
Port Facility Security Plan (PFSP) 67
Port of: Alameda 54; Klang 54; Newark 50
Port State Control 41, 43, 46, 62, 74, 204, 234,
    273; authorities 61, 74
Potter's Rot 40; tuberculosis 40
proficiency in: security awareness 13; Survival
    Craft and Rescue Boats 13–15
promenade deck 96
propeller 33, 84, 93, 98, 101–105, 131–133,
    163, 184, 214; clearance 164; shaft 53,
    83, 101–104
Provision and Use of Work Equipment
    Regulations (PUWER) 17
public address system 33, 37, 48
Puppis 96
Pure Car and Truck Carrier 365
Pure Car Carrier 365
purifier 45, 116, 120, 121, 123, 178, 179, 268,
    281; room 281; sludge tank 178, 179

Qatar 6
Queen: Elizabeth 99; Elizabeth II 4; Mary 99

radar 21, 25, 73, 96, 99, 100, 188, 189–191,
    194, 196, 201, 204, 207, 208, 268,
    293, 295; antenna 207, 295; frequency
    295; screen 207, 295; reflector 308
radioactive material 230
rating 8, 12, 22–24, 27, 156–158, 186, 197
Red Ensign 4
reefer container 39, 237, 240, 250, 253,
    254, 257
rescue craft 295, 299
research vessel 7

respiratory protective equipment 37, 48
risk assessment 36, 45, 161
RMS Titanic 43, 100, 291
Roll-On Roll-Off (RORO) 5, 33, 50, 51, 55,
    59, 233
ROPAX 55
row 50, 54, 248, 249, 251
Royal Fleet Auxiliary 3
Royal Navy 3, 7, 12, 61, 97, 201, 271;
    *Navigational Watch Keeping Officers
    Course* 12; *Senior Ratings' Command
    Course* 12

safety: committee 27, 28; Management
    Certificate (SMC) 68, 69, 75;
    Management Plan (SMP) 27;
    Management System (SMS) 26–29, 36,
    68, 69, 193; officer,
Safety and Environmental Policy 27
Safety of Life at Sea (SOLAS) 18, 28, 29, 35, 40,
    41, 55, 61–64, 67–71, 73, 74, 81, 89–
    91, 92, 96, 99, 109, 111, 131, 135, 148,
    149, 163, 184, 189, 190, 195, 202–205,
    207, 227, 252, 267, 270, 283–287, 291,
    293, 296, 297, 299–301, 303, 305–309
safe weight limit (SWL) 39, 158, 159, 243, 297
Samsung Heavy Industries 56
Search and Rescue Transponder (SART) 20, 42,
    63, 195, 292, 293, 295, 304, 308
scavenge fire 45, 282
Scottish Professional Diploma (SPD) 11
Search and Rescue (SAR) 13, 20, 61, 293, 295
secondary explosion 178, 280
second engineer 7, 23, 42, 44, 197
second officer 7, 20, 41, 44, 155, 197, 202, 273,
    299, 301
Shipboard Oil Pollution Emergency Plan
    (SOPEP) 171
Ship Safety Manual (SSM) 366
Ship Safety Officer (SSO) 28
Ship Security Alert System (SSAS) 195
ship security and intruder alarm 266, 267
Ship Security Officer 19, 65
ship security plan (SSP) 18, 19, 26, 65
sickbay 97, 98
silicosis 40
slips, trips, and falls 38, 39, 251, 265, 272
Solent University 11
South Tyneside College 11
special purpose container 242
stagnation point 84
Standing Orders 187, 188, 196, 205
starter airline fires 281
Starvationer 49
Steward 8, 24: department 7, 8, 24, 42
Storage Roll Container 242
stowaway 209–211
strake 81–83, 90
Suez Canal 6

316 Index

suitably qualified and experienced person
(SQEP) 24
surge 125, 136, 178, 198, 282
swap bodies 232
swinging circle 196
Switzerland 4, 60, 227

tail shaft 101–103, 184
tennis elbow 37
thermal protective aids 268, 302
third engineer 3/E 7, 23, 197
third officer 3/O 7, 11, 20, 23, 42, 47, 155, 197
thrusters 99, 131–133, 157, 187, 198, 199, 275
thrust shaft 101–103
tier 54, 55, 108, 155, 248, 249, 253
torsion box 83, 84
Toyota Maru No.10 56
tramp sector 4
Trans-Siberian Railroad 59
transverse stiffening 79
twenty-foot equivalent unit 20ft/TEU 5, 52–54,
56–60, 235, 236, 249, 253, 277, 285

UK Border Agency 7
Ultra Large Crude Carrier (ULCC) 6
UN Classification Numbers 228
unique identifier number (UIN) 294
United Kingdom (UK) 3, 7, 10–12, 14–17, 19,
24, 29, 30, 35, 61, 72–74, 105, 150,
160, 221, 238, 253, 267
United Nations 227, 366
United Nations Conference on Trade and
Development (UNCTAD) 4, 53, 58

United Nations Convention on the Law of the
Sea (UNCLOS) 69
unmanned machinery space (UMS) 32, 33, 50,
163, 175, 234
upper bridge 96
upper deck 96, 97, 131
uptake fire 46

very high frequency (VHF) 195–198, 206, 268,
269, 273, 291–295, 302
Vessel Traffic Information Management System
(VTIMS) 270
Volkswagen AG 55
Voyage Data Recorder (VDR) 96

Wallenius Wilhelmsen 56
Warsash Maritime Academy 11
Wärtsilä 105, 117
watchkeeping 7, 15, 19–21, 23, 24, 26, 63, 122,
188, 196, 205
Waterman Steamship 50
Wave Making Resistance 84
waybill 221, 224
weather deck 49, 50, 53, 86, 89, 90, 96
welding 22, 36, 110, 155, 159–161,
265, 272
West Africa 41, 256
wiper 24, 266

Yantian Express 277, 278
yaw 135, 136

ZIM Integrated Shipping 56

CPSIA information can be obtained
at www.ICGtesting.com
Printed in the USA
BVHW012117160422
634394BV00003B/113